Nation within a Nation

UNIVERSITY PRESS OF FLORIDA

Florida A&M University, Tallahassee
Florida Atlantic University, Boca Raton
Florida Gulf Coast University, Ft. Myers
Florida International University, Miami
Florida State University, Tallahassee
New College of Florida, Sarasota
University of Central Florida, Orlando
University of Florida, Gainesville
University of North Florida, Jacksonville
University of South Florida, Tampa
University of West Florida, Pensacola

Nation within a Nation

The American South and the Federal Government

Edited by Glenn Feldman

University Press of Florida
Gainesville · Tallahassee · Tampa · Boca Raton
Pensacola · Orlando · Miami · Jacksonville · Ft. Myers · Sarasota

Copyright 2014 by Glenn Feldman
All rights reserved
Published in the United States of America

This book may be available in an electronic edition.

First cloth printing, 2014
First paperback printing, 2019

24 23 22 21 20 19   6 5 4 3 2 1

Library of Congress Cataloging-in-Publication Data
Nation within a nation : the American South and the federal government / edited by Glenn Feldman.
pages cm
Includes index.
ISBN 978-0-8130-4987-8 (cloth)
ISBN 978-0-8130-6448-2 (pbk.)
1. Southern States—Politics and government. 2. United States—Politics and government. 3. Federal government—Southern States—Historiography. I. Feldman, Glenn.
F209.N38 2014
320.0975—dc23
2013047852

The University Press of Florida is the scholarly publishing agency for the State University System of Florida, comprising Florida A&M University, Florida Atlantic University, Florida Gulf Coast University, Florida International University, Florida State University, New College of Florida, University of Central Florida, University of Florida, University of North Florida, University of South Florida, and University of West Florida.

University Press of Florida
2046 NE Waldo Road
Suite 2100
Gainesville, FL 32609
http://upress.ufl.edu

To the memory of Sheldon Hackney

Contents

List of Illustrations   ix
Acknowledgments   xi

Introduction   1
Glenn Feldman

PART I. PAST TO PRESENT

1. First to Secede, Last to Accede: South Carolina's Resistance to the Republic, 1780–Present   19
Thomas F. Schaller

PART II. RACE, WAR, AND CULTURE

2. Tom Watson and Resistance to Federal War Policies in Georgia during World War I   67
Zachary C. Smith

3. "Negroes, the New Deal, and . . . Karl Marx": Southern Antistatism in Depression and War   102
Jason Morgan Ward

4. Dixiecrats, Dissenting Delegates, and the Dying Democratic Party: Mississippi's Right Turn from Roosevelt to Johnson   122
Rebecca Miller Davis

5. Right Turn? The Republican Party and African American Politics in Post-1965 Mississippi   149
Chris Danielson

PART III. A NATION WITHIN A NATION?

6. Texas Philosophy, Nashville Agrarianism, Reagan Republicanism, and the Neo-Confederacy: The Influence of M. E. Bradford   181
Fred Arthur Bailey

7. The Evil Empire Within: Southern Nationalism and
   the Washington Problem   205
   David R. Jansson

Part IV. Economic Development and Reform

8. Getting Farmers—and Tourists—"Out of the Mud": Alabama's
   Nineteenth-Century Experience with Public Projects and Its Response
   to the Federal Road Aid Acts of 1916 and 1921   229
   Martin T. Olliff

9. "From Nothin' to Somethin'": The Tennessee Valley Authority and
   Federal-Local Cooperation in the Sun Belt South, 1940–1960   261
   Matthew L. Downs

10. Lighting the "Dark and Evil World": Judge J. Smith Henley, Arkansas,
    and the Federal Judiciary's Reform of the Southern Prison   287
    Gregory L. Richard

Part V. Tax Fury and the Tea Party

11. The Tea Party in the South: Populism Revisited?   303
    Allan B. McBride

12. Deal or No Deal: Taxes, Government Spending, and Alabamians
    Having Their Cake and Eating It Too   325
    Natalie Motise Davis

List of Contributors   343
Index   345

Illustrations

Figures

    1.1. Democratic fortunes in South Carolina, 1960–2012 47
    12.1. Is the South different from the rest of the country? 329
    12.2. Confidence in state and federal government 329

Tables

    1.1. Political legacies of the Ninety Six District 54
    11.1. Obama approval levels among Tea Party supporters 311
    11.2. Blame Obama (or Bush) for weak economy by region, controlled for Tea Party support 311
    11.3. Trust for Obama (or congressional Republicans) on economic issues by region, controlled for Tea Party support 311
    11.4. Support for economic regulation by region, controlled for Tea Party support 313
    11.5. Support for smaller government and *Row v. Wade* by region, controlled for Tea Party support 313
    12.1. Federal dollars returned to states, 2010 328
    12.2. Alabamians on religion and child rearing 332
    12.3. Perceptions of tax fairness 332
    12.4. Types of federal benefits reported 334
    12.5. Number of federal benefits reported 334
    12.6. Perceptions of return of federal taxes to Alabama by respondent's belief about tax fairness 335
    12.7. Number of benefits received by perceptions of tax fairness 335
    12.8. Benefits received by perceptions of tax fairness 337

12.9. Benefits received by perceptions of return of federal taxes to Alabama   338
12.10. Predictors of perceptions of return of federal taxes to Alabama   339

Acknowledgments

I would like to thank the University Press of Florida, especially Meredith Babb, press director, and Sian Hunter, senior acquisitions editor, who provided invaluable encouragement and guidance. Thanks also to project editor Marthe Walters for guiding the project, and to copy editor Jonathan Lawrence for doing an expert job. I am grateful to them all, as well as everyone else at the press. This book has also benefited from the insightful and intelligent comments of two external readers, and I am appreciative for them.

I am most grateful for the support of my family and friends. I especially thank my wife, Jeannie, for her unfailing support, my daughters Rebecca and Hallie, beautiful inside and out, my brother Richard Feldman for his constancy and devotion, and my parents, Julia Garate Burgos Feldman and Brian Feldman, for a lifetime of guidance and friendship. My brother Danny Feldman, sister Vicky Menke, and niece Julianna Menke have also been great supporters. Lifelong friends Jak Karn and the late Judy Karn and Johnny Sherman have a special place. Becky and Owen Stayner, Vince and Mary Morgan, Yvonne Carlson, Lori Jack, Frank LaRussa, Glenda Curry, Jimmy and Tracy Wooten, Mike and Liz Cleckler, Jason Marchant, and so many others have been stalwart friends.

Deep thanks also to my colleagues at the University of Alabama at Birmingham, especially my department chair, Colin J. Davis, and associate dean for the College of Arts and Sciences, Rebecca Ann Bach. Their enthusiastic support of my research has been so welcome. I am profoundly grateful as well to Dean Robert Palazzo of the CAS for providing a positive and supportive atmosphere for research at the College, as well as my colleagues in the History Department, particularly George Liber, Brian Steele, and Steve Miller. I am indebted to so many other colleagues throughout the profession, especially Wayne Flynt, Dan Carter, and the late Sheldon

Hackney, who are special models and inspirations. Throughout the years I have also enjoyed conversations and learned much from Jacquelyn Dowd Hall, Marjorie Julian Spruill, Don Doyle, Allen W. Jones, Donna Bohanan, Larry Gerber, the late Gordon C. Bond, Robin Fabel, Guy Beckwith, Natalie Motise Davis, the late H. Irvin Penfield, Patrick J. Hawley, Lance Grahn, Edwin L. Brown, Carol Ann Vaughn Cross, and so many others. This book is dedicated to the memory of Sheldon Hackney.

Glenn Feldman

Introduction

GLENN FELDMAN

No other region has been more important than the South in determining the course of U.S. politics and history. This was so in 1776, and 1865, and is still true today, although in vastly different ways.

The South's relationship to the federal government has been intriguing and unique, and it vitally informs the region's continued import to American politics, society, and culture. No other state played a larger role than Virginia in the founding of the United States and the early Republic. Figures of the Virginia Dynasty such as Washington, Jefferson, Madison, Monroe, Edmund Randolph, Richard Henry Lee, and Patrick Henry loom over the founding and early years of the American experiment. Other giants—southern as well—played outsized roles in these early decades and throughout the antebellum period: Andrew Jackson and James K. Polk of Tennessee, Henry Clay of Kentucky, John C. Calhoun of South Carolina, and John Marshall, John Randolph, and John Tyler of Virginia to name but a few. Indeed, southerners have actually lent their names to two of the most important early eras in American history: the Jeffersonian and Jacksonian periods.

The long-accepted notion of southern distinctiveness has, of late, come under assault from a generation of younger scholars who mostly grew up in the "post–civil rights" and "post-racial" South, its metropolitan exurbs, or in environs outside Dixie.[1] When weighing their arguments against the well-established and, yes, empirical concept of southern distinctiveness, the careful reader should keep in mind at least the following: No other region has waged armed rebellion against the federal government. No other region has been militarily defeated and occupied by the Armed Forces of the United States. And no other region has profited more—or more consistently over time—from federal projects, programs, tax expenditures, and public spending: what is often fashionably derided today, within and without the South, as "socialism." Of course there is much more to southern distinctiveness, especially in the way of enduring de jure Jim Crow laws and practices, debt peonage, convict-lease, various outbreaks of the Ku Klux Klan, "massive resistance" and the White Citizens' Councils, black codes, legal mechanisms of disfranchisement, deep and profligate anti-union animus and pro-business boosterism, the pervasiveness of conservative religiosity, manners, climate, pace of life, college football as religion, and kneejerk militarism as a widely accepted substitute for patriotism. Indeed, the relationship between the South and the federal government may be said to be (with varying degrees of accuracy) curious, ironic, even petulant; one of perpetual adolescent rebellion. Certainly there is considerable paradox in the coexistence of the southern states' long and continuing dependence on the federal treasury with the region's persistent resentment of all things federal and Washington.

This book is an attempt to get at the essence, as well as the variety, of Dixie's sometimes tortured relationship with the federal government. Each chapter addresses an intriguing part of the South's relationship to the central state, some through state studies and others through a region-wide approach. The sum of the chapters provides a fascinating window into a region that, while insisting—even to the point of violence—on the sanctity of individualism, local control, and states' rights, has been willing to receive (and even be solicitous of) federal grants, monies, and largesse both for its people and for the region at large. Sectional resentment of the central government as something wholly separate, alien, even hostile, meanwhile, has persisted and, one might argue, grown over time. Obviously, the South's relationship to the federal government has been nothing if not complex, often hypocritical, and at times even perverse.

For example, it may be argued that libertarianism does not exist. Not really; not strictly speaking. It does not exist in a concrete or experiential sense—only, almost, in a parallel if conversely utopian universe from communism. Libertarianism—at the level of individuals and firms—devolves, far too often in practice, into something radically different from what it claims. It would be unkind, and perhaps a bit unfair, to refer to it as a form of perpetual intellectual adolescence. But its actual state *is* something that should be more accurately termed "profitarianism."

That is, in reality, no one and no corporation really wants to be left completely alone by the state—the laissez-faire imaginings of neoliberal economic theory and the Chicago and Austrian Schools notwithstanding.

Government interference is routinely welcomed—indeed millions are spent on the acquisition of it. Only it must manifest in the form of state aid to individual merchants, entrepreneurs, and firms in the form of police and fire protection, taxpayer-funded infrastructure, and grants and subsidies for research, development, and all manner of things. Tax bonuses, land grants, incentives, public investment in transportation, communications, and banking, and even government bailouts of failing firms are also part of the equation. There is no such thing as libertarianism. Despite the deafening noise about it in so many areas—academic and otherwise—it exists only in an abstract state, suspended in the ether of historical and academic imagination—and political cover. Perhaps the purest expression of this paradox is the insistence by individuals and firms on the publicly funded preservation of law and order domestically—and U.S. military protection overseas—for private ventures that result in the making of (even the guaranteeing of) private profits.

The American situation is not unlike the relationship that once existed between Parliament and the British East India Company—a relationship decried as incestuous, corrupt, and perverse by such champions of the free market and classical economics as the conservative giant Edmund Burke.[2] The most serious commonality between the *profitarianism* of individuals, groups, and firms—and that of the American South—is the predictably allergic reaction profitarians have to government involvement in the economy in the form of regulation and oversight. The relationship between the American South and the federal government may thus be largely understood as a form of such profitarianism, only on a microcosmic and regional scale.

The present collection—divided topically into five parts—consists of an introduction and twelve chapters. A variety of disciplinary perspectives are mined, with a heavy emphasis on history. Nine of the contributors are professional historians, three are political scientists, and one is a human geographer. The contributors teach in, and hail from, every section around the country, even overseas. Given the remarkably important role the southern states have played, and continue to play, in the course of our national political and cultural development, this volume aspires to contemporary resonance as well as lasting relevance.

Nationally known political scientist Thomas F. Schaller kicks off the book by examining in great detail the unique role of South Carolina in American history and politics.[3] The center of the Nullification Crisis of the nineteenth century, as well as the first state to secede, the Palmetto State has consistently been at the forefront of opposition to the federal government and a virulent insistence on the sanctity of states' rights. Its importance continues today, as Schaller demonstrates, including the prominent role the South Carolina primary and customary visits to Bob Jones University play for the Republican presidential nominating process.

From the earliest days of the Republic, the Maryland political scientist tells us, South Carolina embraced the resister's role with relish. Largely to appease South Carolina slaveholders, Thomas Jefferson removed language condemning slavery from the Declaration of Independence. In 1780 colonial Tories in South Carolina helped the British recapture the state from the American revolutionaries. John C. Calhoun—vice president, senator, and perhaps the Palmetto State's favorite son—is virtually synonymous with the antebellum "nullification" movement and the doctrine of interposition. South Carolina was not only the first to secede in the lead-up to the Civil War; at one point it actually threatened to secede *from the Confederacy* because its sister states refused to reopen the slave import trade. Deep into the twentieth century, many white South Carolinians chose to celebrate Confederate Memorial Day rather than American Independence Day and the Fourth of July. As might be predicted, Schaller explains, South Carolina was the original litigant in the various cases that were eventually folded together into the epic *Brown v. Board of Education* ruling. South Carolinians actually declined to ratify the Nineteenth Amendment (women's suffrage) until almost half a century after it took effect. In the opening chapter, Schaller examines why it is that South Carolina has repeatedly distinguished itself as a federal outlier to the Republic—a state first to secede, and often last to accede—to the laws and norms embraced by much of the rest of the nation. In doing so, he links the past to the present.

Part 2 examines the South-federal relationship through the often contentious—and sometimes explosive—prisms of race, war, and culture. This section of the book comprises chapters by Zachary C. Smith, Jason Morgan Ward, Rebecca Miller Davis, and Chris Danielson.

Smith's chapter on the life and career of Tom Watson of Georgia will certainly raise eyebrows and stimulate thought and discussion. In his study of the famed Georgia politico, Smith adopts a starkly different perspective than those that have been customarily employed on Watson, including that by the dean of southern historians, C. Vann Woodward. While giving a nod to what may only be called Watson's pathological anti-Semitism, anti-Catholicism, Negrophobia, and venomous stance toward the federal government, the chapter wrestles with both the anti-war and anti-capitalist rhetoric of the former Populist leader during the years of the Great War. In Watson's vitriol against the central government—increasingly conflated in his mind and that of many of his rural Georgia followers with the big-moneyed interests of the North and East—Smith also finds continuity with Watson's Populist past, supposed by many to have disintegrated after the People's Party vanished in 1908. Weighing the nature of the Wilson administration's wartime suppression of Watson and those who supported his crusade against the draft, Smith argues that a region-wide appeal of Watson's resistance to federal war policies denotes a persistent, if sporadic, tradition of anti-capitalistic *and anti-militaristic* thought and rhetoric in the South.

Watson's arguments against the central state were, well, Watsonian, and provide a fascinating window into the growing conflation of the "North" and the "federal government" in the southern mind. Smith tells us that the Georgia politico was especially exercised about what he felt was the inordinate influence of wealthy northeastern elites in gaining a commutation of the death sentence of Leo Frank, a Georgia Jew accused of rape and murder, and also in the Wilson administration's wartime policies, which the ex-Georgia Populist saw as a type of exploitative treason against poor farmers in Georgia and elsewhere who faced conscription to fight a rich man's war in which the country had no business being involved. Smith suggests a degree of long-term ideological consistency (if the word "consistency" can be applied with any degree of accuracy to Tom Watson) that few have recognized in this important southern figure. Readers may be struck by the particular irony of Watson defining the "producing classes" in terms starkly antithetical to those of Ayn Rand—so in fashion for much of today's American right. For Watson, the "producers" in society were poor dirt farmers and the like as opposed to "parasites" located in the financial offices and banks of northern and eastern cities.

Next, Jason Morgan Ward explores southern attitudes toward the New Deal, beginning with the widely derided "demagogic stunt" of the 1936 National Grass Roots Convention in Macon, Georgia. Organized by deep-pocketed financial and industrial elites and featuring demagogic Georgia governor Ol' Gene Talmadge and the aging white supremacist and North Carolina novelist, the Reverend Thomas F. Dixon, the convention of conservative, white, southern opponents of the New Deal would cry racial revolution and increasingly substitute the specter of communists for carpetbaggers as the fomenters of that revolution.

While Talmadge, Dixon, and their corporate sponsors' efforts to tar the

New Deal as a racial revolution met resistance in an impoverished section, and even ridicule in some quarters, the vanguard continued to hammer away at the idea that the expansion of federal power in the New Deal threatened the southern status quo on race. As more and more blacks joined in the New Deal, and its focus shifted from relief and recovery to reform, the region's most confirmed white supremacists and industrial powers damned FDR for using the New Deal as a Trojan horse to upset southern racial customs and bring social equality to Dixie. Right-wing industrialists were especially adamant that federal involvement in the economy would destroy their racialized, preferred, version of capitalism—one that included a not-inconsequential amount of hegemony over the lives of their workers and others regarded as below them on the totem pole of southern society.

Ward demonstrates that, while these charges took some time to establish a foothold, they became increasingly commonplace after U.S. involvement in World War II. Although America joined the Allies as opponents of fascist dictatorships, military struggle against the Axis contributed new rhetorical ammunition for southern conservatives intent on linking Rooseveltian liberalism to communism. "Totalitarianism" became the enemy, Ward tells us, as differences between the communist and the fascist kind blurred during the greatest military struggle the world had ever seen. Efforts by black and civil rights activists to demand improvements on race from Washington only accelerated southern, white tarring of the whole New Deal project as some kind of federally funded racial revolution aimed at remaking the South. By comparing the New Deal to slavery, federal officials to carpetbaggers, and racial liberals to Nazis, Ward argues, later segregationists fused their fears into a racially charged antistatism that threw up considerable resistance to the modern civil rights movement and continues to affect American politics today.

Rebecca Miller Davis turns our attention away from incipient hard-right opposition to New Deal liberalism to Mississippi as she explores politics in the Magnolia State from the presidential administrations of FDR to Lyndon Johnson. Specifically, the chapter focuses on one of the South's most notoriously segregationist states and the political changes that occurred between the end of World War II and passage of the Civil Rights Act of 1964. Davis argues that Mississippi politics took a decided "right turn" after World War II as the federal government showed itself determined to include black people in New Deal, Fair Deal, and successive government programs and activist initiatives. In other words, the federal government's growing commitment to racial justice and equality in the form of the Democratic administrations of Roosevelt, Truman, Kennedy, and Johnson especially (and Republican Dwight Eisenhower to a lesser degree) played the primary role in Mississippi becoming ever more conservative in its politics. Davis covers Mississippi's considerable involvement in the 1948 Dixiecrat Revolt and extends her analysis through Mississippi's famous "Freedom Summer" of 1964.

Davis documents the appeal of Barry Goldwater to white Mississippians upset by racial liberalism on the part of national Democrats. As she elucidates, the Republican Goldwater appealed to disenchanted white Mississippi Democrats not only because he opposed the 1964 Civil Rights Act but also because he singled out the NAACP as his main enemy, rejected the idea that the U.S. Supreme Court was the highest law of the land, and supported Governor Ross Barnett's 1962 segregationist stand at Ole Miss. Former Democrats such as Prentiss Walker profited in Mississippi by riding Goldwater's coattails to become the state's first Republican congressman since 1883.

Chris Danielson takes up the Mississippi story after 1964 and provides a somewhat different interpretation of succeeding events than Davis implies. Danielson acknowledges that race did play a major role in the Republicanization of Mississippi, but he contends that the move toward a Republican-controlled state was not seamless or without significant internal division. The essay explores the growth of a large, black electorate in the Magnolia State after passage of the 1965 federal Voting Rights Act and contends that state Republican leaders were not immediately warm to the idea of an all-white party. The chapter argues that Mississippi GOP leaders held conflicting ideas about the viability of the black vote in post-1965 Mississippi and that this division was further complicated by Republican presidential administrations pursuing a more nuanced path than simply embracing the raw white supremacy of the Ross Barnetts and George Wallaces. Despite attempts by Republican presidents to weaken renewals of the federal Voting Rights Act of 1965, Danielson argues, GOP administrations actually expanded black office-holding through their *enforcement* of the act's provisions.

It should be pointed out that one may accept Danielson's specific findings without, in fact, concluding that race was not the primary factor in the building of a Republican-dominated Mississippi. GOP wunderkind Kevin Phillips, in his 1969 blueprint, *The Emerging Republican Majority*, had recommended precisely (if in a Machiavellian way) that the GOP would best be served in the South by actually *enforcing* federal voting rights laws in order to hasten the process of disgust with, and departure from, the national Democratic Party on the part of most white southerners, whites who already blamed Democrats for civil rights and voting rights legislation and liberal court decisions.[4] Political scientist Abigail Thernstrom has demonstrated that this is exactly what happened. Harry Dent, the South Carolina political adviser of Strom Thurmond and tutor of the legendary Lee Atwater, worked closely with Phillips on Richard Nixon's "southern strategy" and, at a state level, with white Republicans such as Mississippi GOP chair Clarke Reed and Gil Carmichael, whom Danielson describes as a "progressive" Republican. Danielson does acknowledge that a "progressive" in Mississippi was far more conservative than a progressive elsewhere in the country.

But perhaps most important in weighing the give-and-take between these two chapters on Mississippi—and the recent spate of books and articles addressing the colossally important issue of race and partisan realignment in the South—we should proceed with a healthy acknowledgment of reality. To expect or demand the wholesale, unqualified, and immediate exodus of southern whites from the Democratic Party to the GOP instantly after passage of the 1964 Civil Rights Act is, to be certain, to expect too much. Noting that the movement of southern whites to the GOP took some time (precisely *because* of the strength of ten decades of attachment to the Solid Democratic Party based principally on white supremacy) is not the same as arguing that the exodus did not happen, or that, when it did, it did not happen primarily because of race. In fact, it might very well be posited that the 1965 Voting Rights Act was even more influential in pushing southern whites out of the Democratic Party and into the arms of the GOP. Again, taking stock of realities is critical here. The post-1965 realities involved in dealing with a southern electorate that—for the first time since Reconstruction—included significant numbers of black voters should not be forgotten or brushed aside. After 1965 it was no longer a viable strategy for southern politicians to stand in schoolhouse doors or yell "Segregation now, segregation forever" from the steps of state capitols. Speaking in the code and dog whistles of the "southern strategy"—which has been amply documented by scholars and even apologized for by some of its most notable Republican practitioners—should not now be confused for ambivalence or, worse, real division in the ranks of the modern GOP in its successful use of race to wrest the South away from the Democratic Party. Only the most exotic of southern Republicans and Democrats-in-transit to the GOP dissented from the dominant strategy. And, while appreciating complexity is a an essential part of mature scholarship, we should be wary about exalting the pursuit of nuance for nuance's sake to the level of an academic vogue. When that happens, isolated whirlpools and eddies may be confused for predominant and overwhelming currents.

Part 3 of the collection shifts our attention to the question of to what degree the South has allowed itself to become so alienated from the federal government that it has, at times, actually considered itself something apart and different from rest of the country. Or as W. J. Cash famously put it in *The Mind of the South*, "not quite a nation within a nation, but the next thing to it."[5] In this section of the book, Fred Arthur Bailey and David R. Jansson do their best to shed some light on this enduring question.

Bailey, one of the preeminent historians of southern intellectual thought, provides a compelling, and even chilling, view into the mind of one of modern conservatism's foremost intellectual heroes: Melvin E. Bradford. Bailey's chapter dwells on Bradford's Texas background as well as his intellectual growth in one of the South's foremost incubators of southern conservatism at the time—Vanderbilt University—home to the famous Nashville Agrarians. Bailey's exposition on Bradford and Bradford's views makes important connections between the English professor's philosophy and the modern incarnation of Republican conservatism, increasing party extremism, and partisan change in the South.

The Bailey chapter explores what made Mel Bradford and his theories so appealing to George Wallace and, later, President Ronald Reagan and his advisers—as well as other leading conservative politicians and intellectuals, even those associated with the neo-Confederate movement. Particularly interesting is Bailey's discussion of Bradford's infamous attacks on Abraham Lincoln, his defenses of slavery, his paeans to inequality and anti-egalitarian thought, and the religious underpinnings of much of his thought.

David R. Jansson brings the vantage point of human geography to the following chapter. He takes for his task an examination of contemporary attitudes of southern nationalists toward the central government both from a critique of American "empire" by groups such as the neo-Confederate League of the South and the role that Latin American, particularly Mexican, immigration has played in antagonizing southern nationalists. The presence of dark-skinned people who speak Spanish in the local cultural landscape is interpreted, Jansson tells us, as a betrayal by the federal government of the South's largely homogeneous communities. This fascinating chapter is based on interviews with League of the South members and leaders as well as e-mail correspondence and materials from the League and other southern nationalist groups such as the Southern National Congress.

In Part 4 of the collection we switch gears to focus on economic development and reform. In doing so, we encounter a South somewhat at odds with the intransigent, recalcitrant, and often intractable "nation within a nation" that the region has presented when cultural and racial questions have been at stake. Southerners and their states have interacted with the federal government in a number of ways over the years—from political to militaristic to racial to cultural to economic, among others. In this section, chapters by Martin T. Olliff, Matthew L. Downs, and Gregory L. Richard demonstrate that the federal-South relationship has actually been, at times, beneficial, productive, and benign. This applies, most often, to areas of economic development and, occasionally, reform as opposed to the more antagonistic encounters over race and culture that have dominated the relationship. In doing so, these contributors also lay bare the obvious fact that the South has been, as a rule, a whole lot more congenial to federal "involvement" when it has taken the form of federal dollars, projects, and economic development instead of directives on race or clashes over cultural issues.

Olliff informs us that, like the epic railroad construction of the nineteenth century, a system of roads and highways that were sturdy enough to serve all Americans, and their heavy automobile and truck traffic, required enormous outlays and concentration of capital—far more than could be supplied by private industry alone. Alabama's nineteenth-century experience with public projects involved sweetheart deals, bank chicanery, and massive public indebtedness. These experiences, along with the region's notorious allergy to taxation, soured many on the issue of public projects, especially when the demigod of self-reliance led to an individualist worldview that saw roads and other public goods in terms that were primarily personal. Although Alabamians had consistently refused to support the railroads with public monies, they simultaneously viewed roads and highways as a public necessity and a fundamental duty of the government to build and maintain. Yet actually providing the capital necessary to finance a full and modern roadway system required more money than local or state governments had, especially in a region as averse to paying taxes as Dixie.

Thus the construction and maintenance of public roads fell to county governments that employed the "statute-labor" system: a tax payable in cash or physical labor on the roads themselves. Although Alabama created a state highway commission in 1911, it consisted of only a handful of engineers who worked in a merely advisory role with the counties. Persistent disagreements between proponents of "good roads" and opponents of taxes stymied the state from letting bonds to support the projects.

But everything changed in 1916, Olliff tells us, when Congress passed the first Federal Road Aid Act. The law provided matching federal funds to states for the improvement of post roads for states that had highway commissions. Predictably, Alabama and other southern states scrambled for the federal money. Five years later a second Federal Road Aid Act supplied additional matching funds for the creation and improvement of a system that would connect roads and highways to those of neighboring states: a rudimentary interstate system that would link the improved, heavy-duty roads. With the federal money available, the Alabama Legislature leaped into action to pass a $25 million bond issue (huge for the time). Even an adverse decision by the state supreme court, based on a constitutional technicality, could not stop the road-improvement juggernaut once federal funds were available. Famous for its aversion to taxation, fearful of and hostile to the federal government, and still so resentful of defeat in the Civil War that it did not recognize Memorial Day until 1916, Alabama's government showed itself to be quite pragmatic, and persistent, when it came to securing federal money to build a decent system of state roads.

Our next chapter turns, again, to federally sponsored improvements to the South and its material conditions. In it Matthew L. Downs takes on the role and expansion of the Tennessee Valley Authority (TVA) and focuses specifically on the effects of the federal agency on the town and area around Decatur, Alabama. Downs tells us that the twentieth-century Tennessee River Valley perfectly embodied the modern southern "Sun Belt" economy, one built on a firm and expansive foundation of directed federal investment. Indeed, Decatur perhaps best exemplified the complex relationship that developed over time between southern civic leaders such as Decatur editor Barrett Shelton and agents of the federal government, particularly the TVA's David Lilienthal.

Like many other regions, the Tennessee Valley was devastated during the Great Depression to such an extent that people who had never done so before turned their eyes and their hands toward assistance from the federal government. The result was a massive, perhaps unprecedented, construction of dams, reservoirs, and recreational facilities, along with regional planning and, especially, the expansion and availability of electricity to countless rural inhabitants. The area's economy expanded markedly through the 1940s and 1950s, and a close relationship developed between southern civic leaders and TVA officials. As time went on, though, the relationship changed from one centered on regional development to one that became more and more concerned with attracting, and then retaining, industry, investment, and economic development to the seven affected southern states. Eventually, Downs argues, the Valley's residents were successful in shifting the focus of federal agents from large-scale resource management to the attraction of business that was designed to appeal to local industry and foster continued growth. As a result, he maintains, by 1960 the TVA had largely abandoned its ideological foundation and converted to full cooperation with local civic leaders in a Sun Belt pattern of modernization, commercialization, and the attraction of new industry and profits to the region.

Gregory L. Richard shifts our attention to Arkansas and the issue of federal penal reform beginning with the June 1969 decision of Arkansas federal district court judge J. Smith Henley on the inhumane treatment of prisoners at the Cummins and Tucker Prison Farms. Henley's decision, Richard informs us, launched a series of lawsuits that spanned more than two decades and resulted, eventually, in the district court's declaration that the entire Arkansas prison system was unconstitutional: it violated the Eighth Amendment prohibition against "cruel and unusual" punishment.

The chapter focuses on the life and thinking of Judge Henley because, though it was a federal decision, it was also the fruit of a peculiarly southern outlook in the form of the jurist's thinking. This was important because the Arkansas decision would serve as the model for much of the review and reform of more than thirty-five state prison systems, both in the South and outside the region. In fact, it was the Arkansan Henley's judicial philosophy that set the stage for much of subsequent penal reform in the United States.

Henley's view of federalism and the proper place of judges within the system is perhaps the most intriguing part of Richard's chapter. As he tells us, Henley had no problem with the concept of federal judges "making law"—as they were often accused of doing. In fact, he believed that making law was a vital and inherent part of a judge's job; a responsibility derived from the impossibility of legislation (no matter how far-seeing) being able to cover every crack, crevice, and new opening in society not anticipated by the original lawmakers or in existence at the time a measure became law. Hence the proper task of the judge was to "try to adapt the basic constitutional and statutory provisions to circumstances that are new," Henley explained. And if that constituted making law, then so be it. The trick was to be moderate and reasonable and to act as an administrator from above—to say "Look, this is wrong, you've got to stop it and fix it, now you tell me how you want to fix it"—rather than compelling people to institute preconceived reforms and appointing administrators from outside the court to ensure that directives were carried out.

Richard's chapter consequently focuses attention on the relationship between Arkansas and the federal government—one that was tenuous at best. The study explores more than ten years of complex litigation and procedural history that sheds light not only on the South's notorious prison farms but also on how Arkansans and their state government reacted to a federal judge and his decisions.

The final part of the book closes out with two chapters on the recent phenomena of tax fury and the rise of the Tea Party wing of the national GOP. Allen B. McBride and Natalie Motise Davis, both political scientists, bring the tools of that discipline to focus on these important and more contemporary questions. McBride tells us that the Tea Party erupted on the political scene virtually overnight, in the immediate aftermath of the election of America's first black president. Despite its northern origins, McBride cites the anti-statist ideology of the Tea Party as the main reason for its strong support in Dixie. The chapter argues that the Tea Party may be better described as a movement than an actual party and that it is actually the latest incarnation of populism in the United States—an observation that should not extend to confusing present-day Tea Party policies for those of the 1890s Populists.

More important, perhaps, through the use of polling data and the monitoring of social media, among other sources, this chapter concludes that, like the People's Party of the 1890s, preliminary data suggest that today's Tea Party is neither distinctively southern nor expressly racist. McBride provides important caveats to both points, stressing that these conclusions are based only on preliminary data, that the South may be in the process of losing its regional distinctiveness or exporting it to the nation, and that public-opinion survey data have long been known to underestimate attitudes and behaviors that fall outside the political mainstream. The last disclaimer is particularly compelling. How many respondents, after all, leap to answer polling data about race and racism by admitting that yes, in fact, they retain racist assumptions and prejudices, that their political attitudes are colored by race and stereotypes, and that they fully realize that public enunciation of such realities is something to be avoided in the modern age?

While analysis of the chapter's data obviously provides insight into the Tea Party phenomenon, additional caveats may be in order. Although McBride emphasizes that regional differences are slight in the preliminary data, they are still present and consistently so. The South repeatedly registers more intense anti-Obama and anti-statist feelings than other parts of the country. While the data set used here shows these differences to be small among Tea Partiers of various regions, the more important point may be the *consistency* of such regional differences. And because blacks are not factored out of what are discussed as "southern" data, southern numbers on matters of Obama, government regulation, and the free market may be unduly "liberalized" compared to what they would be had the data polled only southern whites. Perhaps this point is most obvious in the chapter's speculation that southerners may be ambivalent when it comes to market values. Certainly it is when the subject is the region's alleged ambivalence toward individualism—and McBride correctly cautions the reader to regard earlier work by political scientist Daniel Elazar on this topic with a healthy dose of skepticism. An important factor that is not measured in the data on Tea Party attitudes on the "deservedness" of recipients of government benefits—even by those who receive Social Security and Medicare themselves—is the importance of the Calvinist streak in southern religiosity that runs so strong in the dominant Southern Baptist, Southern Presbyterian, and even Southern Methodist denominations that reject Wesleyan and Arminian traditions.

Natalie Motise Davis, a recognized regional and even national expert on public-opinion polling, is less tentative in her conclusions. In her chapter on Alabama she takes on the paradox of a consistently churlish attitude toward the federal government on the part of so many white southerners along with the region's equally consistent disproportionate benefiting from federal funding and public spending. Southern states benefit the most from federal programs and tax expenditures, Davis tells us, yet southerners tend to have more negative opinions about the role and performance of the federal government than do others around the country. Not only is the reality of the degree of southern reliance on the federal government not common knowledge in Dixie, it actually has little bearing on southern white opinions of the central government. Only 20 percent of Alabamians, for example, believe the state gets back more in federal spending than it contributes in federal tax dollars. But when presented with a list of twelve federal benefits, only a minuscule 7 percent claim not to have received a single one. Davis attempts to explain why there is such a serious disconnect between the fact that Alabamians benefit disproportionally from federal programs and tax policies and the belief by 40 percent, for example, that they pay "more than their fair share" in federal taxes. The chapter employs both aggregate and survey data, and multiple-regression analysis, in an accessible way to shed light on this apparent and important contradiction.

Like many of the other pieces in this book, the final one wrestles with the South's basically dual personality when it comes to the federal government: one of persistent resistance, even antagonism, as well as one of reliance and even dependency. What follows is endlessly fascinating as well as often disquieting. It suggests that, perhaps, there is a psychological link (rather than a disconnect) between the magnitude of southern dependence on Washington and the region's famed contempt for and fear of the federal government.

Notes

1. Representative works of the "Sunbelt" or "Suburban School" are Matthew D. Lassiter, *The Silent Majority: Suburban Politics in the Sunbelt South* (Princeton: Princeton University Press, 2006); Byron Shafer and Richard Johnston, *The End of Southern Exceptionalism: Class, Race and Partisan Change in the Postwar South* (Cambridge: Harvard University Press, 2006); and Matthew D. Lassiter and Joseph Crespino, eds., *The Myth of Southern Exceptionalism* (New York: Oxford University Press, 2009). See my reviews of two of these works: Glenn Feldman, "Review of *The Myth of Southern Exceptionalism*, ed. Matthew D. Lassiter and Joseph Crespino, in the *Journal of Southern History* 77 (August 2011): 783–86; and Glenn Feldman, "Review of *The End of Southern Exceptionalism*, by Byron E. Shafer and Richard Johnston, in the *Journal of Southern History* 73 (August 2007): 146–48. See also Orville Vernon Burton's comments on the "Suburban School" in the extended version of his 2012 Southern Historical Association presidential address, "The South as 'Other,' the Southerner as Stranger," *Journal of Southern History* 79 (February 2013): 7–37.

2. For Edmund Burke's war against what he viewed as the depredations and perversions of capitalism made by the British East India Company and its principal Parliamentary representative, Paul Benfield, see, e.g., Jerry Z. Muller, *The Mind and the Market: Capitalism in Modern European Thought* (New York: Knopf, 2002), 125.

3. In this section I have relied heavily not only on the contributors' chapters but also on their descriptions of their own chapters.

4. Kevin P. Phillips, *The Emerging Republican Majority* (New Rochelle, N.Y.: Arlington House, 1969).

5. W. J. Cash, *The Mind of the South* (New York: Knopf, 1941), viii (quoted).

I

PAST TO PRESENT

1

First to Secede, Last to Accede

South Carolina's Resistance to the Republic, 1780–Present

THOMAS F. SCHALLER

My constituents are highly alarmed at the large and rapid strides which this new government has taken towards despotism. They say it is big with political mischiefs, and pregnant with a greater variety of impending woes to the good people of the Southern States, especially South Carolina, than all the plagues supposed to issue from the poisonous box of Pandora.... They say they will resist against it; that they will not accept of it unless compelled by force of arms.

Delegate Patrick Dollard, before voting "nay" at South Carolina's convention to ratify the U.S. Constitution, May 20, 1788

To bring [desegregation] about, the federal government would set up a super-police force with the power to rove throughout the states and keep our people in constant fear of being sent to a federal jail unless we accepted the decrees turned out by a bunch of anti-Southern bureaucrats in Washington.

States' Rights Democratic Party presidential candidate Strom Thurmond, *ABC Radio* broadcast, November 1, 1948

From the founding period to the Civil War, from the Progressive Era through the civil rights revolution, the South has distinguished itself as America's most conservative region. Southerners have repeatedly fought against the major social and political transformations of American history, sometimes violently so. The South rejected efforts to end slavery, protected the all white primary, defied attempts to desegregate its public facilities, challenged the constitutionality of the 1965 Voting Rights Act, and continues to express outward hostility toward affirmative action programs. Beyond matters of race, the South thwarted collective bargaining efforts, balked at child labor reforms, opposed the women's suffrage amendment, and today recoils at the notion of reproductive choice or gay rights. Simply put, the South has consistently demonstrated a penchant for resistance— for preferring at the very least a continuation of the status quo, if not an outright reversal of the natural course of America's civil, social, and economic progress.

From the earliest days of the Republic, South Carolina has embraced the resister's role with particular relish. To appease South Carolinian slaveholders, Thomas Jefferson removed language condemning slavery from the Declaration of Independence. Four years later, backcountry loyalists in South Carolina helped the British army recapture the state in 1780 from the revolutionaries. By 1828, Palmetto State native and vice president John C. Calhoun was agitating for state "nullification" of federal powers, generating secessionist calls a full generation before the outbreak of the Civil War. South Carolina narrowly averted a more serious secessionist threat in 1850–51, but South Carolina congressman Preston Brooks was so overcome with anger that in 1856 he bludgeoned abolitionist Massachusetts senator Charles Sumner on the floor of the U.S. Senate because Sumner criticized a South Carolina senator for his devotion to that "mistress . . . the harlot, Slavery." On December 20, 1860, South Carolina became the first state to secede, and four months later Confederate forces in Charleston fired the opening shots of the Civil War on the Union garrison at Fort Sumter.

South Carolina's belligerence and recalcitrance did not abate in the century following the war. During Reconstruction, so horrified were South Carolina's white citizens at the prospect of freed blacks running the state that in 1865 they voted overwhelmingly, if unsuccessfully, to continue northern political occupation. Soon after the state's chapter of the Ku Klux Klan formed, "red shirt" Democratic rifle clubs used physical intimidation and ballot manipulation to alter results of the 1876 election. In the 1890s, Governor Ben "Pitchfork" Tillman—who earned his nickname by threatening to stab President Grover Cleveland in the ribs with said implement—served two terms as governor before embarking on a twenty-three-year Senate career during which he defended segregation as vigilantly as his fellow Edgefield County native Strom Thurmond later did for most of his career. Fully three decades after ratification of the Thirteenth Amendment abolished slavery, South Carolina still relied upon the amendment's convict-lease exemption to exploit prisoners for cheap labor.

Well into the twentieth century, South Carolina's black citizens observed the Fourth of July mostly alone because the majority of whites preferred instead to celebrate Confederate Memorial Day, May 10. State politicians repeatedly averted their eyes as textile industry executives employed children and quashed attempts by mill workers to organize for fair wages. In 1920 the South Carolina legislature rejected the proposed women's suffrage amendment; it took almost a half century to finally ratify it, in 1969. In 1948, the same year the South Carolina legislature declared President Harry Truman's new civil rights commission "un-American," favorite son Strom Thurmond's full-throated advocacy of racial segregation as the States' Rights Democratic Party presidential nominee helped him carry four Deep South states, including the Palmetto State. Six years later, the Clarendon County school district—where per-pupil spending on whites quadrupled that for blacks—was pooled with three other districts in a failed defense of the "separate but equal" standard in the landmark *Brown v. Board of Education* case. And when Congress passed the 1965 Voting Rights Act, a law that finally banned the creative and vicious methods used to disfranchise blacks, South Carolina became the first state to challenge its constitutionality. By 1968, Harry Dent, the most legendary of Thurmond's political protégés and a key architect of the "southern strategy," was helping Richard Nixon translate racial antagonisms into crucial Republican votes, a victory in South Carolina, and a ticket to the White House. In turn, Dent left his scorched-earth policies and tactics to his best-known pupil, the legendary South Carolina operative Lee Atwater, who became head of the Republican National Committee under George H. W. Bush and schooled an entire generation of Republican strategists, including Karl Rove.

If all of this seems like so much ancient history, consider that South Carolinians are still debating the merits of public displays of the Confederate Battle Flag. Indeed, more than a few pundits believe Republican David Beasley won the 1994 governor's race in part because of his pledge to support displaying the Confederate flag over the state capitol—then promptly lost his 1998 reelection bid later after a "religious epiphany" caused him to reverse position. After two decades of adverse judicial rulings, in 2000 Bob Jones University, the state's largest private liberal arts college, founded by its anti-Catholic and Klan-linked namesake, finally ended its policy of prohibiting interracial dating. While other states issue "choose life" vanity license plates, in 2012 South Carolina was sued for issuing the plates while refusing the same option to pro-choice citizens, justifying its decision by claiming that the anti-abortion message constitutes protected government speech.[1] And in 2013, more than eight decades after women first won the right to vote, the South Carolina state legislature remained the only one in America where women did not hold at least 10 percent of all seats.

Other Deep South states may stake their own claims, but South Carolina is America's most conservative state and, as often as not, finds itself at the top or bottom of some lists of negative distinction. Indeed, South

Carolinians who cringe at thought of being distinguished as worst in the nation in this or that category have been known to "Thank God for Mississippi." From a strictly constitutional-historical standpoint, however, South Carolina's legacy of firsts and lasts reads like a rap sheet: first to overturn a provincial government during the revolutionary period; last to abandon the Atlantic slave trade; first to call for nullifying the Constitution's federal authority; first to secede from the Union; last to abolish the white primary; first to litigate against the integration of public schools; first to challenge the Voting Rights Act. Whenever America finds itself at some social or political crossroads and in need of direction, perhaps the best thing to do is ask, "What would South Carolina do?" And then do the opposite.

History can be painful to revisit. But even the most selective of revisionists cannot soothe this discomfiting truth: For the past two centuries, the South has served as a regional brake against the civil, social, and political advances in American history—and South Carolina has provided the lead foot on the pedal. From the revolutionary period through today's new federalism, this most rebellious of states from the nation's most rebellious region has consistently opposed, defied, or ignored the expectations and edicts of the rest of the Republic, and the state's belligerence, racism, misogyny, and violence have provided the key signposts along the route. Of the many democratic blessings to which Americans point proudly as proof that we merit the title "leader of the free world," most were achieved despite the opposition of southern conservatives and, in particular, recalcitrant South Carolinians. Such is the legacy—such is the "heritage"—of South Carolina, the state that has consistently proved itself least likely to pledge its allegiance to the flag of the United States of America, or to the Republic for which it stands.

The Path of Most Resistance

South Carolina was the state most dependent upon slavery. At the height of slave importation in the mid-eighteenth century, enslaved blacks outnumbered whites in South Carolina by a two-to-one ratio. Although that ratio narrowed slightly during the next century, by the outbreak of the Civil War there were still three slaves for every two white citizens in the state. Capitalizing on the constitutional provision allowing twenty more years of slave importation through 1808, South Carolina responded to rising in-state labor demands by resuming the Atlantic slave trade in 1803 and continuing to import slaves until the constitutional deadline. Despite their numbers, or perhaps because of them, for the state's black population liberty was scarce. From the colonial period through the Civil War, the share of freed black men in South Carolina never exceeded 1.5 percent and was consistently lower than almost any other state.[2]

The distribution of slaves and pro-slavery sentiments varied dramatically across South Carolina. The more densely populated coastal areas comprising Charleston, Georgetown, and the surrounding low country featured large plantations with high rates of slave ownership among wealthy elites, many of whom were of English and French ancestry. The area least dependent on slave labor was the rural backcountry of the piedmont, which was dominated by Scots-Irish and German farmers and traders of lower pedigree than their coastal counterparts. Regardless of the intrastate variance, "by almost any index South Carolina whites had a larger stake in slavery than their counterparts elsewhere in the South," says John Barnwell in *Love of Order*, his chronicle of events leading to the state's eventual secession, in 1860. "Taking the antebellum period as a whole, South Carolina had more slaveholders than any other southern state. Too, the average number of slaves per owner was higher in South Carolina than in the rest of the South."[3] In terms of its dependence upon slavery—not to mention the vigilant perpetuation of this oppressive but profitable institution—South Carolina knew no peer.

For South Carolina, slavery (and later, segregation) was more than a regional dispute over racial oppression or economic competition. It was also a litmus test for the interdependent relationship between state and nation, of the explicit and implicit federal compact between South Carolina and the United States government. Delegates from South Carolina and the other southern states in Philadelphia during the summer of 1787 wielded great influence in drafting the Constitution, a fact reflected most obviously in the slavery provisions, including the infamous three-fifths rule for counting slaves, which exaggerated southern representation in the U.S. House of Representatives and the Electoral College. Since then, South Carolina's political leaders have consistently tried to renege on the very constitutional bargain they helped design.

Opposing the Union: 1775 to 1786

Ninety Six is a curious name for a town that played a curious role in the revolutionary experience of South Carolina and the nation. Named during the early eighteenth century because it was believed to be located ninety-six miles from the closest Cherokee settlement, at Keowee, Ninety Six later became site of a frontier fort where, on November 19, 1775, the first southern blood of the Revolutionary War was spilled. But unlike the Battle of Lexington and Concord six months earlier, where Redcoats searching for rebel munitions were thwarted by Massachusetts militiamen, the fighting at Ninety Six was between South Carolina Whigs committed to the revolution and South Carolina Tories who either remained loyal to the British Crown or simply wished to be left alone. According to Walter Edgar, a preeminent historian of South Carolina, within the larger revolutionary struggle Ninety Six became a symbolic flashpoint for a simultaneous civil war fought *among* South Carolinians.

The philosophical divisions revealed by the Revolution were at root regional, and in many respects they persist to this day. South Carolina's low-country elites generally supported, even stoked, the revolutionary fervor spreading through the colonies. By contrast, reports of military victories by Washington's army and the political achievements of the Continental Congress were not always cheered by South Carolina's backcountry whites. These subsistence farmers tended to be more focused on their crops and the threat of Cherokee attacks than on philosophical talk emanating from Philadelphia and Charleston.

Coastal leaders sent political delegations into the heart of the backcountry to persuade frontier whites of the new provincial government's legitimacy and the merits of the Revolution because, as Edgar asserts, without backcountry support "the revolutionaries would be in difficult straights." At first, these overtures appeared to pay off. With the signing of the Treaty of Ninety Six in the summer of 1775, coastal Whigs and upcountry Tories reached a temporary truce. "Under the terms of this agreement, backcountry opponents of the Provincial Congress agreed not to render military aid to any British forces that might enter South Carolina," writes Edgar. "In return, they received a vague promise that they would be left alone."

Backcountry residents constituted a majority of the state's white population, and they remained skeptical about the revolution. For decades, the Charleston-based elites who were suddenly calling themselves revolutionaries had used malapportioned and strategically gerrymandered districts to dilute upcountry white voices in state politics. Little wonder, then, that the truce at Ninety Six disintegrated quickly when revolutionaries hauled off several backcountry Tories in chains, Tories captured a patriot supply train as retribution, and the provincial Congress had to dispatch a five-hundred-man militia led by Major Andrew Williamson to recover the war supplies. An estimated fifteen hundred Tories then attacked the fort that Williamson established at Ninety Six, and "the first blood of the Revolution in South Carolina was shed."[4]

After the patriots seized control, the provincial government in 1777 and 1778 purged the coastal regions of British loyalists by passing "allegiance and fidelity" laws. Prominent Charlestonians who chose loyalty to the Crown liquidated their assets and booked private passage to Europe or the West Indies. With neither the means nor the desire to expatriate, backcountry loyalists simply blended back into their rural communities far from the coastal centers of commerce where they would be difficult to identify and, therefore, served as a latent and potentially nettlesome pool of British sympathizers. The Ninety Six District bordering Georgia was a Royalist haven.

To gin up support among these embedded rural southerners living along the Appalachian frontier, the British devised a "southern strategy" of recapturing Georgia and South Carolina by providing military and political assistance to rural resisters willing to join the Crown to fight the revolutionaries. The response from South Carolina was so overwhelming that the British commissioned the South Carolina Royalists as a provincial regiment within the British army, and with their support Britain recaptured Charleston and South Carolina in 1780.[5] The patriots were literally on the run. The fort at Ninety Six was transformed into a stockade where captured patriots were jailed and often executed. Those lucky enough to avoid being swept up and summarily imprisoned, tortured, or killed by patrols of British legionnaires and their Tory sympathizers beat a hasty retreat to neighboring North Carolina.

Matters soon got out of hand in South Carolina's backcountry. Indiscriminate violence, plundering, and unspeakable crimes were committed by both sides. The atrocities committed by Redcoats and Royalists converted to the revolutionary cause many South Carolinians who had previously favored the British or preferred neutrality. After regrouping in the Catawba River valley along the border between the Carolinas—and blessed with the courageous leadership of men like Thomas Sumter and Francis "the Swamp Fox" Marion—the patriots fought and won key South Carolina battles in "Huck's Defeat," at King's Mountain, in the coastal swamplands, and, most decisively, at Cowpens. In May and June 1781, patriot forces led by Nathaniel Greene laid siege to the Star Fort at Ninety Six. The civil war between South Carolina's patriots and loyalists had turned the tide of the Revolution itself. But the resistance to the Revolution should not be forgotten, for it prefigured many rebellions to come.[6]

When the newly drafted U.S. Constitution reached South Carolina in the fall of 1787, the regional fractures between lowcountry plantation elites and rural backcountry farmers resurfaced. As a proposed replacement for the Articles of Confederation, the Constitution provided for a stronger chief executive and central government—a federal Republic that demanded more of its component states than the articles had. It also lowered the ratification threshold from unanimous consent under the Articles of Confederation to a three-fourths supermajority of member states. Although the Tenth Amendment proposed by the first Congress assuaged anti-Federalist critics by reserving all powers not assigned to the national government "to the states, or the people," the proposed charter clearly heralded an expansion in national power.

Predictably, reactions in South Carolina split along regional lines. Coastal leaders who influenced the Constitution's drafting and had the greatest financial stake in its passage led the ratification push. All four signatories from South Carolina—John Rutledge, Charles Cotesworth Pinckney, Charles Pinckney, and Pierce Butler—were Charlestonians. The backcountry again formed the backbone of resistance. In May 1788, convention delegates voted to ratify the Constitution by a wide margin, 149-73. But the final count is highly misleading, because the apportionment of convention delegates was skewed such that coastal whites were overrepresented by a margin of roughly six to one. Anti-Federalist protests at the convention, led valiantly by Sumter and Aedanus Burke, were suffocated by the dint of sheer numbers.[7]

South Carolina was not the only state wary of the Constitution. New York, Rhode Island, and Virginia came close to rejecting the charter, and anti-Federalist sentiment ran strong in many states. But these constitutional critics tended to focus on the document's lack of civil liberty guarantees; their concerns led to promises of a Bill of Rights in the form of a series of twelve amendments, which the First Congress promptly delivered.[8] The objections raised by South Carolina's anti-Federalists, by contrast, were rooted in narrow, parochial fears about the closing of the slave trade after 1808, a navigation law that might advantage northern shipping interests, and state debt relief. Before adjourning, delegates at South Carolina's ratification convention recommended "several amendments that included the states' unequivocally keeping control of all election procedures for national offices; the states' retaining all powers not specifically given to the central government; and prohibiting direct taxes except in the case of extreme exigency."[9]

In short, South Carolina's anti-Federalism was precisely that: a fear, bordering on paranoia, about potential encroachments by the national government on *states' rights*, rather than libertarian worries about the document's failure to protect *individual rights*. With two-thirds of the state's inhabitants deprived of any citizenship rights by virtue of their skin color, the absence of civil libertarian protests by South Carolina during the heady revolutionary moment also foreshadowed the state's aggressive resistance to the Civil War amendments of the 1860s and the civil rights movement a century later.

Defying the Union: 1789 to 1833

The political transformations in South Carolina before the Civil War arose from the state's desire to protect its economic self-determination and thwart rising abolitionist sentiments. These twin objectives, in turn, required South Carolina to maximize local control by minimizing interference from national elites. Beyond slavery, no single issue during this period defined the state-federal tensions more than national tariff policy. And no figure from antebellum South Carolina epitomized the delicate and inevitably explosive balance between state autonomy and national power more than John Caldwell Calhoun.

Born in a backcountry town of the old Ninety Six District, the Yale-educated Calhoun represented South Carolina in almost every political capacity: in the state legislature; in the U.S. House of Representatives; as secretary of war under James Monroe; as vice president in the successive administrations of John Quincy Adams and Andrew Jackson; and, finally, with two storied turns in the U.S. Senate sandwiched around a brief stint as John Tyler's secretary of state. Suppressing his own presidential ambitions, in 1824 Calhoun was the vice presidential running mate for both Adams and Jackson in a post-Federalist election in which all four candidates ran under the Democratic-Republican banner. With support split four ways among Adams, Jackson, William Crawford, and Henry Clay, Jackson won a plurality of the popular and electoral votes but did not get the requisite majority of electors. The election was thrown into the U.S. House of Representatives, where Clay used his influence as Speaker to swing enough delegations to Adams, depriving Jackson of the White House.[10] Calhoun was chosen to be Adams's vice president.

In office, Calhoun attempted to forge compromises between the surging Jacksonian wing of the party, led deftly by his New York nemesis, Martin Van Buren, and the old-guard Federalist wing, headed by Adams. By 1828, however, Calhoun found himself in the bizarre position of running for vice president on Jackson's new Democratic Party ticket against his own administration. Promising universal suffrage for white men, Jacksonian Democracy allayed the fears of the same frontier, agrarian South Carolinians who fretted during the revolutionary period about an elite-dominated American government that would differ little from the oppressions of British colonialism. In 1828, Jackson won his much-anticipated rematch against Adams, and Calhoun was again elected vice president.

Poor Calhoun couldn't savor the electoral or philosophical benefits of his and Jackson's victory, however. He assumed that Jackson, a fellow southerner, would be sympathetic to South Carolina's position on the export tariff policies Adams enacted in 1828 before leaving office. When Jackson instead endorsed what many southerners called the "Tariff of Abominations," Calhoun could no longer abide the decisions of his own government. Anonymously, he penned the *South Carolina Exposition of Protest*, a theory of state nullification asserting the right of any state to negate federal decisions it opposed. Essentially, Calhoun was arguing for an interpretation of the Tenth Amendment that would distort the Constitution's meaning to reach an illogical conclusion:

> The powers of the General Government are particularly enumerated and specifically delegated; and all powers not expressly delegated, or which are not necessary and proper to carry into effect those that are so granted, are reserved expressly to the States or the people. The Government is thus positively restricted to the exercise of those general powers that were supposed to act uniformly on all the parts, leaving, the residue to the people of the States, by whom alone, from the very nature of these powers, they can be justly and fairly exercised.... Our system, then, consists of two distinct and independent Governments. The general powers, expressly delegated to the General Government, are subject to its sole and separate control; and the States cannot, without violating the constitutional compact, interpose their authority to check, or in any manner to counteract its movements, so long as they are confined to the proper sphere. So, also, the peculiar and local powers reserved to the States are subject to their exclusive control; nor can the General Government interfere, in any manner, with them, without violating the Constitution.[11]

By asserting that two separate and inviolate spheres of government—one state, one national—ran parallel to each another, with neither overlap between them nor superseding national authority, Calhoun was brazenly attempting to undermine the very foundations of American Federalism.

South Carolina's elites called for a convention in late 1832 to address the matter. Foreshadowing Strom Thurmond's presidential campaign 116 years later, opponents of federal tariff policies ran on a ticket labeled "State Rights and Nullification." They won handily, and then passed an "Ordinance of Nullification" declaring the 1828 and 1832 tariffs "null, void, and no law, nor binding upon this State." In effect, South Carolina asserted for itself the Supreme Court–like authority to rule on the constitutionality of federal laws. Historian Manisha Sinha explained Calhoun's underlying motives:

> By 1832, a majority of Carolinian planter politicians, led by Calhoun, were determined to act on nullification. The discourse of slavery and separatism perfected by the state's political elite had imparted an urgency and a broader dimension to the controversy, which the tariff by itself could never have generated. And Calhoun's break with Jackson pushed him to vindicate his pet theory. He best understood the political and constitutional implications of nullification. State interposition would not only nullify the tariff but it would also act as a permanent constitutional mechanism to protect the southern slaveholding minority in a democratic republic.[12]

Despite the region's exaggerated power courtesy of the three-fifths rule and the malapportioned Senate and Electoral College, Calhoun realized that the inevitabilities of American and human history were closing around him and his fellow South Carolina nullifiers. With the deadline for slave importation more than twenty years past and abolitionist sentiment rising in the North and pockets of the South, "Cast-iron" Calhoun made a desperate bid to construct a constitutional Trojan horse through which he could sneak a more permanent, more powerful device to negate the authority of the U.S. government.

Andrew Jackson responded in January 1833 with a stinging presidential rebuke. "If these measures [passed in South Carolina] can not be defeated and overcome by the power conferred by the Constitution on the Federal Government, the Constitution must be considered as incompetent to its own defense, the supremacy of the laws is at an end, and the rights and liberties of the citizens can no longer receive protection from the Government of the Union," he wrote.[13] The nation sided with its president. Politically, Calhoun would survive the gambit. But the damage done to his home state was considerable. "Through the twists and turns of successive interpretations, commentators have agreed upon at least one point: in the final crisis South Carolina found herself utterly alone," says John Barnwell. "After 1828, as the nullifiers demonstrated an increasing appetite for confrontation, their extreme state-rights philosophy attracted only scattered, ineffective support outside South Carolina."[14] But South Carolina would not be isolated for long.

Abandoning the Union: 1834 to 1875

By the mid-nineteenth century, South Carolina's slaveholders were feeling pinched between the rising abolitionist movement and domestic labor pressures. They could tolerate the Union no longer. Despite Calhoun's failure, the nullification movement fueled the sentiments that would lead to an aborted secession attempt in 1850–51 and the successful, nation-shattering one a decade later.

The long-standing internal divisions among South Carolina's whites again pitted slave-dependent coastal elites against the backcountry whites who were either less dependent on slavery for their livelihoods, non-dependent, or actually threatened economically by competition from black laborers. Half of South Carolina's white families owned no slaves, and many resented rising black competition in the trades. An 1848 census of Charleston revealed that about three-fifths of artisans and laborers were either freed blacks or slaves hired out for fee. "Complaints were frequently voiced about black competition, coupled with demands that slaves be limited to agricultural pursuits," wrote Blake McNulty in his account of the events that nearly led to secession in 1850.[15] Meanwhile, the abolitionist movement was gaining traction among a small contingent of courageous progressives in South Carolina. "Local abolitionists were rare, but the presence of only a handful was a nightmare to an already apprehensive slaveholding society," McNulty said. "The confidence of Carolina masters was also shaken by several members of their class leaving the state and embracing the abolitionist credo." William Henry Brisbane, a Baptist minister who left his Beaufort farm for Cincinnati, had a particularly unsettling effect. Writing abolitionist tracts from Ohio under the pen name "Brutus," Brisbane caused a stir by arranging to have his pamphlets distributed to post offices throughout South Carolina.[16]

In an effort to pacify the country, Congress forged the Compromise of 1850, settling five slavery-related questions by passing two pro-slavery measures and two anti-slavery measures, and splitting the difference on the fifth.[17] In one of his most impassioned Senate speeches, on March 31, 1850, Calhoun protested the Compromise. Calhoun was physically so weak that his speech had to be read for him, and he died a few weeks later.

Convening in Nashville with six other southern states in June 1850, a group of South Carolinians led by Robert Barnwell Rhett formed the core group of "fire-eaters" who would repeatedly agitate for secession and a southern confederacy during the next decade.[18] To comprehend the heat emanating from these fiery secessionists, consider how one South Carolina pamphleteer concluded his 152-page screed by turning Patrick Henry's famous revolutionary call to arms inside out: "There is Union and Abolition on one hand, and Disunion and Slavery on the other. Which of the two shall we choose? Give us SLAVERY or give us death."[19] Radicals like Rhett wanted South Carolina to secede even if that meant forming a lone-state nation. More prudent voices, urging caution, won out.

The 1860 presidential election was the breaking point. Soon after Republican Abraham Lincoln's victory, Armistead Burt and others met on what came to be known as "Secessionist Hill" in Abbeville, South Carolina. On December 20, 1860, South Carolina bolted the Union. The fire-eating separatists had triumphed over the unionists, and the Palmetto Flag was raised as the Stars and Stripes was lowered. Ten other southern states followed South Carolina into the newly formed Confederacy. The Civil War—known to some southerners as the War against Northern Aggression—began a few months later when the opening shots were fired by Confederate troops on the Union garrison at Fort Sumter in Charleston Harbor. According to legend, the first salvo belonged to South Carolina's Edmund Ruffin, a secessionist so devoted to the Confederacy that he also fired a final shot at the end of the war: upon learning that Robert E. Lee had surrendered at Appomattox, Ruffin turned his rifle on himself.

Within the Confederacy, South Carolina agitated for the Atlantic slave trade to be reopened. Doing so risked isolating Britain and other cotton importers, however, and threatened to pit the "upper" South states like North Carolina, Tennessee, and Virginia against the Deep South states. Nevertheless, South Carolina's delegation to the Confederate Congress moved to eliminate the slave trade prohibitions from the Confederate constitution.[20] Charleston newspaperman Leonidas Spratt suggested that "another revolution" against the Confederacy might be needed to reestablish the practice. As ever, South Carolina was a rebel even among rebels.

The war brought death and destitution to the South and to South Carolina especially. Fatalities and casualties affected a higher proportion of

South Carolina's population than that of any northern state. Confederate war bonds made worthless by the South's military defeat led to poverty and personal bankruptcy for many survivors. The insult added to these injuries was the possibility of the black majority assuming power over its former masters, a prospect that instilled in southern whites a sense of doom mixed with abject fear. After Congress passed two major Reconstruction Acts in March 1865, South Carolina again rebuked Washington—but this time, curiously enough, by voting *for* federal intervention. New federal mandates called for military supervisors in the occupied states to register all eligible male voters and call conventions to amend state constitutions to guarantee black suffrage. Unlike other southern states, where whites attempted to maximize their representation in the constitutional conventions, South Carolina took the contrarian's path. Historian Richard Zuczek explains:

> For South Carolina, with a black majority, [constitutional enfranchising of blacks] meant whites faced the possibility of becoming less powerful at best, *ruled* at worst. A consensus soon emerged in opposition to the new convention. If no convention were held—if the vote were somehow defeated—the state would remain under military supervision. This situation would be temporary, lasting only until Congress developed a new plan or Northern opinion shifted; besides, conservatives had already demonstrated their ability to undermine federal authority. On the other hand, once a new constitution granted blacks political power, they might control the legislature, the judiciary, and the governorship, and whites would face a grueling uphill struggle to reclaim power. So, contrary to the logic and the course pursued by other Southern states, Carolina whites attempt to derail the convention.[21]

Because the law required a majority of *registered* voters rather than votes cast, conservative whites organized a "register-and-reject" movement to prevent the necessary majority to establish a convention. Despite the fact that blacks were 63 percent of the 127,550 registrants, the ploy almost worked: a total of 68,768 votes were cast for the convention, barely 5,000 more than needed. Few of the defiant registered whites turned out to vote nay, but enough of them had registered and abstained—nearly 56,000 in all—that the final margin was smaller than expected.

Lincoln's successor, Andrew Johnson of Tennessee, was far more palatable to southerners. Johnson thwarted his party's Reconstruction efforts by vetoing the 1865 Civil Rights Act, the Freedmen's Bill, and the Military

Reconstruction Act. Undeterred, congressional Republicans in June 1866 proposed what became the Fourteenth Amendment, promising due process and equal protection for every citizen. The confederate states had to ratify the amendment as a condition of readmission, and GOP victories in the 1866 midterm elections were perceived as a national vindication of Republican policies. With symbolic effect, an obstinate South Carolina legislature expressed its displeasure a few weeks later. On December 20, 1866, six years to the day after South Carolina seceded from the Union, state legislators overwhelmingly rejected the Fourteenth Amendment, and South Carolina joined Louisiana and Texas as the only states without voting members in the Fortieth Congress. "Radical" Republican rule now governed the state.

South Carolinians who never took kindly to federal interference viewed the postwar legal and constitutional battles as a redefined struggle between Columbia and Washington—a war by other means. The first big salvo was fired by Republican president Ulysses S. Grant, who deployed federal troops to South Carolina in 1871 to stabilize a situation made increasingly unstable by the activities of the state's newly formed Ku Klux Klan. (Not until Dwight D. Eisenhower dispatched paratroopers and assumed command of the Arkansas National Guard in 1957 to enforce the school desegregation would another president send troops into the South.) "After the establishment of Radical rule in 1868, disorganized, locally-based resistance appeared, along with trial-and-error attempts at cooperation, abstention, fraud, and economic intimidation in an effort to weaken the state Republican machine," says Zuczek. "Over the years the violence grew more coherent, political, and widespread, and so did conservative politics and political opposition. White Carolinians grew more unified and deliberate, and their resistance became more organized, directed, and effective. By 1876 resistance had evolved into war."[22]

Ignoring the Union: 1876 to 1912

The American centennial was a critical turning point for South Carolina and the South. The Panic of 1873 had created severe economic hardship throughout the region, forcing northern creditors to call in outstanding debts. Economic worries had swept the Democrats into power in the 1874 congressional elections while President Grant watched scandals surround him and his popularity fade. Then, in 1876, something astonishing happened: Governor Samuel Tilden of New York became the only Democratic presidential nominee between the Civil War and the New Deal to win a popular-vote majority, an achievement that eluded even Grover Cleveland and Woodrow Wilson in their four combined presidential victories. In what historian Roy Morris aptly calls "the fraud of the century," however, Tilden was denied the presidency.

Election results were disputed in three southern states: Florida, Louisiana, and South Carolina. Republican nominee Rutherford B. Hayes would need all twenty-two disputed electors if he hoped to eke out a 185-184 electoral majority.[23] The contested election dragged on for months, creating so much tension across the country that some feared war might break out anew. Eventually a highly partisan, fifteen-member national commission composed of five members each from the House, Senate, and Supreme Court voted 8-7 to certify the three states' disputed electors for Hayes, making him America's nineteenth president. Behind the committee's superficial machinations, a private deal between the Hayes and Tilden camps was struck at the Wormley House Hotel in Washington on February 26, 1877—just days before the March 4 inauguration date.[24] In exchange for conceding the presidency to Hayes, the southern states were promised that federal troops would be removed from the South. Five weeks later, on April 10, Hayes delivered. South Carolina's seven electoral votes had been willingly sacrificed upon the altar of southern autonomy.

South Carolina's 1876 state elections were just as messy and more controversial. Democrats claimed that Republican officials, their carpetbag governor Daniel Chamberlain, and other "scalawag" sympathizers "siding with the Negroes" had manipulated the results to deprive the Democratic nominee, legendary Confederate general Wade Hampton, of his rightful place as the state's next governor. Republicans countered with the claim that bands of Democratic gun club members riding on horseback had used terror and intimidation techniques to suppress the black vote.[25] The "Red Shirt" movement arose in the aftermath of the July 8 massacre of black militiamen by local whites in Hamburg, a town then located in the same Edgefield County that later produced governor-senators Benjamin Tillman and Strom Thurmond. These renegade bands "roamed the state in defense of their candidate . . . [w]earing red shirts and armed with pistols and shotguns,"[26] instructing their members that "every Democrat must feel honor bound to control the vote of at least one Negro, by intimidation, purchase, keeping him away or as each individual may determine, how he may best accomplish it."[27] A few black leaders even rode alongside whites or in their own Red Shirt gun clubs, promoting the "straightout" Democratic ticket of 1876.[28]

Republicans challenged the validity of ballots from Edgefield and Laurens Counties, where the vote totals appeared to outnumber the registered populations. Meanwhile, *both* parties assumed legislative power in Columbia, the state capital. "The impasse was ridiculous, yet grave," says Ernest McPherson Lander. "For four days Democrats and Republicans ate and slept in the legislative chamber. To add to the confusion, each group tried to conduct regular business." The state's supreme court declared the Democrats victorious. Emboldened by the presence of federal troops, Republicans re-inaugurated Chamberlain as governor anyway. Ultimately, the dispute was resolved by the same backroom bargain that settled the presidential election, which itself turned on the fact that South Carolina's electoral votes were available for political horse-trading in the first place. Within hours of Hayes's order to withdraw federal troops, the Republicans relented and Hampton and his Red Shirt rebels took over. Reconstruction in South Carolina had ended.[29]

The 1876 election demonstrated the value of manipulation and intimidation to rig outcomes. Though threats and violence were powerful tools, a premium was also placed on creativity. For example, Democratic officials began to tinker with what came to be known as the "eight-box system," a vote-suppression method that required voters to place their ballots for each of the eight statewide offices into separate boxes, with any miscast ballot voided. The eight-box method effectively disfranchised the vast, illiterate majority of former slaves, but it also invalidated the votes of many poor whites—a fact that bothered few members of the white ruling classes.[30] With slavery outlawed and the textile industry growing, those hoping to suppress proletarian ambitions had to be inventive. "In a free South Carolina, the twin pillars of race *and* class stood on an inherently unstable foundation," writes Charles J. Holden. "Black South Carolinians were not slaves. With the rise of the textile mills, poor whites were not bound to lives of hardscrabble farming and later tenantry. Postwar conservatives, therefore, were constantly being forced to aim their salvos in defense of hierarchy at moving targets."[31]

With the Republicans and their federal troops gone, the biggest domestic threat was a divided white populace. The upcountry, farmer-populist "Reformer" wing of the Democratic Party specifically worried that the lowcountry, elitist "Conservative" wing would exploit black votes to their intraparty advantage. The era called for crafty, pseudo-populist politicians capable of disabusing the mill-working classes of any notions they might be harboring about political or economic parity, for such thoughts might pit poor and rich whites against one another. At the end of the nineteenth century, nobody fit that bill better than Benjamin Ryan Tillman.

"Pitchfork Ben" Tillman, who lost an eye to illness, was leader of the Reformers. Because they had the numerical advantage, Tillman advocated a statewide referendum in 1894 to form a constitutional convention to restructure state government to solidify white control in the post-Reconstruction era. The referendum passed, and in 1895 the convention brought Reformer and Conservative Democrats into alliance to achieve Tillman's stated aspiration of establishing the franchise for "every white who is worthy of the vote, while at the same time reducing the negro voters at least one half, probably more."[32] With a ruthless, unbridled efficiency, South Carolina's Democrats were soon exercising one-party rule on behalf of "worthy" whites. The last of the seven black U.S. congressmen from South Carolina to serve between 1870 and 1897 was soon gone, and the age of Jim Crow had begun.[33]

Slavery in South Carolina, meanwhile, was finally coming to an end. The language of the Thirteenth Amendment drafted by southern congressmen permitted slavery "as a punishment for crime," creating a built-in incentive for former slaveholders and local sheriffs to collude in rounding up freed blacks and putting them in prison for the pettiest of crimes—which is precisely what many of them did. The Radical Republican governors during Reconstruction for the most part resisted using the convict-labor clause, but upon his assumption in 1877 of the statehouse Governor Wade Hampton called a special legislative session to establish convict leasing. South Carolina's leasing system was rather limited, neither as large nor as abusive as it was in Arkansas and Georgia. Nor was South Carolina the last state to abandon the practice.[34] But the treatment of South Carolina prisoners leased out to make shoes or mine phosphates was scandalous, as were the conditions of state penitentiaries; scurvy was rampant, and convicts who didn't die from sheer exhaustion suffered from malnutrition and disease. Soon after the legislature created a state-owned farm to profit from convict labor, politicians realized that using prison labor was economically inefficient.[35] In 1897 the state finally banned the practice for good.

Tillman protégé Cole Blease was the next in a long line of leaders who continued South Carolina's tradition of rural white political power. Blease became one of the state's most beloved—and hated—politicians during the early years of the new century, and he built his base of support among the same working-class, backcountry whites Tillman had. South Carolina was a regional outlier because it did not exclude poor whites from electoral participation, as Jim Crow laws in other southern states did. In fact, South Carolina was the first southern state to extend the franchise, at least de jure, to all white males.

But Carolina life was anything but egalitarian for white men. According to labor historian Bryant Simon's account of the South Carolina textile industry during the early twentieth century, race-based and class-based politics were regularly invoked to divert mill workers' aggressions. The number of textile mills in South Carolina had increased fifteen-fold between 1880 and 1920, and most were located in backcountry communities. The industry's growth offered rural whites a chance for economic opportunity beyond the subsistence farming and pelt trading, altering the political calculus for strategic politicians like Blease. Though Blease exhibited the same populist temperament, talents, and tactics of Louisiana's Huey Long, his policies were decidedly different.[36] A stump speaker nonpareil, Blease used bait-and-switch appeals to whites' racism, sexual anxiety, and antiaristocratic sensibilities. Explains Simon:

> Blease rode to power on the backs of white workers . . . [but] did almost nothing to enhance workers' material well-being. These white men feared that their control over their families was dwindling and that their masculinity was under attack. Blease politicized them along divide-and-conquer class lines, but his mobilization produced a misogynist, racist, nonradical, and antireform version of class politics. He directed the ire of male workers against the middle classes, not against the mill bosses, and he aroused them to safeguard their manhood by blocking change, not by proposing reforms of their own. Another politician might have urged workers to enlist in the trade movement or called for child labor legislation linked to minimum wage statutes, but no one in South Carolina, at least not before the Great Depression, put forth these positions.[37]

The politics of angered distraction worked splendidly for Cole Blease long before abortion, gay rights, and evolution emerged as issues to divert voters' attentions from the types of serious reforms that would improve their economic situation. For white and black workers alike, race hatred was a cheap emotion with expensive consequences.

Defying the Union: 1913 to 1968

South Carolina during the next four decades confronted the same cataclysms as the rest of the nation: the Great Depression, the New Deal and two world wars. But South Carolina's response to these events was different.

For example, the women's suffrage movement met with great resistance in the South, and South Carolina was no exception. The Southern Woman's League for the Rejection of the Susan B. Anthony Amendment and the Southern States Woman Suffrage Committee, both of which opposed amending the Constitution to establish women's suffrage, drew significant support from the Palmetto State. When Congress finally proposed the suffrage amendment in the summer of 1919, South Carolina's two senators, Ellison D. "Cotton Ed" Smith and Nathaniel B. Dial, plus all nine members of its U.S. House delegation, voted against it.[38] In Columbia, the all-male South Carolina state legislature voted against ratification by wide margins: 93-21 in the House, and 32-3 in the Senate.[39] Although a 1921 amendment to the state constitution made women eligible to run for office, South Carolina has consistently been at or near the bottom in terms of its share of female elected officials. With fourteen female representatives and a lone state senator (Linda H. Short), South Carolina is the only state where today the percentage of women legislators—a lowly 8.8 percent—is in single digits.

At the outbreak of World War I, South Carolina's population was still majority-African American, but to their chagrin, black South Carolinians who fought in segregated units in Europe returned from battle to find that little had changed back home. There were no black elected officials, and black veterans who dared to call for voting rights were greeted with scorn or violence. During the same summer of 1919 that the state was rejecting women's suffrage, white sailors provoked a race riot in Charleston that culminated in the deaths of three black citizens. The legendary political figure, James F. "Jimmy" Byrnes, then a young Democratic congressman, summarized the mood of South Carolina's white population when he declared that "the war has in no way changed the attitude of the white man toward the social and political equality of the negro."[40]

A limited Progressive movement began to gain traction in South Carolina prior to and immediately following the war. But when cotton and tobacco prices plunged as a result of boll weevil crop damages and the postwar decline in export demand, wholesale economic deprivation quickly scuttled any talk about progressive reform or racial equity. Thousands of farmers, black and white, left the state in search of better lives.[41] Following the 1930 census, South Carolina dropped from seven U.S. House seats to the six-member delegation it has had since. As rumrunners ran and flappers flapped during the roaring 1920s, South Carolina was getting a head start on the Great Depression.

Like many southern states, South Carolina benefited immensely and disproportionately from the New Deal. The Public Works Administration and the Works Progress Administration put citizens to work and infused much-needed developmental capital into the state. The Santee-Cooper dam project did for the state what the Tennessee Valley Authority did for its northwestern neighbor and other southern states. Governor Olin Johnston and U.S. senator Byrnes strongly supported the policies of President Franklin D. Roosevelt, who later appointed Byrnes to the Supreme Court. But the state drew a hard distinction between the "first" New Deal's recovery efforts in banking relief, agricultural legislation, rural electrification, and public works and the anti-lynching and labor reforms of the "second" New Deal. This cleave was made plain when Johnston challenged "Cotton Ed" Smith in 1938 for his Senate seat. FDR came to South Carolina to bolster Johnston's candidacy, but in the end voters were swayed by Smith's unvarnished appeals to white supremacy. "For farmers, the New Deal brought price supports, agricultural credit, a reduction in farm tenancy, soil-conservation measures, and rural electrification. For mill workers, there were better wages and hours, the right of collective bargaining, and an end to child labor," wrote historian Jack Irby Hayes. "Yet, because of Smith's race baiting, the farm vote and part of the mill vote went to him in 1938."[42] The long shadows of Tillman and Blease still darkened South Carolina politics.

Johnston remembered the lessons of 1938 when Smith's turn for reelection came around again in 1944. That April, the Supreme Court issued the first of several decisions over the next two decades that would rattle the entrenched white power structure in South Carolina. In *Smith v. Allwright*, the Court ruled that Texas's "white primary"—which southern states relied upon to prevent black participation in the nominating process—violated the Fifteenth Amendment's suffrage guarantees.[43] With no serious Republican challenge, for decades the white primary ensured that every South Carolina elected official was not only a Democrat but a white Democrat. The *Allwright* ruling outraged the state's two U.S. senators, Smith and Burnet R. Maybank, who warned that the Supreme Court was not going to tell South Carolina how to conduct its elections.

Not to be outdone, Governor Johnston called the general assembly into special session to recommend the elimination of all public primary election laws so that the Democratic Party, as a private entity, could control the nomination process however it saw fit. "White supremacy will be maintained in our primaries," said a defiant Johnston. "Let the chips fall where they may." Within a week, the legislature enacted 147 laws "separating party primaries from state government control." For good measure, the public approved an amendment that eliminated any mention of the Democratic primary from the state constitution.[44] South Carolina would eventually hold out as the last state to abolish the white primary.

Seizing the opportunity to finally dethrone "Cotton Ed" Smith from the Senate seat he had held since 1908, Johnston used the *Allwright* decision to flip the race card on him. In one breath the governor depicted Smith as too soft on the "negro" question, and in the next he complained that Smith's race-baiting speeches brought undue national attention on the state. Having reinforced his own white-supremacist credentials during the special session, Johnston beat Smith by a wide margin in the 1944 Democratic primary, thus guaranteeing his election that November.[45] (Smith, who had been a U.S. senator for thirty-six years, died just a few weeks after the primary, saving him from seeing Johnston ascend to his Senate seat. Johnston himself served almost another two decades, until his own death in April 1965 spared him by four months from having to watch fellow southerner Lyndon Johnson sign the Voting Rights Act into law.)

Despite the late–New Deal reforms, Franklin Roosevelt had managed to pacify white southerners and keep the Democratic coalition together by foot-dragging on civil rights. With the war over and FDR gone, however, President Harry Truman found it increasingly difficult to repair the growing breach within the national Democratic Party. Though Truman knew that the slightest provocation might cause a southern revolt, two incendiary events in the 1940s drew his attentions to the Palmetto State. His responses created a partisan fissure that southern Democrats have yet to repair.

The first incident involved a decorated black war veteran, Isaac Woodard, who, on February 12, 1946, got into an argument with a white bus driver while he was heading home on a long bus ride. When the bus reached Batesburg, a police officer summoned by the driver hauled Woodard off to a local jail, where he was billy-clubbed in the face so badly he lost sight in both eyes. The second incident occurred almost a year to the day later, when a white mob of thirty-five Greenville men armed with shotguns hauled from prison and lynched Willie Earle, a black man who had been arrested for killing a white cab driver.[46] In both trials, all-white juries acquitted the defendants.

Truman, who often mentioned the Woodard story in his speeches, created the President's Committee on Civil Rights by executive order on December 5, 1946. The following October, the committee issued a report that recommended greater federal supervision of civil rights violations in the South. In a special speech to Congress on February 2, 1948, Truman called for sweeping civil rights reforms. Ten days later, the South Carolina legislature passed a resolution condemning the president's plan as "un-American." When Truman announced his reelection bid the next month, his press secretary told disgruntled southerners to "put up or shut up."[47] They put up South Carolina's new governor, Strom Thurmond, as the States' Rights Democratic Party candidate for president.

Born in 1902 in the small, upcountry town of Edgefield, James Strom Thurmond attended what later became Clemson University. A self-taught lawyer who easily passed the state's three-day bar exam, Thurmond by the age of thirty had been elected the state's youngest school superintendent, one of its youngest state senators, and appointed the youngest state circuit judge in South Carolina.[48] At forty-one, he put his political career on hold and volunteered for World War II, where the highly decorated Thurmond flew gliders behind German lines during the Normandy invasion.

Thurmond was a reputed Lothario, and his first wife, Jean, who died in 1960, was twenty-four years younger. His second, now widowed, wife is a former Miss South Carolina forty-four years his junior who interned in Thurmond's Senate office before marrying him and bearing Thurmond two children while he was in his seventies. Thurmond was known to kiss beauty queens in public and had a reputation for groping young women on Capitol Hill; in 1994 he grabbed Senator Patty Murray of Washington in an elevator. Following his death in 2003, Thurmond's family revealed that the same man who ran as a segregationist presidential candidate had fathered a child in 1925 with a black house servant.

Thurmond is beloved in South Carolina. A legendary constituent servant, he sent cards, congratulations, and condolences to what seemed like every family in the state, and often when they least expected his personal touch. The longest-serving and oldest member ever to serve in the U.S. Senate, Thurmond is the most significant politician in South Carolina history except Calhoun—and perhaps including him.[49] A seventeen-foot-tall, thirty-two-ton bronze statue of Thurmond graces the state capitol grounds in Columbia, and countless schools, facilities. and other public sites around the state are named for him. About a year after it was dedicated, the monument was changed to include Essie Mae Washington's name along with that of Thurmond's four other children.

Thurmond won an eleven-candidate Democratic primary in 1946 to become governor. As governor he supported the New Deal, tried to repeal the poll tax, and supported the prosecution of the men who lynched Willie Earle. But any chance of Thurmond emerging as a true southern progressive was forever erased when he ran against the Democratic Party and President Truman as the States' Rights Democratic Party candidate for president. The "Dixiecrats," as they were known, aimed not so much to win as to siphon away enough electoral votes from Truman to deny him reelection. Their plan failed, but Thurmond and his running mate, Mississippi governor Fielding Wright, won thirty-nine electoral votes in four Deep South states, including South Carolina, and the Thurmond-Wright ticket captured over a million votes and at least 10 percent of the vote in every former Confederate state except Texas. Though he lost the election, Thurmond firmly established himself as the nation's most prominent defender of segregation—an issue that once more put South Carolina at center stage in the battle over school equality.

Represented by Thurgood Marshall of the National Association for the Advancement of Colored People, black plaintiffs from Clarendon County were the first to challenge the Supreme Court's separate-but-equal standard for school districts. Even before the U.S. Court of Appeals in 1952 upheld South Carolina's segregated school system in *Briggs v. Elliott*, Governor James Byrnes threatened to shut down the entire public school system and replace it with private schools rather than allow integration to proceed.[50] For good measure, South Carolina voters approved a referendum that gave the legislature "standby power" to shut down the schools as a preemptive signal that schools would not adhere to any court's decree.

In 1952 the Clarendon County case was pooled with three others into *Brown v. Board of Education of Topeka*.[51] Governor Byrnes, who fretted about South Carolina's national image, helped ensure that the Kansas school board was made the lead-named litigant even though Clarendon had pioneered the case. The segregationists were defended by John W. Davis. The 1924 Democratic presidential nominee and former U.S. solicitor general was regarded as one of the top legal minds in the country. But

Marshall prevailed. In its first major decision under newly appointed chief justice Earl Warren, the Supreme Court voted unanimously to overturn the separate-but-equal standard.[52]

When Davis died a few months later, S. Emory Rogers took his place during the 1955 decree stage of the case.[53] Rogers said the state's ability to conform with *Brown* depended on the Court's decree, adding that he hoped "something can be worked out." According to Richard Kluger's account in *Simple Justice*, Warren viewed Rogers's response as "close to heresy." When Rogers asserted that the U.S. District Court for the Fourth Circuit, which contains South Carolina, could best supervise compliance, a testy exchange between the chief justice and "the feisty little Summerton attorney and scion of the plantocracy" ensued:

> WARREN: But you are not willing to say here that there would be an honest attempt to conform to this decree, if we did leave it to the District Court?
> ROGERS: No, I am not. Let us get the word "honest" out of there.
> WARREN: No, leave it in.
> ROGERS: No, because I would have to tell you right now we would not conform—we would not send our white children to the Negro schools

Eyewitnesses recall seeing Rogers point his forefinger at Warren upon requesting that the word "honest" be removed from the discussion. The chief justice looked angry, and some thought he might charge Rogers with contempt, which would have added Rogers's name to the list of martyred southern heroes. Though Rogers escaped the literal charge, for all practical purposes he *was* treating the Court and the Constitution with contempt—even if he was merely trying to be candid with the chief justice about the on-the-ground political situation back home in South Carolina.[54]

The threat of court-ordered desegregation created a political firestorm in South Carolina. Along with Virginia senator Harry Byrd, in February 1956 Strom Thurmond took the lead in drafting the "Declaration of Constitutional Principles," which flatly declared that the Supreme Court's *Brown* ruling violated the U.S. Constitution. The "Southern Manifesto," as it came to be known, cited the intent of Congress at the time the Fourteenth Amendment was crafted and the state of public schools during that period to justify continued school segregation. Beneath Thurmond's lawyerly language and historical references, the manifesto was based on the same premise invoked by southern conservatives since the founding of the Republic: tradition trumps truth. The self-deluding, revisionist tone of the manifesto is striking:

> This unwarranted exercise of power by the Court, contrary to the Constitution, is creating chaos and confusion in the States principally affected. It is destroying the amicable relations between the white and Negro races that have been created through 90 years of patient effort by the good people of both races. It has planted hatred and suspicion where there has been heretofore friendship and understanding.

The manifesto episode bore an eerie resemblance to Calhoun's nullification ploy a century earlier. Indeed, after Thurmond asserted in a floor speech that the white people of the South were the nation's true minority, Republican senator Frank Morse of Oregon said it felt like Calhoun was still walking the floors of the Senate—a comment Thurmond biographers Jack Bass and Marilyn Thompson say Thurmond likely took as a compliment.[55] Thurmond, Olin Johnston, and every southern senator except Majority Leader Lyndon Johnson and Tennessee's Al Gore and Estes Kefauver signed the manifesto. So did eighty-one House members, including the entire delegation from South Carolina.[56]

Like most southern states, South Carolina in the 1960s still used counties as the representational unit in its state legislature, which meant that rural, sparsely populated counties wielded power beyond their numbers. Moreover, one of the legacies of the Tillman era was that county and local officials were not chosen locally; rather, they were appointed by the governor upon the recommendation of the respective county's state legislators, which "effectively eliminated the opportunity of African Americans to elect local officials of their choice, even where they were an overwhelming majority."[57] A series of Supreme Court decisions in the early 1960s outlawed malapportionment, forcing the entrenched powers to yet again seek creative solutions to the problem of suppressing black voting power. Congress then passed the Voting Rights Act in 1965, requiring states like South Carolina to ensure voting rights and gain pre-clearance from the U.S. Department of Justice for redistricting plans.[58]

South Carolina had not elected any black officials since 1902, something these rulings and the 1965 Voting Rights Act were intended to correct. But white leaders were not going to stand idly by as the voting rolls burgeoned with black voters, and courts created majority-minority districts. County election officials used dilatory tactics to discourage or suppress black registration, such as limiting registration times and door-to-door techniques, or forcing blacks who wanted to register to visit intimidating, all-white areas of power like the county courthouse. Electoral discrimination in the period after the Voting Rights Act merely required still more creative mechanisms to dilute the black vote, such as runoff provisions and at-large districts. For those fighting the voting-rights revolution, the lone upside to the passage of the Voting Rights Act was that previously apathetic white voters began to register as a counterbalance to the nascent power of newly enfranchised blacks.[59]

Partisan changes during the post–World War II period paralleled the growing threats to South Carolina's political autonomy posed by the Supreme Court rulings and civil rights legislation passed by the Congress. Events in Washington created a partisan dissonance in the southern states, a problem reflected most obviously in the presidential voting results in South Carolina and other states. Between 1900 and 1940, every Democratic presidential nominee got at least 91.4 percent of the South Carolina vote. In 1944, FDR slipped a bit, to 87.6 percent, and of course Thurmond carried the state as a Dixiecrat in 1948.

By 1952, however, the Republicans were already competitive. Dwight D. Eisenhower lost the state by a bare two percentage points to Adlai Stevenson. Though Stevenson carried the state again in 1956, more than half the votes that year were cast either for Eisenhower (25.2 percent) or a slate of unpledged electors (29.5 percent). In 1960, John F. Kennedy won by a whisker over Vice President Richard Nixon; amazingly enough, the Catholic Democratic senator from Massachusetts won a majority of southern electoral votes that year—an unthinkable feat today, as John Kerry's 2004 campaign proved. Still, Nixon carried Florida, Tennessee, and Virginia, and unpledged electors in Alabama and Mississippi cast fourteen electoral votes for Democratic senator Harry Byrd of Virginia for president and Thurmond for vice president. If the Byrd-Thurmond ticket had been on South Carolina's ballot, or if the state allowed voting for unpledged delegates, it is unlikely that Kennedy would have captured all eight of South Carolina's electors.

In South Carolina during the 1960s, according to political historian Bruce H. Kalk, core Republican support derived mostly from "urban cosmopolitans."[60] The Democratic brand name retained much of its potency, particularly in rural areas. For example, other than Thurmond's Edgefield County, the only upcountry jurisdictions Nixon carried in 1960 were Greenville and Pickens Counties, situated along the Appalachian border with North Carolina. It would take a special southerner—a partisan pioneer—to spark a wholesale and permanent change in the partisan identity of the state and region. That task fell, of course, to Thurmond.

In 1964 Thurmond became the first major southern politician to switch to the Republican Party. Along with his support that year for Republican Barry Goldwater's presidential candidacy, Thurmond's defection sent shock waves from Washington to Columbia and back again. With Thurmond's endorsement, Goldwater carried five southern states, including South Carolina—making him the first Republican to win the Palmetto State since the contested election of 1876. President Lyndon Johnson's signing that summer of the 1964 Civil Rights Act had driven many Democratic boats far from shore, and Thurmond's conversion gave them safe harbor to join the GOP. Political scientists Glen T. Broach and Lee Bandy describe the geography of the partisan transformation unfolding in South Carolina during the mid-1960s:

> It is perhaps inevitable that the Republican appeal to South Carolina whites has had a racial component that belies the party's otherwise reformist image. While the national Democratic party moved from its earlier policy of tolerance for southern segregation to an aggressive stance in favor of civil rights, Republican and third-party alternatives drew their greatest strength within South Carolina's virtually all-white electorate from the Lowcountry and black-belt counties historically most responsive to segregationist appeals. After the reenfranchisement of blacks by the 1965 Voting Rights Act gave rise to a significant African American electorate, especially in the Lowcountry, Republican strength in the predominantly black rural counties of the Lowcountry declined substantially and began to shift to the upstate counties with predominantly white populations.[61]

After a century of one-party rule had muted them, the timeless regional divisions in South Carolina were resurfacing.

By 1966, in the words of state Democratic Party chair Don Fowler, being identified as a Democrat "was about as popular as . . . the bubonic plague," and LBJ had come to be viewed as "Satan incarnate."[62] For the first time in the twentieth century, the South Carolina GOP in 1966 not only fielded a candidate for Senate, in Thurmond, as well as in the special-election contest to replace the late senator Olin Johnston, but also in statewide races for governor, lieutenant governor and superintendent of education.[63] With Thurmond's support, Richard Nixon wrestled South Carolina away from

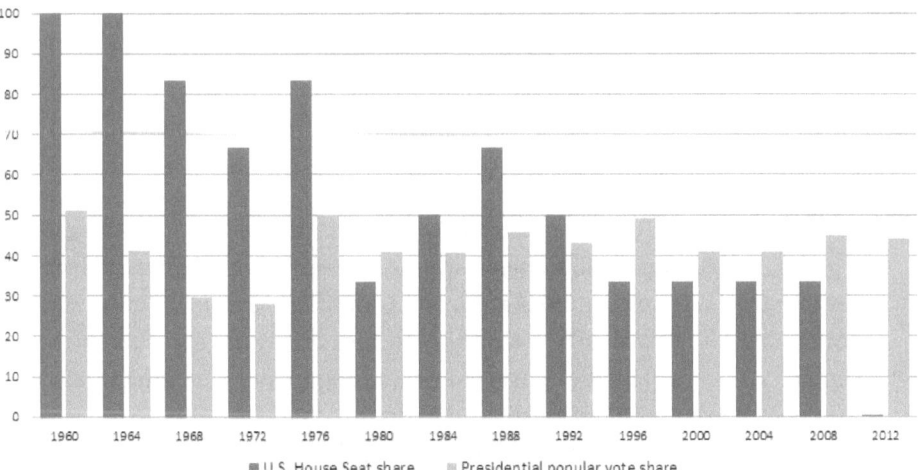

Figure 1.1. Democratic fortunes in South Carolina, 1960–2012

George Wallace in 1968, making it the only southern state the Republicans carried back-to-back in 1964 and 1968. In the late 1960s the Republicans elected their first wave of state legislators to Columbia, and by 1974—an otherwise horrible, post-Watergate year for Republicans across the country—South Carolina elected its first Republican governor of the twentieth century, James B. Edwards. The most consistently loyal Democratic state in the Union had undergone *the most rapid* partisan transformation. No Republican presidential candidate since 1968 has gone on to win the White House without first winning the South Carolina primary.

As the partisan Pied Piper of his state, his region, and his generation, Strom Thurmond was the catalyst for many of these changes. His Dixiecrat presidential candidacy in 1948, his lead role in drafting the Southern Manifesto in 1956, and his conversion to the GOP in 1964 were directly responsible for South Carolina's partisan realignment, and indirectly triggered the broader Republican revolution in the South. Harry Dent, his most storied political protégé, is regarded as the principal architect of Nixon's 1968 "southern strategy" for winning the White House in 1968. But without a builder, an architect's work is little more than white lines on blue paper. James Strom Thurmond was the builder.[64] "The Dixiecrats and, in particular, Strom Thurmond initiated a national political discussion on the dangers of an expansive federal government and on interest group politics that threatened issues of 'local control,'" wrote historian Kari Frederickson. "When a majority of South Carolina voters in November 1996 walked into the voting booth and pulled the lever for Thurmond, honoring with him another term as their senator, they may have recalled his earlier pledge to 'fight the forty-year wrongs of liberalism.' Who better to fight that war than the man who fired the first shot?"[65]

Resenting the Union: 1969 to 2002

In 1968, the New Deal governing majority imploded and America entered a period of partisan dealignment with no majority party. Richard Nixon became the first president in American history who, upon his initial election, failed to carry a party majority with him in at least one chamber of Congress: the era of divided government had begun. But in South Carolina, the era of divisive politics merely continued.

Courtesy of Earl Warren's retirement and the financial scandal that brought down Abe Fortas, early in his first term Nixon was blessed with two Supreme Court openings to fill. Harry Dent visited the White House in the early months of the administration to gain assurance that Nixon was not going to betray the southern agenda by initiating any aggressive civil rights actions or regulations. Seeking to assuage their fears and repay a debt to the state and region that put him in office, Nixon nominated U.S. Court of Appeals judge Clement F. Haynesworth Jr. of South Carolina for the nation's highest court.

Haynesworth earned his legal reputation representing South Carolina's textile mill owners in their battles with labor unions. South Carolina was not a southern pioneer in passing "right to work" statutes, but Haynesworth was a leader of the state's anti-union movement. As a federal judge, he slow-footed the implementation of school integration laws and advocated the "freedom of choice" solution to integration—a sanguine label segregationists concocted for the policy of allowing each school district to decide its own fate without regard for federal case law or statutes. After looking carefully at Haynesworth's civil rights record, Republican senator Edward Brooke of Massachusetts, the first African American elected to the Senate, personally asked Nixon to withdraw Haynesworth's nomination.[66] Nixon would not, and the Senate rejected the nominee, 55-45. But politically, Nixon scored big points merely by attempting to put a Deep South judge on the Court.

Although South Carolina cast its lot with neighboring Georgia boy Jimmy Carter in 1976, by 1980 the states' rights message had risen anew in the figure of Ronald Reagan. The state voted for Reagan by a slim margin in 1980 but gave him a staggering 63.6 percent of its votes during his 1984 reelection—a plateau even George W. Bush never reached. Reagan's "new federalism" assault on the size and power of the national government rang sweetly in South Carolina ears, no matter that Reagan grew the government and South Carolina itself depended on Washington largesse for its economic livelihood then as it does today. Despite their claims of fierce self-reliance, South Carolinians still receive about $1.36 from the federal government for every tax dollar they send to Washington.[67]

Like Governor Edwards's 1974 win, Republican gubernatorial candidate Carroll Campbell's victory in the otherwise down Republican year of 1986 affirmed South Carolina's reputation as an against-type partisan state. Four years later, Campbell became the first Republican governor to be reelected in the state since Reconstruction. The Greenville native clobbered his Democratic opponent, Theo Mitchell, an African American lawyer who drew a paltry 30.5 percent of the vote.

Despite the fact that about 30 percent of South Carolina's statewide population was black, the 1970 and 1980 rounds of redistricting produced no majority-black congressional seats and therefore no black member of Congress from any of the state's six congressional districts. Finally, the 1990 redistricting increased the black share of residents in the Sixth District from 40 percent during the 1980s to more than 60 percent, and in 1992 the district elected James Clyburn as the first and, to date, *only* black congressman from South Carolina to serve since 1897.[68]

In 1994 the Republicans nominated former Democrat and longtime state legislator David Beasley for governor. Beasley had first won election to the state legislature in 1978 as a twenty-one-year-old Democratic college student at Clemson University. He moved up the ladder in the South Carolina House, becoming the youngest speaker pro tempore in the country by the early 1990s. In 1994, that glory-filled Year of the Republican, the now-converted Republican Beasley rode the national partisan wave into the governor's mansion. Following popular Greenville native Carroll Campbell's back-to-back terms, with Beasley's win the GOP had strung together an unprecedented three consecutive gubernatorial wins. Then Beasley committed political suicide.

Citing a "religious epiphany," in 1996 Beasley announced to a televised audience that he had reversed his position on the issue of flying a Confederate flag over the state capitol. "While the beseeching and invocation of heavenly guidance in the matter was appealing to his base on the religious right, it destroyed his credibility among white-flight Republicans almost overnight," writes Citadel political scientist John C. Kuzenski. "The South

Carolina Republican Party lost hundreds of thousands of dollars in nickel-and-dime contributions over a period of a few months, usually chronicled with hate mail that indicated that if the donor was not planning on going back to the Democrats, he or she certainly was not going to the polls to provide support to the anti-Confederate party led by Beasley."[69] The demand for "Dump the Governor—Keep the Flag" bumper stickers was so great that novelty suppliers couldn't keep them in stock.

Failing to articulate a defense of his flip-flop, Beasley got dumped. Democrat Jim Hodges defeated Beasley, who captured only 45 percent of the vote. In May 2003, Beasley received the John F. Kennedy Profile in Courage Award. In his acceptance speech at the JFK Library in Boston, he recalled the difficulty of his decision and the scorn and death threats that followed. "We all know people who have stood for right when it cost them nothing," said Beasley, lamenting that he was destined to be the last casualty of the Civil War (something Sonny Perdue's 2002 takedown of Democratic governor Roy Barnes of Georgia on the Confederate flag issue would rectify). "They beat their chests in the public square and roar from the top of their lungs their righteous indignation against the evil of the day, but they do so only when there is nothing to lose. This is of little value."[70]

Beasley's story is a cautionary tale for southern politicians who dare to ignore the residual animosities of the rural South, where the Confederate capitulation and symbolic power of the battle flag still resonate in the "Lost Cause" mentality. "The defeat of the Confederacy, and the reimagination of the society that had been defeated, laid the foundation for the creation of a conservative culture," asserted W. Scott Poole in *Never Surrender*, his chronicle of the historical roots of the South Carolina's conservative orthodoxy. "Southern conservatism flourished in South Carolina through the medium of the Lost Cause, an aesthetic representation of memory and yearning. Confederate memory provided southerners with an ideology of historical declension, the notion that Confederate loss meant the triumph of materialism, irreligion, and social anarchy."[71] South Carolina is a place where the past is present, and failure to give heritage its due can quickly extinguish the otherwise promising careers of politicians like David Beasley.

South Carolina Today: A State in Transition

With Strom Thurmond's 2002 retirement, South Carolina found itself in transition. Thurmond left his mark on the state for much of the mid-twentieth century. But the two South Carolina politicians more likely to be remembered as having a lasting impact on the state's economic future and political maturation are Senators Fritz Hollings and Lindsey Graham.

In many respects, Hollings and Graham could not be much different. Born in 1922, Hollings is a Charleston Democrat who, despite coming of political age during the segregation era, steadily adopted more-progressive stances on racial and cultural issues. A graduate of The Citadel and a decorated veteran of World War II, Hollings enjoyed a political career that spanned the same half-century as Thurmond's but was more varied. Hollings served in the South Carolina House (1949–55), followed by turns as lieutenant governor (1955–59) and governor (1959–63), before serving thirty-eight years in the U.S. Senate (1967–2005)—all but the final two years alongside Thurmond as the Senate's longest-serving junior senator—before finally retiring from six decades of public service in January 2005. He railed against rural poverty and hunger in his famed 1968 state tour, which culminated in his 1970 book, *The Case against Hunger: A Demand for a National Policy*. He supervised the racial integration of Clemson University in 1963 (future Charlotte mayor and two-time Democratic Senate nominee from North Carolina, Harvey Gantt, was the African American student). Hollings voted in 1982 to strengthen the Voting Rights Act. A pioneer in protecting coastal wetlands, he is the oft-forgotten third co-sponsor on the famed Gramm-Rudman-Hollings bill, which attempted to curtail Reagan-era deficits.

In December 2005, the South Carolina Democratic Party held a fundraiser at the Francis Marion hotel in Charleston in honor of the four living former Democratic governors. I asked Hollings if his long political life would have been made a lot easier had he switched parties several decades ago, as Thurmond had. "It would have been easier—it would have been much easier financially, let's put it that way," he said. "But you wouldn't have been able to have the right position on the issues. We in the Democratic Party are for paying the bills, for jobs and industry and economic development. We said you can't improve the economic ability of any unless you improve the education level of all."[72]

Graham, by contrast, is a lifelong Republican who grew up or worked in Pickens and Oconee Counties, located almost as far across the state in physical distance and political experience from Hollings's Charleston as possible. Born in 1955, the year Hollings became lieutenant governor, Graham came of age during the Reagan-Bush era and, after serving two years in the state legislature, was elected to the U.S. House as part of the 1994

Republican revolution. In 2002 he was elected to fill the impossible-to-fill Senate seat Thurmond had held for almost a half-century. Some conservatives in the state look upon Graham warily because he represents the same maverick wing of the GOP as former governor Mark Sanford. Graham cemented his maverick reputation during the 2000 Republican presidential primary by emerging as one of John McCain's most prominent supporters. (Unfortunately for the Arizona senator, Graham could not protect him from the smear tactics perpetrated by George W. Bush's allies in the state.) In 2005 Graham joined McCain again as part of the bipartisan "Group of 14" that prevented Senate Republicans from deploying the so-called nuclear option to end Democratic filibusters of President Bush's judicial appointments. Graham is studiously passionate about wonky subjects, like hydrogen fuel development, that cannot harvest the kind of votes that push-button cultural issues do. His vibrancy and energy—and his frequent appearances on the national talk show circuit—provide a striking contrast to the representation South Carolina received from Thurmond during the last two decades of his career, when senility reduced the legendary senator to little more than a reliable source for Republican roll-call votes and pork-barreling projects for the state.

In short, Graham's ideology should not be confused with the movement conservatism of the state's other Republican U.S. senator, Jim DeMint, and in that sense his independent streak links Graham to Hollings, who courageously held his ground as a Democrat when he could well have followed Thurmond into the Republican ranks. In bucking partisan traditions and departing from the reflexive, resist-first mentality that has long insulated and isolated South Carolina from national politics, Hollings established for himself in the final third of the last century a legacy that Graham may well duplicate in the first third of the current century. Although Hollings was replaced in the Senate by DeMint, it is telling that the retiring Hollings gave his Senate desk to Graham instead.

Graham has had his work cut out for him. Recent statistics indicate that South Carolina ranks fiftieth in the nation in high school graduation rates, forty-seventh in percentage of high school graduates deemed academically prepared for college, and near the bottom in terms of need-based college grants and college affordability. The state's median income is lower ($37,092) and its poverty rate (14.1 percent) higher than national averages. At 822 incidents per 100,000 households, South Carolina has the highest violent crime rate of any state in America, a fact surely connected to its high unemployment rate (6.8 percent). Most disconcerting are South Carolina's birth statistics for low-weight babies and single-mother and teen births, all of which are among the worst in the country. But the state is competitive in terms of student participation rates in after-school programs and early childhood education attendance, and South Carolinians have a high level of home ownership and a low divorce rate. South Carolina's future is bright.[73]

Ninety Six Today

What's most striking about the history of South Carolina is that political resistance almost inevitably found its roots in the old Ninety Six District, the place where the fate of the American Revolution turned in the South. Today, the boundaries of the Ninety Six District map almost perfectly with those of Abbeville, Edgefield, Greenwood, McCormick, and Saluda Counties. This area, the self-proclaimed Cradle of the Confederacy, comprises just 7.6 percent of the state's land area and only 3.6 percent of its population.[74] Add the five neighboring counties of Aiken, Anderson, Laurens, Lexington, and Newberry, and the result is a small, rural northwestern corner of the state that has produced far more than its share of notable figures from South Carolina political history, including John Calhoun, Preston Brooks, Ben "Pitchfork" Tillman, Cole Blease, Olin Johnston, and, of course, Strom Thurmond. Table 1.1 provides a partial list of key politicians who come from either the five counties of the original Ninety Six District or its five neighboring counties.

In 2005, I toured the historic Ninety Six District. Entering from the southern end, I drove up State Route 25, which bisects Edgefield County, across the low, flat farm terrain dotted here and there with signs advertising the area as part of the state's designated "Heritage Corridor." Out front of one large home along Route 25 I saw a hand-painted, wood sign placed in the yard, with red and blue letters against a white background declaring the occupant's identity: "Patriotic Veteran—Born Southern by the Grace of God." Continuing north I passed the Edgefield Inn, the town's most upscale hotel, which had just a single car in the parking lot. A quarter-mile up the road was one of countless Dollar General chain stores found across the state, every one of which features yellow signs with large-print, black letters assuring customers that the chain accepts both federal food stamps and the state's "EBT card" welfare card.

Easing into the town of Edgefield proper, I noticed that the parking lot at the Strom Thurmond Armory, home of the 122nd Engineering Battalion of the South Carolina National Guard, was overflowing. I pulled in and asked

Table 1.1. Political legacies of the Ninety Six District

Name	Hometown (county)	Political biography
John C. Calhoun	Mount Carmel (McCormick)	U.S. House: 1811–17
		Secretary of War: 1817–25
		Vice President: 1825–32
		U.S. Senate: 1832–43, 1845–50
		Secretary of State: 1844–45
Armistead Burt	Abbeville (Abbeville)	U.S. House: 1843–53
Andrew Butler	Edgefield (Edgefield)	U.S. Senate: 1846–57
Richard Simpson	Pendleton (Anderson)	U.S. House: 1843–49
Preston Brooks	Edgefield (Edgefield)	U.S. House: 1853–57
Matthew Butler	Edgefield (Edgefield)	U.S. Senate: 1877–95
George Tillman	Curryton (Edgefield)	U.S. House: 1879–82, 1883–93
Benjamin Tillman	Trenton (Edgefield)	Governor: 1891–95
		U.S. Senate: 1895–1918
William Talbert	Edgefield (Edgefield)	U.S. House: 1893–1903
Cole Blease	Newberry (Newberry)	Governor: 1911–15
		U.S. Senate: 1925–30
Frederick Dominick	Peak (Newberry)	U.S. House: 1917–33
Olin Johnston	Honea Path (Anderson)	Governor: 1935–37, 1943–45
		U.S. Senate: 1945–65
William Dorn	Greenwood (Greenwood)	U.S. House: 1947–49, 1951–74
Strom Thurmond	Edgefield (Edgefield)	Governor: 1947–51
		U.S. Senate: 1954–2003

Note: The list of names is hardly exhaustive of politicians from these counties, and reports only their service as governor, in Congress, or in other major federal office. It should also be noted that, prior to the 1890s, Abbeville and Edgefield were larger counties that contained what are today the five counties (Abbeville, Edgefield, Greenwood, McCormick, and Saluda) of the old Ninety Six District, which explains the prominence of Edgefield County, and to a lesser degree Abbeville County, in this table before Greenwood (1897), McCormick (1916), and Saluda (1895) Counties were formed.

two fatigue-clad African American guardsmen taking a break outside from weekend drill duties if their unit has been to Iraq and if they had suffered any fatalities. They confirmed that the unit had indeed been to Iraq but, fortunately, they had not lost anyone. About three minutes on foot from the armory named for him is Thurmond's childhood home, a three-story white house with black shutters at 305 Columbia Road. It's privately owned, so I lingered only long enough to read the commemorative sign posted out front and snap a quick mental picture before heading north toward the town square at the center of Edgefield.

The layout of downtown Edgefield is typical of rural county seats in the South. The county courthouse overlooks a small, grassy park in the middle of the square in which local notables and war heroes who died in battle are commemorated. A one-way driving roundabout with local business arrayed around it encircles the park. In the brick building at the south end of the square is the Ten Governors Cafe, which was open, and Sanken's ice cream shop, which looked as if it had been closed for a long time. The eastern, exterior brick wall of Sanken's has been painted with big letters welcoming travelers to "stop, visit and linger" in Edgefield County—"Home to Ten Governors," each of whom is listed across the top of the wall.[75] Beneath their names, in impossible-to-miss, six-inch black letters, there is this quote:

> Edgefield has had more dashing, brilliant, romantic figures, statesmen, orators, soldiers, adventurers, and daredevils, than any other county of South Carolina, if not of any rural county in America."
> W. W. Ball, *The State That Forgot*[76]

A few steps away, in the center of the courtyard and directly in front of an old obelisk donated by the women of Edgefield "to the memory of their confederate dead," is a statue of Thurmond, his right arm raised in an oratorical pose. Erected in 1984—perhaps out of worry that the town's most famous son, then still a youthful eighty-two, might not be around for, say, another two decades—the dedication plaque reads, "Take him all in all. He is a man. We shall not look upon his like again." It is followed by a two-word source of clarification, "After Shakespeare."

Edgefield's glory days of state political power, it seems, have faded like so many of the businesses in its main square. Crouch Hardware (an Ace retailer) is still a going concern, as is the Edgefield Billiard Parlor. The Plantation House hotel, the awning of which suggests that it was at some point folded into the Village Inn chain, was padlocked shut—although one of its street level spaces still houses the *Edgefield Advertiser*, which proudly proclaims in its painted window-front its distinction as the state's oldest newspaper. Catty-corner to the *Advertiser*, on the southeast corner of the square, was the town's larger paper, the *Citizen News*, as well as the Edgefield County Public Library. The previous night Strom Thurmond High School, led by star quarterback Coco Hillary, smothered Clinton, 21-3, to win the Class AAA state football championship—the aptly named Rebels' first state title since 1968.[77] Aside from two young families enjoying after-church snacks on the picnic tables outside the Ten Governors Cafe, there was no fuss or celebration in the center of Edgefield on that Sunday afternoon.

I continued north along Route 25, crossing Turkey Creek into Greenwood County and over the Guffytown Creek before finally picking up Route 248 toward Ninety Six and the National Historic Site located two miles south of town. Roughly thirty thousand people visit the site each year. More emphasis is placed on the loyalists' surrender of the fort following the siege than on the town's earlier significance as a backcountry crossroads the British used to foment their own "southern strategy" aimed at restoring the Crown to power in the colonies by recapturing South Carolina and Georgia and pushing north from there. In May 2006 a special two-day event commemorated the 225th anniversary of the siege.

When I arrived the parking lot was nearly empty, and my entrance to the visitor center startled the young National Park Service ranger in the office behind the greeting desk. I knew from the National Park Service website that the visitor center shows a ten-minute documentary video about the history of Ninety Six and the patriots' fateful twenty-eight-day siege during May and June 1781 led by Polish-born revolutionary hero Thaddeus Kosciuszko and Colonel "Light-horse" Harry Lee. "When does the video play next?" I asked the ranger. "Whenever you're ready," she replied, not missing a beat.

After the video, I headed out along the one-mile walking trail around the battlefield site, which I also had to myself. Sitting on the bench in the one-story overlook shelter built to give visitors a higher view of the grounds and the "Star Fort's" octagonal ramparts, only the mob of beetles that had overrun the shelter were there to keep me company. Visitors could still see the colonial-era horse-and-wagon trails that once connected Ninety Six to Augusta, Charleston, Island Ford, and the Cherokee settlement at Keowee, and they were so wide, flat, and clear of overgrown foliage that you could have driven a tractor-trailer through their canopied rows. The mounded-earth outlines of the eight-sided fortress and the zig-zagged set of trenches that Kosciuszko ordered "sappers" to dig to provide cover for the troops were still visible. Ninety Six's importance to colonial military history is overshadowed by Saratoga and Valley Forge, but its significance in the revolutionary period, especially to South Carolina and the South more broadly, cannot be overlooked.

In 2005 a total of 1,936 people lived in the town of Ninety Six. The town's racial mix of three whites for every African American was only slightly higher than statewide proportions, and its per capita annual income of $15,648 much lower than Greenwood's average, and only slightly ahead of Lee County, the state's poorest. Neighboring counties Edgefield and McCormick were the next two poorest, with income levels a little more than half the national average. Abbeville and Saluda Counties, which complete the old Ninety Six District, aren't much wealthier.[78] On Main Street in Ninety Six, there were no chain restaurants besides Hardee's, and no national retailers other than the local Allstate agent. There were two local hair salons, two cafés, the Ninety Six Pharmacy. and a few thrift shops. The hardware store was closed up, and the second-floor apartments above the store and the two flanking it were either boarded up or their windows busted in. Ninety Six had seen better days.

The next morning in Abbeville, seat to the county of the same name and home of John C. Calhoun, the rain poured down so hard that the brick-lined streets of the town's center square were nearly filled to the curb. A quarter-mile from the center of town is Secessionist Hill, where on November 22, 1860, local leaders including Armistead Burt first called for South Carolina to secede from the Union. Resolutions were approved unanimously, and a twenty-member committee appointed delegates to attend the December 17 convention in Columbia to urge secession. Just north of town a few blocks, that movement met its demise in Burt's private home, which Burt had previously offered to Jefferson Davis as a place to retreat should the Confederate president be run out of Richmond. On the night of May 2, 1865, Davis took Burt up on his offer and, after conferring with his cabinet and military leaders in the first-floor meeting room, signed papers authorizing the political surrender of the Confederacy, went upstairs, and collapsed.[79] Though Appomattox is better remembered as the site of the Confederacy's military capitulation, it was actually Burt's home where Davis famously uttered "All is indeed lost." And thus the Civil War started and ended in Abbeville, at sites less than a mile apart. The memorial erected in 1906 at the center of the town square by the Daughters of the Confederacy, dedicated to the soldiers of the Abbeville district, boasts of the town's role as witness to the war's opening and closing moments. More than sixty years after the war's conclusion, hopefully defiant Abbeville residents were still predicting that "the world shall yet decide, in truth's clear, far-off light, that the soldiers who wore the gray and died with Lee were in the right."

Leaving the old Ninety Six District, I found it difficult to believe that this small area provided the beating conservative heart for the most rebellious state in America's most rebellious region; that eight of the nine delegates this area sent to the 1788 state convention voted *against* ratifying the U.S. Constitution; that thousands of residents from Ninety Six and neighboring towns, burning hot in 1856 with the "fire-eating" talk of secession, held a dinner to honor their beloved congressman, Preston Brooks, and many of them symbolically brought him canes to replace the one he used to bludgeon Charles Sumner on the Senate floor; that sixty miles down Route 25, in what is today the Aiken County portion of the original Ninety Six District, the 1876 "Red Shirt" massacre took place in sleepy little Hamburg; that white vigilantes in the Phoenix section of Greenwood County murdered as many as a dozen blacks on election day in 1898. It is so quiet, so quiescent here.

Like Hampton, Tillman, Blease, and Johnston who served during the years between them, the two iconic political figures who bookend South Carolina's century-long, steadfast defense of states' rights—John Calhoun and Strom Thurmond—drew their strength from the upcountry, rural, white power base of the old Ninety Six District. Thurmond's advocacy of states' rights during the late 1940s in defense of segregation echoed Calhoun's nullification movement in defense of slavery during the 1830s. Though Calhoun and Thurmond were on the wrong side of history, they correctly predicted the political changes that awaited them and their beloved home state. For Calhoun that meant physical force to bring about abolition, though he did not live to see it. For Thurmond it meant judicial force to bring about desegregration, which he survived to see and, to some grudging degree, eventually came to accept.

America chose routes different from those preferred by Calhoun and Thurmond. Yet in the great conservative tradition of South Carolina rebellion, these sons born into and raised within the Confederate cradle of the old Ninety Six District relied upon this very same base of power to impede the steady march of American progress. And they birthed to the country a tradition of political resistance that thrives to this day and is sustained by the people from these same small towns.

Notes

Epigraph sources: South Carolina Ratification Convention debates, May 12–23, 1788, Charleston, South Carolina; Jack Bass and Marilyn W. Thompson, *Ol' Strom: An Unauthorized Biography of Strom Thurmond* (Athens, Ga.: Longstreet Press, 1998), 97.

1. "Court Declines License Plate Case," *Associated Press*, January 25, 2005.
2. John Barnwell, *Love of Order: South Carolina's First Secessionist Crisis* (Chapel Hill: University of North Carolina Press, 1982), 10. The only possible contender to South Carolina for slave dependency was Virginia. According to minutes from the 1788 debates in South Carolina about whether to form a convention to decide whether to ratify the newly proposed Constitution, Virginia's "negro" population of 280,000 was slightly larger as a percentage of its 420,000 whites than South Carolina's.
3. Ibid., 11.
4. Walter Edgar, *Partisans and Redcoats: The Southern Conflict That Turned the Tide of the American Revolution* (New York: William Morrow, 2001), 26–33. Quotations in two previous paragraphs found here.
5. Robert Stansbury Lambert, *South Carolina Loyalists in the American Revolution* (Columbia: University of South Carolina Press, 1987), 59–72.
6. For a fascinating account of events in South Carolina during the 1780s, see chapters 4 and 5 in Edgar's *Partisans and Redcoats*.
7. Walter Edgar, *South Carolina: A History* (Columbia: University of South Carolina Press, 1998), 250–52. The irony is that the same rural backcountry whites who later exploited malapportionment for a century after the Civil War to exaggerate their own power were victimized by this most in-egalitarian of representational devices.
8. The ten that passed are what we now commonly refer to as the Bill of Rights. As for the other two proposed amendments, one regulating congressional pay was ratified by states sporadically during the next two centuries and was finally certified in 1992 as the Twenty-seventh Amendment. The other, which would expand the size of the U.S. House by setting the maximum number of persons in each congressional district, remains alive before the states.
9. Edgar, *South Carolina*, 251–52.
10. Adams's appointment of Clay to be secretary of state led to complaints that the two men had struck a "corrupt bargain" to deny Jackson the presidency. Incidentally, the South Carolina legislature cast the state's eleven electoral votes for Jackson, and the state's U.S. House delegation also voted for Jackson.
11. John Calhoun, *South Carolina Exposition and Protest*, December 1828, http://en.wikisource.org/wiki/South_Carolina_Exposition_and_Protest (accessed October 21, 2013).
12. Manisha Sinha, *The Counterrevolution of Slavery: Politics and Ideology in Antebellum South Carolina* (Chapel Hill: University of North Carolina Press, 2000), 32.
13. President Jackson's Message to the House and Senate Regarding South Carolina's Nullification Ordinance, January 16, 1833, http://avalon.law.yale.edu/19th_century/ajack001.asp (accessed October 21, 2013).
14. Barnwell, *Love of Order*, 40.

15. Black McNulty, "Uncertain Masters: The South Carolina Elite and Slavery in the Secession Crisis of 1850," in *Looking South: Chapters in the Story of an American Region*, ed. Winfred B. Moore Jr. and Joseph F. Tripp (Westport, Conn.: Greenwood, 1989), 82.

16. Ibid., 80–81.

17. The two anti-slavery components of the Compromise were the admittance of California as a free state and the abolition of slavery in the District of Columbia. The two pro-slavery measures were the formation of Utah and New Mexico as states that could decide slavery on their own and the passage of a strengthened fugitive slave law for the return of escaped slaves. The fifth part of the Compromise involved the ceding of portions of west Texas in exchange for $10 million.

18. Philip M. Hamer, *The Secessionist Movement in South Carolina, 1847–1852* (Cambridge, Mass.: De Capo Press, 1971).

19. Ibid., 67.

20. Sinha, *The Counterrevolution of Slavery*, 183–85.

21. Richard Zuczek, *State of Rebellion: Reconstruction in South Carolina* (Columbia: University of South Carolina Press, 1996), 39, emphasis in original.

22. Ibid., 4–5.

23. In addition to the twenty-one electors from the three southern states, there was a smaller dispute involving one Oregon elector whose eligibility was challenged because of his status as a federal postal employee.

24. An ironic twist to the "Compromise of 1877" brokered at the Wormley House Hotel—which, by helping restore local autonomy to southern politicians, led inevitably to one-party white rule and systematic political and economic suppression of African Americans—is that the popular hotel's respected proprietor, James Wormley, was someone rather rare for that era: a prominent black entrepreneur. See Nicholas A. Hollis, "A Hotel for the History Books," *Washington Post*, March 18, 2001.

25. Ernest McPherson Lander Jr., *A History of South Carolina, 1865–1960* (Chapel Hill: University of North Carolina Press, 1960), 17–22.

26. Ibid., 21.

27. Paul D. Escott et al., eds., *Major Problems in the History of the American South*, vol. 2 (New York: Houghton Mifflin, 1999), 37–38.

28. Edmund L. Drago, *Hurrah for Hampton! Black Red Shirts in South Carolina during Reconstruction* (Fayetteville: University of Arkansas Press, 1998).

29. Lander, *A History of South Carolina*, 22.

30. Michael Perman, *Struggle for Mastery: Disfranchisement in the South, 1888–1908* (Chapel Hill: University of North Carolina Press, 2001), chapter 5.

31. Charles J. Holden, *In the Great Maelstrom: Conservatives in Post–Civil War South Carolina* (Columbia: University of South Carolina Press, 2002), 57, emphasis in original.

32. Ibid., 92–105.

33. They were Richard Harvey Cain (1873–75, 1877–79), Robert C. DeLarge (1871–73), Robert B. Elliott (1871–74), Thomas E. Miller (1890–91), George W. Murray (1893–95, 1897–97), Alonzo J. Ransier (1873–75), and Robert Smalls (1875–79, 1882–83, 1884–87). See Mildred L. Amer, *Black Members of the United States Congress: 1789–2001* (Congressional Research Service report updated July 12, 2001).

34. That (dis)honor fell to Alabama, which finally abolished the lease in 1928. Of course, one can argue that chain gangs continued the practice in a more diluted form of convict leasing well before the 1920s, when the U.S. Supreme Court essentially ended the practice for good. The hire-and-deport practices that exploited Mexican laborers by the south Texas farmers who funded Lyndon Johnson's political career, and the twenty-first-century abuses of migrant workers in Immokalee, Florida, are just two examples that raise the question of whether slavery in its more insidious incarnations has yet to be fully expunged from American soil.

35. Matthew J. Mancini, *One Dies, Get Another: Convict Leasing in the American South, 1866–1928* (Columbia: University of South Carolina Press, 1996), chapter 12, "The Carolinas," 198–212.

36. Bryant Simon, *A Fabric of Defeat: The Politics of South Carolina Millhands, 1910–1948* (Chapel Hill: University of North Carolina Press, 1998), chapter 1.

37. Ibid., 34–35.

38. The state's nine members of the U.S. House delegation were James F. "Jimmy" Byrnes, Frederick H. Dominick, Asbury F. Lever, Edward C. Mann, Samuel J. Nicholls, James W. Ragsdale, William F. Stevenson, Philip H. Stoll, and Richard S. Whaley.

39. Edgar, *South Carolina*, 471.

40. Ibid., 481.

41. Ibid., 483–85.

42. Jack Irby Hayes Jr., *South Carolina and the New Deal* (Columbia: University of South Carolina Press, 2001), chapter 9, quote on 157.

43. Smith v. Allwright, 321 U.S. 649 (1944).

44. Lander, *A History of South Carolina*, 169–71.

45. Ibid., 171–72.

46. Strom Thurmond, to his credit, insisted that those arrested for allegedly participating in Earle's lynching stand trial, which, as Bass and Thompson point out (*Ol' Strom*, 84–86), was by itself a momentous and pathbreaking signal of changes to come in South Carolina.

47. Kari Frederickson, *The Dixiecrat Revolt and the End of the Solid South, 1932–1968* (Chapel Hill: University of North Carolina Press, 2001), chapter 2.

48. Thurmond's political career stretches across so much of South Carolina's two-degrees-of-separation political history that the opponent he defeated in the 1932 Democratic state senate primary was none other than Benjamin Tillman Jr., son of the inimitable "Pitchfork" Ben Tillman.

49. Bass and Thompson, *Ol' Strom*.

50. Briggs v. Elliott, 342 U.S. 350 (1952).

51. Brown v. Board of Education, 347 U.S. 483 (1954).

52. Fred Vinson was chief justice when the arguments in the case began in December 1952, but Warren had replaced him by the time final voting and the announcement of the ruling came in May 1954.

53. Brown v. Board of Education II, 349 U.S. 294 (1955).

54. Richard Kluger, *Simple Justice: The History of* Brown v. Board of Education *and Black America's Struggle for Equality* (New York: Knopf, 1976), 729–33.

55. Bass and Thompson, *Ol' Strom*, 157–59.

56. South Carolina's six-member House delegation in 1954 was Robert T. Ashmore, W. J. Bryan Dorn, John L. McMillan, James P. Richards, John J. Riley, and L. Mendel Rivers.

57. Orville Vernon Burton et al., "South Carolina," in *Quiet Revolution in the South: The Impact of the Voting Rights Act, 1965–1990*, ed. Chandler Davidson and Bernard Grofman (Princeton: Princeton University Press, 1994), 202.

58. The precedent-setting cases were Baker v. Carr, 369 U.S. 186 (1962), and Reynolds v. Sims, 377 U.S. 533 (1964), for state legislative districts, and Wesberry v. Sanders, 376 U.S. 1 (1964), for congressional districts.

59. Burton et al., "South Carolina," 191–232.

60. Bruce H. Kalk, *The Origins of the Southern Strategy: Two-Party Competition in South Carolina, 1950–1972* (Lanham, Md.: Lexington Books, 2001).

61. Glen T. Broach and Lee Bandy, "South Carolina: A Decade of Rapid Republican Ascent," in *Southern Politics in the 1990s*, ed. Alexander P. Lamis (Baton Rouge: Louisiana State University Press, 1999), 70.

62. Bass and Thompson, *Ol' Strom*, 221.

63. Kalk, *Origins of the Southern Strategy*, 69.

64. According to Bass and Thompson in *Ol' Strom*, Dent and other top advisers to Thurmond were very wary about his partisan conversion, not to mention other bold strokes the senator took during his career, including marrying his second, much younger wife. But Thurmond neglected their advice and proved Dent and the others wrong.

65. Frederickson, *Dixiecrat Revolt*, 238.

66. Kalk, *Origins of the Southern Strategy*, 103–5.

67. Sumeet Sagoo, "Federal Taxing and Spending by State," Special Report #132 published by the Tax Foundation, Washington, D.C., November 1, 2004.

68. Historical data on congressional district data files for the 93rd (1973–74), 98th (1983–84), and 103rd (1993–94) Congresses are courtesy of the website maintained by University of Colorado political scientist E. Scott Adler: http://sobek.colorado.edu/~esadler/districtdatawebsite/CongressionalDistrictDatasetwebpage.htm.

69. John C. Kuzenski, "South Carolina: The Heart of GOP Realignment in the South," in *The New Politics of the Old South: An Introduction to Southern Politics*, ed. Charles S. Bullock III and Mark J. Rozell, 2nd ed. (Lanham, Md.: Rowman & Littlefield, 2002), 25–26.

70. Remarks by Governor David M. Beasley, John F. Kennedy Library, Boston, Massachusetts, May 12, 2003, http://www.jfklibrary.org/Events-and-Awards/Profile-in-Courage-Award/Award-Recipients/David-Beasley-2003.aspx?t=3.

71. W. Scott Poole, *Never Surrender: Confederate Memory and Conservatism in the South Carolina Upcountry* (Athens: University of Georgia Press, 2004), 17.

72. Hollings, interview with author, Charleston, South Carolina, December 7, 2005. By eerie coincidence, earlier on the day when the four former governors came together at the Francis Marion Hotel for the banquet, former governor Carroll Campbell died.

73. Education statistics and rankings taken from *Education: The State We're In*, report from Renewing Our Schools, Securing Our Future: A National Task Force on Public Education, August 2005, based on data from the National Center for Education Statistics. Income, poverty, housing and divorce data are taken from U.S. Census Bureau 2000. Birth rate, unemployment, and crime statistics are taken from the *South Carolina Statistic*

Abstract 2005, published by the South Carolina Budget and Control Board's Office of Research and Statistics.

74. A comparison of Edgar's (1998) map computed from 2000 U.S. Census Bureau data, reported on the website of South Carolina Association of Counties: www.sccounties.org.

75. They are, listed both here and on the building in chronological order: Andrew Pickens II, George McDuffie, P. M. Butler, J. H. Hammond, Francis Pickens, M. L. Bonham, J. C. Sheppard, Ben Tillman, J. G. Evans, and, of course, Strom Thurmond.

76. Ball's book, interestingly subtitled "South Carolina's Surrender to Democracy," was published in 1932 (Bobbs-Merrill).

77. Kenton Makin, "Rebels Win State Title," *Aiken Standard*, December 4, 2005, B1.

78. According to a report by the South Carolina Association of Counties based on 2000 census data, only Lee County ($15,386) had a lower per capita income than Edgefield ($16,221) or McCormick ($16,546) Counties. In relative terms, the counties were far below the statewide average of $29,000—and 55 percent and 56 percent, respectively, of the U.S. average of $29,469.

79. I am grateful to the Abbeville Chamber of Commerce and to my tour guide, Pat, who was kind enough to meet me on a cold and rainy Monday morning when the Burt-Stark Mansion (as it is now known) is otherwise closed to give me a detailed, private tour.

II

Race, War, and Culture

2

Tom Watson and Resistance to Federal War Policies in Georgia during World War I

ZACHARY C. SMITH

Hundreds of people packed the McDuffie County courthouse in Thomson, Georgia, on February 12, 1916, to hear the most influential and controversial figure in Georgia politics. The speaker, the former Populist Party leader Thomas E. "Tom" Watson (1856–1922), was soliciting the crowd's support in the face of federal obscenity charges that stemmed from the hate-filled rants in his newspaper and magazine concerning the case of Leo Frank. Frank, a Jewish factory superintendent, was lynched in Cobb County by a Georgia mob in August 1915 after his death sentence for murder was commuted by the governor. In Watson's remarks, as in much of the rhetoric in *Watson's Magazine* and his weekly newspaper, the *Thomson Jeffersonian*, the razor-tongued Georgian described the federal charges in terms of a corrupt, tyrannical outsider imposing its will on the white rural South, whose interests and values were embodied by none other than Watson himself. "From the foundation of this Government to this very moment," he claimed, "the South has never had justice in history or in legislation." According to Watson, the federal government had favored northern manufacturing interests since the earliest days of the republic, while "those infamous laws have become more and more outrageously unjust to the South." For the past hundred years, he contended, the national administration had allowed northern moneyed interests a free hand in business and a comfortable position above the law. His obscenity charge, Watson argued, was merely a continuation of this trend: "She [the South] has never got it [justice], and now the proposition is that this Government of one hundred millions of men, with criminals every which way going unwhipped, this great Government, will pick out one southern man and use the powers of the Government to grind him to powder."[1]

In the same courthouse, in June 1917, Watson addressed another large crowd—between five hundred and six hundred listeners—about what he saw as another example of federal power being abused for the benefit of "Big Money," an epithet he used often. More than two months earlier, President Woodrow Wilson and members of Congress had thrust the United States into a war with Germany that, at best, only a large minority of Americans supported. The point of the meeting was to organize support for a legal challenge to the Selective Service Act, which Congress had passed on May 18, 1917. Again crafting his appeal in sectional terms, Watson began his two-hour speech by addressing the growing inequality between rich and poor, claiming that economic conditions were worse in the South in 1917 than during the Civil War. The Wilson administration, Watson argued, had begun implementing plans to conscript poor southern men, both white and black, to act as cannon fodder on faraway battlefields to further the interests of northern capital.[2] In the case of wartime conscription, the sons of working-class Georgians were those whom the federal government wished to grind into powder.

This article's examination of the power of Watson's wartime rhetoric suggests that the Populist reform impulse of the 1890s was central to the popularity of his antiwar and anti-draft crusade in the South and in Georgia, in particular. The effectiveness of Watson's class-based arguments against the Selective Service Act of 1917 inspired federal repression of his publications and his followers. Repression of the latter, in at least one instance, resulted in violent resistance to a display of federal force in the Georgia upcountry. When examined alongside the language that he used throughout the life of the Populist Party, returned to in the Leo Frank matter, and spouted during the period of American neutrality, the antiwar and anti-draft sentiment that Watson provoked in rural Georgia during World War I reveals the persistence of class antagonism, antimilitarism, and southern nativism, as well as important intellectual and emotional continuities, in his long public career. To the aging Populist and his followers, it was southern men's duty to combat the evil forces that looked to usurp local justice in the Frank case and conscript southern manhood and wealth in the interests of Big Money and the federal state.

A close assessment of Watson's life from roughly 1914 to 1918, the span of World War I, suggests that past portrayals of him deserve reexamination. Although C. Vann Woodward's widely accepted depiction of Watson as an inspiring reformer turned uncompromising reactionary is not altogether inaccurate, the Populist editor's actions during the war years suggest that he did not cross the proverbial Rubicon into full-blown psychosis. Instead, it appears he merely straddled that line. Despite his harsh anti-Catholic, anti-Semitic, and racist ravings in his publications, twice during his anti-draft crusade Watson displayed a surprising ability to work with and in behalf of the religious and racial minorities he professed to despise when Populist issues were at stake.[3]

The rural South during World War I has not received a great deal of attention from historians. The most recent and complete work is Jeanette Keith's study of antiwar sentiment among rural whites and blacks throughout the region. Keith explores how the "premodern, traditional aspects of southern rural society affected war mobilization." This clash between time-honored notions of local control and the emerging federal state was most evident, she claims, in rural southerners' attitudes toward conscription. Keith argues that draft exemption standards and the race and class prejudices of local middle-class draft administrators turned many southerners against the idea of conscription.[4] The current study differs from Keith's in that, at least in the case of Watson and his ardent followers, resistance to conscription in the rural South began long before federal, state, and local draft machinery was even put in place.

Yet along with work by historians such as Keith and Anthony Gaughan, this chapter attempts to complicate the supposition that the South is and always has been fundamentally militaristic. According to Gaughan, the South between Reconstruction and World War I contained "a deep reservoir of pacifist and isolationist sentiment" based in a fear of expanding federal power over the states. Gaughan claims that this anxiety toward potentially militaristic policies had its origins in southern memories of federal abuses during Reconstruction. Gaughan credits the Wilson administration's "'100 percent' Americanism campaign" and the president's purging of antiwar southern Democrats in the 1918 election with overcoming southern resistance to war policies in Congress and remilitarizing the South.[5]

As Keith, Gaughan, and others have made clear, Watson may have been the loudest and most persistent voice of discontent, but he was not the only source of class-based, sectionally charged anti-administration rhetoric reaching southerners in rural north Georgia and beyond. During the early years of the Great War in Europe, the Georgia Farmers' Union (GFU) stood alongside Watson by speaking out against administration assistance to northern bankers and cotton speculators at the expense of cotton farmers. During American involvement, popular southern Democratic politicians such as House majority leader Claude Kitchen of North Carolina, Senator

James K. Vardaman of Mississippi, and Senator Thomas W. Hardwick of Georgia were consistent opponents of federal war measures—including the draft—that transferred local, state, and congressional power to the federal executive branch.[6]

Although southerners elected men such as these to represent them in Washington, public-opinion polls did not exist at this time. In order to better understand how rural southerners viewed Europe's war, historians must turn to the editorial pages of local newspapers. Most rural town and county newspapers were curiously silent about the buildup to war and the United States' role first as a neutral and then as a belligerent power; however, Watson in the *Jeffersonian* explained the war in the context of how it affected Georgia and the South. Most of what rural Georgians learned about the war came from individuals or groups who, to varying degrees, defined the war as inimical to the South's interests and way of life. This silence among local editors implies how little these communities believed the war in Europe—or international affairs in general—meant to their lives.[7] Combining this factor with rural southerners' historical antipathy toward centralized authority and the region's proclivity for self-sufficiency suggests that rural Georgia was fertile soil in which the seeds of anti-draft sentiment could flourish.

The Georgia upcountry appears to have been especially sensitive to arguments espousing the Populist principles of economic independence and contempt for federal authority.[8] The Populist Party's electoral strength in the 1890s, the violent reaction to the Frank case (especially to the commutation of his sentence), and the significant antiwar and anti-draft opposition in the rural hill country reflected long-standing class and sectional sentiments brought to a boil again in 1917 by the words of Tom Watson. Only during World War I did the federal government actively intervene to suppress the so-called lawless elements in the area. On August 11, 1917, several hundred men from Cobb and neighboring Cherokee Counties met in Marietta to pass resolutions supporting Watson's plan to contest the constitutionality of the draft in federal court.[9] Similar groups inspired by Watson's words cropped up all across rural Georgia and as far away as San Antonio, Louisville, and Sanford, North Carolina.[10] In July 1918, after a five-month investigation into Watson's part in instigating region-wide opposition to the draft, the Bureau of Investigation (BI) in the U.S. Department of Justice organized a raiding party, including fifty fully armed federal soldiers, to physically intimidate the leaders of the Cobb County anti-draft group and arrest the roughly twenty draft evaders they had allegedly assisted.[11]

Before drawing national attention through the Frank case and attracting the federal government's ire through draft opposition, Cobb and Cherokee were relatively obscure southern cotton counties. They lay in a region, though, that had seen drastic changes over the previous three generations. Steven Hahn has argued that poor upland farmers accrued large debts because the economic and political circumstances following the Civil War and Reconstruction forced white yeomen in the hills of north-central Georgia to convert from semi-subsistence farming to commodity production to satisfy the demands of invisible market forces. Blaming established politicians and greedy bankers for their new and uncomfortable roles as dependent cotton farmers and debtors, white yeomen in this section of the state began casting votes against local, state, and national Democrats and for independent and, by the 1890s, Populist Party candidates. According to Hahn, the Populist Party tapped into the divide between the yeomen's preindustrial, communal principles and "the tenets of bourgeois individualism and the free market" followed by small-town merchants and cotton speculators. The Populist message that "the corruption of the political process" was to blame for the increasingly unequal distribution of wealth and power fell on receptive ears in the Georgia hill country. When Populists ranted against speculators, banking interests, and those who became "'richer and richer . . . at the expense of those who produce," concludes Hahn, the upcountry farmers were emphasizing not just the expanding gap between the economic and political interests of producers and financiers but also the growing divergence between the values these classes held.[12] After the catastrophic 1896 election and the formal collapse of the Populist Party in 1908, Watson continued to preach this sentiment, using it as ammunition against whatever external forces appeared to threaten Georgia, the South, and himself.

Tom Watson was the most trusted Populist in Georgia in the early 1890s and continued upholding Jeffersonian ideals until his death in 1922. In an 1891 speech he railed against "the cold-hearted and hard-hearted men . . . who consider the mere getting of gold the gospel of life." Their greed led them to "utterly despise" and exploit the producing classes. The Spanish-American War of 1898, he argued, strengthened the historic bond between the federal government and moneyed interests. While "the privileged classes profit[ed] by this war," imperial expansion also "perpetuate[d] the unjust system" placed on the laborers. That exploitative system, he claimed, led to "military domination, military despotism." Watson opposed Theodore Roosevelt's 1904 presidential reelection campaign for the same reasons he later opposed the Wilson administration before and during World War I: "He stands for governmental policy which puts the dollar above the man, which puts the corporation above the people, which puts the few above the many, which puts the class above the mass." Watson also blamed federal legislation that favored northeastern capital for the South's "comparative lack of wealth" in 1907. This inequity, he claimed, was "not by nature, not by the fault of the people . . . but of the legislators who passed laws in favor of New England against the other section of the Union."[13] Despite his often bitter and hateful rhetoric directed toward blacks, the Catholic Church, and Jews, Big Money continued to be the enemy Watson cited most consistently in his speeches and writings throughout his career after the final collapse of the Populist Party.

Although the Populist revolt largely failed, its ideological tenets persisted in the Georgia upcountry.[14] This continuity became abundantly clear well before Watson's wartime crusade against conscription. In April 1913 a thirteen-year-old factory worker named Mary Phagan was brutally raped and murdered at the Atlanta Pencil Factory, where she worked. A jury found Leo Frank, the Ivy League–educated Jewish factory superintendent, guilty of the crimes and sentenced him to death. A heated national debate ensued concerning Frank's guilt and the fairness of his trial. According to Frank's defense team, his wealthy benefactors, and the northern press, the jury voted unanimously to convict Frank out of the fear that an acquittal would rouse violent mob activity against themselves and their families. Frank's lawyers claimed that the evidence instead pointed toward Jim Conley, a black custodian at the factory. Convinced that Frank was innocent, his legal team appealed his case to the highest state court in November 1914 and eventually to the U.S. Supreme Court in April of the next year, losing there in a seven-to two-decision.[15]

Coverage of the Frank case in the Georgia press did not begin to reach critical mass until March 1914, when the *Atlanta Journal* called for a retrial on the grounds that mob activity precluded Frank from receiving a fair hearing. The *Journal*'s editorial, however, raised the ire of Tom Watson, who up to this point had been largely indifferent toward the case. Watson initially became involved because of his personal dislike of Senator Hoke Smith, former owner of the *Journal*, who was "dragging the Frank case into politics."[16] The Populist editor's decision to inject himself into the Frank controversy is critical to understanding not only his personal popularity after the defendant's trial and subsequent murder but also Watson's reemergence as a trusted defender of the producing class at a time when Americans were about to brave the choppy seas of wartime neutrality.

With his involvement in the Frank affair, Watson again became a household name throughout the United States, the South in particular. As his federal obscenity charge indicates, the attention those outside the region (and some even in Georgia) paid to Watson's fiery editorials on Frank's case was decidedly negative. Yet Watson's class-based arguments against the influence of northern moneyed interests on the trial and the commutation of Frank's sentence struck a chord with many rural southerners. The reported increase in the circulation of the *Jeffersonian* resulting from the Frank case (from 25,000 subscribers in March 1914 to 87,000 in September 1915) suggests that the paper's readership was at an all-time high in Georgia and the South during the early months of U.S. involvement in World War I.[17] In short, Watson's increased popularity and newspaper circulation stemming from the Frank case placed him in a position to define, for a greater number of southerners than otherwise would have been possible, the South's relation to the war and Woodrow Wilson's policies in class terms. At the same time, Watson's class-based editorials on Frank likely left readers positively predisposed toward similar opinion pieces concerning Wilson's neutrality and war policies.

When responding to Frank's appeal to the Georgia Supreme Court, Watson began to claim that what was at stake in the Frank affair was the state's political independence from northern banking interests. An organized crusade of Big Money, Watson felt, was working to overturn the state's laws in order to free a twisted, perverse killer. Watson believed that for "the capitalists of Big Money" to throw their weight on the side of such a man revealed their lack of "regard [for] the poor man's daughter."[18] In the November 19, 1914, issue of the *Jeffersonian*, Watson proposed forming a "Vigilance Committee" that would constantly observe the activities of Frank and his benefactors, "whose Money and whose resources seem *so insolently determined that his crime shall go unpunished!*"[19]

Watson also took offense at the northern press's representation of the case, which he implicitly blamed on the *Atlanta Journal*'s allegation that an Atlanta mob forced the jury's hand in the Frank decision. Editorial opinion outside Georgia had largely portrayed the state as lawless and Georgians as unruly.[20] Watson presented this tendency as nothing more than "*the propaganda of Big Money against the Law*," which Frank's supporters hoped would "divide public opinion, create mawkish sentiment, and manufacture a sympathy which will influence the authorities."[21] In an apparent attempt at irony, Watson equated the diffusion of northern editorial opinion with the spreading of a mob mentality. Through the press, he claimed, preachers and lawyers in the North had become infected with the Big Money virus and begun bashing Georgia's reputation in the pulpit and courthouse. He asked, "Shall a lot of preachers and lawyers, living in a distant State, usurp the functions of our Courts?" The more widespread northern sentiment in favor of Frank and against the state's legal system became, the more Big Money was able to interfere with the legal process. In Watson's eyes, Frank's supporters' use of the northern press was proof that the case was not only "a contest between Money and the Law, between the Big Purse and the little one, between the Rich and the poor," but also one between the North and the South.[22]

Watson's class-based arguments during the Frank case were tightly mingled with anti-Semitic rhetoric. Much worse than wealthy northerners' hold on the Georgia judicial system and national press was what Watson considered Big Money's sponsorship of the sexual exploitation and murder of young Gentile girls by wealthy Jews. The Frank case indicated to Watson that "Jews of [Frank's] type have an utter contempt for law, and a ravenous appetite for . . . *girls of the uncircumcised!*"[23] In the same issue in which he called for the creation of the vigilance committee, Watson questioned the ability of Georgia courts to stop the endless mocking of the law by Big Money. "*How much longer,*" he railed, "*is the innocent blood of little Mary Phagan to cry in vain to Heaven for vengeance?* How much longer is Big Money . . . to mock justice and defy the law of Georgia?"[24]

As rumors began circulating that Governor John M. Slaton was considering commuting Frank's death sentence, Watson ramped up the rhetoric. In a June 3, 1915, article he described the murder in the vilest and most graphic terms: "*Frank was choking the neck, ripping the drawers, and bloodying the private parts of Mary Phagan.*" Blood and affronts to southern honor became central features in Watson's almost weekly rants about the case in the *Jeffersonian*. In the same article, he wrote that the thousands of men who had followed the case "had their eyes on Mary Phagan's innocent blood." Those with daughters or granddaughters "felt the blood run cold in their veins at the thought that, what Leo Frank did to the little Phagan girl, some other lustful beast might do to these idols of their own hearts."[25] In the next issue, discussing the possibilities of a commutation, Watson claimed that all Georgians knew "that a commutation, *in this case*, means that Mary Phagan's blood will forever cry in vain to Heaven!"[26] In late July, a month after Slaton commuted Frank's sentence, Watson warned that if the "Big Money campaign" did not end soon, Georgia men must show how they were willing to "shed every drop of our blood to protect the honor of our Womanhood, and the sacred principle of Home Rule."[27] Having already established Big Money's support for Phagan's alleged murderer in earlier issues of the *Jeffersonian*, Watson employed graphic references to bloody scenes to both rile up the emotions of Georgians and direct their men toward an outlet for their wrath.[28] Many of his readers bought in. With Frank's Big Money benefactors out of their reach, Watson targeted the accused and arguably the state's second-most-hated figure, John Slaton.

In Atlanta, before the June 20 commutation, a mass meeting of three thousand was held near the state capitol "to protect the laws of the State against the disgraceful seige [sic] of Big Money being handled in violation of law to defeat Justice." Retribution was on the minds of those in attendance: "This rape and murder stinks above the earth and cries to God for vengeance, Who says 'Vengeance is Mine,'" the meeting's organizers wrote.[29] Watson was quick to accuse Governor Slaton of being bought by Big Money, and the charge fell on angry eyes and ears. Letters began pouring into Watson's publishing house in Thomson, so many that to print them all he had to set aside two full pages in two different issues of the *Jeffersonian*. A Savannah man "expect[ed] that the jingle of gold" from Frank's Jewish supporters "was so loud around the Governor's ears and eyes that it drowned out poor little Mary's voice." One Georgia woman wrote that "Big Money and the Devil" worked in tandem during the case and that she hoped "that Frank will be lynched yet, and Slaton with him." One letter charged that daily newspapers throughout the state had "sold out" the state's reputation "for Jew gold" and that Slaton had also "disgraced the grandest State in the Union for money."[30] A minister in Union Ridge placed Slaton's treachery in a biblical context: "Slaton should do as Judas did—go and offer his thirty pieces of silver to the family of poor Mary Phagan, then have his friend [Big Money] bury him in the Potter's field."[31]

The ultimate and horrifying display of the power and persuasiveness of Watson's words came with the mob attacks on Slaton's home and the lynching of Leo Frank. In the afternoon on June 20, 1915, the day Slaton commuted Frank's sentence, a boisterous crowd formed in front of the capitol while a much larger horde, five thousand strong, gathered at the Atlanta city hall to protest the governor's actions. That night, four thousand people began the six-mile journey along Peachtree Street from downtown to Slaton's mansion in Buckhead. Despite several police barricades, half the mob was able to reach the governor's property. Hearing of the mob's size, Slaton declared martial law and called for a regiment of the state militia to protect his home and his family. The mob lobbed rocks and glass bottles toward the troops while sarcastically singing the popular antiwar tune "I Didn't Raise My Boy to Be a Soldier." With bayonets fixed, the militiamen were able to drive off the angry mass of Georgians. At the same time, two hundred men from Cobb County had organized and were marching toward Slaton's residence from a different direction; however, they were turned back without a confrontation. Later that week, another mob of two hundred, this time heavily armed, approached the militia troops. The ensuing skirmish ended quickly. The cache of dynamite and fuses the militia found in the woods after the fight revealed the mob's intent. Martial law remained in effect around Slaton's home even after the newly elected Nathaniel E. Harris took over the governorship. Only days after leaving office, Slaton and his wife boarded a train for New York City, Big Money's supposed headquarters, never to return to their home state.[32]

Watson and the mob had not finished expunging their enmity toward Big Money's alleged attempt to trounce over the rule of law in Georgia. Watson plainly expressed the main issue in the commutation and the case at large in a July 22 article: "This assumption of rich outsiders that they have the right to run our Courts, and to run over our people, and to dictate to us how we shall manage our own domestic affairs, *must stop!*"[33] The mob was one way Georgians could get this done. Since justice had been overturned, "lynch law" was "*better than no law at all.*"[34] Watson attempted to show that without the interference of northern Big Money and those in its employ, mob justice would not be necessary: "Let the rulers *treat the people right*, and there will be no mobs, and no riots."[35]

But one more mob had yet to form. On August 17 a group of twenty-five Mariettans, several from the Phagan family, pulled Leo Frank from his cell in the state penitentiary in Milledgeville and hanged him outside Marietta, not far from the final resting place of his alleged victim.[36] Watson's reaction in the *Jeffersonian* was triumphant and lacked any semblance of remorse:

> *By the highest court on earth*, Leo Frank's trial was pronounced legal and fair.
> *By the highest court in Georgia*, the evidence was declared to be sufficient to support the verdict of the jury.
> *By the judicial department of our State government*, Frank's guilt had been ascertained, and the death penalty imposed.

By one of his own Lawyers, the verdict and the decisions were all brushed aside.
BY THE PEOPLE, that void act of Frank's lawyer was ignored, *and the sentence was carried out.*
The Law forfeited this man's life, for a horrible crime, *and he has paid.* That's all.
Now let outsiders attend to their own business, AND LEAVE OURS ALONE.[37]

With the lynching of Leo Frank, Georgians felt they had exacted revenge for a major insult to their honor and reclaimed the power and sovereignty Big Money had supposedly seized.

Historians studying Watson and the Frank case have cited widespread anti-Semitism and affronted honor as the primary factors that motivated Watson and many Georgians to oppose commutation, confront Slaton, and revel in Frank's murder. Although those factors may have spurred much of Watson's dangerous rhetoric, Frank's murder, and the rebirth of the Ku Klux Klan in the fall of 1915, these issues were not the only ones that inspired the majority of demonstrators at Slaton's mansion or the thousands who waited to view Frank's body in Atlanta after his death.[38] Conceding that an especially virulent strain of anti-Semitism made some Georgians more susceptible to the words flowing from Watson's poisonous pen should not minimize the class and regional implications of his argument. Moreover, Barton C. Shaw has argued that instances of outright anti-Semitism among Georgia Populists were rare in the 1890s. "Wool-hat boys" used such anti-Semitic terms as *Shylock* and *Rothschild* to describe Democrats, Big Money, and any other enemy charged with exploiting their state. Anti-Semitic remarks, according to Shaw, were mostly metaphorical.[39]

Although a visceral hatred for Jews likely motivated many members of the 1915 mobs, it is unclear whether Populist-minded Georgians in general viewed Jews as any more of a threat at that point than in the 1890s; however, there is no denying that Watson's ability to strike the nerves of class, regional, and masculine pride set many Protestant white Georgians alight with anger. Watson's popularity increased in the state after the Frank affair not necessarily because of intensive anti-Semitism but because of arguments based in the same ideology that had effectively mobilized his followers in the past. One indication of this strategy may be the words of one follower in an October 1915 issue of the *Jeffersonian*: "One blast from Watson's horn would put 50,000 men in the field at any central point as quick as the iron horse could carry them."[40] Similar arguments against Big Money's influence in national politics during the period of neutrality and wartime soon inspired a similar emotional reaction. Falling prey to Frank's team of Big Money benefactors was no different than allowing the federal government to trample white southern men's individual rights. Yet with the war, the stakes were higher. Unlike with the Frank case, Watson and his followers perceived the battle against federal wartime policies as a life-and-death struggle.

As many Georgians focused their indignation on Leo Frank, John Slaton, and northern moneyed interests, a war raged in Europe. Despite Watson's preoccupation with the Frank case, his *Jeffersonian* was the only newspaper in Cobb and Cherokee Counties prior to the U.S. declaration of war against Germany on April 6, 1917, that consistently tried to explain how the European conflict affected Georgia. Watson was like most Americans in his disdain for the war and his sorrow over Europe's self-inflicted implosion. When writing directly to southern farmers about the war, he was quite clear: "But *you* have nothing to do with it. The quarrel is not yours."[41]

Watson's vitriol against federal policies also had firm roots in his long-held hatred for Woodrow Wilson, which appears to have gone back as far as 1905. Wilson had allegedly said, "Trusts can never be abolished. We must moralize them." In response, Watson called Wilson an "insufferable, impractical prig" with a clear affinity for exploitative capitalists. Watson strongly disliked Wilson's five-volume *A History of the American People* (1903) because it exposed Wilson's "cold cynicism toward popular movements [and] a deference to wealth and social power." According to C. Vann Woodward, Watson saw this attitude as tantamount to treason against Wilson's native South.[42] As the United States inched closer to war, the disgruntled Populist began attacking Wilson's moral character—in sectional and class terms, as usual. For instance, in October 1916 Watson printed an article in the *Jeffersonian* admonishing the president for allegedly spending thousands of dollars on jewelry for his present wife while leaving the "*grave of* [his] *GEORGIA WIFE*—the mother of his grown daughters" without markings or even flowers. The first southern Democrat to occupy the White House since Andrew Johnson, then, was a traitor to his family, his wife's former home state, and his native South. "*Gentlemen, the facts are ugly!*" Watson exclaimed. "But they are characteristic of Woodrow Wilson."[43]

Once the war began in Europe, Watson was quick to charge that the Wilson administration and northern Big Money were using the drop in cotton prices, which resulted from the U.S. refusal to challenge Britain's blockade of Germany, as a way to exploit southern farmers and rob them of their income.[44] Before the war, rising prices and rising production resulted in unprecedented profits in the cotton South. In August 1914, though, the fear that exports to Europe would be cut off led the major cotton exchanges to close for three months—during harvest season. In the interim, farmers were left with no reliable indication of prices. Most farmers had little choice but to sell their crop to speculators at eight cents a pound (the price had been thirteen cents a pound before August). Many who refused to sell low found no other outlet for their crop. According to historian George Brown Tindall, the severe drop in price cut the value of the 1914 crop in half, a loss of $500 million.[45]

Cotton speculators' alleged abuses during the crisis raised Watson's ire. Northern banks, he claimed, made low-interest loans to speculators for the purpose of buying up cheap cotton. In the December 10, 1914, issue of the *Jeffersonian*, he charged the Wilson administration with the crime of loaning $78 million—straight from the U.S. Treasury—at 2 percent interest to "such demi-gods" as J. P. Morgan, Jacob Schiff, and Hoke Smith. These "demi-gods" then used this money to grant loans to speculators at low rates. The government had secured the money for the original loans "partly by taxing it out of the farmers" and partly through the Treasury's ability to print money. The speculators, Watson charged, also refused to lend any money to farmers unless they agreed to cut their 1915 cotton crop in half and thereby boost the value of the cotton the speculators had already bought.[46] As with most of his ramblings, the accuracy or inaccuracy of Watson's assessment is not as relevant as his underlying message. By refusing to make direct loans to farmers, Watson argued, the administration and Big Money were holding southern cotton farmers hostage with their own tax money.

Watson's tirades concerning cotton prices continued into the fall of 1915. The Democratic administration, he continued, offered little assistance to farmers while buttressing the already dominant political and economic position of Big Money. Having broken a pledge to give rural credits to struggling farmers and instead handing the money to banking interests—the Democratic Party was essentially in a position to "*safely kick its own dog*" in the solid South. The administration sold out its base when it "hurriedly stamped $400,000,000 of new money" so "Wall Street gamblers" could exploit the cotton farmers' desperate position and the party could "curry favor with the North and East."[47]

In the case of the federal government and cotton speculators, Watson was not only shaping rural opinion but also mimicking it. In November 1914 two Georgians, a preacher and a "plain country man," sent letters to the *Jeffersonian* grumbling about how the federal government had sold out Georgia cotton farmers to outside financial interests. The preacher's letter addressed President Wilson, accusing him of using the war as "subterfuge by which you can escape the just criticism which you deserve." The man condemned Wilson and his "gang of political prostitutes" for putting "the neck of the government under the heel of high finance."[48] Explaining his opinion on cotton speculation, the "plain country man" wrote, "But the muddy recesses of Hades must be yawning for legislation when the bankers, business men, and Congressmen and other starched shirt farm doctors make statutes and penalties against us poor farmers for making cotton."[49] In short, from the winter of 1914 to the fall of 1915, Watson bombarded his readers with the message that the Wilson administration viewed the war in Europe as an opportunity to placate northern financial interests at the expense of the cotton-producing South. One of rural Georgia's first encounters with federal war policies, therefore, was a decidedly negative one.

The Georgia Farmers' Union spoke out in favor of rural credits and against the protective cover the administration allegedly gave to speculators.[50] At a September 1915 meeting in Atlanta, the GFU adopted resolutions condemning federal protection of cotton speculators and the lack of support for farmers. One resolution stated in Watson-esque prose, "Never in the history of our nation has there been such an example of bad faith or high-handed double-dealing" as the administration's refusal to make loans directly to farmers. Like Watson, the GFU threatened an electoral revolution (voting Republican) if the Democrats did not follow up on their promise in 1912 to enact rural credits at the same interest rate given to speculators. To encourage farmers to make up for the loss they took on their 1914 crop, the GFU passed a resolution echoing Watson's suggestion that the farmers hold their cotton until wartime prices reached a more favorable rate.[51] The same feeling of betrayal that came across in *Jeffersonian* editorials was clearly visible in the words of the GFU resolutions. Unlike Watson, the GFU's statements did not cite conspiracy theories about whom the cotton speculators were or the source from which their money came. Yet Watson's influence with the GFU was strong enough that in November 1915 it formally endorsed his stance on the rural credits issue.[52] Soon thereafter, in February 1916, Watson gave the speech concerning his obscenity charge before a gathering of farmers in Thomson; GFU president J. J. Brown was scheduled to speak at the same event.⁵³ The GFU's endorsement of Watson's rural credit proposition and the scheduling of Watson's speech before a GFU crowd suggest that Watson and the GFU saw each other as partners in the fight against the alliance of federal authority and Big Money.

While the GFU continued to battle cotton speculators, Watson railed against what he perceived as American imperialism and the growth of militarism in the United States—just as he had in 1898. During the military preparedness campaign throughout 1916 and early 1917, he continued to spit fire at Wilson's attempts to increase the power of the federal government through militaristic policies.⁵⁴ Playing on the rural South's general antipathy toward militarism, a strong and intrusive federal government, and northern industrial and financial greed, Watson cautioned against the dangers of compulsory military service. "Our people have yet to learn, and may learn it too late," he wrote in October 1916, that the money the administration was spending on a larger military was "simply meant to prepare the country for a change of government . . . from a Republic, to a military despotism."⁵⁵ To Tom Watson, the United States, by producing "*big armaments*" for itself and the Allies, "*instead of insuring* PEACE, *insure*[d] WAR." The most dangerous aspect of military preparedness and universal military service was the prospect of "millions of young men" being "trained into blind obedience to Authority," an authority that his readers had been taught to mistrust.⁵⁶ Calls in the press and Congress for compulsory military training, then, were signs that despotism was on the rise in the United States. "Men are always the same," he asserted; "give any one man, or any one class, too much power, *and it will be abused*." Germany might be deadly on the high seas, "but the real truth is, *our deadliest foes are within the gates*."⁵⁷

In the *Jeffersonian* on December 21, 1916, Watson opened his legal crusade against universal military conscription, emphasizing the urgency of the moment. A shift toward militarism was "taking place under [our] eyes," he warned, and there was "no time to lose" in combating "these revolutionary changes." The old Populist hoped to empower his readers to play their part in creating a widespread public reaction against the administration and the business leaders who advised the president. The Constitution, which Watson claimed could not "be so stretched as to legalize this monstrous proposition," would be their ammunition. Compulsory military service, he argued, "destroys personal liberty and annuls *Habeas Corpus*, in time of peace." Neither Wilson nor Congress could legally institute conscription "without trampling upon the fundamental law of the Union."⁵⁸

Watson, though, was not the only voice of class-based antiwar and antidraft rhetoric in the United States. Eight days after the April 1917 war declaration, the Socialist Party of America (SPA) passed several resolutions claiming that U.S. entry "was instigated by the predatory capitalists in the United States who boast of the enormous profit . . . from the manufacture and sale of munitions" and foodstuffs to Europe. The SPA also called for repeal of the Selective Service Act and promised to support other parties toward that end. Likewise, the American Union against Militarism saw universal military training as a threat to individual liberty and a step toward militarism. It also saw military preparedness as the Wilson administration's attempt "to feed the war trust." Although the People's Council of America did not blame Wall Street for American belligerency during its meeting in May 1917, it too opposed conscription and warned against the exploitation of the working class by munitions makers.[59] Other organizations with class-based platforms—such as the local farmers unions, the Nonpartisan League, and the Industrial Workers of the World—opposed the war as a capitalist scheme, but their protests did not single out the administration.[60] Although these organizations were relatively popular in several corners of the country, only the local farmers unions held much sway in the South. Yet the war opponents' uniformity in argument speaks to the effectiveness of Watson's message in Georgia, the South, and the nation at large.

Several key southern politicians in Washington, along with several of their midwestern and western colleagues, shared Watson's class, regional, and antimilitarist reasons for opposing the Wilson administration's buildup to war and, after April 1917, its war legislation. Their arguments and language were similar to those in the *Jeffersonian*. The leader of southern congressional opposition to military preparedness and wartime legislation was House majority leader Claude Kitchin of North Carolina. Reminiscent of Watson, Kitchin referred to those who favored military preparedness and universal military training as "New York people" or "jingoes and war traffickers." Staying true to his prewar antimilitarist stance, Kitchin voted against the declaration of war and the Selective Service Act.[61]

Kitchin's votes largely mirrored the attitudes of his constituents, who saw the war and the pending Selective Service bill as a means of protecting the financial investments of northeastern war profiteers. Having believed the United States would enter the war only in the case of invasion, J. B. Eastwood of Lakeview, North Carolina, had "voted for Wilson because he kept us out and because he would keep us out of war." "Only the profit dollars of a few powerful . . . men have been attacked" by German U-boats, Eastwood asserted, concluding that he would neither "fight for dirty dollars" nor "kill for sordid gain." A man from Waxhaw, North Carolina, claimed to speak for "us poor working people who are expected to do the *fighting*, and *dying*, and the *feeding*, and after the war the paying of the bills"; he argued that the purpose of the war and conscription was "only the protection of the men who are engaged in High Seas commerce." The president of the North Carolina Farmers Union also wrote to Kitchin, asking him to vote against conscription because Wilson knew "that the casus belli does not appeal to the masses of the people." Wilson wished to force the people "to make a useless and unjust sacrifice for the benefit of others."[62]

Mississippi senator James K. Vardaman also viewed preparedness and the entry into the war from a class perspective. Writing to Kitchin in October 1915, Vardaman expressed a hope that others would join the fight against preparedness "and save the farmers and wealth producers of this Republic from being plundered in the interests of the manufacturers of munitions of war."[63] Vardaman's attitudes toward Wilson, the war, and alleged war profiteers mirrored those of Watson but without the Georgian's unbridled anti-Catholicism. Like Watson, Vardaman blasted the Wilson administration for its halfhearted attempts to relieve struggling cotton farmers in late 1914 and 1915, blamed bankers and businessmen for arousing war hysteria, and feared that conscription would result in a permanent standing army and eventually a militarized republic.[64] This rhetorical similarity may be traceable to Vardaman's subscription to the *Jeffersonian*. Vardaman wrote Watson in June 1913 asking for the issues he had not received since moving to Washington. The newly minted senator badly wanted Watson's advice on a currency bill being debated in Congress. Watson happily obliged, promising to forward the newspaper to Vardaman's office and then explaining the historical position of the "Jeffersonian Democrats" on the issue.[65] If Vardaman's subscription to the *Jeffersonian* and his letters are any indication, Watson's influence and appeal had the potential to reach beyond rural Georgians to those representing other southern states in Washington.

Watson and Georgia senator Thomas W. Hardwick were on less friendly terms. Hardwick's roller-coaster relationship with Watson had begun in 1902 when the latter threw the weight of his well-oiled statewide political machine behind Hardwick's run for Congress. Hardwick won but refused to be as subservient as Watson demanded. In 1910 Watson withdrew his support for Hardwick, citing the congressman's growing political allegiance to Watson's in-state archrival and then-governor Hoke Smith. Yet despite their rift, Hardwick and Watson shared a decidedly dim view of military preparedness, the influence of northern financial interests on the government, and conscription. During the Senate debates about preparedness in March 1916, Hardwick feared that the dramatic expansion of powers that Congress had granted the administration through the organization of a Council of National Defense and advisory commissions of businessmen (the War Industries Board) was a step toward the strangling of democratic principles and individual liberties.[66] When universal military training came up for debate that same month, the senator seconded Watson's misgivings about a large, permanent standing army and compulsory military service. The hostility among the people to increasing the size of the army was "not only deep-seated and general but," in Hardwick's opinion, also "well founded and insuperable." European-style universal training was not necessary in a country that enjoyed "happy geographical isolation" and where "the democratic and peaceful instincts of its people" precluded a move toward militarism.[67]

Seeing Germany's sinking of neutral American shipping as blatantly belligerent, Hardwick voted in favor of the war declaration. Yet he stayed true to his opposition to compulsory military training by arguing that the U.S. contribution to the Triple Entente cause should be mostly naval in character, with only a few regular army units being sent to France "for the moral effect it would have over there." Conscription, he said, would transform the United States into what it despised: "In our fight on Prussian militarism has it become necessary to establish in this country a more drastic and a more burdensome militarism than that under which Prussia has groaned and which we profess to hate? I think not; I believe not. Has the time come when, in order to democratize the balance of the world, we must lose our own democracy?" Citing his agreement with Vardaman, Hardwick asserted that if the country were under threat of invasion, American men would volunteer for service. But to require a man to go to battlefields three thousand miles and an ocean away was to "treat him as a subject, not as a citizen; as a serf, not as a freeman."[68] Hardwick's assault on compulsory training almost mirrored what Watson printed in the *Jeffersonian* throughout 1916 and until the newspaper's demise in August 1917. The fundamental difference, one that might have made Watson's message more threatening in the eyes of federal authorities but more appealing to many Georgians, was Senator Hardwick's failure to cite northern bankers and industrialists as the source of the perceived militaristic policies.

As several southern congressmen took up the fight in Washington, Watson continued to put forth conspiracy theories linking the administration to Big Money. The cause for which the administration was preparing to fight, he argued, was not the spread of democratic ideals; moreover, universal military training, or "American Prussianism," was not a means of combating German militarism. Instead, the policy was "aimed *at* the plundered American producers; and aimed *by* the plundering non-producers." "Now, when you regard [J. P.] Morgan as a *type*, rather than as an individual," Watson explained, "and remember that he represents the greed of soulless Capitalists incorporated by law, favored by legislation ever since the War between the States, fortified by court decisions made by lawyers when they are elevated to the bench, and constantly guarded from the peril of reformatory measures by their docile serfs in the Governmental livery, you can begin to see what are the selfishly sordid *sources* of all this fanatical clamor for an American army in Europe." In other words, Watson viewed the push for conscription as a move toward a form of militarism that "perpetuat[ed] an infernal system of class-legislation" that enriched the "non-producing classes, by the pillage of the producing masses."[69]

He also saw American entry into the war as official sanctioning of "the most ravenous *commercialism* that ever cursed a nation."[70] When explaining why he thought Wilson wanted war with Germany, Watson again evoked J. P. Morgan. Wilson had sent U.S. soldiers to fight in France to protect Morgan's investment in the Allies from the prospect of a German victory that would reduce *"their war paper to the status of Confederate money."* Watson could not have summed up his point more succinctly when he exclaimed, *"Where Morgan's money went, your boy's blood must go,* ELSE MORGAN WILL LOSE HIS MONEY!"[71] To Watson and his supporters, Big Money had already vilified the South in the northern press, interfered with Georgia's internal legal affairs in the Frank case, and robbed yeoman farmers of their tax money and much of their cotton-dependent livelihood. Big Money's close ties to the administration, the drive for military preparedness, and wartime conscription signified the final steps toward complete regional subservience to federal power and corporate wealth.

What made Watson especially threatening to the war effort was that his seductive theories of a northern financial conspiracy inspired active and widespread resistance to conscription. The aging Populist brought the war home to the backcountry with his claim that the Wilson administration would conscript rural sons to die in a war that was not theirs to fight. Watson did not advocate armed resistance but encouraged followers to contest the constitutionality of conscription in the federal courts. His wartime antidraft campaign began in the *Jeffersonian* on May 10, 1917, when he printed a petition against sending soldiers to die on European battlefields. The petition's third point was the most important regarding the draft: "We most respectfully contend that the Federal Government has no constitutional authority to adopt and enforce any law requiring the citizen, *against his will*, to serve in the Army or Navy." Conscription was no different than slavery and "would violate the 13th Amendment to the Constitution."[72] Selective conscription, though, became law when Wilson signed the bill on May 18, 1917. Watson soon suggested that community leaders from across the South convene in Macon, Georgia, to discuss "*the recent unconstitutional and revolutionary acts of Congress.*"[73] The meeting, planned for August 23, was canceled due to death threats directed toward Watson by war supporters in Macon.[74]

Watson's staunch resistance to the new law infected rural communities across the South, leading the Department of Justice to send agents to various Watson-inspired anti-draft meetings in the summer of 1917. Near Dothan, Alabama (in the extreme southeastern corner of the state), a group of *Jeffersonian* subscribers held a meeting where it was reportedly claimed that "if an attempt was made to conscript them they would set up a government of their own."[75] An agent stationed in Cornersville in central Tennessee reported that the *Jeffersonian* had created "a strong spirit of animosity toward the Government" by urging local people to raise money to fight the draft in court. In the same report, the agent also claimed that he had gotten wind of communities in Arkansas and Mississippi that were also raising money for Watson. According to the agent, the Populist editor was doing "what he has always done; stirring up strife and confusion among the more illiterate people, appealing especially to country folk."[76] In early August, local authorities arrested a man in the town of Sanford in central North Carolina for "advising young men not to answer the call of the Exemption Board" and for "soliciting funds" for a Watson-led legal challenge to the draft.[77] The Bureau of Investigation's regional agent asserted, "All of the trouble here in this state [North Carolina] is traceable to Watson, and I think a few arrests of agitators will keep the ones who are against the draft quiet and inactive."[78] Bureau agents filed reports about groups raising money for Watson from Louisville, Kentucky; near Birmingham, Alabama; and outside Austin and San Antonio, Texas.[79]

During August, the last month of the newspaper's existence, the *Jeffersonian* was overwhelmed with letters from similar groups in Georgia and elsewhere in the South. At first the letters only trickled in. The August 9 issue included three reports of resolutions passed during meetings in Warren

County and Fairview, Georgia, as well as one from Iron Springs, Mississippi. The resolutions these groups passed mirrored those in Watson's petition from May and his first editorial challenge to compulsory training in December 1916. The Mississippi letter mentions the stance of Watson's old acquaintance James K. Vardaman against the Selective Service bill in the Senate as being part of the group's inspiration to support the Georgian's legal challenge. The club, consisting of people from Iron Springs and Leeville, wished to "thank our noble Senator . . . for the brave and noble stand taken for real true 'Democracy'" by contributing a total of $68.75 to Watson's legal fund.[80] These letters were a sign of things to come and perhaps inspired the formation of more anti-draft clubs that based their principles on Watson's rhetoric.

In the issue of August 16, Watson printed more than twenty letters from anti-draft clubs and individuals sympathetic to his cause under the headline "Is Congress Blind and Deaf to This Sentiment of the People?" Again, the majority of letters echoed Watson's declaration that conscription was big business's and the federal government's attempt to violate the Thirteenth Amendment, infringe on blood-bought individual liberties, and steer the nation toward autocracy. For instance, after admitting that each man would "willingly fight and die in defense of our country in case of invasion," members of a Howard, Georgia, group indignantly refused to die for the "moneyed and blue-blooded oligar[ch]ies of the old world" or to add billions of dollars to "the already busting coffers of Wall Street[']s money ogress." The northern Big Money interests, they concluded, sought "to destroy the lives of millions of their fellow citizens and plunge their families into endless wars." The other letters printed in the same issue were sent from all over Georgia and the South, including Alabama, Mississippi, and Arkansas.[81] Not every set of resolutions from the anti-draft clubs used the language of "us versus them" or the "haves versus the have nots," but their opposition to the war and their financial support for the legal fund imply that Watson's antiwar rhetoric—consistently coated in class conflict—either inspired rural southerners or, at the very least, gave them an excuse to protect themselves and their kin from being shot at on distant battlefields.

On August 18 Watson put his people's sentiment and their donations (approximately $100,000) to use in front of Judge Emory Speer of the U.S. District Court for the Southern District of Georgia. Public attendance for Watson's formal legal assault on the draft was so large that Speer was forced to move the proceedings outdoors in Augusta's oppressive summer heat. The sweat on Watson's brow that afternoon contrasted sharply with his reportedly cool and measured demeanor.[82] Similar to his petition in the May 10 *Jeffersonian*, Watson spared the court any direct rants against Big Money and its influence on the White House. Instead, he grounded his reasoning in common law and the Constitution: most important, he argued that the draft violated states' rights and the Thirteenth Amendment by handing near-imperial powers to the president and Congress. Not only did federal conscription allow Congress to "forfeit the Constitutional rights of millions of citizens" by "authoriz[ing] their despotic control" in war zones overseas, Watson argued, but the draft also gave the federal government the right to assign certain undrafted men a place in a war industry or on a large commercial farm. "Has Congress the power to authorize a system of industrial servitude?" he asked.[83] Without making the accusation directly, as he had done so consistently in the *Jeffersonian*, Watson pegged the federal government as militaristic by implying that northeastern industry and capital as well as wealthy planters in the South and West benefited and likely played a hand in bringing about the war declaration and conscription.

Although Speer ruled against Watson on the basis that calling a soldier a slave in a time of war was "degrading" to the men and the nation, the unsurprising outcome of the case is not as important as two often-overlooked details.[84] First, Watson chose to employ his supporters' donations in the defense of two African American men charged with failing to register for the draft. It is unclear why he chose to defend John Story and Albert Jones. It may have been to further drive home his point that conscription was tantamount to slavery, or perhaps Story and Jones were Watson's only options as plaintiffs in the short time he had before the U.S. postmaster general denied mailing rights to his mouthpiece the *Jeffersonian*. Regardless, during the trial Watson's words harked back to his more racially inclusive days of the 1890s: "The liberty of one is the liberty of all: in defending these two negroes, we defend everybody."[85] By defending Story and Jones, then, Watson was acknowledging the legal and moral equality of African Americans in the fight against conscription and militarism.

Second, the case led to "an unlikely alliance" between Watson and Harry Weinberger, a Jewish attorney from New York, the capital of Big Money. Weinberger, a socialist and self-proclaimed Jeffersonian Democrat, began the correspondence in July with the hope that Watson could assist in Weinberger's defense of anarchists Emma Goldman and Alexander Berkman. The relationship blossomed as the men collaborated on Watson's ill-fated appeal of Speer's decision to the U.S. Supreme Court. By winter Watson and Weinberger wrote each other almost daily about the appeal, with Watson occasionally asking his new partner for advice on how to revive his publishing career. Watson and Weinberger's relationship lasted until Watson's death in 1922. The point here is not to imply that Watson was not a white supremacist, an anti-Semite, or at the very least suffering from mental illness or emotional hardships during the final ten to fifteen years of his life. The evidence does suggest, however, that the generally accepted portrait of Tom Watson as the working-class hero of the 1890s who lost his way (or his mind) needs to better account for the consistency of his rhetoric over time and for his ability to forge mutually beneficial relationships with members of groups he had derided in the past.[86]

Yet the editor's army of donors no longer had the opportunity to write to the *Jeffersonian* about how they felt about his defense of two African Americans and his relationship with Weinberger, making it practically impossible to measure their surprise, horror, indifference, or any combination of these reactions. Before Speer could make a decision in the case, the *Jeffersonian* fell victim to the clause in the 1917 Espionage Act that allowed U.S. postmaster general Albert Sydney Burleson, a Texan of long Confederate lineage, to deny mailing privileges to publications he deemed seditious. In case Burleson's agency faced resistance from Watson or his supporters, Attorney General Thomas W. Gregory offered the assistance of his department. "So far as Mr. Watson's paper" was concerned, Gregory wrote to Burleson, "the attitude of this Department . . . is that of sustaining your department in every way practicable."[87] After government censorship had proved incapable of squashing Watson's influence, Gregory's Department of Justice followed through on this promise with direct action.

Although it appears that most of Watson's supporters across the South chose to fight federal intrusion through legal means, the Department of Justice had grave doubts about the track Georgians would take. Federal investigators portrayed the vast majority of the anti-draft groups as militant and potentially violent. The U.S. attorney for north Georgia, Hooper Alexander, warned a Bureau of Investigation agent about a Watson-inspired group of roughly eighty-five men in Roswell, about twenty miles north of Atlanta. The members of the organization "were alleged to have . . . signed a pledge that they would fight this country against conscription" before allowing their sons or themselves to be sent to France. Alexander's phrasing implied that the group planned to resist violently. As it turned out, the men met merely to circulate an appeal to Congress contesting the draft, not to physically confront federal authorities.[88]

The next month, July 1917, Alexander received a letter from Lithonia in

DeKalb County saying that an undisclosed number of men had "armed themselves with Winchester rifles and [were] preparing to resist any attempt" to draft anyone in their group. Although the letter's author could not be sure, he was "inclined to believe" that the armed men were "ardent supporters of 'Tom' Watson." It is unclear whether federal officials responded to the allegations; however, as the DeKalb club's resolutions printed in the *Jeffersonian* indicated, the Lithonians planned to resist the draft through legal channels only.[89] A Bureau of Investigation agent sent to Carroll County likewise did not find evidence of a planned violent insurrection. Interviewing county elites to garner information on a possible anti-draft group, he found that meetings were held in the rural areas of the county to petition Congress and to raise money "for the purpose of employing Watson and his associate lawyers" to "test the constitutionality" of conscription.[90]

The one place agents had clear evidence that violent resistance was in the works was in mountainous Union County, on the Georgia-Tennessee border. In late May 1918 the Justice Department caught wind of a sizable band of so-called slackers—all fifty to seventy-five of them believed to be armed—who allegedly had bought their local sheriff's protection with moonshine.[91] Despite the apparent lawlessness and strong potential for armed resistance, the federal officials chose not to send a raiding party into Union County. One possible explanation is the county's relative isolation due to its largely mountainous terrain, which would have made a raid difficult to carry out. At the same time, Union did not have a national reputation for vigilante violence, and it was not clear if Watson's anti-draft rhetoric was the source of local support for the slackers, as was the case in these other counties.

Instead, the Justice Department targeted the alleged organizers of one of the largest anti-draft meetings in the state. Men from Cobb and Cherokee Counties met on August 11, 1917, in Marietta, the site of the Leo Frank lynching two years earlier. According to the club's secretary, J. B. Petrie, the crowd at the meeting "was variously estimated at from eight hundred to one thousand" men who "all heartily endorsed the enclosed resolutions." Their resolutions cited both Watson's and Senator Hardwick's public stances against militarism as inspiration. The Marietta group insisted that "fully 75 per cent" of Georgians did not support conscription and that the law was unconstitutional, and its members planned to send a delegation from the group to Watson's proposed convention in Macon. Their opposition to the draft, as in all the other groups' resolutions, was to be peaceful. Most striking, though, the Marietta resolutions did not rail against northern greed or attack the administration, and President Wilson was not seen to be at fault. The letter claimed that the president had been misled by the state's congressional delegation into believing that Georgians supported his plan for conscription.[92] In this sense, the Marietta resolutions were un-Watsonian in tone. Most important, however, the resolutions said nothing of armed resistance.

Despite the peaceful tone of the resolutions, Bureau of Investigation officials, aware of the national reputation for violence that Cobb County earned in the Frank affair, were perhaps warranted in assuming that the evaders and anti-draft clubs were armed and itching for a fight. Eighteen to twenty draft evaders reportedly hid in the hills of the two counties, supposedly with the active support of the anti-draft group's leaders. The federal agents anticipated facing armed resistance to federal law: fifty federal soldiers accompanied federal and state civil authorities on a raid into Cobb and Cherokee.[93]

Eleven months after the club's meeting, on the morning of July 16, 1918, the posse set off from Marietta to interrogate and intimidate the alleged ringleaders of the Cobb anti-draft organization as well as catch any slackers the authorities might come across. The size and makeup of the expedition reveals the importance the Department of Justice placed on the mission: two bureau agents, four revenue officers, a U.S. deputy marshal, a local informant, and two trucks, each filled with twenty-five fully armed soldiers. Despite confronting each suspected anti-draft organizer with the federal government's most effective means of coercion, the raiders failed to achieve the primary objectives of the operation, which were to obtain evidence against Watson for a potential Sedition Act violation and to nab the rural draft dodgers. Instead, the raid ended in disaster when one truck carrying soldiers crashed through a wooden bridge in Cherokee County, falling forty feet into the Etowah River. The crash left three dead, eight seriously wounded, and approximately ten with less severe injuries. The Bureau of Investigation agent on the scene suspected that the bridge was sabotaged by locals: he cited the lack of a caution sign along the road, the sudden emergence of several men on the riverbank after the crash, and what he believed to be freshly cut support beams.[94] If the agent was correct, it appears that the tactic Watson's supporters in the Georgia upcountry employed against Governor John Slaton in 1915—attempted violence against outside invaders with seemingly bad intentions—had reared its ugly head again. The Justice Department did not attempt another raid in Georgia, perhaps because it viewed the results in Cherokee County as indicative of Watson's support and further evidence of the seemingly inherent lawlessness permeating the state.

To wage war effectively, nations must mobilize minds, men, and matériel efficiently and with the least possible resistance. This is especially true in a liberal democracy. The raid on Cobb and Cherokee Counties and the move to shut down the *Jeffersonian*, then, reflected the federal government's concern over Watson's regional and national capacity to foster anti-draft dissent. Through his widely circulated newspaper, his antimilitarist and anti–big business message spread quickly. The basis of the aging Populist's opposition to American involvement in World War I and the Selective Service Act likely resonated with a large number of rural white Georgians because the argument was one they had been hearing from Watson and other Populist-minded politicians for decades.

The actions in Cobb County in response to Watson's rhetoric concerning Big Money's influence—in not only the Frank case but also the Wilson administration's war policies—reveal both Watson's powers of persuasion and Georgians' deep-seated mistrust of external moneyed influences. Watson's somewhat self-referential definition of the southerner was similar to that of his readers: Protestant white men native to the South who had not sold out to northern finance or centralized national authority. Aspects of this definition were evident in all of his arguments in the wartime era. In the Frank case, Big Money and northern Jews, categories Watson often lumped into one entity, made a mockery of Georgia law and southern honor by bribing witnesses and state officials as well as vilifying the state's good name in the northern press. Northern bankers in cahoots with the Wilson administration used southern operatives to buy Georgia cotton on the cheap before selling it at inflated wartime prices. During the neutrality period and the first five months of the war, the federal government looked to implement policies that would usurp individual rights, safeguard northern investments, and impose autocratic rule from afar. Therefore, by resisting federal and moneyed interference in southern life and politics, Watson and his followers fought to preserve the ideals of southern nativism and keep Georgia free of alien influence.

Of course, many Georgians may not have seen the war in class terms. Just as many who violently protested Frank's commutation did so out of religious and ethnic hatred, some who joined Watson's legal crusade against the draft or headed for the cover of the foothills did so simply out of fear of being shot. Yet to chalk up southern draft evasion as a whole to cowardice undermines the cultural relevance of the Lost Cause tenet that a white southern man's responsibility was to take up arms to protect his home, his women, and his way of life. To Watson and his followers, this sense of honor did not apply in the case of a war with Germany as it had in the Frank case because no German soldier had set foot on American soil. The only regimes to directly threaten the state of Georgia, in their view, were Big Money, "Kaiser" Wilson, and their wartime alliance. When making the decision to avoid military service, Georgia draft evaders likely had more in mind than their own safety. Ducking the draft, like demonstrating against the federal government's protection of cotton speculators, was also a means of protesting the burgeoning power of the American state and the slow disintegration of a premodern communal southern society.

When arguing against preparedness, the war, and conscription, Watson's message was clear: compulsory military training was the ultimate usurpation of power by the federal government and its moneyed partners. Not only would it make automatons out of American men, but the undemocratic, militaristic society that would result from such policies would leave the fabric of the republic in tatters. As on many other occasions, the Populist editor saw the war and conscription as the abuse of government power to benefit northeastern Big Money at the expense of the so-called producing classes. To bow to conscription and the administration's war polices would be to give in to the same faction that had exploited struggling cotton farmers early in the war, supported a murderer and rapist with money and positive press, bribed a governor for the commutation of Frank's sentence, and tried unjustly to jail and muzzle what many—including Watson himself—saw as the true voice of the people. Anti-Semitism, conservative beliefs about sexuality, and the fear of death clearly attracted many to Watson's various but related causes from 1914 to 1918. Yet these beliefs were not the only factors that mobilized rural men and women in Georgia and the South over the previous three decades. Watson's ability to marshal thousands of his followers against Frank and his supporters, cotton speculators, Woodrow Wilson, and American involvement in the World War I is proof that Populist sentiment was by no means dead in rural Georgia and the South as a whole. To Tom Watson and many in the Georgia upcountry, the fight against the Wilson administration and conscription was merely another skirmish in a decades-long battle for economic and political independence against the greed and corruption of both northern Big Money and federal power.

Notes

1. Speech, February 12, 1916, Thomas E. Watson Papers, microfilm, Series 1.7, Thomas E. Watson Papers (34 microfilm reels; Bethesda, Md.: University Publications of America, 1991; originals at the Southern Historical Collection, Wilson Library, University of North Carolina at Chapel Hill) [hereafter cited as TEW Papers], microfilm, reel 18. Watson eventually was cleared of all charges.

2. George G. Calmes, report, June 25, 1917, Old German File 17,761, Records of the Federal Bureau of Investigation, Record Group [hereafter cited as RG] 65, National Archives and Records Administration [hereafter cited as NARA], College Park, Maryland, National Archives Microfilm Series M-1085, reel 349 [hereafter cited as OGF, RG 65]; Thomas E. Watson, *Speech against the Conscript Act, Delivered by Thos. E. Watson at Thomson, Ga., June 23, 1917* (Thomson, Ga., 1917).

3. See C. Vann Woodward, *Tom Watson: Agrarian Rebel* (New York: Macmillan, 1938). An example of Watson's prejudices being less than pathological that did not occur during the war was his defense of Sigmund Lichtenstein, a Jewish man tried for murder in Swainsboro, Georgia, in 1901. While Watson spoke of his client in racial terms ("It is written on the face of Sigmund Lichtenstein that he is a member of that noble race of people in whose veins flow the godly blood of Moses, David, and the prophets"), he spoke of the alleged racial characteristics in a positive manner. Watson told the jury, "No Jew can murder. And you know I am not telling you anything that's not true." Watson took the case partly because he was short on money but also to save the "little guy" from a lawless mob. Louis E. Schmier, "'No Jew Can Murder': Memories of Tom Watson and the Lichtenstein Murder Case of 1901," *Georgia Historical Quarterly* 70 (Fall 1986): 433–55 (quotations on 453).

4. Jeanette Keith, *Rich Man's War, Poor Man's Fight: Race, Class, and Power in the Rural South during the First World War* (Chapel Hill: University of North Carolina Press, 2004), 10.

5. Anthony Gaughan, "Woodrow Wilson and the Rise of Militant Interventionism in the South," *Journal of Southern History* 65 (November 1999): 771–808 (first quotation on 774; second quotation on 784). Practically all historians who have examined the period of American neutrality from 1914 to 1917 acknowledge that western and southern states were the most staunchly isolationist and pacifist regions of the country. The bastion of interventionism was clearly the great metropolises of the Northeast, most significantly New York City. See Arthur S. Link, *Woodrow Wilson and the Progressive Era, 1910-1917* (New York: Harper Torch, 1954), chaps. 4–10; John Milton Cooper, *The Vanity of Power: American Isolationism and the First World War, 1914-1917* (Westport, Conn.: Greenwood, 1969); and Justus D. Doenecke, *Nothing Less Than War: A New History of America's Entry into World War I* (Lexington: University Press of Kentucky, 2011).

6. Hardwick, though, voted in favor of the declaration of war. Josephine Newton Cummings, "Thomas William Hardwick: A Study of a Strange and Eventful Career" (M.A. thesis, University of Georgia, 1961), 21.

7. The *Marietta Journal and Courier* carried almost no news of the war and briefly mentioned on only one occasion the sinking of the *Lusitania*, a British ship, by German submarines in May 1915, which killed more than one hundred Americans. The *Cobb County Times*, also published in Marietta, reported sparingly on the war as well. In December 1916

the *Times* ran two articles during the Christmas season deploring the massive loss of life in Europe. The *Cherokee Advance*, in contrast, dedicated significant space in its May 14, 1915, issue with news of the *Lusitania* disaster and, two weeks later, printed the full text of President Woodrow Wilson's response to Germany. Yet the *Advance* paid scant attention to the war afterward and did not publish editorials or letters to the editor about the war. The primary source of war news in rural Cobb and Cherokee Counties were the *Atlanta Journal* and the *Jeffersonian*. The *Journal* likely had the larger circulation in these counties during the public debates over Frank and the war, but its rural readership declined in the wake of its March 1914 editorial espousing Frank's innocence. In contrast, Watson's involvement in the Frank affair led to a sharp increase in the *Jeffersonian*'s circulation throughout the state and region after that same month. Despite the *Journal*'s larger rural circulation, Watson's harangues against the influence of Big Money in Georgia appear to have positioned him as the more authoritative voice on the war to many rural residents of Cobb and Cherokee Counties. "Lusitania Is Sunk by German Torpedo," *Marietta Journal and Courier*, May 14, 1915, 1; "Christmas Longings," Marietta *Cobb County Times*, December 21, 1916, 8; "Dealers in Death," ibid., December 28, 1916, 8; "Lusitania Sunk and Many Lives Are Lost," Canton *Cherokee Advance*, May 14, 1915, 2; "Text of Note Sent Germany by Mr. Wilson," ibid., May 28, 1915, 3; *N. W. Ayers & Son's American Newspaper Annual and Directory* (Philadelphia, 1915), 147; and Woodward, *Tom Watson*, 437–38, 442. Most issues of the *Jeffersonian* are now available online as part of the Thomas E. Watson Papers Digital Collection, www.lib.unc.edu/dc/watson.

8. Steven Hahn defines the Georgia upcountry as comprising the hill counties just south of the north Georgia mountains. Although his study focuses primarily on Carroll (west) and Jackson (east) counties, he expands his research to the remaining upcountry counties: Floyd, Bartow, Cherokee, Forsyth, Hall, Banks, Franklin, Hart, Polk, Paulding, Cobb, Milton, Gwinnett, Madison, Walton, DeKalb, Rockdale, Fulton, Douglas, Haralson, Campbell, Clayton, Fayette, and Heard. Hahn, *The Roots of Southern Populism: Yeoman Farmers and the Transformation of the Georgia Upcountry, 1850–1890* (New York: Oxford University Press, 1983), 7–8.

9. "Resolutions om [sic] Meeting Held at Marietta, Cobb County Georgia, Aug. 11, 1917," Thomson *Jeffersonian*, August 30, 1917, 8; "Cobb County Has Meeting," ibid., 9.

10. H. F. Rape, report, August 4, 1917; Hilton D. Campbell, report, August 20, 1917; J. J. Lawrence, report, August 8, 1917; Manuel Servia, report, August 17, 1917; and Willard Utley, report, August 8, 1917; all in OGF, RG 65.

11. Howell Jackson, report, June 15–18, 1917, OGF, RG 65.

12. Hahn, *Roots of Southern Populism*, 282. In a similar vein, C. Vann Woodward describes southern Populism as a cultural as well as a political revolution. Southern Populists confronted not only the unequal distribution of wealth in the South but also the region's political and social traditions, most notably the tenet of white solidarity. Most recently, Charles Postel has written that the Populist movement was not a political and cultural battle between premodern and modern worldviews. Instead, Postel depicts Populists like Tom Watson as offering an alternative vision of modernity, not an alternative to modernity. Like Hahn, Barton C. Shaw focuses on Georgia Populists, but Shaw highlights the threat distant economic forces posed to small landowning farmers, a tradition of political nonconformity, and the magnetic appeal of fiery leaders like Tom Watson. Woodward,

Origins of the New South, 1877–1913 (Baton Rouge: Louisiana State University Press, 1951), 249–50; Charles Postel, *The Populist Vision* (New York: Oxford University Press, 2007); Shaw, *The Wool-Hat Boys: Georgia's Populist Party* (Baton Rouge: Louisiana State University Press, 1984).

13. "Labor-Day Address," May 1891, in Thomas E. Watson, *Life and Speeches of Thos. E. Watson* (Thomson, Ga., 1911), 61 (first and second quotations); "Summary of Mr. Watson's Speech," July 27, 1898, ibid., 179–80 (third, fourth, and fifth quotations); "Speech in Nashville, Tenn.," September 1904, ibid., 204 (sixth quotation); "How the Law Controls the Distribution of Wealth," January 22, 1907, ibid., 255 (seventh and eighth quotations).

14. Historian Richard Nelson has argued that Watson's political rhetoric and philosophy remained consistent from the 1890s to the Leo Frank affair (which lasted, for Watson, into 1916) because of Watson's interpretation of republican government and inability to cope with a rapidly modernizing world. Nelson's analysis, though, does not extend into Watson's antiwar stance in 1917. Nelson, "The Cultural Contradictions of Populism: Tom Watson's Tragic Vision of Power, Politics, and History," *Georgia Historical Quarterly* 72 (Spring 1988): 1–29.

15. The standard study of the Frank case is Leonard Dinnerstein, *The Leo Frank Case* (Athens: University of Georgia Press, 1968). Journalist Steve Oney provides a more recent and exceptionally detailed account in *And the Dead Shall Rise: The Murder of Mary Phagan and the Lynching of Leo Frank* (New York: Pantheon, 2003). For a detailed analysis of Watson's involvement in the case, see C. Vann Woodward's classic biography, *Tom Watson*, 435–49.

16. Woodward, *Tom Watson*, 437–38 (quotation on 437).

17. Ibid., 442.

18. "Leo Frank, as a Regular Newspaper Contributor," Thomson *Jeffersonian*, December 3, 1914, 1, 8–9.

19. "The Leo Frank Case Again Decided by the Supreme Court," Thomson *Jeffersonian*, November 19, 1914, 5. Emphasis in quotations from the *Jeffersonian* is in the original.

20. Oney, *And the Dead Shall Rise*, 384, 451–57.

21. "Leo Frank Sentenced Again," Thomson *Jeffersonian*, December 17, 1914, 1, 8–9 (quotations on 9).

22. "Where Ought Law Cases Be Tried? And How? And by Whom? *In Re* Leo Frank," Thomson *Jeffersonian*, December 31, 1914, 1.

23. "Leo Frank, as a Regular Newspaper Contributor," Thomson *Jeffersonian*, December 3, 1914, 1, 8–9 (quotation on 9).

24. "The Leo Frank Case Again Decided by the Supreme Court," Thomson *Jeffersonian*, November 19, 1914, 5.

25. "Further Consideration of the Case of Leo Frank," Thomson *Jeffersonian*, June 3, 1915, 2 and 4.

26. "Possibilities and Peculiarities of the Frank Case," Thomson *Jeffersonian*, June 10, 1915, 3.

27. "The Frank Case; John M. Slaton; A Forgery or Two; and a Hidden Mesh-Bag," Thomson *Jeffersonian*, July, 22, 1915, 1–8 (quotations).

28. Two significant articles have analyzed Tom Watson and the Frank case in the context of gender and honor. Nancy MacLean has argued persuasively that a "reactionary

populism"—an ideology that found solutions to social problems in racism, murder, and the subordination of women—was just as important in rallying white Georgians against Frank and in the revival of the Ku Klux Klan as class or regional arguments were. Mary Phagan became the symbol of the paternalism inherent in reactionary populism and many Georgia men's fear of losing "possession" of "their" women. Bertram Wyatt Brown concentrates on personality and emotional disorders from which Watson potentially suffered and how these affected Watson's politics in the post-Populist Party years. Wyatt-Brown depicts a sad figure overcome by a sense of personal inadequacy and a possible genetic predisposition toward depression. Like Richard Nelson, though, Wyatt-Brown pays scant attention to Watson's antiwar stance in 1917. MacLean, "The Leo Frank Case Reconsidered: Gender and Sexual Politics in the Making of Reactionary Populism," *Journal of American History* 78 (December 1991): 917–48 (quotations on 929); Wyatt-Brown, "Tom Watson Revisited," *Journal of Southern History* 68 (February 2002): 3–30.

29. Jos. S. Barnwell et al., "Mass Meeting in Atlanta," Thomson *Jeffersonian*, June 17, 1915, 3.

30. J. M. Gardner, "A Voice from Savannah," Thomson *Jeffersonian*, July 8, 1915, 11 (first and second quotations), A Woman, "A Woman's Indignation," ibid., 11 (third and fourth quotations); C. W. McDade, W. C. Glass, et al., "Gentiles Think It Time to Fight Back," ibid., 12 (fifth, sixth, and seventh quotations).

31. T. E. Fears, "Resolutions of Union Ridge (GA.) Church," Thomson *Jeffersonian*, July 22, 1915, 2.

32. Dinnerstein, *Leo Frank Case*, 132–33; Oney, *And the Dead Shall Rise*, 503–6, 510–11.

33. "The Frank Case; John M. Slaton; A Forgery or Two; and a Hidden Mesh-Bag," Thomson *Jeffersonian*, July 22, 1915, 8 (quotation).

34. "The Old Paths—and the New Path Taken by the Frank Case," Thomson *Jeffersonian*, June 24, 1915, 3.

35. "When 'Mobs' Are No Longer Possible, Liberty Will Be Dead," Thomson *Jeffersonian*, July 8, 1915, p. 6.

36. Oney, *And the Dead Shall Rise*, 561–72; Dinnerstein, *Leo Frank Case*, 139–47.

37. "The Wages of Sin Is Death," Thomson *Jeffersonian*, August 26, 1915, 1.

38. The odd requests and purchases some Georgians made after the Frank lynching reveal the pride many felt in serving what they saw as justice. More than fifteen thousand people attempted to catch a glimpse of Frank's corpse at the undertakers' establishment in Atlanta. Several well-off Georgians offered $250 for the tree from which Frank was hanged. The owner refused. Finally, two years later, in 1917, photographs of the lynching could still be purchased in Marietta. Photographing a lynching victim and taking body parts from the corpse were common methods whites used to sanctify and remember such acts, especially when the prey was African American. But treating Frank's ethnicity as the only cause of the acts mentioned above ignores the fact that race was one of many factors shaping Georgians' opinions of the Frank case. Oney, *And the Dead Shall Rise*, 567–72; Dinnerstein, *Leo Frank Case*, 143–45.

39. Shaw, *Wool-Hat Boys*, 178–80.

40. Woodward, *Tom Watson*, 425.

41. "The European War and the Farmer," Thomson *Jeffersonian*, January 7, 1915, 1.

42. Woodward, *Tom Watson*, 368–69 (first quotation on 368; second quotation on 369), 426 (third quotation).

43. "Woodrow Wilson's Neglect of His First Wife's Grave," Thomson *Jeffersonian*, October 26, 1916, 1.

44. Despite historical Populist antipathy toward Great Britain and its bankers for their alleged conspiracy to keep the United States on the gold standard (and thus destroy the drive for free silver), Watson rarely depicted Wilson, Congress, or banker John Pierpont Morgan as tools of England. Although Populists in the 1890s believed, as one wrote, that "[a] war with England would be the most popular ever waged on the face of the earth," Watson showed no interest in such a conflict from 1914 to 1917. For quotation see Richard Hofstadter, *The Age of Reform: From Bryan to F.D.R.* (New York: Knopf, 1955), 88.

45. George Brown Tindall, *The Emergence of the New South, 1913–1945* (Baton Rouge: Louisiana State University Press, 1967), 33–34.

46. "What Right Have the Bankers to Dictate to the Government and to the Farmers?" Thomson *Jeffersonian*, December 10, 1914, 1. The size of the alleged federal loan to northern banks changed from issue to issue, with Watson at one point putting it at $300 million. The reason for his inconsistency is unclear.

47. "How the Government Has Aided the Wall Street Gamblers to Rob the Southern Cotton Growers," Thomson *Jeffersonian*, September 23, 1915, 7–8 (quotations on 8).

48. "A Georgia Preacher Writes to the President," Thomson *Jeffersonian*, November 5, 1914, 3.

49. Jas. M. Elders, "A Plain Country Man's View of the Present Democratic Administration," ibid., 4.

50. Woodward claims that Watson enjoyed a position of influence with the GFU because he had chosen a "loyal lieutenant" to head the organization. With the support of Watson's rural followers, that political subordinate, J. J. Brown, became the state's commissioner of agriculture in 1917 while continuing to lead the GFU. The head of the largest nonparty political organization in Georgia, therefore, owed his success, and allegiance, to Watson. Woodward, *Tom Watson*, 431; Walter J. Brown, *J. J. Brown and Thomas E. Watson: Georgia Politics, 1912–1928* (Macon: Mercer University Press, 1988).

51. "Resolutions Adopted by Farmers' Union," *Atlanta Constitution*, September 26, 1915, E7.

52. "J. J. Brown to Again Head Farmers' Union; Indorses Tom Watson's Rural Credit Proposition and State Bonded Warehouse System," *Atlanta Constitution*, November 12, 1915, 2.

53. "Brown and Watson to Address Farmers," *Atlanta Constitution*, February 9, 1916, 7.

54. Prior to the declaration of war, advocates of military preparedness and universal military training primarily consisted of political and economic elites in the Northeast (such as Theodore Roosevelt and J. P. Morgan) and high-ranking military officers (such as Leonard Wood). Wilson was a reluctant participant in the campaign for preparedness. The president publicly announced his support for increased readiness for war while working behind the scenes to push a very weak army bill through Congress. The definitive work on the preparedness campaign is John Patrick Finnegan, *Against the Specter of a Dragon: The Campaign for American Military Preparedness, 1914–1717* (Westport, Conn.: Greenwood, 1974).

55. "A Size Up of the Presidential Situation," Thomson *Jeffersonian*, October 5, 1916, 1 and 3 (quotations).

56. "It Happened in the Year 1916, Thomson *Jeffersonian*, December 21, 1916, 1 and 4.

57. "Historical Facts Bearing upon 'Military Preparedness,'" Thomson *Jeffersonian*, January 25, 1917, 4.

58. "It Happened in the Year 1916," Thomson *Jeffersonian*, December 21, 1916, 1 and 4 (quotations).

59. "Socialist Party Position on American Belligerency," April 14, 1917, in *The Eagle and the Dove: The American Peace Movement and United States Foreign Policy, 1900–1922*, ed. John Whiteclay Chambers II (New York: Garland, 1976), 114–16 (first quotation on 115); "Crystal Eastman: Suggestions for the American Union against Militarism for 1916–1917," ibid., 92–96 (second quotation on 94); "Resolutions of the People's Council," May 31, 1917, ibid., 117–19.

60. H. C. Peterson and Gilbert C. Fite, *Opponents of War, 1917–1918* (Seattle: University of Washington Press, 1957), 23–24, 44–45, 65–67; Tindall, *Emergence of the New South*, 46–48.

61. Tindall, *Emergence of the New South*, 42–43.

62. J. B. Eastwood to Claude Kitchin, April 9, 1917, in *Draftees or Volunteers: A Documentary History of the Debate Over Military Conscription in the United States, 1783–1973*, ed. John Whiteclay Chambers II (New York: Garland, 1975), 265 (first through fourth quotations); S. S. Dunlap to Claude Kitchin, April 28, 1917, ibid., 266 (fifth and sixth quotations); H. Q. Alexander to Claude Kitchin, April 23, 1917, ibid. (seventh and eighth quotations).

63. Tindall, *Emergence of the New South*, 42.

64. William F. Holmes, *The White Chief: James Kimble Vardaman* (Baton Rouge: Louisiana State University Press, 1970), 298–302, 307, 318–21.

65. James K. Vardaman to Tom Watson, June 17, 1913, and Watson to Vardaman, June 20, 1913, TEW Papers, microfilm, reel 11.

66. Cummings, "Thomas William Hardwick," 6–11, 17–18.

67. Thomas W. Hardwick, *Extracts from the Speeches of Hon. Thomas W. Hardwick of Georgia, in the Senate of the United States, Between December 30, 1914, and September 7, 1917* (Washington, D.C., 1918), 5.

68. Ibid., 8–10.

69. "Common Sense Comments on the Great War," Thomson *Jeffersonian*, May 17, 1917, 3.

70. "Short Notes on the Great War," Thomson *Jeffersonian*, April 12, 1917, 4.

71. "Kaiser Wilson's Administration Shuts the Jeffersonian Out of the Mails," Thomson *Jeffersonian*, August 16, 1917, 6.

72. "Sign This! Petition against Sending Our Young Men to War in Europe," Thomson *Jeffersonian*, May 10, 1917, 6.

73. Woodward, *Tom Watson*, 455–56.

74. "Macon Meeting of Draft 'Antis' Now Called Off," *Atlanta Constitution*, August 22, 1917, 1.

75. George C. Smith, report, July 1, 1917, OGF, RG 65.

76. W. E. McElveen, report, July 31, 1917, ibid.

77. D. E. Haley to A. B. Bielaski, August 5, 1917, ibid.

78. D. E. Phillips, report, August 5, 1917, ibid.

79. H. F. Rape, report, August 4, 1917; Hilton D. Campbell, report, August 20, 1917; J. J. Lawrence, report, August 8, 1917; Manuel Servia, report, August 17, 1917; Willard Utley, report, August 8, 1917; all ibid.

80. "Resolutions of Meeting Warren County, Signed by Many," Thomson *Jeffersonian*, August 9, 1917, 12; L. O. Hopkins et al., "Minutes of Fairview Mass Meeting, Aug. 1st, 1917," ibid., 10; C. E. Chisolm, "From Senator Vardaman's State," ibid. (quotation). In June 1918 federal authorities sent soldiers into Neshoba County, Mississippi (home of Iron Springs), to smoke out thirteen slackers hiding in the area. According to Keith, the details of the story are murky, but it appears that the federal officers preferred reason over force. Four of the thirteen fugitives soon surrendered to authorities. Keith, *Rich Man's War*, 190.

81. C. L. Searcy, "Meeting at Howard, GA," Thomson *Jeffersonian*, August 16, 1917, 9.

82. Woodward, *Tom Watson*, 456. Woodward describes Watson's speech as "one of the most impressive [he] ever made." Had Watson the trial lawyer ranted and raved in a manner similar to his writings in the *Jeffersonian*, it would be difficult to describe his performance in such a light.

83. "Will the U.S. Judiciary Permit, and the People Ratify, the Congressional Overthrow of Our Constitutional System of Government? Mr. Watson's Argument Against the Conscription Acts, Before Judge Emory Speer, at Mt. Airy, August 18, 1917," *Watson's Magazine*, September 1917, 314–26 (quotations on 324).

84. John Story and Albert Jones, Petition for Habeas Corpus, August 20, 1917, Cases 77 and 78, Box 4, Records of the U.S. District Court, N. E. Division, Southern District of Georgia, Augusta, Records of District Courts of the United States, RG 21 (NARA, Morrow, Ga.). Judges' decisions made outside the bounds of legality were actually quite common in the United States during the country's involvement in World War I. The wartime hysteria that permeated American society infected judges and juries and clearly factored into their decisions. Emory Speer is merely one of hundreds of federal, state, and county judges across the country who ruled on the basis of unsound legal pretexts or prosecuted allegedly disloyal or dangerous defendants with little or no solid evidence. Most such trials—nearly all Espionage Act or Sedition Act cases—were overturned or sentences were reduced in the early 1920s after the wartime hysteria had fully subsided. See David Kennedy, *Over Here: The First World War and American Society* (New York: Oxford University Press, 1980), 83–86; Peterson and Fite, *Opponents of War*, 237–40; Kathleen Kennedy, *Disloyal Mothers and Scurrilous Citizens: Women and Subversion during World War I* (Bloomington: Indiana University Press, 1999); and Richard Polenberg, *Fighting Faiths: The Abrams Case, the Supreme Court, and Free Speech* (New York: Viking, 1987).

85. "Will the U.S. Judiciary Permit, and the People Ratify, the Congressional Overthrow of Our Constitutional System of Government?" *Watson's Magazine*, August 1917, 324.

86. Fred D. Ragan. "An Unlikely Alliance: Tom Watson, Harry Weinberger, and the World War I Draft," *Atlanta Historical Journal* 35 (Fall 1981): 19–36.

87. T. W. Gregory to A. Burleson, August 15, 1917, file 190,740, box 2822, Straight Numerical File, Central Files, Records of the Department of Justice, RG 60 (NARA, College Park, Md.). The denial of mailing privileges to the *Jeffersonian* and the death of his only remaining daughter left Watson in a deep state of depression and squelched his desire to

combat the administration's war policies until his unsuccessful last-minute campaign for Congress in August 1918. Woodward, *Tom Watson*, 458–59.

88. Russell M. Anderson, report, June 26, 1917, OGF, RG 65.

89. "Mass Meeting Held at Rockland, DeKalb County, GA," Thomson *Jeffersonian*, August 16, 1917, 9.

90. George G. Calmes, report, July 31, 1917, OGF, RG 65; George G. Calmes, report, August 1, 1917, ibid. (quotes from August 1 report).

91. "Testimony of Mr. Felix Crawley," May 30, 1918, file Ga. 17-179, box 110 States File, Selective Service System Records (World War I), RG 163 (NARA, College Park, Md.).

92. "Cobb County Has Mass Meeting," Thomson *Jeffersonian*, August 30, 1917, 9 (first and second quotations); "Resolutions Om [sic] Meeting Held at Marietta, Cobb County Georgia, August 11, 1917," ibid., 8 (third quotation).

93. Howell Jackson, report, March 28–April 1, 1918; Howell Jackson, report, June 7–12, 1918; Howell Jackson, report, June 8–13, 1918; Howell Jackson, report, June 15–18, 1917; all in OGF, RG 65.

94. Howell Jackson, report, June 15–18, 1917, ibid.; "Three Soldiers Killed and Many Injured When Steele's Bridge Over Etowah Falls," *Atlanta Constitution*, June 17, 1918, 1.

3

"Negroes, the New Deal, and ... Karl Marx"

Southern Antistatism in Depression and War

JASON MORGAN WARD

In early 1936, Georgia governor Eugene Talmadge invited the South's most vocal Roosevelt critics to Georgia for a National Grass Roots Convention. Talmadge hoped the gathering, sponsored by his shadowy Southern Committee to Uphold the Constitution, would springboard his bid for a presidential nomination. The response was sobering—a few hundred non-Georgians mingled with a much larger contingent of Talmadge's loyal followers. Undaunted by a half-empty Macon Auditorium, the Georgia governor and a dais of disgruntled "Jeffersonian Democrats" vowed to derail Roosevelt's reelection.[1]

The defeat of the president and his New Deal was the convention's stated purpose, but the gathering's racially charged atmosphere energized the crowd. Convention organizers festooned the stage with a giant Confederate battle flag and placed a copy of Talmadge's partisan newspaper in each seat. On the front page, a Talmadge lieutenant bragged, was "a picture of Mrs. Roosevelt going to some nigger meeting, with two niggers, on each arm." Delegates applauded Texas lumber and oil baron John Henry Kirby, the convention's chief sponsor, when he departed from his prepared remarks to highlight the distributed tabloid's revelations concerning the Roosevelts' "friendly attitude towards the Negroes." Aging novelist, the Reverend Thomas Dixon, famous for his turn-of-the-century paeans to the Reconstruction-era Klan, lashed out at the National Association for the Advancement of Colored People (NAACP), while multiple speakers stressed Roosevelt's hostility toward "states' rights."[2]

The Grass Roots Convention's inflammatory rhetoric and electoral pipe dreams invited scorn from the South's political mainstream. Talmadge, who just four years prior had paraded down Atlanta's choked streets with then candidate Roosevelt, cemented his reputation as the South's most infamous rabble-rouser. Unfazed, the governor lashed out at the ballooning federal bureaucracy, and, increasingly, the New Deal's alleged threat to the racial status quo. With the region's Democratic establishment lined up squarely behind the New Deal, Talmadge faced an uphill battle convincing everyday southerners that white supremacy was under attack. But while most contemporary observers dismissed Talmadge's warnings as premature at best and demagogic at worse, the Georgia governor blazed a trail for a racially charged revolt against the New Deal. By linking the emerging New Deal state to the death of Jim Crow, Talmadge anticipated and advanced a trend that would become commonplace after Pearl Harbor—attacking the president and his domestic agenda in explicitly racial terms.

As southern racial conservatives stepped up their attacks on Roosevelt, their strategic and rhetorical flexibility allowed them to emerge from a decade of depression and war with a white-supremacist critique of the New Deal order. Even as the New Deal undercut regional isolation and eroded a thoroughly racialized political economy, Roosevelt's reform program precipitated a countermovement that played on themes of race and region to mobilize southern conservatives. From the New Deal's inception, far-sighted economic elites warned that federal reforms would undermine Jim Crow. Especially in the plantation regions of the Deep South, conservatives portrayed the emerging welfare state as the corruptor of a seemingly organic racial hierarchy. Meanwhile, a chorus of politicians, journalists, and everyday southerners pondered the implications of a New Deal coalition that included black voters. Increasingly, southern conservatives argued that subversives and malcontents had captured *their* Democratic Party, and they advocated a variety of strategies for overcoming their political dispossession.

While they embraced their identity as regional insurgents, southern anti–New Dealers believed they were defenders of traditional Americanism. From prewar red-baiting to wartime comparisons between New Deal liberalism and Axis totalitarianism, southern conservatives characterized their anti-Roosevelt revolt as a patriotic endeavor. By racializing the New Deal order and Americanizing their anti–New Deal crusade, southern conservatives crafted an antistatist rhetoric that echoed in future decades.

*   *   *

Talmadge was the loudest Roosevelt critic south of the Mason-Dixon, but he was not the first. Three years before the ill-fated Grass Roots Convention, conservative businessmen founded the Southern States Industrial Council (SSIC) to fight New Deal wage regulations that threatened their segregated supply of cheap labor. According to SSIC president John Edgerton, the South's segregated, low-wage labor system not only provided a competitive advantage but also protected "labor's racial purity." By pressuring the Roosevelt administration to accept a lower wage scale in southern industry and avoid demands for equal pay for black workers, conservative business interests preserved the economic underpinnings of Jim Crow. "Colored labor has always been paid less than whites," an SSIC member explained, "and for good reason."[3]

Talmadge's grandstanding obscured southern industrialists' measured counteroffensive, but right-wing business interests carried more weight on Capitol Hill. The SSIC applauded southern New Deal critics like North Carolina senator Josiah Bailey, who in 1937 co-authored a "Conservative Manifesto" that stressed limited government, free enterprise, and states' rights. One of Roosevelt's earliest southern congressional critics, Bailey framed his critique of the New Deal in distinctly regional terms. In a rollicking keynote before SSIC members in Washington, Bailey praised his "fellow feudalists" for resisting New Dealers' attempts to make over the region. "They can't reform us," Bailey declared, "and they can't reconstruct us." The right-wing industrialists hooted and clapped as Bailey likened New Dealers to carpetbaggers and praised the "unchangeable character" of the South. "I like her ability to withstand criticism," Bailey concluded, "and to repel the advances of uplifters."[4]

By 1938, congressional conservatives like Bailey echoed the defiant bluster once confined to "Grass Roots" demagogues. This growing anti–New Deal sentiment stemmed from the intertwined fears of racial subversion and economic disruption. Since his public break with Roosevelt in late 1935, Talmadge had argued that federal relief programs would undermine white supremacy in Georgia. After his campaign to oust Roosevelt failed to gain steam, the sitting governor attempted to unseat Georgia senator Richard Russell. Branding the senator a "rubber stamp" for the president, Talmadge used his propaganda machine to spread lurid rumors of racial mixing in Georgia's New Deal programs. In one widely circulated account, Talmadge claimed that Works Progress Administration (WPA) officials in Atlanta forced "refined and educated" white women to use "the negro toilet" at their project site. Talmadge deployed such rumors to link Russell and the rest of Georgia's pro–New Deal establishment to a federal conspiracy "to break the will of our people and force social equality with the negro." Unfazed, Russell publicly scolded Talmadge for "crying nigger" and cruised to a resounding reelection. In South Carolina, another key Roosevelt ally, junior senator James F. Byrnes, easily fended off two race-baiting challengers.[5]

While demagoguery failed to unseat pro–New Deal politicians in 1936, those lawmakers returned to Capitol Hill to discover that racial controversy had followed them. In April 1937, New York congressman Joseph Gavagan reintroduced an anti-lynching bill days after a gruesome double lynching in Mississippi grabbed national headlines. While the bill passed the House by a three-to-one margin, southern senators staged the longest filibuster in five decades to kill the latest round of anti-lynching legislation. Less than two years after fending off primary challengers who argued that the New Deal undermined white supremacy, Russell and Byrnes joined their southern comrades in a seven-week tirade against federally imposed racial reform. Almost two years to the date after Talmadge launched his crusade against "Negroes, the New Deal, and . . . Karl Marx," Russell announced from the Senate floor that northern liberals had transformed the party of Jefferson and Jackson into a leftist "Afro-Democratic Party."[6]

The filibuster's success gave cold comfort to southern conservatives who saw the seven-week operation as parrying the opening salvo from an administration beholden to black voters and bent on remaking the region. Southern conservatives repeatedly blamed the clamor for federal anti-lynching legislation on the growing influence of African Americans in the New Deal coalition. Politically astute southern Democrats noted that three-quarters of black voters had cast ballots for Roosevelt in 1936, just eight years after giving the same ratio of support to Herbert Hoover. "The shift of the Negro to Democratic ranks establishes him now as a prize to be sought in every election," warned Birmingham columnist John Temple Graves. "The future of the Democratic Party here may depend upon what it is willing to pay for this prize." For southern Democrats increasingly skeptical of Roosevelt's intentions, the anti-lynching controversy dramatized growing black political influence and a national party establishment increasingly responsive to their concerns.[7]

The more attention Roosevelt paid the South, which he deemed "the Nation's number one economic problem," the more southern Democrats used race to discredit his reform program. While Roosevelt refused to endorse anti-lynching legislation, he spoke out forcefully against southern conservatives who stood in the way of his economic prescriptions for the region. In Georgia and South Carolina, two states where Roosevelt openly supported liberal challengers to sitting senior senators, establishment politicians dabbled in demagoguery. In Georgia, the courtly Walter George lashed out at the same unholy trinity—blacks, liberals, and leftists—that Talmadge and company had campaigned against in 1936. "I wear as a shining emblem the condemnation I have received from James Ford, the Negro Vice-Presidential nominee of the Communist Party," George bragged in one stump speech. At another campaign stop, he warned that racial liberals wanted "to send a Connecticut judge down here . . . to try you on an anti-lynching charge." In South Carolina, Ellison "Cotton Ed" Smith reminded voters that he had walked out of the 1936 Democratic National Convention to protest black participation. He denounced New York senator Robert Wagner, New Deal powerbroker and co-sponsor of the Senate anti-lynching bill, "for being willing to humiliate and punish the South to win negro votes in Harlem." By reelecting "a white supremacy Democrat," Smith's campaign literature promised, South Carolinians would send "a wholesome warning to the East." Two years after Russell and Byrnes trounced anti-Roosevelt race-baiters, these senior colleagues fended off pro–New Deal challengers with white-supremacist appeals.[8]

The backlash against Roosevelt's "purge" attempt melded anti-reformist sentiment with race-infused anticommunism. When confronted with federal challenges to the region's status quo, New Deal opponents linked the liberalism to revolution. Convinced that Marxists had infiltrated the Roosevelt administration, aging author Thomas Dixon updated his Reconstruction-era plotlines by substituting Communists for carpetbaggers in his final novel. A featured speaker at the Grass Roots Convention, Dixon switched his support to Republican Alf Landon after Talmadge's nomination challenge failed to materialize. For his efforts, a Republican judge rewarded Reverend Dixon a patronage post in Raleigh, North Carolina. The author poured most of his federal salary and waking hours into finishing *The Flaming Sword*. Published in 1939, the novel presented African Americans, liberals, and assorted radicals as a mortal threat to white America. Although Dixon did not cite the New Deal by name, his villains included Phil Stephens, a southern-born "racial liberal" whose approach to the "Negro Problem" was to "use him for all he's worth, give him a square deal . . . and let the future take care of itself." While the novel's naive reformers fretted over African Americans, Communist revolutionaries were arming the all-black Nat Turner Legion to invade and conquer the South. The novel ends with The Patriot Union, Dixon's band of white protagonists, pledging to overthrow the newly established "Soviet Republic of the United States."[9]

Critics did not warm to Dixon's "nightmare melodrama," which a southern editor summed up as "an indictment of the liberal concept in race relations which the author scores as an invitation to the radicalism he seems to fear with something like hysteria."[10] Yet the notion that government-imposed reforms provided an entering wedge for revolutionary change gained traction as authoritarian regimes pushed Europe to the brink of war. Lumping "New Dealism" with "socialism, fascism, collectivism, bolshevism, communism, [and] Nazism," the Talmadge propaganda machine warned that the end result of any of these "isms" would be ""a Christless, regimented, controlled state of slavery." Determined to root out subversives of all stripes, East Texas congressman Martin Dies used the newly established special House Un-American Activities Committee (HUAC) to link a New Deal establishment "politically controlled by foreigners and transplanted Negros" to civil rights groups, labor unions, and even federal agencies infiltrated by Communists. Like Dixon, Dies deemed African Americans particularly susceptible to leftist propaganda and revolutionary appeals. So too did the Connecticut-based Constitutional Educational League, which used its Birmingham branch office to distribute tracts warning that an imminent Communist takeover of the South "would make Sherman's march to the sea seem tame and trivial."[11]

While red-baiters linked New Deal liberalism to a Communist-inspired racial revolution, other southern conservatives warned that federal largesse produced subtler yet no less startling consequences. For Archibald Rutledge, a South Carolina nature writer who presided over an inherited lowcountry estate, the New Deal corrupted the "caste system" that he celebrated in his poems and short stories. "The Negro's welfare has always been close to my heart," Rutledge announced in 1940, "and whenever I discover that he is being morally debased, I cannot keep quiet."[12] Rutledge, who had recently accepted the honorary title of South Carolina's "poet laureate" and retired to his father's defunct plantation, increasingly peppered his hunting tales and paeans to plantation life with a racial critique of the New Deal. Whereas other Roosevelt critics used white-supremacist rhetoric and apocalyptic anticommunism to shock their fellow southerners, Rutledge portrayed an idyllic plantation society ruined by the growing reach of federal relief programs and opportunistic politicians' overtures toward African Americans.

For Rutledge, the New Deal disrupted the symbiotic relationship between white elites and their black dependents. On the plantation, he claimed, "the Negro could always get work, and the employer could always get labor." Yet New Dealers sought to replace this "decent and natural and orderly system" with a "vicious" program of public aid. "Almost to a man," Rutledge claimed, "every able-bodied Negro man and boy of my acquaintance is on relief." Rutledge charged that local jobs provided by the Works Progress Administration contributed to the "physical and moral decay" of his black neighbors. The trouble with the New Dealers, Rutledge argued, was that they failed to recognize the black man's "dim infallible genius in his ability to get along without money." While Franklin Roosevelt promoted social security, Rutledge argued that southern blacks simply needed "rustic security": a little parcel of land, some livestock, and a decent white man to loan them money in a pinch. If rural blacks yearned for something more than this pastoral existence, they did so because government work had undermined their inborn preference for the simple life. "I have been noticing that W.P.A. workers drive cars for the first time in their lives; they have radios; and they consume whole oceans of raw liquor," Rutledge lamented. "The money they make does no good, for they utterly neglect their homes and the good earth about them."[13]

Blending wistful white supremacy with charges of fiscal recklessness, Rutledge painted his black neighbors as the "victim of political ambition sponsoring impractical experiments." The easygoing, apolitical dependents that Rutledge portrayed in his writings were the ideal dupes for government largesse. "Practically every Negro I know is trying to raid the United States Treasury," he warned, "They regard the government as some easygoing Santa Claus; and they will take all that they can get." Blasting relief programs as "arrant bribery," Rutledge charged that bureaucrats were spending "your money and mine" to win black votes in northern cities. This supposedly all-consuming quest for black political favor, he argued, "is contributing to our ruin by piling up debt and by taking from a vast army of our citizens all ambition, all initiative, all self-reliance, and almost all self-respect." By linking the "moral decay" of his black neighbors to the designs of distant politicians, Rutledge betrayed the broader anxieties that united anti–New Deal southerners. "Nothing more revolutionary in American politics has ever occurred," he warned, "than the defection of the Negro from the Republican party, and its consequent alignment with the Democrats."[14]

Rutledge's mix of planter paternalism and anti-government resentment resonated with southern conservatives suspicious of the New Dealers' racial agenda. Rutledge's critiques, the *Charleston News and Courier* opined, "should have the attention of friends of the negroes everywhere. It will not have the attention of the 'humanitarians' . . . who are buying their votes with the money of the America taxpayers." William Watts Ball, the *News and Courier*'s unapologetically aristocratic editor, had lashed out at the New Deal's southern incursions since its inception. Convinced that "the able and astute Negro politicians of the northern cities have captured both political parties," Ball had quietly coached one of Senator James Byrnes's race-baiting primary challengers in 1936. The aging editor exercised less discretion in his disdain for the New Deal. As Charleston's pro–New Deal mayor complained in 1940, "the constant nagging of the newspaper" strained relations between the city and lucrative federal development initiatives. Yet Ball, like Rutledge, countered that "extravagant and wasteful spending of public monies by genial politicians" threatened constitutional government and moral order. "The effort of the government," he lamented, "is to allow the incompetents, the half-competents, the congenital failures to live by the labor of the diligent and ambitious. . . . [T]he only recovery needful or desirable now, is the recovery of common sense and character."[15]

During the 1930s, a growing chorus of southern conservatives attacked the New Deal for encouraging racial liberalism, class conflict, and the decline of private enterprise. But the core conviction that united southern conservatives was the belief that the New Deal defied divinely ordained rules of race and place. Southerners had fought hard to institutionalize this order, and they resented federal efforts to undermine it. While Ball complained that federal aid debased the average southerner, he linked this moral crisis to the racial revolution prophesied by militant white supremacists. Like Thomas Dixon, who traded carpetbaggers for Communists in *The Flaming Sword*, Ball—a Confederate colonel's son—drew on the memory of Reconstruction in his denunciations of the New Deal order. "It seems to me a conclusion of mathematical precision," he confided to a friend, "that if the propertyless shall number enough to decide the elections for president, governors and legislatures they will in time take the possessions of others for their own use. That, of course, was what the carpetbaggers and negroes tried to do and did."[16]

For Ball and other defenders of the southern status quo, class war meant race war. Any disruption to the South's political economy threatened to bring down an organic social system that conservative southerners deemed natural and irrevocable. "Why not abolish the old laws of nature," quipped one resentful Mississippian, "and turn the universe over to the New Dealers?" Yet while men of Ball's generation believed that the existing order honored a divine plan, they also conceded that it had been handed down to them not by God but by their fathers. In the closing decades of the nineteenth century, bloody insurgencies had overthrown Reconstruction, ousted biracial coalition governments, and institutionalized disfranchisement and segregation. Invoking the architects of the white-supremacy campaigns in the Carolinas, another Roosevelt critic urged another conservative counterrevolution. "[Either] our old friends Simmons and Aycock and Ben Tillman and others were wrong," he declared, "or the New Deal is."[17]

By the end of the 1930s, southern conservatives did more than link the New Deal to racial disruption. Increasingly, these critics treated the president's domestic agenda and even his name as synonyms for civil rights. When a southern critic proclaimed "I am no New Dealer" or lashed out at "Rooseveltianism," he indicted not just an economic philosophy or political program but an egalitarian racial agenda as well. Given that the president, eager to conciliate his southern support base, remained decidedly aloof toward civil rights supporters throughout the 1930s, this trend owed more to black activists' determination to wield their unprecedented political and economic leverage. Despite his best efforts to distance himself from civil rights groups, Roosevelt could no longer ignore their demands. When labor leader Asa Philip Randolph announced plans to mobilize tens of thousands of fellow African Americans for a March on Washington in the summer of 1941, he forced Roosevelt to prioritize a looming war emergency over white-supremacist sensibilities. Roosevelt's Executive Order 8802, which prohibited discrimination in federal agencies and defense industries, convinced Randolph to call off the march with just days to spare. For southern conservatives, the unprecedented concession rendered Roosevelt's reform program inseparable from the wartime civil rights movement.

Southern denunciations of the president's newly established Committee on Fair Employment Practice (FEPC) made clear that white supremacists equated Roosevelt and his New Deal with racial agitation. When the agency announced plans to hold hearings in Birmingham in 1942, Alabama newspapers denounced the "Roosevelt racial experts" and "halo-wearing missionaries of New Deal socialism."[18] For southern conservatives, the FEPC dramatized as never before the link between the federal government's growing reach and the disruption of the racial status quo. Anti–New Deal southerners slung similar allegations before Pearl Harbor, but war mobilization created new opportunities for federal challenges to white supremacy. As civil rights activists seized this wartime window of opportunity, southern conservatives fought back with a racial indictment of the New Deal.

Rather than fold in the face of a global crusade against fascist aggression, southern conservatives seized new rhetorical possibilities in their fight against federal encroachment. While scholars have paid significant attention to the African American "Double V" campaign—victory over fascism abroad and over racial discrimination at home—they have largely ignored southern civil rights opponents' attempts to align white supremacy with the war effort. Even as black activists compared lynch mobs and racist demagogues to Nazis, southern conservatives denounced "totalitarian" federal policies in strikingly similar terms. For them, World War II presented an opportunity not to advance reform but to call America back to its "original plan" of limited government, state sovereignty, and white supremacy. The struggle against the Axis, conservative southerners argued, represented a new phase in an ongoing crusade against foreign assailants and alien ideologies. Like the conquered countries of Europe, syndicated Birmingham columnist John Temple Graves argued, the South fought "a war for states' rights, for the right of individual lands not to be invaded by outsiders, not to be dictated to or aggressed against." A powerful Mississippi Delta planter agreed. "This is a conservative war," Oscar Bledsoe declared. "It is a war against aggression. It is not a war for Fascism, Nazism, Communism, Socialism, New Dealism, or Democracy." The only "ism" worth fighting for, declared Mississippi House Speaker Walter Sillers, was the "100% Americanism" embodied by "the white democracy of the South."[19]

The Allied war effort challenged simplistic conflations of New Deal liberalism, Soviet communism, and Axis fascism, but right-wing southerners persisted with an expansive definition of the totalitarian threat. Some linked domestic racial reforms to Nazi policies. Blasting the FEPC in his weekly column, Mississippi congressman William Colmer argued that the federal agency's objectives "could only be reached in a national socialist state. Its provisions are no different in principle than the edicts of Hitler, et al. to ostracize and deny employment to Jews, Negroes and other minorities to be employed. While the objectives are diametrically opposed, the principle is the same." Such comparisons resonated with white conservatives throughout the region, who likened the FEPC to the Gestapo in protest letters and petitions. Others argued that the Axis threat paled in comparison to the threat posed by domestic subversives. "There is no doubt," Walter Sillers declared in 1943, "that this nation faces a serious government crisis at home, regardless of whether we win the war against the Axis or not." Convinced that Marxist egalitarians had exploited the wartime emergency to hijack the New Deal, Mississippi's most powerful legislator believed that "our greatest enemy is within and not without." Like-minded constituents put it more bluntly. Faced with wartime challenges to the poll tax, the white primary, and workplace discrimination, the father of two army volunteers declared that he and "many thousands of true Southerners" felt "that it might be better to lose this war, than to have victory with Negroe [sic] equality and black domination."[20]

Faced with the prospect of federally imposed reform, a few diehards admitted they would rather take their chances with Hitler. For most southerners, however, Axis aggression and federal meddling represented a dual threat to their way of life. As the tide turned in favor of the Allies, southern conservatives mobilized for "the battle on the home front." At stake, Walter Sillers warned his Mississippi Delta constituents in a radio address, was "the overthrow and destruction of our form of government, and loss of liberty and personal freedom." As Sillers's ominous rhetoric suggests, the conflation of domestic subversives, civil rights activists, and the northern Democratic establishment was complete by 1943.[21] As southern conservatives linked the national Democratic Party to alien ideologies and outside influences, the more clearly they defined themselves in oppositional terms. If the Democratic Party had evolved into a "New Deal Party," as conservatives charged, then true southern Jeffersonians could either force the party to reclaim its founding principles or abandon it in favor of independent political action. As a growing chorus of diehards declared the national party beyond redemption, they increasingly clamored for the second option.

The language in which southern conservatives described this impending schism reflected how race and region shaped their anti-government resentments. Anticipating "an all out political battle with the Northern Democrats," a Mississippian proposed a "Southern Democratic Conservative Association, dedicated to the cause of white supremacy, strict interpretation of the Constitution, and freedom in our domestic affairs." Some made the splinter faction's racial objectives explicit, suggesting an "Independent White Democratic League," while others made their anti-Roosevelt animus clear by forming a "Southern Anti–New Deal Association." Sam Jones, ex-governor of Louisiana and an early proponent of an "independent Southern Democratic Party," deemed it "abundantly and increasingly clear that the New Deal high command hopes to use the war as an instrument for forcing the social 'equality' of the Negro upon the South." Only a return to "the original attitude of the Democratic Party toward the race problem in the South," he warned in early 1943, could forestall a southern revolt.[22]

As the anti–New Deal movement gained steam, southern conservatives linked recent history to the enduring lessons of the Lost Cause. Although they continued to compare the New Deal to Reconstruction, Roosevelt's critics increasingly contrasted the emerging welfare state with the Old South. Like Rutledge's paeans to plantation life, these critiques juxtaposed a mythically antebellum order with the modern-day "slavery" of bureaucracy. Lamenting the New Deal's "totalitarian" strategy of "feeding and fattening" the people into dependency, William Watts Ball contrasted Roosevelt's "despotism" with his grandfather's "kind" treatment of his seventy-five slaves. "My grandfather's negroes had 'social security,'" Ball quipped. "By the standards of the 1850s they had good shelter, good food, warmth and medical attention." Whether the treatment was kind or brutal, Ball concluded, slavery was slavery. "No matter how high the New Deal may make the American standard of living," he warned, "under that governance and guidance the Americans would be slaves."[23]

Like Ball, Mississippi newspaperman Clayton Rand deemed Roosevelt's reform program "The New Slavery." The Harvard-educated firebrand had created a buzz in national right-wing circles when he published and distributed 130,000 copies of an anti–New Deal speech he gave to his local Rotary Club. Reaching further back than Ball for his historical lessons, Rand argued that the Roman emperor Diocletian "sprung a New Deal on the empire in 301" and ushered in "the Dark Ages" with lavish spending and unnecessary public-works programs. According to Rand, "the only idea promoted by the Romans not undertaken by WPA was public baths." Encouraged by the success of "The New Deal and Diocletian," Rand updated his critique by applying the lessons of southern history to contemporary events. For Rand, the New Deal program threatened a form of bondage totally different from that practiced in the South. "The most humane type of slavery," he argued, "was that which existed under masters who had a personal and sympathetic interest in their slaves." The South's slave society was also "efficient," unlike the growing bureaucracy run by "federal flunkies and factotums" who were "failures in business life." Rand contended that "the threatened slavery in America . . . is that merciless, insidious type that exists under a completely centralized government in which free men forge the very chains by which they are bound. . . . Much rather would one be owned by an individual than become a chattel under the regimentation of a totalitarian state."[24]

Just months before Frederich von Hayek's *The Road to Serfdom* hit American bookstores, Rand provided an indictment of "bureaucratic bondage" that meshed anti-totalitarian war rhetoric with regional themes. The allusions to slavery resonated strongly in the plantation regions of the

Deep South, where federal incursions threatened white male hegemony. In the Black Belt, where slavery, peonage, and cheap labor had concentrated power in the hands of a privileged elite, economic and racial reforms threatened to turn society on its head. Nothing dramatized this anxiety more forcefully than the image of the region's white elites—planters and industrialists—shackled by state tyranny. This rhetoric also revealed how conservative elites clung to traditional notions of race and place even as regional modernization rendered their plantation system obsolete. In lashing out at the New Deal order, southern conservatives lamented not only their waning political clout in the Democratic Party but also the crumbling of a social order that placed them atop a seemingly organic hierarchy. To resist, many argued, reasserted their natural right to rule—not just in politics and economics but in personal relationships as well.[25]

As southern conservatives plotted a "political secession movement," they counted on fellow white elites to rally behind them. As the anti-Roosevelt campaign peaked in mid-1944, Rand delivered his "New Deal and New Slavery" message to trade conventions, civic groups, and college students across the Deep South."[26] Like Rand, former Mississippi governor Mike Conner believed that the "white man's party" had become a "New Deal Party" of "minorities" and "radicals." Whereas southern white men had built the party on principles of "Jeffersonian Democracy and true Americanism," the New Dealers took their cues from "the platform of the Communist Party." These "political reformers and communistic equalizers," Conner warned a Memphis audience, believed an "impotent" South could not resist their revolutionary schemes. Because New Dealers hoped to "establish over us a political rule and a social order that the white people of the South cannot endure," Conner characterized the anti-Roosevelt movement as a crusade for "civilization" itself. "America is White, not Red, not Black," Conner concluded, "and the time has come for the Democratic Party to tell the New Dealers . . . to keep it White."[27]

Nearly a decade before, Eugene Talmadge attempted to whip up anti–New Deal hostility with sexualized imagery and lurid prophecies. While anti-Roosevelt resentment had deepened and broadened by 1944, this rhetoric of white power and racial purity remained intact. Like Talmadge, Conner vilified Eleanor Roosevelt with allusions to interracial sexuality. He claimed that the president's wife and his closest advisers, like the Communists, wanted to abolish laws prohibiting interracial marriage. The New Deal's alleged threat to racial purity and southern manhood inspired North Carolina industrialist R. M. Prince to distribute his own anti-Roosevelt pamphlet. Under the heading "I Can't Vote for Roosevelt in November," Prince inserted a photograph of an interracial wedding party. A lifelong Democrat and three-time Roosevelt supporter, Prince claimed that the president had "done more to give [negroes] social equality than all men and political parties combined. . . . The picture on the front is the result. . . . [W]hen this white boy gets married, in Connecticut, he gets a negro for best-man."[28]

The masculine rhetoric and sexually charged imagery that southern insurgents deployed could not obscure the political impotence that they alternately denied and lamented. Indeed, the most vocal wartime New Deal critics did not hold public office. Former governors like Jones and Conner could lend political credibility to an insurgency of businessmen, newspapermen, and courthouse cliques, but they did not have to risk their political lives. By early summer, equally disaffected but more politically connected officials conceded that they could not derail the president's renomination. Over the previous year, a diffuse coalition of anti–New Deal southerners had abandoned the third-party plan in favor of sending anti-Roosevelt delegates to the Democratic National Convention. In Texas, Mississippi, and briefly in South Carolina, anti–New Deal factions took control of state conventions. The Supreme Court's April ruling in *Smith v. Allwright*, which declared the white primary unconstitutional, fueled the anti–New Dealers' racial anxieties. Tellingly, these state conventions adopted resolutions that demanded pro–white supremacy and pro–states' rights planks in the national party platform. But when the Democrats convened in Chicago in July 1944, only 89 southerners, out of 1,158 total voting delegates, cast protest ballots against Roosevelt's renomination.[29]

It should surprise no one that a diffuse anti–New Deal insurgency failed to oust a popular three-term president, in the midst of a war, by arraying the nation's most solidly Democratic region against him. However, in the midst of a resounding tactical failure, southern diehards set the stage for an ongoing revolt against the federal government. From its inception, the anti–New Deal movement had capitalized on fears that further consolidation of power in Washington would undermine the South's segregated status quo. By war's end, southern conservatives had crafted a critique of the modern welfare state that rendered federal power and racial disruption inseparable—even synonymous. The Dixiecrat movement of 1948, which has received far more scholarly attention than earlier southern protests against the national Democratic establishment, dramatized this trend. However, the focus on the Dixiecrat revolt tempts scholars to portray southern racial backlash as a delayed reaction against the New Deal's racial implications. Yet the key tactician of that movement, Alabama-born lawyer Charles Wallace Collins, hatched his blueprint for southern insurgency not in response to Truman's 1948 civil rights program but rather in the midst of wartime political controversy.

When southern insurgents attempted to siphon off electoral votes from Truman and throw a deadlocked election into the House of Representatives, they lifted their strategy from the pages of 1947's *Whither Solid South?* Collins, a Black Belt native and an unreconstructed white supremacist, wrote the bulk of the manuscript during the waning months of World War II. This wartime context shaped his characterization of civil rights not as a postwar development but as a New Deal initiative. Collins repeated southern conservatives' well-worn claim that civil rights activists had hitched their cart to opportunistic northern liberals during the 1930s. Yet Collins, in language stronger and clearer than ever before, characterized racial reform as an unavoidable consequence of federal expansion. Indeed, the New Deal rendered these political projects inseparable. "The whole Negro program," Collins warned, "is infected with the deadly virus of stateism."[30]

Collins cemented the link between a powerful federal government and the demise of white supremacy, and at the same time he provided the most farsighted strategy for turning back the tide of racial liberalism. While he advocated a short-term electoral scheme by which southern insurgents could force the Democratic Party to barter away its civil rights plank, Collins argued that the South's ultimate salvation rested upon "the conversion of the present Republican-Southern Democratic coalition into a new conservative political party." By realigning the two-party system along ideological lines, a national conservative majority "would save the United States from stateism." Although the Dixiecrats failed to unite the South and derail Truman's reelection, the racialization of New Deal liberalism fueled an ongoing antistatist critique. By 1952, former Roosevelt and Truman administration official James F. Byrnes had overtaken Dixiecrat presidential candidate and fellow South Carolinian Strom Thurmond as the symbol of southern insurgency. As Byrnes urged southern conservatives to reject big-government Democrats, he reminded them that federal expansion and racial change proceeded apace. A former New Dealer himself, Byrnes recalled how "Negro politicians . . . interested only in race problems" had forced the party of his forefathers to adopt "a platform more socialistic than democratic."[31]

The anti–New Deal rhetoric of the 1930s and 1940s reveals that the segregationist movement of the 1950s and 1960s did not invent a political narrative of dispossession and betrayal. Instead, they inherited the historical rationale for their plight from like-minded conservatives who simultaneously battled the emergence of the modern welfare state and the early rumblings of a civil rights revolution. By war's end, white supremacists had honed arguments against state action and federal power that they deployed in later battles against the civil rights movement. From its inception, the southern critique of the New Deal order drew on long-standing ambivalence toward federal power and fears that future incursions would undermine the social and economic imperatives that drove Jim Crow. Whether comparing the New Deal to slavery, federal officials to carpetbaggers, or racial reformers to Nazis, postwar segregationists fused their fears into a racially charged antistatism that echoed in future battles over the fate of the welfare state. Later denunciations of civil rights legislation and Great Society initiatives built on anti–New Deal rhetoric that linked white supremacy, racial capitalism, and constitutional conservatism. Rather than view these arguments as some strategic innovation on the part of segregationists and opportunistic "Southern Strategy" Republicans, scholars should view this rhetorical continuity as further evidence of southern conservatives' long-standing ambivalence toward the federal government. In the current political climate, where right-wing activists posit that African Americans may have been better off as slaves than as wards of a welfare state, and diehards simultaneously denounce the nation's first black president as a Nazi and a Communist, the rhetorical flexibility and broad vision of the South's New Deal–era antistatists demands thoughtful attention.

Notes

1. Stetson Kennedy, *Southern Exposure* (New York: Doubleday, 1946), 128; William E. Leuchtenburg, *The White House Looks South: Franklin D. Roosevelt, Harry S. Truman, Lyndon B. Johnson* (Baton Rouge: Louisiana State University Press, 2005), 126.

2. Arthur M. Schlesinger Jr., *The Politics of Upheaval, 1935–1936* (Boston: Houghton Mifflin, 1960), 522; William Anderson, *The Wild Man from Sugar Creek: The Political Career of Eugene Talmadge* (Baton Rouge: Louisiana State University Press, 1975), 139; Andrew Michael Manis, *Macon Black and White: An Unutterable Separation in the American Century* (Macon, Ga.: Mercer University Press, 2004), 118–19.

3. George Brown Tindall, *The Emergence of the New South, 1913–1945* (Baton Rouge, 1967), 444; Bruce Schulman, *From Cotton Belt to Sunbelt: Federal Policy, Economic Development, and the Transformation of the South, 1938–1980* (New York: Oxford University

Press, 1991), 24. For the most comprehensive study of the Southern States Industrial Council, see Katherine Rye Jewell, "As Dead as Dixie: The Southern States Industrial Council and the End of the New South, 1933–1954" (PhD diss., Boston University, 2010).

4. "Southern States Industrial Council, Dinner Session Minutes," May 2, 1938, pp. 7–8, box 1, folder 4, Southern States Industrial Council, Tennessee State Library and Archives, Nashville.

5. "Is the Junior Senator from Georgia a Rubber Stamp or Ain't He?" *Georgia Woman's World*, August 14, 1936, 1; Eugene Talmadge to Richard B. Russell, December 5, 1935, and n.t., n.d. [attached to Eugene Talmadge to Richard B. Russell, December 5, 1935], both in Series IV, Subseries B, box 19, folder 15, Richard B. Russell Papers, Russell Library for Political Research and Science, University of Georgia, Athens; Winfred B. Moore Jr., "The 'Unrewarding Stone': James F. Byrnes and the Burden of Race, 1908–1944," in *The South Is Another Land: Essays on the Twentieth-Century South*, ed. Bruce Clayton and John A. Salmond (Westport, Conn.: Greenwood, 1987), 13–14; Howard N. Mead, "Russell vs. Talmadge: Southern Politics and the New Deal," *Georgia Historical Quarterly* 65 (Spring 1981): 37.

6. Tindall, *The Emergence of the New South*, 552; *Congressional Record*, 75th Cong., 3rd sess., 1102, 1098–1103.

7. John Temple Graves, "South Discusses a Two-Party Plan," *New York Times*, November 8, 1936, E10.

8. Allan A. Michie and Frank Ryhlick, *Dixie Demagogues* (New York: Vanguard Press, 1939), 197; "'Georgia's George Relies on Prejudice to Save His Seat,'" *New York Amsterdam News*, August 27, 1938, A3; "Race Is Issue of Primaries in the South," *Chicago Defender*, September 3, 1938, 4; *Record of Ellison D. Smith as United States Senator . . . Written, published, and distributed by friends of Senator "Cotton Ed" Smith who desire to see this great individualist returned to the Senate* (Columbia, S.C., 1938), 12, copy in South Caroliniana Library, University of South Carolina, Columbia.

9. Thomas Dixon, *The Flaming Sword*, rev. ed (Lexington: University Press of Kentucky, 2005), xi, 83, 453. In his introduction to the latest edition of *The Flaming Sword*, historian John David Smith emphasizes the negative and dismissive reaction to the novel and deems it an "utter failure" because most Americans ignored Dixon's "sick fantasies" of Communist takeovers and race war. At the same time, the attempts of southern conservatives and militant white supremacists to lend credence to Dixon's "final warnings" point to concerted resistance to racial reform in the prewar South. *The Flaming Sword*, xxv.

10. K. W., "A Novel of Conflict," *New York Times Book Review*, August 20, 1939, BR10; Frank Smethurst, "Americans in Black, White, and Red," *Raleigh News and Observer*, August 6, 1939, M4.

11. "In Issue," *Georgia Women's World*, September 15, 1937, 2; "Uncle Ralph Observe," *The Statesman*, June 17, 1941, 4; Martin Dies, *The Trojan Horse in America* (New York: Dodd, Mead, 1940), 118–29; Joseph P. Kamp, *The Fifth Column in the South* (New Haven: Constitutional Educational League, 1940), 5, 8.

12. Archibald Rutledge, "A Southerner Comes Home," *South Atlantic Quarterly* 37 (October 1938): 346; Rutledge, "The Negro and the New Deal," *South Atlantic Quarterly* 39 (July 1940): 281.

13. Rutledge, "The Negro and the New Deal," 282, 287, 286, 281, 287.

14. Ibid., 284, 289, 281, 288, 281.

15. "New Dealers Not to Reply," *Charleston News and Courier*, n.d., n.p., clipping in scrapbook, Rutledge Manning Rutledge Papers, South Caroliniana Library, University of South Carolina, Columbia; W. W. Ball to Fitz Hugh McMaster, June 27, 1936, and W. W. Ball to Mother, June 8, 1936, both in box 26, folder "1936, June," William Watts Ball Papers, Rare Books, Manuscripts, and Special Collections Library, Duke University, Durham, North Carolina; "The Press: Editor, Old Style," *Time*, March 18, 1940, http://content.time.com/time/magazine/article/0,9171,763669,00.html (accessed October 26, 2013); W. W. Ball to J. Heyward Gibbes, March 25, 1936, box 26, folder "1936, March–April," Ball Papers.

16. Kari Frederickson, *The Dixiecrat Revolt and the End of the Solid South, 1932-1968* (Chapel Hill: University of North Carolina Press, 2001), 11-12; W. Ball to J. Heyward Gibbes, March 25, 1936, box 26, folder "1936, March–April," Ball Papers. Glenn Feldman has written for some time about the interrelated factors of white supremacy, economic rightism, religious conservatism, and a distinct type of southern patriotism in southern opposition to the New Deal. See, e.g., Feldman, *From Demagogue to Dixiecrat: Horace Wilkinson and the Politics of Race* (Lanham, Md.: University Press of America, 1995), conclusion, esp. pp. 194-95; Feldman, *Politics, Society, and the Klan in Alabama, 1915-1949* (Tuscaloosa: University of Alabama Press, 1999), 280-82, 387 n. 67; Feldman, "Ugly Roots: Race, Emotion, and the Rise of the Modern Republican Party in Alabama and the South," in *Before Brown: Civil Rights and White Backlash in the Modern South*, ed. Feldman (Tuscaloosa: University of Alabama Press, 2004), esp. 275; Feldman, "The Status Quo Society, the Rope of Religion, and the New Racism," in *Politics and Religion in the White South*, ed. Feldman (Lexington: University Press of Kentucky, 2005), 287-352; Feldman, "Race, Class, the Southern Conference, and the Beginning of the End of the New Deal Coalition," in *History and Hope in the Heart of Dixie: Scholarship, Activism, and Wayne Flynt in the Modern South*, ed. Gordon E. Harvey, Richard D. Starnes, and Glenn Feldman (Tuscaloosa: University of Alabama Press, 2006), 124-57; Feldman, "Race, Sex, Class, and the Status Quo Society: Developing Racial, Political, and Religious Attitudes in 1940s Alabama," *History* 94 (July 2006): 360-85; Feldman, "Southern Disillusionment with the Democratic Party: Cultural Conformity and 'The Great Melding' of Racial and Economic Conservatism in Alabama during World War II," *Journal of American Studies* 43, no. 2 (August 2009): 199-230; and Feldman, ed., *Painting Dixie Red: When, Where, Why, and How the South Became Republican* (Gainesville: University Press of Florida, 2011), 13, 328-32.

17. W. H. Rucker to Theodore Bilbo, April 7, 1944, box 1076, folder 8, Theodore Gilmore Bilbo Papers, Special Collections, McCain Library, University of Southern Mississippi, Hattiesburg; "Extracts from a Letter Written By a Prominent Newspaper Correspondent in Washington, D.C.," box 11, folder 3, Walter Sillers Papers, Charles W. Capps Archives and Museum, Delta State University, Cleveland, Mississippi.

18. Roi Ottley, *New World A-Coming: Inside Black America* (Boston: Houghton Mifflin, 1943), 302.

19. W. W. Ball to J. Heyward Gibbes, March 25, 1936, box 26, folder "1936, March–April," Ball Papers; "Let's Face the Race Question," *Town Meeting*, February 17, 1944, 7; O. F. Bledsoe, "Agriculture and the Federal Government," p. 3, box 29, folder 5, Sillers Papers; Walter Sillers to James O. Eastland, February 5 and May 13, 1943, box 98, folder 2, Sillers Papers.

20. "Wake Up, America! Should a Permanent Fair Employment Practice Commission Be Created by Congress," May 21, 1944, box 421, folder 19, William Colmer Papers, Special Collections, McCain Library, University of Southern Mississippi, Hattiesburg; Port Gibson [Miss.] Lions Club, "A RESOLUTION," n.d., box 1022, folder 8; "RESOLVED," Men's Club of Trinity Methodist Church, Savannah, Georgia, May 15, 1945, box 1024, folder 12, Bilbo Papers; Walter Sillers to Rev. N. G. Augustus, September 17, 1943, box 1, folder 11, Sillers Papers; Earle C. Douglas Sr. to TGB, May 29, 1943, box 1076, folder 7, Bilbo Papers.

21. Walter Sillers, "Radio Talk," April 21, 1943, p. 2, box 1, folder 11, Sillers Papers.

22. Brinkley Morton to Bilbo, November 19, 1942, box 1076, folder 1, Bilbo Papers; M. Bracey to The Dixie Press, October 10, 1944, box 11, folder "Correspondence: South Betrayed (1/1)," andHarvey G. Fields to The Dixie Press, May 24, 1944, box 7, folder "Correspondence: 'New Deal and Diocletian . . . Louisiana (3/4) 1944," Clayton Rand Papers, Special Collections, Mitchell Memorial Library, Mississippi State University, Starkville. Stetson Kennedy identified a variety of anti-Roosevelt groups active in the 1944 campaign season, including the "Southern Democrats," the "Anti–New Deal Democrats," and the "Independent White Democrats." Kennedy, *Southern Exposure*, 129; Sam Jones, "Will Dixie Bolt the New Deal?" *Saturday Evening Post*, March 6, 1943, 21.

23. W. W. Ball to F. H. Prince, June 23, 1942, box 36, folder "Letters, 1942, June," Ball Papers.

24. Clayton Rand, *The New Deal and Diocletian* (Gulfport, Miss.: Dixie Press, 1943), n.p., copy available in folder "Brochures: The New Deal and Diocletian," box 26, Rand Papers; Rand, *The New Deal and the New Slavery* (Gulfport, Miss.: Dixie Press, 1944), n.p., copy available in folder "Brochures: The New Deal and the New Slavery," box 26, Rand Papers. Rand, who owned and operated the Gulfport-based Dixie Press, reported in March 1944 that he had printed 130,000 pamphlets and received nearly 4,500 letters praising his stance and requesting additional copies. Rand to H. E. Bush, March 18, 1944, box 8, folder "Correspondence: "New Deal and Diocletian . . . Mississippi (3/5)," Rand Papers.

25. Kari Frederickson, "As a Man, I Am Interested in States' Rights: Gender, Race, and the Family in the Dixiecrat Party, 1948–1950," in *Jumpin' Jim Crow: Southern Politics from Civil War to Civil Rights*, ed. Jane Dailey, Glenda Gilmore, and Bryant Simon (Princeton: Princeton University Press, 2000), 260–74.

26. Rand, *The New Deal and the New Slavery*, n.p. The pamphlet included a sampling of locations where Rand delivered this speech in May and June 1944: a Lions Clubs conference in Birmingham, a Mississippi Bankers Association convention in Biloxi, the Southeast Louisiana College commencement, and the Mississippi Cotton Seed Crushers Association convention.

27. Martin S. Conner, "The Case against the New Deal," April 17, 1944, n.p., box 29, folder 5, Sillers Papers.

28. Ibid.; R. M. Prince, *I Can't Vote for Mr. Roosevelt in November*, n.p., copy in Series X, box 113, folder 1, Russell Papers.

29. Robert A. Garson, *The Democratic Party and the Politics of Sectionalism, 1941–1948* (Baton Rouge: Louisiana State University Press, 1974), 94–130. Conservative senator Harry Byrd, who had earlier made clear that he would not accept the presidential nomination, received all the votes from his home state as well as the entire Mississippi and Louisiana

delegations. He received twelve votes from the anti–New Deal contingent from Texas and a handful of votes from South Carolina, Alabama, and Florida.

30. Charles Wallace Collins, *Whither Solid South? A Study in Politics and Race Relations* (New Orleans: Pelican, 1947), x. Joseph Lowndes provides a trenchant anaysis of Collins's link between racial reform and the New Deal order. As Lowndes argues, Collins "viewed civil rights advancements and increased federal power as distinct political projects, but ones that were becoming fused to the mutual benefit of black activists and New Dealers." Lowndes, *From the New Deal to the New Right: Race and the Southern Origins of Modern Conservatism* (New Haven: Yale University Press, 2008), 22.

31. Collins, *Whither Solid South?* ix, 257; James F. Byrnes, "Two Addresses of Governor James F. Byrnes," pp. 14–15, Series 9, box 12, folder 15, James F. Byrnes Papers, Special Collections, Clemson University.

4

Dixiecrats, Dissenting Delegates, and the Dying Democratic Party

Mississippi's Right Turn from Roosevelt to Johnson

REBECCA MILLER DAVIS

When Lyndon Johnson signed the Civil Rights Act, he famously concluded that he had lost the South to the Republican Party for a generation. This statement proved prophetic, as no presidential Democratic candidate has won the majority of white southern votes since 1964.[1] LBJ's landslide victory that year was a decisive moment for southern political culture and identity, as it signaled the southern "right turn." It was the culmination of a defection twenty years in the making, however, not a singular event. In no state was this shift more pronounced than in Mississippi, often considered the deepest Deep South state. It is clear that Mississippi's desertion from the Democrats began long before, seen in the intertwined issues of race and politics stretching back to the 1940s and gradually building over time, most evident in the Dixiecrat Revolt of 1948, the Unpledged Elector movement in 1960, and finally the complete denunciation of the Democrats in 1964. In the process, Mississippi revealed how truly out-of-step it was with the rest of the nation, and sometimes even the rest of the South. The state's willingness to attach itself to a losing cause reveals its role in the larger narrative on the inextricably linked issues of white backlash to the growing civil rights struggle and the resurgence of conservatism in America. To say that Lyndon Johnson "lost" the South in 1964 ignores nearly twenty years of political turmoil, because white Mississippians had left long before.

Southern Democrats enjoyed nearly universal control of their politics dating back to the Redeemer governments following Reconstruction. The former Confederate states completely rejected the party of Lincoln, putting the South in the Democrats' pocket for nearly a century. This one-party system stifled real progress in the region, limiting labor initiatives and industrialization, thereby separating it from the national political scene and leading to graft and corruption under such demagogues as Theodore Bilbo and James Vardaman of Mississippi, Gene Talmadge of Georgia, and Huey Long of Louisiana. Fissures within the party emerged in the early 1940s, however, as southern Democrats watched the Roosevelt administration put more emphasis on racial politics.[2]

As odd as it sounds, Franklin Delano Roosevelt—the blue-blooded, Harvard-educated, native New Yorker—was, in many respects, a southerner at heart. As historian William Leuchtenburg points out, FDR spent so much time at his Georgia vacation home that he came to regard the state as his own, even thinking of himself as a native. A local reporter dubbed the president "neighbor Roosevelt," explaining how southerners "'took' to this 'Yankee' who was part-time Georgia 'Cracker,'" often seeing him as an "adopted son." FDR embraced many aspects of southern culture, developing a penchant for barbeque, collard greens, possum hunts, coonhounds, and even a touch of white supremacy. The president at times sank to such racial epithets as calling blacks "semi-beast[s]," "darkies," and "niggers," making this highbrow Ivy Leaguer sound more like a lowbrow redneck.[3]

A Roosevelt White House, therefore, seemed amenable to white southerners, who believed they had an ally in Washington. The president catered to the South by avoiding the race issue altogether. He never advocated for civil rights legislation, allowed blatant racism and discrimination in New Deal programs, disregarded attempts to abolish the poll tax, and refused to back an anti-lynching bill. Ignoring racial inequality maintained his party's firm grip on the "solid South," but as the head of the Tennessee Valley Authority put it, this made the president "a prisoner" of southern Democrats. Any outright support of civil rights would jeopardize the party and his administration, and FDR therefore kept his distance. "Dixie is in the saddle on Capitol Hill, all right," one Washington paper reported only a month after Roosevelt's first inaugural, but his twelve years in office yielded significant shifts on race, which made some white southerners consider changing horses.[4]

Even though FDR never officially supported civil rights measures, his administration put wheels in motion that prompted momentous changes for African Americans. These shifts, Leuchtenburg explains, "shook established racial patterns" and, in the process, "stirred up resistance to the old order that would reverberate for decades to come." The president selected many blacks for high-ranking positions in his administration, including

William Hastie and Mary McLeod Bethune, leading to what some called his "Black Cabinet." Nearly fifty blacks worked in federal posts and New Deal programs, more than three times as many as in any previous administration. Some New Deal agencies, especially the Works Progress Administration and its Federal Arts Project subsidiaries, had special black divisions to ensure more opportunities for African Americans.[5] As U.S. involvement in World War II drew closer, Roosevelt stunned the white South in June 1941 by establishing the Fair Employment Practices Committee (FEPC), which prohibited racial discrimination in the defense industry. This decision made civil rights a national issue for the first time, and the white South began worrying about the president's commitment to his supposed "second home."[6]

Well into the war, the white South suffered yet another blow to its cherished way of life when the U.S. Supreme Court outlawed the white primary with the *Smith v. Allwright* (1944) decision. The white primary, poll tax, and literacy test were key factors in disfranchising nearly all southern blacks, thereby protecting the South's one-party, all-white rule. Most blacks could not afford the poll tax, but the white primary excluded even those who could pay, barring them from voting in the only election that really mattered in the South—the Democratic primary. In a sweeping eight-to-one decision, however, the Supreme Court removed this barrier.[7]

White southerners immediately mounted challenges to the Court's perceived violations of their "sovereign states' rights" and the national party's "betrayal." Tom Hederman, editor of the *Jackson Clarion-Ledger*, Mississippi's highest-circulating daily paper, acknowledged the white-primary ruling as "the most serious threat in years to white supremacy" but maintained that "one thing is certain, however. This decision will not be 'accepted' in Mississippi, and Mississippi Democrats will not voluntarily open their primaries to any but white voters, without resistance." State congressman William Colmer, who later served as Republican Senate leader Trent Lott's mentor, claimed that "radical" national politicians were using blacks for political gain, just as they had during the "dark days" of Reconstruction. Abolishing the white primary, Colmer reasoned, was a ploy to woo black voters to Roosevelt and the Democrats in an election year. This was not a drive for civil rights, he argued, but for political domination. Even though the national party "coveted" the black vote, he urged it to consider how the "mad rush" to obtain it might cost it the white southern vote. Black equality in the voting booth would push southerners over the edge, Colmer concluded, and "certainly there is a limit to which the Solid South can be kicked around."⁸

As many white southerners cast blame on everyone from "treacherous" Supreme Court justices, communists, radicals, and "deceitful" national Democrats, some took direct aim at the president. FDR was the root of the problem, they reasoned, as he had appointed all eight justices who ruled against the white primary. As journalist Peter Molyneaux observed, "many regarded the decision as practically the act of President Roosevelt himself," and the South saw it "as the latest treacherous blow from the national Democratic party." Mississippi editor Hazel Brannon, who later won a Pulitzer Prize for racially progressive editorials and her fight against local white supremacists, wrote in her weekly column that the *Smith* decision was a disaster of the highest order and evidence of "the Roosevelts in action."⁹ White southerners should see the writing on the wall, Brannon reasoned, and vote the president out in the next election. Four more years of FDR, she claimed, "will mean a death blow to every tradition held dear to Southern hearts." She argued that both the president and the First Lady stood for integration, pointing out that Eleanor Roosevelt had attended a function where "white girls and negroes danced and sang together . . . singing 'Let Me Call You Sweetheart,' if you please." Roosevelt's twelve years in office were enough, she insisted, because "he has gone too far. It is time for him to go." For Democrats to survive in the South, she argued, the party needed "to purge itself entirely of the taint of the New Deal and its half-baked ideas and get a real Democrat to run for president. . . . Even then we fear that the day of the Democrat is limited."¹⁰

Such criticisms did not keep Roosevelt from another term, as he defeated Thomas Dewey handily and swept every southern state for the fourth straight time. Winning 69 percent of the southern popular vote seemed promising, but some saw problems looming on the horizon. One journalist commented that, despite carrying the South, "there are danger signals flying for [Roosevelt] all over the old Confederacy." Many once-loyal, pro–New Deal Democrats were so disillusioned with FDR that they stayed home on election day, unwilling to support the man who "betrayed" their values but not quite ready to cast their ballot for the much-hated Republican Party. FDR won over 97 percent of Mississippi voters in 1936, but he steadily lost ground in the state over the next two elections, falling four points by 1944. While such drops seem insignificant for a man who garnered over 90 percent of Mississippi votes in each election, they do show a state slowly moving away from the national Democratic Party. As Leuchtenburg argues, FDR's victory in 1944 was not as impressive as it appeared. Yes, "the South was 'Solid' for the Democrats in yet another election, but, though no one could know this at the time, 1944 was the last year it would be."[11]

On April 12, 1945, much of the nation mourned Franklin Roosevelt's death and feared having a new, unseasoned president at the helm. For white southerners, however, having Harry Truman in the White House promised a "new day" for the party and their way of life. Truman's pro-southern roots ran deep, as the native Missourian's grandfather was a slave owner and his mother did not allow anyone wearing Union blue on her front porch. He also owed his political livelihood to southern Democrats, who had successfully mounted a campaign to have him put on the Roosevelt ticket in 1944. Once Truman ascended to the presidency, they expected his loyalty and gratitude. As Mississippi senator James O. Eastland wrote: "[Truman] is friendly to the South, respects its traditions, and appreciates the support we gave him," leading him to believe that the new president would step back from racial issues.[12]

The error in this thinking became obvious almost immediately. Less than two months after taking office, Truman publicly asked the House Rules Committee to restore the FEPC's funds. Employer discrimination against qualified people because of race was, in Truman's opinion, "un-American," and abandoning the FEPC was "unthinkable." The president then went one step further by insisting that the temporary wartime organization be made permanent, a proposal he took to Congress in September. Although the FEPC bill died at the hands of a southern filibuster, Truman's pro–civil rights stance proved to be a decisive opening shot in what became a war within the Democratic Party.[13]

Truman's continued commitment to civil rights only exacerbated tensions between southern Democrats and the national party leading up to the 1948 election. Truman created the President's Committee on Civil Rights in 1946, which called for sweeping federal action to end racial inequality. In its 178-page report, *To Secure These Rights*, the committee recommended anti-lynching and anti–poll tax legislation, a new civil rights division of the Justice Department, a permanent Commission on Civil Rights, and an end to segregation in public education, the military, employment, public accommodations, housing, and interstate transportation. Southern Democrats responded angrily, denouncing Truman, his committee, and its findings as "anti-South." If he continued down this road, one Florida man promised the president, "you won't be elected dogcatcher in 1948."[14]

As 1948 approached, the president and his advisers formulated a campaign strategy that drastically underestimated the South, a decision that nearly cost Truman the election. In a forty-three-page memo, top aide Clark Clifford mistakenly assured the president that all was well in Dixie. "It is inconceivable," he reasoned, "that any policies initiated by the Truman Administration, no matter how 'liberal,' could so alienate the South in the next year that it could revolt. As always," Clifford concluded, "the South can be considered as safely Democratic. And in formulating national policy, it can be safely ignored." Heeding this advice, Truman proceeded with his racial agenda. In February 1948 he sent a special message to Congress proposing the most ambitious civil rights bill since Reconstruction. The southern firestorm that erupted, however, showed that the South was not as solid as Truman had hoped.[15]

The president's endorsement of civil rights proved to be more than Dixie Democrats could bear. A meeting of southern governors produced a joint resolution warning the national party not to take their constituents for granted, insisting that "the South is no longer 'in the bag.'" Two weeks later, fifty-two southern congressman and twenty-one senators seconded the resolution, promising to "stand guard" against any attempt to make Truman's civil rights legislation a reality. Mississippi congressman John Bell Williams was so disgusted that he draped one of Truman's portraits in his office in black and turned the other toward the wall. He railed against the evils of "communism," "mongrelization," and "moral disintegration" that surely went hand-in-hand with racial integration, laying blame directly at the president's feet. "The people of the South are directly responsible for Mr. Truman's ascendency to the Presidency," Williams insisted, and "yet, despite this, he has seen fit to run a political dagger into our backs and now he is trying to drink our blood." Southern Democrats put the president where he was, and this was "a mighty poor way for him to evince his gratitude."[16]

Politicians were not the only ones expressing their disdain for the president. In only five months, Truman's approval ratings in the South plummeted from 59 to 35 percent, making his reelection prospects more questionable by the day. Fred Sullens, the vicious, race-baiting editor of the *Jackson Daily News,* knew that Truman would never win Mississippi. He maligned the president for his "deceit," chastising him for being "a renegade from his own race. He has quit the white folks and gone over to the negroes. He has declared himself an enemy of the South and the Southern people." This treachery meant just one thing as far as Sullens and Mississippi were concerned: "Truman is through, finished, washed up, blotted out."[17]

Truman was indeed through in Mississippi, but white voters were not ready to defect to Thomas Dewey and the Republicans. Instead, anti-Truman southern Democrats established a States' Rights faction that fought to block Truman's nomination at the national convention and, in the process, garner support for inclusion of states' rights, rather than civil rights, in the party platform. When they failed on both counts, delegates from Mississippi and Alabama staged the infamous Dixiecrat Revolt by walking out of the convention in Philadelphia and reconvening in Birmingham, where they nominated Strom Thurmond of South Carolina and Fielding Wright of Mississippi as their own states' rights, pro-segregation candidates.[18]

The Dixiecrats made it clear that their defection was not a condemnation of the entire party but simply a rebellion against Truman and his "radical" racial policies. White Mississippians, however, had their fair share of criticisms for both. J. Oliver Emmerich, editor of the *McComb Enterprise Journal,* participated in the walkout himself and fiercely defended the party's actions. He called Truman "a disease," claiming that his "harsh," "anti-South" civil rights bill threatened the nation with "totalitarian rule." Defecting from the national party was a point of pride for Emmerich, as it showed that the South "has something in her backbone that amounts to more than sawdust." They had been "kicked around, abused, [and] ignored," Emmerich claimed, and the time had come to put an end to it by finally standing up for southern values and demanding the dignity southern voters deserved. "We will win the party," he wrote on the front page, naively believing that the entire South would rally behind the Dixiecrats to punish Truman.[19]

By a margin of two to one, most southerners understood that bolting from the national ticket was a mistake bound for failure, one that could plunge the region into political obscurity. This did not stop Mississippians from supporting the revolt, however. When polled a week before the convention, they voted for a defection by a three-to-two ratio, showing how drastically out of step the state was with much of the South. Some realized that the Thurmond-Wright ticket could not possibly take the White House, but they still exuded great pride in the attempt. "Southern Democrats," Sullens explained, "of course, realize their cause is hopeless," but by taking a stand for their values and rights, they wrote "a new chapter" in political history and "set a precedent. They have put the nation on notice that we will not surrender our most sacred constitutional rights in order to placate a vicious minority that seeks to rupture present race relations and established social equality. If damnfool Democrats in other sections want to eat, sleep and drink with Negroes," Sullens concluded, "that is their business. We can only deplore their degeneracy and declare we will have none of it." After all, southern pride and heritage was more important than loyalty to "what is now called the Democratic Party."[20]

President Truman was a natural target for many white Mississippians, as seen in the pages of their daily newspapers. They echoed Strom Thurmond's contention that passage of Truman's civil rights bill guaranteed a "virtual revolution" and "police state in this country." Political enemies could hardly agree on anything, the *Clarion-Ledger* reported, "but they all hate Truman." Sullens used his typical acerbic editorials to attack the president as a "Negrocrat" and race traitor, maligning "Truman and His Negroes" for hijacking the party and playing Democrats like "a bunch of suckers." The Dixiecrat insurrection was patriotic, many journalists argued; its supporters were merely trying to protect the Constitution and save the country from a tyrannical executive.[21]

Any hopes that a Dixiecrat ticket would "doom Truman" in the general election vanished when Truman defeated Dewey and Thurmond. Many had predicted a "Solid South" for the Dixiecrats, but the party only carried Mississippi, Alabama, Louisiana, and South Carolina, hardly the desired outpouring. The *Delta Democrat-Times,* Mississippi's most moderate newspaper, had anticipated as much, commenting as early as the convention about the Democratic Party's "bad case of split personality.... There were fissures within fissures," the reporter observed, "cracks within cracks.... The 'solid South' was hardly more solid than a pile of jackstraws." As the election drew closer, the paper published stories on how the "once solid South [was] shaken and split," dashing any hopes of putting a Dixiecrat in the White House. The one bright point, the paper's Pulitzer Prize–winning editor Hodding Carter Jr. wrote, was the possibility of a two-party system in the South. If enough voters questioned the Democrats, they might seriously consider the Republican alternative for the first time since Reconstruction. The election promised to "leave big dents, if not wide-open holes, in Dixie's Democratic armor," Carter argued, which would be the best possible outcome. The South, after all, "has suffered for a long time from an aggravated case of political sterility and political neglect," and a viable second party was, in Carter's opinion, its "salvation."[22]

The Dixiecrat Revolt did not bring about the two-party system Carter had hoped for. Thurmond won Mississippi with nearly 90 percent of the popular vote, higher than any other state, even Thurmond's native South Carolina.[23] Most were disappointed with the lack of southern solidarity, but they remained proud of the brave, though unsuccessful, battle for their rights. The Dixiecrats successfully restored much of the South's "political dignity and prestige," Emmerich argued, as well as beating back the threat of "totalitarian rule." If the national party wanted to punish the recalcitrant Dixiecrat rebels, Sullens editorialized, so be it. "If the worst comes to the worst," he reasoned, "we can secede again and go off in a small crowd by ourselves."[24]

The Dixiecrat Revolt was the first dramatic break from the national party, but Mississippi and the rest of the South quickly returned to the Democratic fold. It did signal a significant change in the region, however. States' Rights Democrats and Republicans represented 50 percent of southern voters in 1948, an alliance that grew over time. As historian Michael Perman explains, southern Democrats failed to produce a new party, but they "did encourage disloyalty to the Democratic Party and undermine the electoral mechanisms that had maintained party unity in the South for decades." The election of 1948, therefore, "opened the door for further, and more explicit, disloyalty," which grew steadily in the coming decades. For the time being, however, "many Southerners still prefer a Democrat for President," a Georgia editor argued, "but not one of the Truman stripe."[25]

In 1952 and 1956, Dwight D. Eisenhower won the presidency handily over his Democratic opponent Adlai Stevenson, who drew most of his support from the solid South. The Mississippi Democratic Party opened old wounds to scare voters away from the popular war hero, blaming the Republicans for everything from Reconstruction to World War II. It reminded voters of "pillaging carpetbaggers" in the 1860s and 1870s, as well as the bloodthirsty Republicans who turned on "our beloved Woodrow Wilson['s]" League of Nations, which ushered in World War II. Sullens urged his readers to "stand by the faith of your fathers" and remember that "the Republican Party is still our hereditary enemy." He painted Eisenhower as a vicious integrationist, urging parents to "tell your children to move over in school seats and make room for Negro children" and to be prepared to have "anti-lynching, anti-poll tax and FEPC laws rammed down throats still sore from shouting for Eisenhower." Southerners had contributed to the GOP victory, many critics complained, as Eisenhower had "split [the] Solid South to bits," stealing three traditionally Democratic southern states.²⁶ Misguided southern voters had "sown the wind," Sullens chided, and should "now prepare to reap the whirlwind."²⁷

As president, however, Eisenhower focused on foreign affairs, not civil rights, and this placated southern Democrats. His tepid response to the momentous *Brown v. Board of Education* decision suggested that he was not committed to racial equality, and his inaction fueled southern resistance. If the president would not force the issue, then white southerners could maintain separate schools for years, if not decades. They did not believe their way of life was in jeopardy, and *Brown* was yet another Supreme Court decree to be ignored. The Little Rock crisis of 1957 changed this, however, and sent shock waves through the South.²⁸

In the wake of *Brown*, Little Rock's school board decided to comply on its own terms, rather than waiting for forced integration. The night before school opened, however, the board's careful plans fell apart when Governor Orval Faubus ordered the National Guard "to prevent tumult, riot and breach of the peace," but everyone understood that he really intended to block integration. Outright defiance of federal law forced Eisenhower's hand, and he responded by federalizing the National Guard and ordering the U.S. Army's 101st Airborne Division to integrate Central High School. Little Rock was the first true test to states' rights since the *Brown* decision, and Eisenhower's use of force shocked the white South. Governor Faubus became nothing short of a hero, with southern editors and their readers lauding his "courageous action" and "gallant fight to save both races from communism." He stood as a protector of southern heritage against yet another display of "northern aggression."²⁹

Unsurprisingly, Eisenhower's decision to send in the army made him the villain, which hurt his party even more in the South. For many, his actions signaled the beginning of "a second Reconstruction," and Mississippi editors and their readers compared him to Thaddeus Stevens, Charles Sumner, and even Ulysses S. Grant. One letter to the editor of the *Jackson Daily News* noted that the worst president during Reconstruction was "a military man and a Republican," and in 1957, he argued, that still held true. Tom Ethridge, a popular but virulently racist columnist at the *Jackson Clarion-Ledger*, said that Eisenhower was "even more pathetic than U.S. Grant," quite a condemnation coming from the South. When he plunged them into another Reconstruction, Ethridge continued, "we suddenly wondered if John Wilkes Booth had any descendents."³⁰

According to many editors, Eisenhower wanted dictatorial control over the South and was willing to trample on the Constitution to get it. Some depicted him as a "despotic" tyrant or totalitarian dictator, even likening him to Adolf Hitler. Eisenhower wanted to become "A New Fuehrer," one editor claimed, while a Shreveport newspaper encouraged readers to practice their "Heil Eisenhower" salute. The press compared the president to Rome's most corrupt emperors, claiming that "Emperor Nero fiddled while Rome burned. Emperor Eisenhower played golf as federal troops knifed the South in the back." Some presented Eisenhower as an out-of-touch president who preferred playing golf to leading. Instead, they argued, he allowed his attorney general, the NAACP, and Communists to pull the strings and "do his thinking for him."[31]

As Eisenhower's second term came to a close, white Mississippians welcomed the opportunity to rid the White House of Republican "filth" and put a sympathetic Democrat in its place. They tired of threats to states' rights and the growing attention to civil rights, but the 1960s brought them no solace. As the candidates took shape for the 1960 election, the white South became increasingly worried by the prospects. John F. Kennedy's successful nomination posed a serious dilemma for the solidly Democratic South, because the Harvard-educated candidate from Massachusetts, with his thick Boston accent and proclaimed dedication to civil rights, hardly represented the South's interests. Mississippi's two major daily newspapers, the *Jackson Daily News* and *Clarion-Ledger,* argued that Kennedy was subservient to the Pope and the NAACP, two entities that riled white readers. Tom Ethridge wrote that Kennedy would lead the nation "straight to the NAACP's slaughter pen" and that anyone voting for him was simply a "docile sheep who can be herded and driven at will by mix-minded shepherds." Jimmy Ward, who became editor of the *Daily News* after his mentor Fred Sullens died in 1957, wrote that Kennedy's "liberal gang" planned a "hatchet job on constitutional rights." Their first objective, he claimed, was to steal rights from southern whites and pass them along to blacks. Many also cited Kennedy's platform, which called for "first-step compliance" to the *Brown* decision by 1963, the centennial of the Emancipation Proclamation. If Kennedy won, they argued, the South had to brace itself for the "return of Negro rule."[32]

Kennedy's running mate, Lyndon Johnson, was supposed to be a political asset in the South, but many Mississippians attacked his civil rights record. Even though the native Texan had deep southern roots, he had established a reputation by pushing through civil rights legislation as Senate Majority Leader, and this did not sit well with many southern voters. As an expert politician, Johnson collected as many votes as he could, calling in favors and wooing both southern and black voters. In a letter to the Jackson *State Times,* one reader argued that Johnson "showed his true color" when he told black delegates to "just wait till we're elected—and we will have four long years ahead and you'll see that you will have more progress in four years than in the 104 years before." This solidified a common belief that a Kennedy-Johnson White House would "bow to the wishes of the NAACP."[33]

Richard Nixon seemed even less viable for the South. The long tradition of anti-Republican sentiment ran deep, and Nixon's connection to Eisenhower and the bitter memories of Little Rock further damaged his credibility. The Citizens' Council, Mississippi's most powerful anti-integration organization, published a string of editorials condemning the GOP in the coming election, reminding readers of Eisenhower's treachery by satirizing the Gettysburg Address. "Forescore and seven Mondays ago," it chided, "my Supreme Court brought forth on this continent a new constitution ... dedicated to the proposition that all segregationists are bayoneted equal." It was in this hope "that the government of the Supreme Court, by the paratroopers, and for the minorities, shall not perish at the next election." The Citizens' Council insisted that Little Rock would haunt the GOP in 1960.[34]

As a result, Nixon finished an unsurprising last in Mississippi with only 25 percent of the popular vote. Kennedy, however, finished second with 36 percent, while the remaining 39 percent of Mississippians voted for "Unpledged Electors," essentially protesting the election and declaring both Nixon and Kennedy unacceptable candidates because of a single issue—race. Governor Ross Barnett championed the Unpledged Elector movement, couching his argument in a way that all white Mississippians could understand, insisting that "a vote for either party is a vote for integration."[35]

Both Kennedy and Nixon had supporters in Mississippi, but the segregationist press joined forces with Governor Barnett and the Citizens' Council to explain why voters should avoid both candidates. Editors compared the Unpledged movement to the "courageous" Dixiecrat Revolt, but the comparison did not hold up. In 1948 the Dixiecrats had a platform and a candidate, but in 1960 the rebels had nothing. They urged Mississippians to vote for no one. Two liberal Mississippi editors, Hazel Brannon Smith and Ira Harkey (who both later won the Pulitzer Prize for their racially progressive editorials), criticized the movement on that very premise. "If Gov. Ross Barnett ... wants to support a Conservative Party," Smith argued, "that's perfectly all right," but the proposition at hand "offer[s] no platform, no candidates, no solutions." In addition, the Unpledged Elector idea did not even have full support from the political hierarchy. Senators Jim Eastland and John Stennis, along with the majority of the state Democratic executive committee, endorsed Kennedy, which damaged the Unpledged movement.[36]

Barnett and his supporters vowed that voting for Unpledged Electors was "more than a vote of protest" and that it could put Mississippi in a unique position of power. In the months and weeks leading up to the election, Nixon and Kennedy were in a tight race, one of the closest in American history, and many believed that it would go down to the wire. If Mississippi voted Unpledged, the argument went, neither candidate would get the necessary number of electoral votes to win. They believed that Kennedy and Nixon would then have to woo Mississippi for its coveted eight electoral votes, and the state could then use its "bargaining position" to decide the presidency. In this situation, Mississippi could dictate the terms—trading electoral votes for civil rights concessions and the promise to ease pressure on the South.[37]

The Unpledged supporters argued that this was "the only course left for Mississippi," because voting for Nixon or Kennedy guaranteed the breakdown of society. They "will weaken and eventually destroy the freedoms that are the heritage of the American people," because they were "puppets on strings worked by minority groups," a *Clarion-Ledger* editorial proclaimed. Voting for either party meant embracing integration and turning their backs on the southern way of life. One voter argued that the election signaled that "the fight between God and the devil is now entering the final stage." When a reporter asked Governor Barnett if he preferred a segregationist Republican or a civil rights Democrat, Barnett made his convictions plain: "I would vote for the devil if he were a segregationist."[38]

Critics charged that anyone who voted Unpledged threw their vote away or handed the election to Kennedy, but the Unpledged supporters insisted that their actions were patriotic and admirable. They criticized Kennedy supporters as "loyalists" to the party that betrayed them, even reminding readers that "George III had his 'loyalists' during the Revolutionary War," likening Unpledged supporters to the Sons of Liberty and the Founding Fathers. Allusions to the Revolution continued, and in a front-page editorial the *Clarion-Ledger* proclaimed that "the United States is a nation because a small group of men were willing to stand alone, at all costs, to resist an oppressive government.... Our unpledged electors could well be the spark that will ignite that tiny light of freedom." Mississippians, they argued, could not allow a tyrannical government to push them around. One voter insisted that "no vote is thrown away if it is for principle," but even so, "I would rather throw away my vote than give it to my enemy to be used to destroy me."[39]

Mississippi's more moderate editors believed that voters could see through the Unpledged ploy and decide on a candidate based on reasons other than race. Hodding Carter editorialized that the state was slowly approaching a time when it understood that segregation was only *one* of the problems it faced, not the only one. He believed that 1960 was the year when Mississippi voters would not "heed the old, familiar yelps of hate, ignorance, and vicious stupidity." Oliver Emmerich concurred, stating that "it's doubtful whether [race] alone can swing" the Mississippi electorate. He also emphasized that an Unpledged vote would not help the state. The reality, Emmerich explained, was that Congress had already enacted civil rights legislation, and they could not change the Supreme Court's decision, no matter how stubbornly they tried. Mississippians had to accept their place in America and not pretend that federal laws did not apply to them.[40]

In the end, Mississippi threw its votes away and sank further into political and national obscurity, casting 30 percent of its votes for Unpledged Electors. The election was the tightest in history to that point, but neither candidate needed Mississippi. John F. Kennedy defeated Richard Nixon by a slim margin in the popular vote (just under 113,000 votes), but soundly won in the Electoral College (303 to 219). The state's eight electoral votes would not have altered the election results at all. Governor Barnett tried to spread the Unpledged movement throughout the South in the weeks leading up to the election, but Mississippi was the only state to completely reject both candidates. Historian Joe Crespino claims that when 87 percent of Mississippians voted for Barry Goldwater in 1964, that "never before in American history had one state been so far removed from the voting mainstream," but the 1960 election is actually more telling in this regard. In 1964, Mississippi stood alongside five other states in its endorsement of Goldwater, but in 1960, the state stood alone, an isolated, insignificant outlier willing to thumb its nose at the entire national political scene.[41]

Despite their inability to impact the election in any way, Mississippi segregationists saw it as a moral victory. "Let not your heart be troubled," the *Daily News* assured its readers, because "Mississippians endorsed the Unpledged Elector cause. It was and is an honorable course of action." Governor Barnett proclaimed his "respect and admiration" for his state, which fought "mighty hard" for its principles. Mississippi's vote showed a fiercely anti-Kennedy sentiment, and one *Daily News* reader called for "Southern Democrats and real Republicans to be on the watchtower" to safeguard against the Kennedys. Mississippi would lead the way to protect southern values, many argued, because all of the other southern states were the real "'laughing stock' of the nation for kissing the feet sworn to kick them hard and often in the next four years."[42]

While the Unpledged supporters congratulated one another for their tenacity and determination, some realized what the election really did to the state. Hazel Brannon Smith admitted feeling embarrassed for Mississippi, claiming that the nation did not see "a gallant Mississippi people standing bravely for principles" but rather "a lone state trying futilely to hold back the curtain of time while the rest of the world went by." Various small-town newspapers also blasted the state's vote, with the *Madison County Herald* announcing that "the result is just the same as if we hadn't voted" and others sarcastically congratulating Mississippi on finally seceding from the Union, showing the rest of the nation exactly what they had "come to expect and to ignore." Emmerich and Carter both commented on their disappointment that "Mississippians have not outgrown their inclination to let the race issue guide their politics." Carter sarcastically compared Ross Barnett and the Mississippi legislature to Pavlov's dog, because "anytime the word segregation is mentioned, an overwhelming majority of the legislators promptly take leave of their faculties and blindly react." He blamed the Unpledged Electors for "using the Negro as a whipping boy" and running to the race issue "like rats returning to the garbage can."[43]

Republicans saw hope for Mississippi in the 1960 results, believing that their party was finally making headway in the previously impenetrable Democratic state. They sensed a turning of the tide, and they were right. The 1960 election revealed a state in transition, and the next four years under Kennedy and Johnson were all the Republicans needed. Even though Kennedy tried to avoid direct action in civil rights, he still proved to be the embodiment of everything Mississippi and the white South feared. Attorney General Robert Kennedy sent federal marshals into Alabama to protect the Freedom Riders, prompting one political correspondent to argue that "every crack of the Democratic whip in the South drives more voters into the Republican Party." The following year, President Kennedy sent troops into Oxford to guarantee James Meredith's admission to Ole Miss after Barnett defied several court orders to do so himself. Most white Mississippians cheered their governor's resistance and sneered at Kennedy's use of fifteen thousand "inexperienced, trigger happy marshals" and "ruthless" troops to protect one black student. Kennedy's already low approval in the South dropped precipitously, and some called Ole Miss his "Waterloo." In the days before the riot, the chairman of the Mississippi Democratic Executive Committee expressed his fear that Kennedy's decision had ruined any chances of winning the state in 1964. By using the might of the federal government, he warned, Kennedy would "wipe Mississippi out of the Democrat column.... If this is done, you can kiss Mississippi and the Deep South goodbye."[44]

Kennedy remained the scorn of the South until his assassination the following year, especially after he called for a comprehensive civil rights bill in June 1963. With Lyndon Johnson in the White House, however, the white South hoped for more preferential treatment from the fellow southern Democrat. The *Daily News* argued that LBJ was "unlikely to press as hard as Kennedy for a tough civil rights program" and would "woo some discontented Dixie Democrats back into the party fold." African Americans feared the same thing, and black writer Louis Lomax stated that "the cracker twang in his voice chilled our hearts. For we know that twang, that drawl," leading them to believe that Johnson would be like every other white southerner.[45]

Others understood that Johnson was a different breed of southern Democrat—one who not only continued the late president's racial agenda but proved to be the civil rights president Kennedy never dared to be. No one was prepared for the new president's passion for civil rights, however. President Johnson told one writer, "those civil rightsers are going to have to wear sneakers to keep up with me. Those Harvards think that a politician from Texas doesn't care about Negroes," he insisted, but "I always vowed that if I ever had the power I'd make sure every Negro had the same chance as every white man. Now I have it. And I'm going to use it."[46]

In the year leading up to the 1964 election, Johnson was true to his word, ensuring passage of the Civil Rights Act, calling for the Voting Rights Act, and sending the FBI into Mississippi to search for three missing civil rights workers. To the white South, Kennedy had been a monster, but Johnson seemed like the Devil himself. The segregationist press berated Johnson endlessly, running a three-part series proving that he was "the arch scalawag" who had "about as much chance of winning Mississippi as a Southern Baptist has of becoming Premier of Israel." Barnett called Johnson a "counterfeit Confederate" prepared to "resign from the white race," reminding voters of the "brotherhood by bayonet" in Oxford and the flood of FBI agents "snooping" around their state during Freedom Summer.[47]

Republicans nominated Arizona senator Barry Goldwater for president to counter Johnson's excesses and the ever-growing strength of the federal government, and Mississippi latched onto Goldwater as their "only hope to restore freedom."[48] Strom Thurmond, the hero of the Dixiecrat revolt, signaled the mass exodus to the Republicans when he publicly switched parties in September.[49] The Arizona senator aligned himself perfectly with white southern ideals, arguing that the Supreme Court was not the law of the land, calling the NAACP his "most vociferous political enem[y]," supporting Barnett's resistance to federal force at Ole Miss, and, most importantly, voting against the Civil Rights Act. Mississippi writer Walker Percy insisted that race and race alone drove the state's support of Goldwater, because "it would not have mattered if Senator Goldwater had advocated the collectivization of the plantations and open saloons in Jackson; he voted against the Civil Rights Bill and that was that."[50]

The vast majority of white Mississippians never dreamed of voting Republican, and the thought took some getting used to. One Jackson man wrote how he was raised believing that voting Republican "would be the same thing as turning my back on my state," but columnist Florence Sillers Ogden assured him and other voters that switching parties was not defiling their heritage. "If our fathers should rise up out of their graves and take a look around," she argued, "they wouldn't recognize the party of their fathers.... I know exactly what my father ... would do. He would vote for Goldwater. So would my two Confederate grandfathers."[51]

The rest of the nation did not have the same affection for Goldwater, however, and Johnson defeated him by the largest margin in American history. Mississippi and five other states, however, strapped their electoral votes to a clearly losing candidate.[52] In its endorsement of Goldwater, in fact, most of the Mississippi press admitted that although he had practically no chance of winning, he pressed on anyway. Even more astounding was the fact that Goldwater won every single county in Mississippi, and 87 percent of Mississippi voters preferred the man whom less than 40 percent of their fellow Americans did. Only Alabama came anywhere close to this, with 69 percent of its vote going to Goldwater, who won only 50 percent in his home state. Mississippi, much like in 1960, showed the nation how out of touch it was with mainstream politics, but Mississippi did not care.[53]

Hodding Carter III was an exception, however, as he and his Pulitzer Prize–winning father often were. He understood how Mississippi's overwhelming support of Goldwater damaged the state and indicated its deeper problems. In a post-election editorial he wrote: "It is time we looked at ourselves and ask why we can be so out of step with most of the rest of the nation. We should ask why our political leaders march us backward and deny man's equality under God and the validity of the system of government under which we live." In another editorial, Carter charged that the state was a "political embarrassment, even to other Southern states," because Mississippi still placed race and civil rights as the overriding issues dictating its course. He pleaded with his readers to stop "walk[ing] down dead-end streets, waving our tattered banners of defiance. No one is going to walk with us anymore."[54]

Following the election, Mississippi political commentators argued that the state voted for a man, not a party, and it "[did] not mean a romantic engagement with the Republican Party." The vote for Goldwater was "an overwhelmingly resentment vote—an expression of complete disgust and anger over the treatment of Mississippi." While this may have been true, they could not deny the GOP's growing strength in the state. As white Mississippians rushed to the polls to defeat Lyndon Johnson, many also voted for Prentiss Walker. Walker was the only Mississippi Republican running for Congress in 1964, and he defeated the eleven-term Democratic incumbent W. Arthur Winstead to become the state's first Republican congressman since 1883. A Republican victory in Mississippi shocked many, including editor Jimmy Ward, who wrote: "We have a new political creature in Mississippi—a Republican congressman . . . whether this is a freak upset or foretells dramatic political changes in Mississippi is a matter to be decided in the future." Mississippians may have simply been voting against LBJ in 1964, but Walker's unexpected victory indicated a larger-scale shift in the very fabric of Mississippi politics.[55]

Goldwater's victory in Mississippi was indeed the death knell to Democratic control of the state in national politics, and it introduced a much-needed two-party system within the state. State Democrats rightfully worried about the challenge posed by GOP candidates, but many admitted that it "produced a healthy political reawakening" and "southernized" the Republican Party. George Wallace's third party run in 1968 showed the power of southern voters, which led to Nixon's "southern strategy" to cement the region for his party. The South became a factor in national elections again, forcing both parties to court southern voters.[56] Some can argue that the South reverted to one-party politics with Ronald Reagan's 1980 election and the culmination the conservative revolution that Goldwater started in

1964, but the South continues to reinvent itself in politics, seen in Barack Obama's victory in 2008 and key southern states like Virginia and North Carolina going for not only a Democrat but an African American.[57]

The rising tide of conservatism in the American South is an integral part of understanding the region. While the current Republican Party appeals to Americans on many different levels, from the Religious Right, Tea Partiers, fiscal conservatives, and advocates of small government, it is undeniable that the conservative backlash in the white South stems from a refusal to let go of antebellum ideas of white supremacy and states' rights. Historians can easily point to 1964 as "the moment" that Lyndon Johnson lost the white South, but this discounts the escalating isolation and frustration that southern Democrats faced as their party morphed around them. Concern over Roosevelt's racial agenda jarred southern Democrats and continued through the 1964 election, while notable events marked the fracturing of the solid South. As one historian wrote, "if Thurmond in 1948 did not lead Southerners directly into the Republican party, he at least led them in a significant way out of the Democratic party." This is true, as the Dixiecrats signaled serious tensions within the party, but they returned to the party fold for the next decade without incident. Clearly, they needed another rallying point.[58]

The *Brown* decision and the Little Rock crisis created that sense of desperation in the South, leading directly to Mississippi's defection in 1960, which forced the state into further political and national insignificance. In a state known for lynchings, church bombings, and demagogues, the act of protesting both candidates was only another indication of its backwardness. This backwardness, however, revealed the struggle over identity in a time where that had always meant white and Democrat. The twenty-year period prior to the 1964 election shows the depths of white southern disenchantment and the lengths they would go to in order to protect their heritage. The era of magnolia blossoms, plantations, demagogues, and Dixiecrats could not survive the growing commitment to racial equality in this country, and the Democratic Party as the dominant power in the solid South was the inevitable casualty.

Notes

1. In 1968, white southerners overwhelmingly voted for states rights' candidate George Wallace, with support for the Democrats dropping below 20 percent. Jimmy Carter won much of the South in 1976 but did not draw the majority of white voters. He saw his support fall off precipitously in 1980 against Ronald Reagan, garnering only 36 percent of

the white electorate in his native South. Scholars roundly mark the culmination of the conservative turn in modern American history with Reagan's sweeping victory, where he won all but six states and more than 90 percent of the electoral vote. Even Arkansas governor Bill Clinton could not win the majority of white southerners, as they stayed solidly in the Republican camp. Barack Obama's historic victory in 2008 revealed slight shifts in southern states, notably Virginia and North Carolina, but today the Republican Party still draws a great deal of support from white southern voters. William Leuchtenburg, *White House Looks South: Franklin D. Roosevelt, Harry S. Truman, Lyndon B. Johnson* (Baton Rouge: Louisiana State University Press, 2005), 325, 396.

2. For studies on the role of civil rights in the Roosevelt administration, see Patricia Sullivan, *Days of Hope: Race and Democracy in the New Deal Era* (Chapel Hill: University of North Carolina Press, 1996); Lauren Sklaroff, *Black Culture and the New Deal: The Quest for Civil Rights in the Roosevelt Era* (Chapel Hill: University of North Carolina Press, 2010); Harvard Sitkoff, *A New Deal for Blacks: The Emergence of Civil Rights as a National Issue* (New York: Oxford University Press, 1978); Kevin McMahon, *Reconsidering Roosevelt on Race: How the Presidency Paved the Road to* Brown (Chicago: University of Chicago Press, 2004); Leuchtenburg, *White House Looks South*, part 1; and Michael Perman, *Pursuit of Unity: A Political History of the American South* (Chapel Hill: University of North Carolina Press, 2009), 194–203, 225–47.

3. Leuchtenburg, *White House Looks South*, 29–37, 56; Sklaroff, *Black Culture and the New Deal*, 17.

4. Leuchtenburg, *White House Looks South*, 55–59; Perman, *Pursuit of Unity*, 243–44; Sklaroff, *Black Culture and the New Deal*, 24–28; Sullivan, *Days of Hope*; Sitkoff, *New Deal for Blacks*.

5. For more on the Federal Arts Project and how it promoted black rights, see Sklaroff, *Black Culture and the New Deal*, especially chapters 2–3.

6. Leuchtenburg, *White House Looks South*, 55, 62–66, 131, 136; Sklaroff, *Black Culture and the New Deal*, 24; Sullivan, *Days of Hope*, 7, 136; Sitkoff, *New Deal for Blacks*; McMahon, *Reconsidering Roosevelt on Race*; Perman, *Pursuit of Unity*, 252–53.

7. For more on the *Smith* decision see Papers of the National Association for the Advancement of Colored People on microfilm, Part 4, Reel 11; Charles L. Zelden, *The Battle for the Black Ballot: Smith v. Allwright and the Defeat of the Texas All-White Primary* (Lawrence: University Press of Kansas, 2004); Darlene Clark Hine, Steven F. Lawson, and Merline Pitre, *Black Victory: The Rise and Fall of the White Primary in Texas* (Columbia: University of Missouri Press, 2003); Michael J. Klarman, *From Jim Crow to Civil Rights: The Supreme Court and the Struggle for Racial Equality* (New York: Oxford University Press, 2004), 236–48; Kari A. Frederickson, *The Dixiecrat Revolt and the End of the Solid South, 1932–1968* (Chapel Hill: University of North Carolina Press, 2001), 39–49; Steven F. Lawson, *Black Ballots: Voting Rights in the South, 1944–1969* (New York: Columbia University Press, 1976); Donald R. Matthews, *Negroes and the New Southern Politics* (New York: Harcourt, Brace & World, 1966); Charles V. Hamilton, *The Bench and the Ballot: Southern Federal Judges and Black Voters* (New York: Oxford University Press, 1973); Sullivan, *Days of Hope*, 120, 147–48, 169–70; Patricia Sullivan, *Lift Every Voice: The NAACP and the Making of the Civil Rights Movement* (New York: New Press, 2009), 282–85; "Justice Roberts Protests Supreme Court Act to Give Negroes Right to Cast Ballot in Texas," *Jackson (Miss.)*

Clarion-Ledger [hereafter *C-L*], April 4, 1944; Klarman, *From Jim Crow to Civil Rights*, 200, 449; Glenda Elizabeth Gilmore, *Defying Dixie: The Radical Roots of Civil Rights, 1919-1950* (New York: Norton, 2008), 394; Keith M. Finley, *Delaying the Dream: Southern Senators and the Fight against Civil Rights, 1938-1965* (Baton Rouge: Louisiana State University Press, 2008), 72-73; Charles M. Payne, *I've Got the Light of Freedom: The Organizing Tradition and the Mississippi Freedom Struggle* (Berkeley: University of California Press, 1995), 24; Perman, *Pursuit of Unity*, 194.

8. "Texans See 'White Supremacy' Decision as Costly to FDR," *C-L*, April 17, 1944; "Democrats May Win Negroes, Lose Whites—Colmer," *Jackson (Miss.) Daily News* [hereafter *JDN*], April 12, 1944; "Justice Roberts Protests Supreme Court Act to Give Negroes Right to Cast Ballot in Texas," *C-L*, April 4, 1944; "It Is Time for the People to Stop, Look, Listen and Act," *C-L*, April 5, 1944; "Reaction on Negro Votes Stirs South," *C-L*, April 4, 1944; "Most Serious Threat in Years to White Supremacy in South," *C-L*, April 6, 1944; "State Democrats Do Not Intend to Let Negroes Vote," *JDN*, April 4, 1944; "Further Legal Action to Give Negroes Voting Privileges in South Forecast in Some Sections," *Delta Democrat-Times* (Greenville, Miss.) [hereafter *DD-T*], April 4, 1944; "Ranking Scores Court for Negro Vote Rule," *C-L*, April 6, 1944; Sullivan, *Days of Hope*, 7; Frederickson, *Dixiecrat Revolt*, 39.

9. Hazel Brannon married Walter "Smitty" Smith in 1950, becoming the better-known Hazel Brannon Smith.

10. "Through Hazel Eyes," *Lexington (Miss.) Advertiser* [hereafter *LA*], April 13, 20, 1944; Peter Molyneaux, *The South's Political Plight* (Dallas: Calhoun Clubs of the South, 1948), 8-9; Leuchtenburg, *White House Looks South*, 131.

11. Leuchtenburg, *White House Looks South*, 139-40.

12. Perman, *Pursuit of Unity*, 261; Leuchtenburg, *White House Looks South*, 158-63.

13. For more on Truman and civil rights, which caused the rift between him and southern Democrats, ultimately leading to the Dixiecrat Revolt of 1948, see Leuchtenburg, *White House Looks South*; Michael Gardner, *Harry Truman and Civil Rights: Moral Courage and Political Risks* (Carbondale: Southern Illinois University Press, 2002); William Berman, *The Politics of Civil Rights in the Truman Administration* (Columbus: Ohio State University Press, 1970); Monroe Billington, "Civil Rights, President Truman and the South," *Journal of Negro History* 58, no. 2 (April 1973): 127-39; Harvard Sitkoff, "Harry Truman and the Election of 1948: The Coming of Age of Civil Rights in American Politics," *Journal of Southern History* 37, no. 4 (November 1971): 597-616; Joseph E. Lowndes, *From the New Deal to the New Right: Race and the Southern Origins of Modern Conservatism* (New Haven: Yale University Press, 2008); Leuchtenburg, *White House Looks South*, 163-65.

14. Leuchtenburg, *White House Looks South*, 158-88; Perman, *Pursuit of Unity*, 257-58, 263-76; Sitkoff, "Harry Truman and the Election of 1948," 599-600.

15. Clark Clifford, memo to Harry Truman, November 19, 1947, Clark Clifford Papers, Political File, box 23, Harry S. Truman Library, Independence, Missouri; Leuchtenburg, *White House Looks South*, 177-85; Sitkoff, "Harry Truman and the Election of 1948," 597, 600-601, 604-5; Perman, *Pursuit of Unity*, 261, 265; Robert A. Garson, *The Democratic Party and the Politics of Sectionalism, 1941-1948* (Baton Rouge: Louisiana State University Press, 1974), 231.

16. Leuchtenburg, *White House Looks South*, 178-85; Perman, *Pursuit of Unity*, 265-66;

Sitkoff, "Harry Truman and the Election of 1948," 602; Richard D. Chesteen, "'Mississippi Is Gone Home!' A Study of the 1948 Mississippi States' Rights Bolt," *Journal of Mississippi History* 32 (1970): 43–59; "Gov. Wright Calls Truman's 'Civil Rights' Message of February 'Straw Breaking Camel's Back' in Article," *McComb (Miss.) Enterprise Journal* [hereafter *EJ*], July 1, 1948.

17. Mississippi Is Through with Truman," *JDN,* February 5, 1948; Chesteen, "'Mississippi Is Gone Home!'"; Leuchtenburg, *White House Looks South,* 181; Sitkoff, "Harry Truman and the Election of 1948," 602–5.

18. For more on the Dixiecrat Revolt itself, see Frederickson's standard text, *The Dixiecrat Revolt and the End of the Solid South,* as well as Leuchtenburg, *White House Looks South;* Morton Sosna, *In Search of the Silent South: Southern Liberals on the Race Issue* (New York: Columbia University Press, 1977); William D. Barnard, *Dixiecrats and Democrats: Alabama Politics, 1942–1950* (Tuscaloosa: University of Alabama Press, 1974); Kent Germany, "Rise of the Dixiecrats: Louisiana's Conservative Defection from the National Democratic Party, 1944–1948" (M.A. thesis, Louisiana Tech University, 1994); Jane Dailey, Glenda Gilmore, and Bryant Simon, eds., *Jumpin' Jim Crow: Southern Politics from Civil War to Civil Rights* (Princeton: Princeton University Press, 2000), 260–74; Jack Bass, *Strom: The Complicated Personal and Political Life of Strom Thurmond* (New York: Public Affairs, 2005); Lowndes, *From the New Deal to the New Right*; Glenn Feldman, *From Demagogue to Dixiecrat: Horace Wilkinson and the Politics of Race* (Lanham, Md.: University Press of America, 1995); Chesteen, "'Mississippi Is Gone Home!'" For more on the Mississippi press response on the Dixiecrat revolt, see Susan Weill, *In a Madhouse's Din: Civil Rights Coverage by Mississippi's Daily Press, 1948–1968* (Westport, Conn.: Praeger, 2002); Susan Weill, "The Dixiecrats and the Mississippi Daily Press," *Journal of Mississippi History* 64, no. 4 (Winter 2002): 259–82.

For more specifics on the Dixiecrat Revolt, see Perman, *Pursuit of Unity,* 266–76; Leuchtenburg, *White House Looks South,* 195; John Egerton, *Speak Now against the Day: The Generation before the Civil Rights Movement in the South* (Chapel Hill: University of North Carolina Press, 1994), 498–501; Weill, "The Dixiecrats and the Mississippi Daily Press," 275; "Fierce Platform Battle on Civil Rights Issue Looming for Convention," *EJ,* July 8, 1948; "Dixie Set to Walk," *C-L,* July 11, 1948; "Mississippi Delegates Walk Out Wednesday; They're Bama-Bound," *JDN,* July 13, 1948; "All State Delegates Pledged to Walk Out If States' Rights Issue Is Flouted at Convention, Wright Says on Eve of Trip," *DD-T,* July 8, 1948; "Dixiecrats Go on 'Warpath,'" *C-L,* July 8, 1948; "Dixie Leaders Say Civil Rights Plank 'Entirely Unsatisfactory,'" *DD-T,* July 13, 1948; "Hot Platform War Rages," *EJ,* July 14, 1948; "Southerners Lose Battle for States Rights Plank," *JDN,* July 14, 1948; "Wright Calls All States' Righters, Truman Opponents to Birmingham Convention," *DD-T,* July 15, 1948; "Truman Is Nominated; Mississippi Takes Walk," *C-L,* July 15, 1948; "Mississippi and Alabama Take a Walk as Truman Is Nominated; Harsh Civil Rights Anti-South Program Is Adopted," *EJ,* July 15, 1948; "Wright Issues Call; Dixiecrats Roll South," *C-L,* July 16, 1948; "Dixiecrats Rolling into Birmingham for Saturday Conference; Republicans Yell 'Trick' at Special Session Call," *EJ,* July 16, 1948; "Thurmond, Wright Hoist Dixie Standard," *C-L,* July 18, 1948; "Thurmond, Wright Accept Dixiecrat Draft," *JDN,* July 18, 1948; "Thurmond, Wright Lead South," *DD-T,* July 18, 1948; "Wild Outbursts Greet Dixiecrat Nominations," *JDN,* July 18, 1948.

19. "Highlights in the Headlines," *EJ*, July 1, 2, 8, November 2, 1948; "It's On to B'ham! Mississippi and Alabama Take a Walk as Truman Is Nominated, Harsh Civil Rights Anti-South Program Is Adopted," *EJ*, July 15, 1948; "We Will Win the Party," *EJ*, July 15, 1948; "South Will Be 'Solid' against Truman, Dewey, Wright Predicts," *DD-T*, September 17, 1948; Perman, *Pursuit of Unity*, 267–69; Weill, "The Dixiecrats and the Mississippi Daily Press," 261; Leuchtenburg, *White House Looks South*, 203.

20. "Will Dixie Survive Bolt? Press Survey Indicates 'No,'" *C-L*, July 1, 1948; "Southern Democracy," *JDN*, July 19, 1948; "The Low Down on the Higher Ups," *JDN*, July 15, 16, 19, 1948; "Dixiecrat Platform Strikes at Truman," *C-L*, July 18, 1948; "States' Rights Movement Is Born, Cradled and Raised by Sympathetic Mississippians," *C-L*, July 25, 1948; "Dixie Shapes Hard Fight on Civil Rights," *EJ*, July 26, 1948; "Odds Greatly against South Leaders Admit," *EJ*, July 27, 1948; Weill, "The Dixiecrats and the Mississippi Daily Press," 280.

21. "Thurmond Says Civil Rights Would Mean 'Virtual Revolution' in South," *DD-T*, August 1, 1948; "Dixiecrats Launch Campaign," *C-L*, August 12, 1948; "Enemies Can't Agree But They All Hate Truman," *C-L*, July 13, 148; "Harry Truman, Renegade," *JDN*, July 28, 1948; "Truman and His Negroes," *JDN*, July 21, 1948; "The Low Down on the Higher Ups," *JDN*, July 19, 1948; "Negroes in the Saddle," *JDN*, July 16, 1948; "Through Hazel Eyes," *LA*, November 11, 1948; "Highlights in the Headlines," *EJ*, November 2, 1948; "States Rights Movement Supports States' Rights," *C-L*, October 4, 1948; "A Hurt and Angered South Is Pondering These Questions," *C-L*, July 16, 1948; Weill, "The Dixiecrats and the Mississippi Daily Press," 262, 275.

22. "Say Dixie Ticket May Doom Truman," *C-L*, July 19, 1948; "Democrats Go to Convention Hall with Bad Case of Split Personality," *DD-T*, July 12, 1948; "Once Solid South Shaken and Split as Presidential Election Nears," *DD-T*, October 28, 1948; "Today's Election May Leave Wide-Open Holes in Dixie Armor," *DD-T*, November 2, 1948; "Today's Election," *DD-T*, November 1, 1948; "Why Truman Won," *DD-T*, November 4, 1948; "South Will Be 'Solid' against Truman, Dewey, Wright Predicts," *DD-T*, September 17, 1948; "Wright Predicts Solid South for States' Rights; Throwing of Election into House," *DD-T*, October 7, 1948.

23. Thurmond also took South Carolina with 72 percent of the vote, Alabama with 80 percent, and Louisiana with 49 percent.

24. "10 States' Rights Achievements," *EJ*, November 2, 1948; "The Low Down on the Higher Ups," *JDN*, November 4, 1948; "Highlights in the Headlines," *EJ*, November 2, 1948; "States' Righters Are Due to Carry Mississippi by Majority of about 4 to 1," *EJ*, November 2, 1948; "Mississippi Casts Votes Proudly for Party Which Was Started by Governor," *EJ*, November 3, 1948; "Amendments Beaten; State Goes Thurmond," *DD-T*, November 3, 1948; "Election Headed for U.S. House? State Nearly 90 Percent for SR," *C-L*, November 3, 1948; "Wright Expresses Pride in People of Magnolia State," *C-L*, November 4, 1948; "Through Hazel Eyes," *LA*, November 11, 1948; Leuchtenburg, *White House Looks South*, 181, 188–213; Perman, *Pursuit of Unity*, 265–76.

25. Perman, *Pursuit of Unity*, 268–74; Leuchtenburg, *White House Looks South*, 220; Egerton, *Speak Now against the Day*, 513.

26. Eisenhower won Tennessee, Virginia, and Florida.

27. "The South's Experience with Republican Rule," *LA*, October 30, 1952; "Stand by the Faith of Your Fathers," *JDN*, November 2, 1952; "The Low Down on the Higher Ups," *JDN*,

November 3, 1952; "Prepare for the Whirlwind," *JDN*, November 6, 1952; "Ike Splits Solid South to Bits; GOP Official Sees Start of Two-Party System," *JDN*, November 5, 1952; "Ike's 'Tidal Wave' Cracks South," *C-L*, November 5, 1952.

28. David A. Nichols, *A Matter of Justice: Eisenhower and the Beginning of the Civil Rights Revolution* (New York: Simon & Schuster, 2007), 66–67; "Ike Asks South to Be 'Calm and Reasonable,'" *DD-T*, May 19, 1954; Sullivan, *Lift Every Voice*, 423; Michael Klarman, "Why Massive Resistance?" in *Massive Resistance: Southern Opposition to the Second Reconstruction*, ed. Clive Webb (New York: Oxford University Press, 2005), 29; John Dittmer, *Local People: The Struggle for Civil Rights in Mississippi* (Urbana: University of Illinois Press, 1994), 52.

29. For more on the Little Rock crisis, see Elizabeth Jacoway, *Turn Away Thy Son: Little Rock, the Crisis That Shocked the Nation* (New York: Free Press, 2007); Melba Beals, *Warriors Don't Cry: A Searing Memoir of the Battle to Integrate Central High* (New York: Pocket Books, 1994); Karen Anderson, *Little Rock: Race and Resistance at Central High School* (Princeton, NJ: Princeton University Press, 2010); Melba Patillo Beals, *White Is a State of Mind: A Memoir* (New York: Putnam, 1999). See also "Telegrams from U.S. Public Backing Faubus' Action 20-1," *C-L*, September 9, 1957; "Major Sullens' Mail," *JDN*, September 10, 12, 1957; "Affairs of State," *C-L*, September 9, 1957; "South's Leadership Seen Saving Nation," *JDN*, September 16, 1957; "Voice of the People," *C-L*, September 13, 1957.

30. "State Editors Blast Ike for Little Rock Invasion," *C-L/JDN*, September 29, 1960; "Return of Carpetbagger Era Predicted for Southerners," *JDN*, September 24, 1957; "Major Sullens' Mail," *JDN*, September 9, 1957; "Mississippi Notebook," *C-L*, September 26, 1957; Gene Roberts and Hank Klibanoff, *The Race Beat: The Press, the Civil Rights Struggle, and the Awakening of a Nation* (New York: Knopf, 2006); Executive Order 10730, September 24, 1957, Box 29, James W. Silver Papers, J. D. Williams Library, Department of Archives and Special Collections, University of Mississippi, Oxford; "Crisis in Little Rock," *Crisis*, November 1957.

31. "The Low Down on the Higher Ups," *JDN*, September 27, 1957; "Guard Federalization Is Unconstitutional," *JDN*, September 27, 1957; "Ike Loses the Confidence of People in Dixieland," *C-L/JDN*, September 29, 1957; "Mississippi Notebook," *C-L*, September 26, 1957; "State Editors Blast Ike for Little Rock Invasion," *C-L/JDN*, September 29, 1960; "It Is War on Arkansas," *C-L/JDN*, September 29, 1957; "We Are Playing for Keeps," *JDN*, September 6, 1957; "Nasty Mess at Little Rock," *JDN*, September 30, 1957; "Editors on Troops in Arkansas," *DD-T*, September 26, 1957.

32. "Kennedy's Busy Little Gang," *JDN*, October 18, 1960; "South to Get Break, Johnson Friends Say," *Jackson State Times* (Jackson, Miss.) [hereafter *ST*], November 12, 1960; "Kennedy Put 'C-R' Plank in Platform," *ST*, October 26, 1960; "Independents Claim They'll Elect Byrd," *EJ*, November 3, 1960.

33. "Poplarville Editor Is for Unpledged," *C-L*, October 18, 1960; "Letters from Readers," *ST*, October 31, 1960; "Readers' Viewpoint," *JDN*, October 27, 1960.

34. "The Little Rock Address," *Citizens' Council*, January 1958; "The Tide Is Turning," *Citizens' Council*, November 1957.

35. Theodore White, *The Making of the President 1960: A Narrative History of American Politics in Action* (London: Cape, 1965), appendix A; "Mississippi Votes 'Unpledged'; GOP Runs Third in State," *DD-T*, November 9, 1960.

36. Both senators disapproved of Kennedy's stance on civil rights but feared that undermining the national party might jeopardize their positions in Washington. Eastland, e.g., chaired the powerful Senate Judiciary Committee, and he worried that Mississippi's Unpledged vote could cost him the job. "South's Politicians Will Still Fight New Civil Rights Laws," *DD-T*, November 10, 1960. See also "The 'Independents' Are Not Democrats," *LA*, September 29, 1960; "Over the Editor's Desk," *Pascagoula (Miss.) Chronicle* [hereafter *PC*], October 21, 1960; "Contrasts in 1948, 1960 Mississippi Party Bolt Movements," *New Orleans Times Picayune*, September 4, 1960.

37. The list of proposed stipulations changed constantly, but key points included no more civil rights legislation (including the promise not to enforce existing legislation) and the appointment of southerners to the Supreme Court, cabinet, and high-ranking positions in the administration. See also "Voice of the People," *C-L*, October 24, 1960; "Elector Plan Is Explained," *JDN*, October 7, 1960; "Readers' Viewpoint," *JDN*, October 27, 1960; "Mississippi Electors Unpledged," *EJ*, November 9, 1960; "Mississippi Votes 'Unpledged'; GOP Runs Third in State," *DD-T*, November 9, 1960.

38. "Poplarville Editor Is for Unpledged," *C-L*, October 18, 1960; "Mississippi Is Being Watched," *JDN*, October 24, 1960; "The South Is Blamed Again," *JDN*, November 4, 1960; "Elector Plan Is Explained," *JDN*, October 7, 1960; "Our Readers' Viewpoint," *JDN*, November 8, 1960; "Letters from Readers," *ST*, November 14, 1960; "Ross Prefers Devil to an Integrationist," *JDN*, May 11, 1960.

39. "The Political Misconception of the Unpledged," *ST*, November 6, 1960; "The Misconception of the Unpledged," *EJ*, November 7, 1960; "Why Unpledged Will Lose Even If They Carry State," *ST*, October 23, 1960; "Why Independents Can't Attain Their Objective," *EJ*, November 1, 1960; "Readers' Viewpoint," *JDN*, October 13 and 20, November 5, 1960; "Mississippi Notebook," *C-L*, November 3, 1960; "Vote for Unpledged Electors," *C-L*, November 7, 1960; "The South a Political Orphan," *JDN*, October 27, 1960; "Unpledged Elector Potency," *JDN*, November 7, 1960; "Voice of the People," *C-L*, October 27, 1960.

40. "With the Rains, Old Demagoguery," *DD-T*, October 31, 1960; "Which Way Will Mississippi Vote?" *EJ*, October 26, 1960; "Why Unpledged Will Lose Even If They Carry State," *ST*, October 23, 1960; "Why Independents Can't Attain Their Objective," *EJ*, November 1, 1960; "Independents Claim They'll Elect Byrd," *EJ*, November 3, 1960; "Our Choice Is Nixon and Lodge," *LA*, November 3, 1960.

41. Georgia, Louisiana, South Carolina, and North Carolina stayed with the Democrats and voted for Kennedy, while Arkansas, Tennessee, and Virginia went for Nixon. Arkansas switched parties from 1956 to 1960, a significant win for Nixon. Some predicted low voter turnout in Mississippi, since many "don't like either guy," but Mississippi voters came out in record numbers. The 1960 election drew over forty thousand more Mississippi voters to the polls than in 1956, but only about four thousand more than in 1952. "State's Black Voters Estimated at Near 25,000," *Times Picayune*, October 16, 1960. See also "Mississippi Votes 'Unpledged'; GOP Runs Third in State," *DD-T*, November 9, 1960; "Voters Cook to Both Candidates," *EJ*, October 26, 1960; "Unpledged Slate Rolls in County," *EJ*, November 9, 1960; Joseph Crespino, *In Search of Another Country: Mississippi and the Conservative Counterrevolution* (Princeton, NJ: Princeton University Press, 2007), 1. Alabama actually had six unpledged electors out of its eleven.

42. "The Kennedy Ship Is Anchored," *JDN*, November 10, 1960; "Acclaim Jack Winner;

Unpledged Leads State," *C-L*, November 9, 1960; "Readers' Viewpoint," *JDN*, November 12, 1960; "Mississippi Notebook," *C-L*, November 10, December 16, 1960; "State's Vote 'Anti-Kennedy,'" *ST*, November 14, 1960; "Rebel State Demos Say Triumph 'Warns' Nation," *EJ*, November 9, 1960.

43. "Through Hazel Eyes," *LA*, November 10, 1960; "Mississippi Editors Look at the Election," *EJ*, November 11, 1960; "Congratulations Sen. Jack Kennedy!" *EJ*, November 9, 1960; "The Election Ends," *DD-T*, November 9, 1960; "Three Constitutional Amendments," *DD-T*, November 6, 1960; "With the Rains, Old Demagoguery," *DD-T*, October 31, 1960.

44. Conversely, some Mississippi politicians actually cheered on Kennedy, hoping he might bury himself. Ole Miss, state senator John McLaurin argued, "may be a God-sent miracle . . . the Kennedys may have fired their big gun too soon. It demonstrates the police-state tendencies to which they will resort, which we have all suspected in the past. This might be the act which will remove them from office." "McLaurin Gives Version Of Ole Miss Story," *C-L*, October 10, 1962. See also "Acclaim Jack Winner; Unpledged Leads State," *C-L*, November 9, 1960; "GOP Is Emerging in 'Solid South,'" *EJ*, July 7, 1961; "Barnett Calls Use of Force Inflammatory," *C-L*, October 2, 1962; "Mississippi Could Be Waterloo for Kennedy," *JDN*, October 6, 1962; "The 'Mess in Mississippi' Could Defeat President Kennedy in '64," *C-L*, October 20, 1962; "Adams Predicts End of Kennedy," *JDN*, October 2, 1962; "Adams Says Democrats Have Lost the South," *JDN*, October 10, 1962; "Affairs of State," *C-L*, October 9, 1962; "Dixie Solons See Oxford Backfire," *JDN*, October 15, 1962; "Tragic Era Is at Hand," *C-L/JDN*, October 7, 1962; "Mississippi Notebook," *C-L*, September 21, 1962.

45. "All Bets Are Off on '64 Election," *JDN*, November 25, 1963; "LBJ, with Roots in South, May Be Able to Heal Old Wounds," *C-L*, November 26, 1963; "Johnson First President from South in 100 Years," *PC*, November 25, 1963; "What of the South Now? Politicians Take a Look," *JDN*, November 26, 1963; Louis E. Lomax, "A Negro View: Johnson Can Free the South," *Look*, March 10, 1964, 34; Leuchtenburg, *White House Looks South*, 288–89, 300; Richard N. Goodwin, *Remembering America: A Voice from the Sixties* (Boston: Little, Brown, 1988), 257–58.

46. Leuchtenburg, *White House Looks South*, 288–89, 300; Goodwin, *Remembering America*, 257–58; "Our Readers' Viewpoint," *JDN*, December 3, 1963; "All Bets Are Off on '64 Election," *JDN*, November 25, 1963; "Dixie Eye on Johnson," *C-L/JDN*, December 1, 1963; "Johnson First President from South in 100 Years," *PC*, November 25, 1963; "Citizens Council Leader Brands Kennedy a Tyrant," *DD-T*, November 26, 1963; "A Negro View: Johnson Can Free the South," *Look*, March 10, 1964; "Proposal Would Do Violence to Constitutional Rights of People," *C-L*, November 30, 1963; "The Progeny of Hate," *DD-T*, November 26, 1963; "President Johnson, an Able Leader," *DD-T*, November 25, 1963.

47. "The Arch Scalawag," *C-L*, September 2, 1964; "The Arch Scalawag, II," *C-L*, September 8, 1964; "LBJ the Arch Scalawag," *C-L*, September 24, 1964; "Mississippi Notebook," *C-L*, October 28, 1964; "Voice of the People," *C-L*, undated; "Our Readers' Viewpoint," *JDN*, November 3, 1964; Leuchtenburg, *White House Looks South*, 313; "LBJ Blasted at Neshoba," *DD-T*, August 14, 1964.

48. Their initial "only hope" was Alabama governor George Wallace, who dropped out after Goldwater received the nomination. Mississippi Democrats immediately shifted

support to Goldwater. Crespino, *In Search of Another Country*, 101; "After Tuesday, What's in Store for the State?" *EJ*, November 2, 1964.

49. Thurmond switched parties the day before Goldwater visited South Carolina. At their meeting, Thurmond was even wearing the GOP's symbol, a gold elephant tie clip. Leuchtenburg, *White House Looks South*, 313.

50. Crespino, *In Search of Another Country*, 100–107; Leuchtenburg, *White House Looks South*, 309–13, 322–23; "Goldwater Calls NAACP 'Loud Political Enemy,'" *C-L*, June 6, 1962; "Mississippi Notebook," *C-L*, October 28, 1964; "LBJ May Not Be Dead in State," *EJ*, September 15, 1964; "After Tuesday, What's in Store for the State?" *EJ*, November 2, 1964; Walker Percy, "Mississippi: The Fallen Paradise," *Harper's*, April 1965, 172.

51. "Voice of the People," *C-L*, August 9, 1964; "Voice of the People," *C-L*, April 11, 1964; Crespino, *In Search of Another Country*, 103.

52. Goldwater's other states in 1964 were Alabama (69 percent for Goldwater), South Carolina (59 percent), Louisiana (57 percent), Georgia (54 percent), and Arizona (50 percent).

53. "Goldwater Could Win without Getting Popular Vote Majority," *C-L*, October 31, 1964; Crespino, *In Search of Another Country*, 1, 100–107; Leuchtenburg, *White House Looks South*, 322; "LBJ Passes FDR in Popular Votes," *JDN*, November 4, 1964; "Republicans Cheer Mississippi Victory," *JDN*, November 4, 1964.

54. "Post Mortem," *DD-T*, November 4, 1964; "Mississippi Walks Alone," *DD-T*, August 31, 1964.

55. The year before, Republican Rubel Phillips ran for governor and carried seven counties, the best showing for a state Republican since Reconstruction. "President's Death Overshadows State's Big News Events of 1963," *C-L*, January 5, 1964. See also Crespino, *In Search of Another Country*, 105; "Republicans Cheer Mississippi Victory," *JDN*, November 4, 1964; "GOP Victory," *DD-T*, November 6, 1964; "Covering the Crossroads," *JDN*, November 4, 1964; "Goldwater Loss Is No Mandate for Any Sweeping Change in US," *C-L*, November 5, 1964; "The Lyndon Johnson Victory," *JDN*, November 5, 1964.

56. During the 1960 election, journalist Bill Minor commented on how Mississippi had been "in the bag" for the Democrats for so long that both parties saw the outcome as a foregone conclusion. In 1960, however, the Republicans saw the strain between southern and national Democrats and used this opportunity to pick up votes. Nixon campaigned in the state, while Kennedy sent Lyndon and Lady Bird Johnson in his stead. The state enjoyed Nixon's attention, even if only 25 percent of them voted for him. "It is the first time in scores of years that a presidential candidate has thought enough of us to come to Mississippi to ask us to vote for him," Minor wrote, and pointed out that the last presidential candidate to campaign in the state was Andrew Jackson in 1828, some 132 years earlier. "Nixon in 1960 First Presidential Candidate to Campaign in State since 1828," *Times Picayune*, September 18, 1960; "Did Lyndon Do What He Came Here to Do?" *C-L*, October 17, 1960.

57. "GOP Victory," *DD-T*, November 6, 1964; "Through Hazel Eyes," November 5, 1964; "Through Hazel Eyes," July 23, 1964; "A New Era," *DD-T*, November 3, 1964; "Mississippi's One-Way Road," *DD-T*, July 28, 1964; "What's Ahead for State Democrats?" *DD-T*, July 22, 1965; "Rising Republicans," *DD-T*, July 14, 1965.

58. Leuchtenburg, *White House Looks South*, 222.

5

Right Turn?

The Republican Party and African American Politics in Post-1965 Mississippi

CHRIS DANIELSON

The state of Mississippi, regarded as the most recalcitrant of the southern states in the civil rights era, might have been expected after the civil rights laws of the 1960s to have immediately seen the surge of an all-white Republican Party that advocated federal restraint and cared little for black voters. That may seem true now in the era of Haley Barbour, but this was not necessarily the predestined path for the Mississippi GOP. While many scholars have commented on the role that race has played in the shift of southern whites to the GOP, southern party leaders did not always immediately embrace the creation of all-white parties. The Mississippi Republican Party experienced a considerable internal schism over the viability of the black vote in post-1965 Mississippi. Federal law also complicated the aims of state GOP conservatives, and GOP presidential administrations pursued a more nuanced path than simply embracing white segregationists. While Republican presidents favored weakening or abolishing the Voting Rights Act when it came up for extension, GOP administrations, especially that of Ronald Reagan, actually expanded the state's black office-holding through their enforcement of the Voting Rights Act.

For much of the pre-1965 era, the Republican Party commanded the allegiance of black Mississippians, but this had changed by the middle of the century. The Mississippi Republican Party, first under the leadership of the Black and Tans and then under the Lily White delegation after 1960, did not provide any examples of leadership for civil rights activists during the 1950s. With the state GOP and Democrats both appealing to white segregationists, black Mississippians relied on their own political efforts during the 1950s and 1960s, through civil rights organizations like the NAACP and the Mississippi Freedom Democratic Party (MFDP).[1]

When federal registrars arrived in Mississippi in 1965 to register black voters under the provisions of the Voting Rights Act, the increase in the number of black voters was not significant enough to have an immediate impact on the state GOP. The party leadership under Wirt Yerger, a Greenville insurance salesman, firmly opposed civil rights legislation. While the Republicans did not indulge in the crude racial demagoguery of Democrats like Ross Barnett, they represented a growing demographic of suburban, white, conservative professionals across the South who had little interest in soliciting black votes. Like the rest of the emerging Sun Belt, Mississippi's suburban areas became the base of Magnolia State Republicanism. Yerger told the national Republican chairman the oft-repeated statement that he did not favor "writing off completely any vote [the black vote specifically], but I do think it is best to go hunting where the ducks are."[2]

The "ducks" were the rural whites who made up much of the state Democratic Party. Prentiss Walker took that approach in 1966 when he challenged Senator James Eastland's reelection bid. A chicken farmer who had won a congressional seat in the 1964 election, Walker joined his Democratic colleagues in opposing the Voting Rights Act and solely focused on the white vote. During the Senate campaign, Walker tried to "outsegregate," in the words of state AFL-CIO chief Claude Ramsey, Eastland, but most white voters stayed with Eastland.[3]

The failed GOP candidacies in the 1960s showed the difficulty the white conservatives of the party had trying to convince white Democrats to leave the party of states' rights and segregation. A two-party system threatened to weaken white supremacy by dividing the white electorate. While white Mississippians voted overwhelmingly for Goldwater in 1964, they did not reciprocate with state Republicans since their Democratic opponents had even more fervent commitments to Jim Crow. The "Great White Switch" had occurred, as Earl and Merle Black labeled the shift of southern white voters to voting Republican in presidential elections, but party identification with the Democrats continued on the state and local level due to the continuing white dominance of the Mississippi Democratic Party.[4]

Black voting continued to grow as registration increased in the late 1960s, and the state GOP could not ignore the numbers. The enfranchisement of black Mississippians under the Voting Rights Act created a major ideological cleavage in the Republican Party that would last for years even as they made another bid for the governor's office in 1967. Since 1960, conservatives like Wirt Yerger had guided party philosophy. The ultraconservatives, or conservative ideologues, favored economic philosophies that promoted an unregulated free market. Many of these conservatives were businessmen who would benefit from such policies. Much like the neobourbons, the rural conservatives who led resistance to school desegregation of the 1950s, they regarded programs that helped the poor and African Americans as government interference.[5] They favored soliciting white voters who had supported George Wallace, but with coded racial appeals, not economic populism.

With the enactment of the Voting Rights Act, the ideologues found their influence in the party contested by a progressive wing. The label "progressive" was relative to Mississippi, since many of the more liberal Mississippi Republicans were still conservative by national standards. The progressives differed from the ideologues with their significant efforts at black voter outreach, which reflected a desire to build a biracial party based on economic development and growth. Although some of their leaders came from the business sector like the conservative ideologues, the progressives did not see government programs as being incompatible with economic growth. The progressives generally supported social programs that favored low-income, predominantly black Mississippians, as well as civil rights legislation.

Between these two factions were the less ideologically committed members of the party. Like the state GOP overall, they were reliably conservative, but they shifted as the situation demanded. These uncommitted members, or pragmatists, may have had sympathies with one faction or the other (usually the conservative ideologues), but they focused on gaining political power and maintaining party unity, even if it meant at times compromising ideology. The pragmatists would eventually become a significant force in the party, holding both party leadership positions and the small number of elected offices Republicans won in the 1970s.

These divisions and philosophies did not mean that the ideologues were unaffected by or ignorant of the changes wrought by black enfranchisement. As Joseph Crespino has shown, conservative Mississippians accepted the reality of black suffrage and made a "subtle and strategic accommodation" to the reality of federal civil rights enforcement. This accommodation did not mean the ideologues gave up resistance; instead, it became part of the "conservative counterrevolution" that enshrined states' rights and white elite privilege in a nonracial discourse.[6] The ideologues gave lip service to black outreach but held it in far less esteem than did their more moderate Republicans. These developments were replicated in other areas of the South and became part of the "silent majority" that developed from the suburban conservatism of the 1960s and 1970s.[7] The counterrevolution was by no means uncontested within the party, however. As Jason Sokol has demonstrated, the acceptance of the civil rights movement by whites was a contested process with no single vision.[8] In effect, the Voting Rights Act and the enfranchisement of black Mississippians created in the state GOP the same conservative-moderate split that divided the national Republican Party in the 1960s and 1970s.

Rubel Phillips, who had run as a Republican for governor in 1963, returned to challenge John Bell Williams in 1967. Unlike his 1963 campaign, he ran as a progressive and racial moderate, blaming Jim Crow for the state's economic underdevelopment. He became the first candidate in modern Mississippi to solicit black leaders through a mailing campaign. Phillips realized that a simple racist appeal would not win him the election, but his black outreach still had its limits. When the state MFDP endorsed Phillips as more palatable than his segregationist opponent, Phillips, conscious of the need for white votes, distanced himself from the mostly black organization, but the damage was done. Phillips received less than 30 percent of the statewide vote, although he did well in some of the black-majority counties and won majorities in some black precincts. However, his failure to take even MFDP strongholds like Holmes County with an anti-segregation position foreshadowed the difficulty the Republican Party would have wooing black voters with moderate positions.[9]

Clarke Reed, who became the chair of the state GOP in 1966, personified the pragmatist wing of the state GOP and its ambivalent balancing act with black voters. The Greenville businessman clashed with civil rights activists like Fannie Lou Hamer and Charles Evers, but he lacked a strong conservative identity. In 1968 he helped swing the presidential nomination to Richard Nixon against the wishes of delegates like Prentiss Walker, who wanted to nominate California governor Ronald Reagan. Reed swayed the right wing of the Mississippi GOP by assuring them that Nixon would move slowly on school desegregation.[10]

Reed's position as the state chairman of the Southern Association of Republicans increased his political influence and thus his pragmatism. He had a warm relationship with Harry Dent, President Nixon's southern political strategist, and advised him on ways to increase GOP gains in the South. Reed had to deal with conservatives angry over school desegregation as well as to attract black voters to craft a conservative but not racist image of the party. He told Dent to make sure that HEW's civil rights division did not answer any queries from white Mississippians "bitching" about school desegregation. "The letterhead alone makes the recipients see red and starts them screaming," he warned. Dent in turn advised Reed on black outreach and set up meetings with Reed and black Republicans. Pragmatists like Reed and the progressives hoped to benefit from a schism in the Democratic Party, where white state Democrats held all the important political offices but were not recognized by the national Democrats (the so-called Regulars) and the mostly black Loyalist Democrats enjoyed national recognition but held few political offices.[11]

If the pragmatic Reed valued victory over ideological purity, that sentiment was not shared by William Mounger of Jackson, the party's finance chairman. Mounger had amassed a fortune as an oil and gas developer and represented the pro-business and antiregulatory outlook of the conservative ideologues. An avid admirer of Barry Goldwater, Mounger opposed "New Deal giveaways" and business regulation. He called himself a "small-government Republican" and had begun raising money for the state party in the early 1960s.[12]

On racial matters, Mounger cloaked his statements in the ostensibly nonracial rhetoric of states' rights. He was not a Ross Barnett demagogue or even a Wirt Yerger when it came to statements on race, and he accepted the need for some integration when he named three black members to the Hinds County Republican Party Executive Committee. However, he defended states' rights despite the negative associations the phrase conjured, even to the point of insisting that the word "sovereign" be kept in the 1968 state party platform. He declared that northern pro–civil rights Democrats "lacked any real understanding of the social pressures weighing down the southern states." He opposed civil rights enforcement, especially what he called the "Gestapo-like" ruling by the IRS denying tax-exempt status to racially exclusive private schools.[13]

GOP leaders showed their skittishness about interracialism by refusing to participate in the major state races in 1971. When Meridian businessman Gil Carmichael told GOP officials that he planned to run for lieutenant governor, they talked him out of the race for fear that white Mississippians would associate his candidacy and the Republican Party with Charles Evers's independent gubernatorial campaign. No GOP candidate for governor ran either, preventing a split in the white vote that might have elected Evers.[14]

Carmichael emerged as the Republican standard-bearer of the 1970s and a leader of the progressive wing of the party. A Volkswagen dealer from Meridian, he described himself as a "progressive conservative" who championed economic development. In 1972 he challenged Senator Jim Eastland, and like Rubel Phillips, he blamed the state Democrats for Mississippi's poverty. Carmichael, who also served on the advisory committee to the U.S. Commission on Civil Rights, worked to reach two very different groups of voters. His campaign staffers contacted prominent black leaders and businessmen to try to garner black voters while also soliciting the aid of white supporters of segregationist politicians like George Wallace. Carmichael had little help from the GOP organization, demonstrated vividly when the Nixon White House publicly snubbed him by excluding him from a Jackson rally headlined by Vice President Spiro Agnew.[15]

One of Carmichael's chief Republican backers was, ironically, Billy Mounger. The party finance chairman did not like Carmichael, and complained about his desire for publicity and "ingratitude." Unlike Wirt Yerger, who was suspicious of Carmichael's moderation, Mounger put more faith at this time in the Republican candidate and raised funds for him. Mounger believed that Nixon had treated Carmichael poorly at the Agnew rally and felt bound by party loyalty to his fellow Mississippian.[16]

Carmichael's campaign worried Eastland enough to force the aging Sunflower County planter to actively campaign, even to the point of dispatching a representative to black college campuses running ads in the state's black newspaper, the *Jackson Advocate*. Eastland later complained that "that son of a bitch cost my friends a half million dollars" in the last month of the election, but Eastland won with a majority of 58.1 percent. Carmichael won eleven counties, but only two were black-majority. Despite increased black voter registration since the 1960s and Eastland's white-supremacist history, Carmichael could not siphon significant numbers of black Loyalist Democrats into the Republican camp.[17]

Other Republicans did have some success in winning black votes. Two Republicans, Thad Cochran and Trent Lott, ran for congressional seats in 1972. Lott, a Pascagoula lawyer who ran in the Fifth District, did not make any significant bid for black votes, since his district did not have a single county with a black majority. Cochran, a Jackson attorney who ran in the Fourth District in southwestern Mississippi, actively campaigned for black votes, a strategy no doubt influenced by the 43 percent black population of the district. Mounger had no quarrel with this strategy and raised the majority of Cochran's campaign funds.[18]

Cochran's strategy included hiring a black aide, but the independent candidacy of Eddie L. McBride, a black minister, aided the Republican lawyer far more. McBride did not win a single county but received more than eleven thousand votes, while Cochran defeated white Democrat Ellis Bodron by a plurality of less than six thousand votes. A black spoiler clearly had more of an effect on the Republican victory than efforts to attract blacks to the GOP. Upper- and middle-class white suburbanites in Jackson, not African Americans, formed the base of Cochran's support in 1972 and in future elections. The "upwardly mobile new reactionaries," as some observers called them, gave Cochran Hinds County by a 57 percent majority. Bodron was no moderate and a product of the segregationist state Democrats, so Cochran did have some pull with a minority of black voters, and in his successful 1974 reelection, he polled a near-majority in Wilkinson County and 42 percent of the vote in Claiborne and Jefferson Counties, all majority-black counties. Cochran's willingness to speak before black audiences and his lack of a segregationist past, since he was a political neophyte and tabula rasa, also aided him in a state where Democrats had openly championed segregation in the recent past and voter discrimination still plagued African Americans at the polls.[19]

The 1975 governor's election led to the healing of the divided Democratic Party before the GOP made significant gains in Mississippi, an action that would weaken the efforts of the GOP progressives. Cliff Finch, a Batesville trial lawyer and former Ross Barnett supporter, embraced a populist-style campaign for governor after winning the Democratic primary. Observers commented that Finch's campaigning resembled that of Alabama governor George Wallace, but unlike Wallace, Finch openly sought black votes. Finch hired black staffers and won the endorsement of prominent black Democrats, but he also received behind-the-scenes support from Klansmen and other segregationists.[20]

Finch likely campaigned for black support because his opponents did the same. Although Henry Jay Kirksey, a sixty-year-old black cartographer and former MFDP member, opposed Finch with an independent campaign, his efforts drew little support. Finch's more serious threat in the campaign for black votes came from his Republican opponent, Gil Carmichael. Carmichael, as he did against Eastland in 1972, ran as a progressive who championed economic development and an end to the cheap export of the state's natural resources. Harry Dent, as part of his strategy for building a viable southern GOP, encouraged Carmichael to run for governor. Carmichael also backed a number of progressive issues, including a new constitution, ratification of the Equal Rights Amendment (ERA), compulsory school attendance, reduced punishment for marijuana possession, and handgun licensing. The last issue, which he proposed in the wake of the two attempts to assassinate President Gerald Ford, cost him some support with white voters and alienated more conservative Republicans like Clarke Reed. His issues-oriented campaign, which he put forth in both personal campaigning and television ads produced by campaign strategist Walter De Vries, contrasted with the vague economic proposals and rhetoric of Finch.[21]

Race remained a significant issue in the election, but not in the same manner as past gubernatorial races. With the absence of race-baiting or a major black gubernatorial candidate, both men freely campaigned for the black vote and sought to create black-white coalitions to help them into office. Carmichael countered Finch's black endorsements by employing state representative Robert Clark, the first black representative elected under the Voting Rights Act, on his strategy committee. Carmichael had also cultivated goodwill with black residents in Meridian when he hired black salesmen at his car dealership in 1968. He also became the first gubernatorial candidate in Mississippi history to visit the all-black town of Mound Bayou.[22]

State representative Robert Clark became one of Carmichael's most prominent supporters and the front man for his outreach to black Mississippians. Clark saw himself not as joining the GOP but as trying to broaden political and economic opportunities for black people. He said that Carmichael's election would "force the [Democratic] party to . . . include all the people." He cited Carmichael's record in Meridian and his pledge to hire blacks and the poor in state agencies. Clark used strong racial imagery, telling black voters that they "can't afford to be a slave to a party."[23]

Carmichael's campaign, which marked the peak of the GOP progressives, exacerbated the Republican intraparty schisms and eventually carried over into the national convention the following year. The pragmatists reluctantly supported Carmichael or at least did not oppose him. Cochran stayed neutral, while Reed swallowed his disdain for Carmichael's positions and said that "for some reason I don't understand, it [the campaign] seems to be working." Some conservative ideologues finally began to break with Carmichael, either publicly or privately. Billy Mounger opposed the proposal for a new state constitution and pressed Carmichael to hire Reagan associate Lyn Nofziger to run his campaign, but Carmichael resisted both efforts. Although he raised money for the campaign, Mounger later recalled that he became "progressively disillusioned" with Carmichael's liberal platform, but he did not publicly voice his concerns. When Carmichael, at De Vries's urging, endorsed handgun registration, Mounger quit the campaign. Still convinced that Carmichael was going to win, Mounger wrote a letter on election night renouncing any links to the candidate. Specifically, he cited Carmichael's support of the ERA, handgun registration, and a new constitution as evidence of his "ineptitude" and "Teddy Kennedy appeal to liberals."[24]

Mounger did not voice an opinion on Carmichael's black outreach, instead opting to frame his critiques in ideological terms. Support of the old Constitution of 1890, which had been created specifically to disfranchise black voters, had racial undertones, however. Voting irregularities and intimidation continued to hamstring black voters in 1975, and the Justice Department continued to deploy examiners to investigate reports of harassment and other irregularities. For the November 1975 election, nineteen counties in the state received federal observers.[25]

With the exception of Clark, Carmichael's efforts did not sway most prominent black political and civil rights figures in Mississippi. NAACP president Aaron Henry publicly endorsed Finch in an open letter to the press but did not even mention Carmichael by name. Henry criticized the GOP as an institution that "has fostered programs that now has all America teetering on the brink of economic, social, and moral decline." He flatly stated that Finch was not his first choice for governor but that he needed black help "to withstand the forces that still exist . . . that would advise him to return to a policy of racism."[26]

GOP conservatives like Mounger avoided racial issues, and Reed said that race was "not even a Mickey Mouse issue anymore" in Mississippi, but some ideological conservatives linked their critiques of Carmichael's liberalism to race. Prentiss Walker, the former congressman, ran a column in the *Clarion-Ledger* blasting Carmichael as "a real discredit to all the true Republican principles." Walker referred to Carmichael's call for handgun registration, but he also attacked the Meridian businessman's proposal for a new state constitution. Walker said that Carmichael would rewrite the constitution "under the direction of Senators [Edward] Brooke and [Jacob] Javits," two liberal northern Republicans (Brooke was the only black U.S. senator).[27]

Walker made the racial nature of his attack more explicit when he invoked memories of the Lost Cause, charging that Carmichael and his associates had "reestablished the old school of Radical Republicanism" in Mississippi. Mississippi Republicans had routinely launched attacks on their liberal northern counterparts, such as when Reed criticized Javits's poverty tour in the Mississippi Delta with Robert Kennedy in 1967. Nor was the bugbear of their Radical Reconstruction ancestors off-limits to Mississippi Republicans. Rubel Phillips expropriated the rhetoric of Ross Barnett in 1963 when he accused the Democratic Party of mimicking the Radical program of the 1870s.[28] Yet the vitriol of Walker's attack harkened back to 1960s Mississippi political discourse; it was also unique in that it was a public attack by one Mississippi Republican on another. Walker's conjuring the ghost of Radical Republicanism against a colleague openly appealing to black voters indicated that some of the ideological conservatives did not want even the appearance of integration in 1975.

A few days after Walker's advertisement, the *Clarion-Ledger* ran another anti-Carmichael ad, this one paid for by a Finch supporter. The ad made no specific reference to race, but it had a very clear pro-segregationist slant in its attack on "Carmichael the cunning." It blasted the national Republican Party and said that Mississippi Democrats "have, since 1948, been in the leadership of all the states in voting independently and for their own rights. . . . [W]e voted Strom Thurmond and Fielding Wright, for Eisenhower, Goldwater, and Nixon. We voted unpledged and for George Wallace." The ad painted Carmichael as the thrall of liberal New York Republicans and said that "Republicanism, like the serpent in the Garden of Eden, comes to us in these latter days full of oily words and soothing assurances." It called on voters to "crush the serpent!" Democrats as well as Republicans could invoke Republican racial moderation in an effort to win segregationist votes.[29]

Carmichael ran a strong race, but Finch won 52.2 percent to Carmichael's 45.1 percent. Finch's populist appeal, along with the traditional identification of black voters to the Democratic Party, gave him 80 percent of the black vote. Finch won sixty-six of eighty-two counties, including most of the predominantly black counties, while Carmichael only won two black-majority counties. Black voters were too firmly entrenched in the state Democratic Party to go to the GOP in 1975. Carmichael made sincere appeals for the black vote, but since the state Republicans had done little substantive groundwork before him, they could not make many inroads. Leslie Burl McLemore, a former MFDP member and black political science professor who supported Carmichael, said that the Republicans had needed to "work on people over time" if they wanted a victory in 1975.[30]

Despite Carmichael's disappointing showing among black voters, the GOP still made serious attempts to woo them after 1975. In 1977, with James Eastland's Senate seat up for election next year, Carmichael and state Republican chairman Charles Pickering both entertained a run. Pickering, a rising star in the party, had won election in 1971 as the first Republican state senator from Jones County since the nineteenth century. Although more conservative than Carmichael, Pickering showed his pragmatism when he solicited black leaders and their votes, a tactic he would try in later elections. Both men courted black state leaders at the NAACP's annual state conference in 1977. The meeting occurred as black leaders in the state began to publicly express their dissatisfaction with the Finch administration over poor minority representation in state offices.[31]

Yet the Republicans, much like Finch in 1975, played both sides of the racial divide in Mississippi. Eastland's Senate seat became an open race when the elderly planter announced his retirement from politics. Thad Cochran and Pickering both announced their candidacy for the GOP nomination. Charles Evers, the black mayor of Fayette, broke with the state Democrats and ran as an independent for the open seat. An Evers victory seemed possible with a black plurality and a divided white electorate. With that in mind, Frank Montague, a Hattiesburg attorney, urged Pickering and Cochran to campaign for black votes to deny Evers a unified black vote. At the same time, he suggested they play to racial fears by reminding white voters that their low turnout could mean a black senator.[32]

Cochran easily defeated Pickering in the Republican primary and moved to attract black voters in the general election. Cochran's conservative record in the House was not very different from that of his fellow Republican Trent Lott or his three Democratic colleagues. All five representatives voted against busing, voted to restrict civil rights lawsuits filed by lawyers for the Legal Services Corporation, and voted to import chrome from Ian Smith's white-minority government in Rhodesia, even though the country was under international sanctions. Yet perhaps the most telling votes concerned suffrage. Despite the increase in black voter registration since 1965, all five representatives opposed the renewal of the Voting Rights Act in 1975. They also voted against the establishment of a nationwide voter registration system to increase voter registration. Outreach to black voters, regardless of the party, had its limits.[33]

Cochran's limited black support and outreach, built during his House campaigns, gave him a veneer of moderation and pragmatism by 1978 that Lott, Mounger, and other conservatives did not possess. Cochran could also look to the recent GOP candidacy of Doug Shanks, who won 46 percent of black voters in Jackson during his failed bid to become mayor of the city. The "Cochran Black Operation," as the congressman's campaign dubbed its outreach, was a similarly structured campaign to get the black vote, funding advertising and fielding a network of black county coordinators, canvassers, and speakers. The Cochran campaign believed that well-educated blacks would be more likely to vote Republican, so it aimed in particular at blacks with high school diplomas and college educations.[34]

Evers's campaign lagged in fund-raising, trailing both Cochran and Maurice Dantin, the Democratic nominee. But Evers helped by siphoning off critical black votes from Dantin. Cochran himself acknowledged the help Evers was giving him by splitting the Democratic vote and said that "if I had to write a script, I couldn't have done a better job."[35] On election day, Dantin received 31.8 percent of the vote while Evers took 22.9 percent, but Cochran won with a 45 percent plurality. The Fayette mayor drew over 133,000 votes, more than enough to cost Dantin the election. Dantin clearly had a significant number of black votes, since he ran competitively or led in the majority-black Delta counties, but the pull Evers had with black voters proved too much for the Columbia attorney.[36]

With a Republican senator now representing Mississippi in Washington, the question that loomed for the 1979 elections was whether the GOP would take the governor's mansion as well. Carmichael prepared another run for the governor's office, but he now faced opposition from the ideological wing of his party over his moderate views. Conservatives in the Mississippi GOP had opposed Carmichael in 1975, but they had kept quiet for the sake of party unity. After Carmichael's loss to Cliff Finch, all of that changed.[37]

The conservative and moderate factions in the state party erupted into a nasty public squabble at the Republican National Convention in Kansas City in 1976. Carmichael backed the nomination of Gerald Ford while Billy Mounger became the state chairman for Ronald Reagan, who challenged the incumbent president. Within the Mississippi GOP, the moderates backed Ford while the conservative ideologues supported Reagan. The state delegation was officially uncommitted, but the Ford campaign diverted its resources elsewhere after Reagan's string of victories in the southern primaries. Yet Harry Dent, the architect of Nixon's Southern Strategy and now a Ford adviser, saw a chance for Ford to win the state's winner-take-all primary by reaching out to the pragmatists, especially Clarke Reed.[38]

Reed had reason to be dissatisfied with Ford, in particular over civil rights issues. As chairman of the Southern Association of Republican State Chairmen, Reed continued to try to exert influence on Ford, just as he had done with Nixon on school desegregation. However, Ford waffled over extending the Voting Rights Act in 1975 to all fifty states, a position Reed supported and also sponsored by Senator John Stennis (D-Miss.). Ford's clumsy endorsement of Reed's position and his subsequent retraction in the wake of liberal Republican concerns angered Reed and led some observers to brand Ford incompetent.[39]

Ford backer Gil Carmichael was a state delegate at the convention and provided intelligence to Dent, giving him information on the delegates so that he could contact and pressure them. Dent said that Reed, despite his conservatism, understood the importance of winning, while one conservative less kindly described Reed as weak "because he wanted to please everybody."[40]

The Dent strategy of working on the pragmatists showed how fluid and circumstantial some of these ideological categories were in the Mississippi Republican Party. Reed wanted to maintain influence by supporting the winner, even if it meant a less conservative nominee, and Dent played to Reed's ambition. Yet Dent also worked on state senator and party chairman Charles Pickering, even arranging a personal audience with Ford. Pickering, a conservative whom Mounger liked and supported, eventually backed Reagan even though he did consider switching his support to Ford.[41]

Mounger used his clout as the party's chief fund-raiser to keep the delegates aligned with Reagan. Mounger had already broken privately with Carmichael, but Reed's vacillation particularly infuriated Mounger, who put a high value on loyalty. In 1975 Reed had encouraged Reagan to run for president, so Mounger interpreted Reed's wavering as a personal betrayal of both Reagan and conservative principles. Reed finally abandoned Reagan when he picked a liberal, Senator Richard Schweiker (R-Penn.), to be his running mate, declaring Schweiker unpalatable, but in reality Reed was looking for an excuse to back Ford. Yet Mounger, despite his distaste for Schweiker, stayed loyal to Reagan, reasoning that a liberal vice president was tolerable as long as the conservative Reagan headed the ticket. The ideological splits carried over to other prominent state GOP figures as well. Ideologues like Wirt Yerger and Trent Lott backed Reagan, while the pragmatist Cochran favored Ford. While Pickering worked to keep the peace at the convention, fallout from the Ford-Reagan feud would also have implications for the state GOP and the direction it would take with black voters.[42]

With the party divisions now publicly laid open after Kansas City, the GOP struggle over black voters became more visible as a key component of the ideological clashes. Carmichael said that his goal was to make sure the Republican Party did not become "lily white and hard right." The conservative faction in the party, by implication, wanted to do the opposite. The Mounger faction of conservative ideologues did not make open appeals to segregationists or use other forms of overt race-baiting as Prentiss Walker and Rubel Phillips did in the first half of the 1960s. Sensitive to charges of racism, they had adopted the nonracist discourse of the New Right discussed by scholars like Joseph Crespino, Matthew Lassiter, and Kevin Kruse. While more astute than Walker had been in his 1975 attack on Carmichael, the ideologues' actions betrayed little interest in party integration. Mounger generally did not support other Republicans who made interracial appeals, and in some cases he actively opposed them, as in the case of Doug Shanks's 1977 bid for mayor of Jackson.[43]

Mounger defended conservative doctrine against another campaign by Carmichael. Carmichael prepared another run for the governor's office in 1979, but Mounger and Yerger rallied Leon Bramlett, a wealthy Clarksdale cotton planter, to oppose him. Bramlett, a former chairman of the Regular Democrats, had opposed fusion with the mostly black Loyalists and switched to the GOP shortly after Cliff Finch's election in 1975, citing "quotas and preferential treatment" as a source of his discontent.[44]

Carmichael won in a close primary victory and faced Lieutenant Governor William Winter, who won the Democratic nomination. Carmichael repeated his earlier theme of economic development, declaring that he would attract high-paying industrial jobs to the state. In speeches before black audiences, he echoed Evers's theme of replacing social programs with jobs. He played to anti-welfare sentiment but also declared that he would not cut spending and took pains to deflect the charge that he was an enemy of entitlement programs.[45]

Although the campaign pitted two racial moderates against each other, some lingering racial issues created tensions. Carmichael irritated some black voters by waffling over the issue of busing, and he avoided a firm stand when he predicted that the energy crisis would curtail it. He continued to emphasize his own record on economic issues, namely, his employment of African Americans at his Volkswagen dealership, and then called attention to the lack of black employees at Winter's law firm. Yet Carmichael admitted his own shortcomings when he apologized before an NAACP meeting for his membership in an all-white country club. Carmichael continued his black outreach, especially to ministers, businessmen, and black elected officials. Winter in turn reminded black voters that his moderation likely cost him the governor's race in 1967, when he lost to John Bell Williams.[46]

Carmichael's biggest handicap, as in 1975, remained his Republican Party label. As one black voter put it, the Republicans "don't really want blacks and poor people to join their club, just vote for them." Carmichael solicited help from national conservatives like Reagan, who did not enjoy wide popularity among black people. Mississippi Republican Jon Hinson, who had won election to Cochran's House seat in 1978, also stirred anger from black voters when he opposed a national holiday for Martin Luther King Jr.[47]

Racial matters also surfaced late in the campaign in another statewide race. In the attorney general's race, political observers favored Republican nominee Charles Pickering over the Democrat, Assistant Attorney General Bill Allain. Pickering ran commercials on several black radio stations the weekend before election day that accused Allain of previous membership in the White Citizens' Councils. The ads made a direct reference to Allain's tenure as assistant attorney general from 1962 to 1975, when he represented the state in the *Conner* cases. One of the radio spots said that "in the reapportionment cases, Bill Allain fought equal representation for blacks." The ads misfired, especially when the Citizens' Council allegation proved to be untrue. Pickering backed off from the ads, but the fallout over them created a last-minute backlash giving Allain a narrow victory.[48]

Billy Mounger, who was unaware of the development of the ad campaign, called it "disastrous" and said he would have opposed it. To Mounger, ever attuned to the racial feelings of conservative whites, the ads had the opposite effect and made Allain more palatable to them by linking him to the councils. He made clear the importance of white racial conservatism to the expanding state GOP when he said after the election that "the greatest errors Mississippi Republican candidates commit are those concerning appeals for liberal or black votes." Mounger recognized, as Dan Carter has pointed out about the GOP generally, that the Wallace Democrats were the GOP's "natural constituency" and that in order to win they could "never alienate these groups."[49]

Although avoiding racist commentary, Mounger laid out his party's direction regarding which voters to pursue in clear racial terms. Black voters were welcome, but only if they shared the totality of Mounger's conservatism. Compromise, so abhorrent to him, would not be tolerated for the sake of party biracialism. Regarding the memory of the civil rights movement, Mounger saw even a rhetorical condemnation of the state's past as undesirable. The wooing of Wallace voters rested squarely on race, as Mounger and other ideologues were opposed to the populist economic agenda of Wallace and instead backed the pro-corporate orientation of the national New Right.

Mounger no doubt felt his views vindicated when Carmichael lost again, with dire consequences for the GOP moderates. On election day, William Winter easily won with 413,000 votes to Carmichael's 263,000. Carmichael failed to carry a single majority-black county; he did not even get the support of some Bramlett Republicans, who voted for Winter or not at all out of their dislike for the Republican nominee.[50] The defeat of Carmichael marked the permanent decline of the moderate wing of the state Republican Party. With the exception of Cochran, GOP pragmatists largely drifted away from interracial outreach.[51]

The Democrats' own problems with race still encouraged some Republicans to make overtures to black voters. In 1980, Governor Winter created a major rift in the state party when he sought to end the biracial chairmanship of the party and appoint a white party head, ostensibly to stymie the movement of white voters to the Republicans. Black Republicans used the Democrats' woes to successfully push for the election of three black alternate delegates to the Republican National Convention by warning of a similar schism erupting in their own party. Mike Retzer, the GOP party chairman and a pragmatist, tried to reap political gain from the Democratic problems by calling for black Mississippians to join the party, but *Clarion-Ledger* reporter Jo Ann Klein dubbed this the GOP's "annual request for blacks." The state GOP sent an all-white delegation to the national convention in 1980, and only three of the twenty-two alternates were black, while the Democratic delegation that year was 34 percent black. Although Retzer accused the Democrats of taking black voters for granted, he refused to endorse a biracial chairmanship for his party, which had no black members on its executive committee.[52] Party ideologues would likely interpret such an approach as racial quotas, which had prompted whites like Leon Bramlett to leave the Democratic Party.

The nomination of Ronald Reagan for president in 1980 satisfied Republican conservatives in Mississippi, who knew the former California governor could attract white southern support. Although black voters were not completely written off in heavily black districts, the Mississippi GOP's limitations on race did not make the party attractive enough for black voters to bolt the Democratic Party, and most stayed with Jimmy Carter. Reagan did not help his standing with black Mississippians when in August 1980 he campaigned at the Neshoba County Fair in Philadelphia, site of the notorious "Freedom Summer" murders in 1964. He had come at the urging of Representative Trent Lott and other Republicans, who felt an appearance could carry the state for Reagan. Carter lost the state by a narrow margin that fall, and lost the election nationally.[53]

A few black Mississippians did make a home in the Republican Party by 1980. The state's Black Republican Council had twelve county chapters by 1980 but only a few hundred members. Like some of the black candidates in the 1960s and 1970s, its members saw themselves less as ideological party loyalists than as activists for their race who believed that an overwhelming black vote for the Democratic Party would lead white politicians to take them for granted. Wilbur Colom, a Columbus attorney and spokesman for the council, criticized "blind loyalty" to the Democratic Party but refrained from attacking black Democrats and called for "structured participation by blacks in both parties." While Colom embraced the economic conservatism of the Republicans, he saw a viable effort by the GOP to win black votes as a way to create meaningful competition for the black vote and thus improve the political status of the African American community. He and other black Republicans reasoned that an independent black vote would only benefit the black community and increase its political influence.[54]

Later attempts at party integration still met the fierce resistance of Mounger. He opposed the renewal of the Voting Rights Act in 1982, telling Reagan it was an "inequitable, invidious, and iniquitous" law. He again dismissed black votes for Republicans, insisting that "they are only for sale through government handouts." In another sign of the rift between him and Thad Cochran over ideology and black outreach, Mounger blasted a proposal from Cochran to add five black Republican delegates to the state party's executive committee, calling it "incestuous proliferation" and "worse than any quota." He admitted that the party needed to attract black voters, but he felt the integration of the executive committee violated conservative principles. Mounger's rhetoric, while ostensibly nonracist, was laden with the racial anxieties of white segregationists and certainly not a color-blind discourse or ideology. The overt hostility of conservatives like Mounger to the institutionalization of racial progress cannot be deemed nonracial in tone or rhetoric, despite what some scholars have argued.[55]

The failure of the moderates in 1979 and the victory of Reagan in 1980 was the death knell of major black outreach by the Mississippi GOP. Although individual candidates continued the efforts, the party preferred the ever-increasing numbers of defecting white Democrats. The second "Great White Switch" of white southern Democrats by the 1980s to a partisan identification with the Republican Party, combined with a comparable black identification with the Democratic Party, ended the efforts of the moderates.[56]

Although the Mississippi GOP had decisively moved toward appealing to the old George Wallace Democrats by the 1980s, the federal government under Ronald Reagan did not always take the same path, to the annoyance of the state party's conservative ideologues. In reapportionment cases during the 1970s and 1980s, civil rights lawyers and black plaintiffs fought against discriminatory gerrymandering, but they experienced limited success until the passage of the strengthened Voting Rights Act in 1982. Mississippi's black voters then found an unlikely ally in the Reagan administration. The federal government's intervention in 1983 greatly increased black representation on the county boards of supervisors and removed yet another mechanism of vote dilution in Mississippi.

The 410 elected county supervisors were among the most powerful local offices in the state's eighty-two counties, controlling road and bridge construction and other public works, but severe malapportionment from demographic changes affected many supervisors' districts. After the Supreme Court ruled in 1969 in *Allen v. State Board of Elections* that the Voting Rights Act covered not just obstacles to voting but also schemes like at-large elections, many Mississippi counties shifted to gerrymandering their single-member districts to prevent or limit the election of black supervisors. Boards of supervisors devised plans that "cracked" black voting strength among several districts to prevent a black majority, or "stacked" white population areas onto black-majority districts to dilute black votes.[57]

Black county residents, with the aid of civil rights attorneys, challenged the new gerrymandering in the courts. Although they filed a series of lawsuits, most notably in Hinds County, they had mixed success, since they often could not prove discriminatory intent in the crafting of the gerrymandering plans. They received a major boost in 1982 when Congress debated strengthened vote dilution standards in the extension of the Voting Rights Act. A bipartisan group of voting supporters introduced an amendment to section two of the act to prohibit any practice "which results in a denial or abridgement" of the right to vote. The change, known as the results test, meant that future suits would be able to focus less on proving racist intent in local governments and election systems and more on effect, regardless of the original circumstances of the examined law or system. Although the proposed change clearly rejected proportional representation, it did utilize the "totality of circumstances" that the courts had established in voting bias cases instead of focusing on narrow remedies.[58]

Prominent conservatives opposed the strengthened section two. William Bradford Reynolds, the head of Reagan's Civil Rights Division, called the revised section "a proportional representations scheme . . . inconsistent with the democratic traditions of our pluralist society." The results test stayed intact, however, and on June 29, 1982, President Reagan signed the renewal into law, extending the Voting Rights Act by twenty-five years and with provisions even stronger than the original 1965 act.[59]

In the spring of 1983, black residents in Bolivar County lobbied the Justice Department to reject the county's redistricting plan, charging that it fragmented black voting power. Local activists received a boost when the Reverend Jesse Jackson arrived in the Mississippi Delta in early June 1983 as part of a voter registration campaign targeting seven southern states. Jackson coordinated the campaign as a precursor to his formal announcement of candidacy for the Democratic presidential nomination in 1984. He criticized lingering barriers in Mississippi such as dual registration, where a voter had to register separately for municipal and county elections. This system, he charged, handicapped poor, black, and rural voters by requiring them to travel to separate locations to register.[60]

When Jackson returned to Mississippi in mid-June, he had a powerful and unlikely companion. Reynolds, head of the Civil Rights Division, seemed to be the last person that would appear publicly with the liberal black preacher. Reynolds, dubbed by one critic "the iceman," was a former corporate lawyer who had alienated the nation's civil rights lobby through his enforcement of Reagan's conservative civil rights policies. Probably his most controversial stance was his fervent opposition to affirmative action programs, which he said "bestowed benefits on people who are not victims of discrimination at the expense of those who have done no wrong at all." He also lacked strong voting rights credentials. In 1982 he urged the Reagan administration to side with an all-white county government in Georgia in a voting discrimination suit. Many Carter-era Justice Department attorneys, including many of the black lawyers in civil rights enforcement, left the administration rather than continue working under Reynolds.[61]

Reynolds's visit may have been motivated by political factors. Although he came at the invitation of Jackson, Reynolds also arrived the week before a scheduled visit by President Reagan. The timing of the visit drew criticism from state Democratic Party chairman Danny Cupit, who called the trip an attempt to interfere in the August Democratic primary. Jackson accompanied Reynolds on a two-day trip across the Delta. At each stop, Reynolds heard local African Americans give testimony of the problems they encountered trying to register and vote, including stories of economic intimidation of black workers by plantation owners and factory managers. White employers used methods such as required overtime and no lunch breaks on election day to prevent voting, and one woman reported an eviction of a black family from a plantation for voting.[62]

Throughout the two days, Reynolds remained noncommittal on what course he would take. Still, he commented that "the ability to register is not as open and accessible as it might be." He recalled numerous and blatant voting irregularities in the Delta and said that some of the "subtle gerrymandering [was] not so subtle." After his return to Washington, Reynolds ordered federal voting registrars into five majority-black counties. He also declared that the Voting Rights Act "is the most precious civil rights legislation ever passed," a marked change from his criticism of portions of the act during the previous year.[63]

Reynolds's actions drew quick condemnation from Representative Webb Franklin of the Second Congressional District, which encompassed the majority-black Delta. Franklin, a white Republican who had won his seat in a racially charged election against black state representative Robert Clark the previous year, had little sympathy for any effort to increase black voter registration in his majority-black district.[64] Reynolds took criticism from the national civil rights establishment as well. Lani Guinier, a former Justice Department lawyer now with the NAACP Legal Defense and Educational Fund, said that the trip was not "an indication that [Reynolds] has seen the light." With the exception of a brief story in *Newsweek* and some coverage in major newspapers like the *Washington Post*, the trip garnered relatively little national attention. When President Reagan came to Jackson the Monday following Reynolds's trip, he made no public mention of Reynolds's visit.[65]

Reynolds objected to thirty-six Mississippi redistricting plans in all, most of them after his June trip. Much of the push for him to act came from the twenty-eight county redistricting lawsuits that black voters and civil rights lawyers filed. Lawsuits delayed many of the elections and led to federal court orders that halted the August supervisors' elections in fourteen counties on the grounds of unconstitutional district lines, an action that Webb Franklin sharply criticized. After the counties held the delayed elections in 1984, the number of black supervisors in the state more than doubled, from twenty-seven to forty-seven. Most of the growth came in counties without black majorities, which marked the first black representation that many African Americans enjoyed in their home counties. Black-majority Madison County and white-majority Pike County made the most dramatic gains, going from zero black supervisors to two apiece. Humphreys County also increased its black supervisors, from one to three, to give them control of the board, and Holmes County added a black supervisor to gain a majority.[66]

Despite the obvious and tangible gains in black representation from Justice Department and court intervention, a survey of all eighty-two counties showed the limits of legal reform in advancing black electoral power. Many counties that gained black supervisors still had low levels of black representation, and many of the Delta counties with black majorities did not increase their black supervisors over their numbers before the lawsuits. Even though twenty years had passed since the Voting Rights Act became law, seven counties with black populations of 45 percent or higher still had no black representation at all on their boards of supervisors. Not surprisingly, the most heavily black counties usually had the highest numbers of black supervisors, with Holmes, Humphreys, Claiborne, and Jefferson having the heaviest black representation, much of this resulting from earlier civil rights organizing, not the actions of Reynolds. Poverty, much as it had in the 1960s, also contributed to the lagging black representation and limited electoral and legal reform in the era of civil rights enforcement, seen vividly in the defeat of black candidates in Quitman County in 1983.[67]

Despite the limited outcomes, the redrawing of the county supervisors' districts in the early 1980s and Reynolds's 1983 trip raise some curious if unanswered questions. Reynolds's motives for the trip and his swift action to redistrict the counties remain unclear. One theory is that he wanted to exacerbate the racial split in the fragile biracial state Democratic Party. The redistricting affected a statewide Democratic primary and pitted white incumbent Democrats against black Democrats, so any fissure could only help the Republicans who would profit from further white defections from the Democratic Party, a charge made by political scientist Abigail Thernstrom. She charged that Republicans favored redistricting that drew up majority-black districts since such plans also created heavily white districts that favored white conservative candidates.[68]

Reynolds could also have been trying to boost Jesse Jackson's candidacy by building a stronger black base and viable candidacy for him so that the national Democratic Party would face a racially divisive presidential nomination process in 1984 and help Reagan's reelection. That is exactly what Jackson's candidacy did to former vice president Walter Mondale in 1984. Many southern whites, inflamed or frightened by Jackson's campaign and his eventual support for Mondale, turned out in large numbers to defeat the Democratic ticket. The 3 million new southern white voters who voted in 1984 overwhelmed the 1.3 million new southern black voters whom Jackson's campaign had helped to register.[69]

Reynolds's actions may also have been what Frank Parker called "the national consensus on voting rights." Parker argued that in the years after the enactment of Voting Rights Act, a broad-based consensus that crossed partisan lines developed to protect minority voting rights. The act won extensions from bipartisan coalitions in Congress despite the attempts of Republican presidents to weaken it. In the case of all four extensions, a Republican president signed them into law, and their Justice Departments enforced the act. The Supreme Court contributed to the consensus by expanding interpretations of what constituted vote dilution and discrimination. Voting rights protections, Parker argued, do not raise the same emotional white opposition as affirmative action and busing. While white officials on the state and local level continued to obstruct political access in various ways, national pressure from Congress and the Justice Department remedied the situation. Reynolds, as a national figure in the Reagan administration, had come to share the views of the voting rights consensus. Legal precedent and his job as an enforcer of the law likely pushed him in this direction despite his earlier objections to the 1982 amendments.[70]

Reynolds denied any ulterior motives, however, and pointed out that conservatives criticized him for his appearances with Jackson. He said that the trip had been an "eye opener" that revealed the continuing problems of racial voting discrimination.[71] According to him, local officials' actions proved their intent to discriminate on race, a clear violation of the original intent of the Voting Rights Act. Reynolds could then enforce the law but still legitimately criticize the broadened provisions of the 1982 extension as an overreaching of the act's 1965 boundaries.

Whatever the reason for his actions, Reynolds profited little from his redistricting orders. His nomination by Reagan to be associate attorney general in the summer of 1985 failed to make it out of committee. The national press made almost no mention of his actions in Mississippi two years earlier, and even his defenders in conservative publications like *National Review* did not point to the change he wrought in numerous Mississippi counties, instead praising his opposition to racial quotas. Reynolds stayed on as head of the Civil Rights Division for the rest of the Reagan administration and continued to serve as a lightning rod for criticism from the civil rights lobby. Despite his positions on other civil rights measures, his intervention on behalf of black voters greatly increased black representation in the county governments of Mississippi.[72]

While the state GOP had by the Reagan administration firmly shifted toward the "lily white and hard right" position that Gil Carmichael feared, the Reagan administration's own enforcement of federal civil rights law displeased many of those same state conservatives. The struggle within the state party over black voting as well as the dichotomy between state Republicans and Republican presidential administrations indicate not only the central role race played in the "Great White Shifts" but also the complex and contested processes in the creation of the Republican South.

Notes

1. Neil R. McMillen, *Dark Journey: Black Mississippians in the Age of Jim Crow* (Urbana: University of Illinois Press, 1989), 60–64, 69; John L. Dittmer, *Local People: The Struggle for Civil Rights in Mississippi* (Urbana: University of Illinois Press, 1994), 200–207; Jack Bass and Walter De Vries, *The Transformation of Southern Politics* (New York: Basic Books, 1976), 204; Alexander P. Lamis, *The Two-Party South* (New York: Oxford University Press, 1984), 45–46.

2. Joseph Crespino, *In Search of Another Country: Mississippi and the Conservative Counterrevolution* (Princeton: Princeton University Press, 2007), 84–85, 87; Bruce J. Schulman, *From Cotton Belt to Sunbelt: Federal Policy, Economic Development, and the Transformation of the South, 1938–1980* (New York: Oxford University Press, 1991), 215; résumé of Wirt A. Yerger Jr., Mississippi Republican Party Papers, box H-1, Biographies folder, Special Collections, Mitchell Memorial Library, Mississippi State University, Starkville; Billy Burton Hathorn, "Challenging the Status Quo: Rubel Lex Phillips and the Mississippi Republican Party, 1963–1967," *Journal of Mississippi History* 47, no. 4 (1985): 240–64; Robert Webb, "Kennedy 'Absolved' of Link to Riders," undated newspaper clipping from State Sovereignty Commission Online, SCR ID# 2-140-1-49-1-1-1. For a detailed narrative of the transition from the Black and Tans to the Lily Whites in Mississippi, see Joseph Crespino, "Strategic Accommodation: Civil Rights Opponents in Mississippi and Their Impact on American Racial Politics, 1953–1972" (PhD diss., Stanford University, 2002), 121–29. Crespino's dissertation has been revised into his book *In Search of Another Country*, but the quotes are only in the dissertation and the account of the Black and Tan overthrow is longer. In Mississippi, urban areas are defined as municipalities of ten thousand or more in population. Frank R. Parker, *Black Votes Count: Political Empowerment in Mississippi after 1965* (Chapel Hill: University of North Carolina Press, 1990), 143.

3. Michael Paul Sistrom, "'The Authors of the Liberation': The Mississippi Freedom Democrats and the Redefinition of Politics" (Ph.D. diss., University of North Carolina at Chapel Hill, 2002), 364; "Negroes Eye State Republican Party," *Jackson Advocate*, May 14, 1966; Lamis, *The Two-Party South*, 45–46; *Mississippi Official and Statistical Register, 1968–1972*, 442.

4. Crespino, *In Search of Another Country*, 89; Earl Black and Merle Black, *The Rise of Southern Republicans* (Cambridge: The Belknap Press of Harvard University Press, 2002), 4.

5. Numan V. Bartley, *The Rise of Massive Resistance: Race and Politics in the South during the 1950s* (Baton Rouge: Louisiana State University Press, 1969).

6. Crespino, *In Search of Another Country*, 4.

7. Matthew D. Lassiter, *The Silent Majority: Suburban Politics in the Sunbelt South* (Princeton: Princeton University Press, 2006).

8. Jason Sokol, *There Goes My Everything: White Southerners in the Age of Civil Rights, 1945–1975* (New York: Knopf, 2006), 17.

9. *Hinds County FDP News*, November 3, 1967; Crespino, *In Search of Another Country*, 217–18; Hathorn, "Challenging the Status Quo," 244; Lamis, *The Two-Party South*, 47; Crespino, *In Search of Another Country*, 217–18; "General Election Vote Equals Primary Tally," *Lexington Advertiser*, November 9, 1967.

10. Biography of Clark Thomas Reed, Mississippi Republican Party Papers, box H-1, Biographies folder; Paul Squires to W. T. Wilkins, May 13, 1970, Mississippi Republican Party Papers, box G-1, Census Civil Rights folder; Bruce Galphin, "Miss. GOP Chief Blocked Evers Aid Bill," *Washington Post*, March 20, 1970; Don Oberdorfer, "HEW Approves Grant Requested by Evers," *Washington Post*, May 4, 1970; Crespino, *In Search of Another Country*, 226; Paul Pittman, "Reed Is Facing Trouble on School Desegregation," *Delta Democrat-Times*, February 20, 1969; W. T. Wilkins to Harry Dent, January 6, 1968, Mississippi Republican Party Papers, box G-3, HEW Coahoma County Schools folder; Wilson F. Minor, "Reed: Chicken-fried Machiavellian or Conservative True Believer?" Eyes on Mississippi column, newspaper unknown, July 11, 1976, Wilson F. Minor Papers, box 10, Eyes on Mississippi folder, Special Collections, Mitchell Memorial Library, Mississippi State University, Starkville.

11. Memorandum from Clarke Reed to Harry Dent, February 9, 1970, Harry Dent Papers, box 5, folder 159, Special Collections, Robert Muldrow Cooper Library, Clemson University; memorandum from Harry Dent to Clarke Reed, November 12, 1969, Dent Papers, box 18, folder 456; Harry Dent to Clarke Reed, July 11, 1969, Dent Papers, box 18, folder 456; Harry Dent to Clarke Reed, December 16, 1971, Dent Papers, box 22, folder 506. For an example of Mississippi Republican complaints about school desegregation under Nixon, see James M. Moye to Harry Dent, August 13, 1970, Dent Papers, box 5, folder 159.

12. William D. Mounger and Joe Maxwell, *Amidst the Fray: My Life in Politics, Culture, and Mississippi* (Brandon, Miss.: Quail Ridge Press, 2006), 58, 69–71, 75.

13. Ibid., 64–65, 88, 125, 145, 350, 371. For coverage of the IRS private school decision, which culminated in the *Bob Jones v. U.S.* case, see Crespino, *In Search of Another Country*, 237–66.

14. Gil Carmichael, interview by author, tape recording, Meridian, Mississippi, October 13, 2004.

15. *Mississippi Official and Statistical Register, 1972–1976*, 475, 480; biography of Gilbert Ellzey Carmichael, Mississippi Republican Party Papers, box H-1, Biographies folder; J. F. Barbour III to Tommy Giordano, Gilbert E. Carmichael Papers, 1972 Campaign Correspondence, folder 150, Special Collections Department, Mitchell Memorial Library, Mississippi State University, Starkville; membership card of Gilbert E. Carmichael for the U.S. Commission on Civil Rights, Carmichael Papers, Organizations, folder 16; Bass and De Vries, *The Transformation of Southern Politics*, 214.

16. Mounger and Maxwell, *Amidst the Fray*, 136–39, 141–42, 155.

17. Carmichael interview, October 13, 2004; advertisement for Sen. Jim Eastland, *Jackson Advocate*, May 27. 1972; Jere Nash and Andy Taggart, *Mississippi Politics: The Struggle for Power, 1976–2006* (Jackson: University Press of Mississippi, 2006), 51; Lamis, *The Two-Party South*, 49–50; *Mississippi Official and Statistical Register, 1972–1976*, 480. Bass and De Vries describe Carmichael's black support in 1972 as "substantial," and while he did run strong in some black-majority counties, in others he trailed badly, including most of the black Delta counties. Bass and De Vries, *The Transformation of Southern Politics*, 215; *Mississippi Official and Statistical Register, 1972–1976*, 480. As an example of Meredith's ever-changing political nature, he ran as a Democrat in 1974 in the Fifth Congressional District, but then he withdrew after leading in the first primary and ran as independent in the general election. "Meredith after Winning Withdraws; Dean, Sturgeon in Runoff," *Fayette Chronicle*, June 6, 1974.

18. Hinds had a 39.3 percent black population in 1970 but was the most populous county in the state. Amite and Copiah actually had slight black majorities in 1970 (50.5 and 50.3 percent, respectively), but they had declined to 47.6 and 48.4 percent by 1980. *1970 and 1980 Census of the Population, Vol. 1, General Characteristics of the Population*; Mounger and Maxwell, *Amidst the Fray*, 139, 143.

19. *Mississippi Official and Statistical Register, 1972–1976*, 149–50; Bass and De Vries, *The Transformation of Southern Politics*, 215; *Mississippi Official and Statistical Register, 1976–80*, 432; Michael Barone et al., *The Almanac of American Politics 1978: The Senators, the Representatives, Their Records, States, and Districts* (New York: Dutton, 1977), 466; Leslie Burl McLemore, interview by author, tape recording, November 19, 2004, Oxford, Mississippi. Bass and De Vries completely omit mention of Eddie McBride's independent candidacy and lead the reader to believe that Cochran won his election solely by siphoning black votes away from his Democratic opponent. Lamis gives attention to McBride and credits his 8.2 percent showing with throwing the race to Cochran. Bass and De Vries, *The Transformation of Southern Politics*, 215; Lamis, *The Two-Party South*, 57. For continued reports of voting discrimination in Mississippi in the early 1970s, see Steven F. Lawson, *In Pursuit of Power: Southern Blacks and Electoral Politics, 1965–1982* (New York: Columbia University Press, 1987), 231–33.

20. "The Common Touch," *Newsweek*, September 8, 1975; Bass and De Vries, *The Transformation of Southern Politics*, 216. Winter also had black staffers in his 1975 campaign. R. W. Apple Jr., "Republican Courts Mississippi Blacks," *New York Times*, August 18, 1975; Fred Banks, interview by author, tape recording, Jackson, Mississippi, June 28, 2005.

21. George A. Sewell and Margaret L. Dwight, *Mississippi Black History Makers* (Jackson: University Press of Mississippi, 1977), 79; Jack Elliot, "Kirksey Charges State, Opponents Trying To Keep Him Off Ballot," *Clarion-Ledger*, August 2, 1975; Linda Buford,

"Kirksey Vote: No Counties Won, No Black Support," *Clarion-Ledger*, November 6, 1975; Lamis, *The Two-Party South*, 50–51; Harry Dent to Gil Carmichael, November 13, 1974, Dent Papers, box 25, folder 554; R. W. Apple Jr., "Republican Courts Mississippi Blacks," *New York Times*, August 18, 1975; "New Breezes Blowing On the Old Magnolia," *Time*, November 3, 1975; Roland Evans and Robert Novak, "Carmichael's Mississippi Is Viewed," *Clarion-Ledger*, October 18, 2005; Jack Elliot, "Batesville's Backing Its Man, Finch," *Clarion-Ledger*, November 1, 1975; telephone interview with Gil Carmichael, August 31, 2006.

22. Bass and De Vries, *The Transformation of Southern Politics*, 210; Carmichael interview, October 13, 2004; Walter C. Gough to Gil Carmichael, Carmichael Papers, 1975 Campaign Correspondence, folder 328.

23. Robert Clark press conference, Carmichael Papers, 1975 Campaign, folder 454.

24. Lamis, *The Two-Party South*, 51; "Cochran Not Endorsing His Fellow Republican," *Clarion-Ledger*, October 16, 1975; Mounger and Maxwell, *Amidst the Fray*, 153–55, 157–58, 160–61.

25. *Exhibits to the Testimony of J. Stanley Pottinger before the Subcommittee on Civil and Constitutional Rights, Committee on the Judiciary, U.S. House of Representatives, March 5, 1975*, J. Stanley Pottinger Papers, box 94, folder 270, Gerald R. Ford Presidential Library, University of Michigan, Ann Arbor; J. Stanley Pottinger to Gerry Jones, October 30, 1975, Pottinger Papers, box 64, folder 133. For an example of harassment of black voters in 1975, see Memorandum for the Attorney General from J. Stanley Pottinger, October 30, 1975, Pottinger Papers, box 64, folder 133.

26. "Finch 'Recommended' for Governor; 'Our Only Viable Choice'; Total GOP Posture 'Unredeemable' for Poor," *Lexington Advertiser*, October 23, 1973.

27. Advertisement by Prentiss Walker, *Clarion-Ledger*, October 18, 1975.

28. Ibid.; Crespino, *In Search of Another Country*, 217; Hathorn, "Challenging the Status Quo," 240.

29. Advertisement by Elmore Douglass Greaves, *Clarion-Ledger*, November 3, 1975.

30. *Mississippi Official and Statistical Register, 1972–1976*, 497, 500; Gil Carmichael to President Gerald Ford, Carmichael Papers, General Political, folder 167; Bass and De Vries, *The Transformation of Southern Politics*, 216; Lamis, *The Two-Party South*, 51; Linda Buford, "Kirksey Vote: No Counties Won, No Black Support," *Clarion-Ledger*, November 6, 1975; Jack Elliot, "Finch Shows Rural, Black Strength," *Clarion-Ledger*, November 6, 1975; McLemore interview, November 19, 2004.

31. "NAACP Object of GOP Wooing," *Clarksdale Press Register*, November 4, 1977; "Finch Displeasing Black Leaders," *Clarksdale Press Register*, May 30, 1977; Ken Faulkner, "State Black Officials Form Organization," *Clarksdale Press Register*, November 8, 1977; biographical sketch of Charles Pickering, Mississippi Republican Party Papers, box H-1, Biographies folder.

32. Frank Montague Jr. to Charles W. Pickering and Thad Cochran, Carmichael Papers, General Political, folder 213.

33. Barone et al., *The Almanac of American Politics 1976* (New York: Dutton, 1975), xiv–xv, 458–65; Barone et al., *The Almanac of American Politics 1978*, xix, 462–67; Bill Pardue, "Senate Approves Delegate Election," *Clarion-Ledger*, January 22, 1975; Calvin Edward Durden, "All Five Opposed Voting Rights Act," *Mississippi Press* (Pascagoula), August 19,

1975. For the Citizens' Councils and their support for Rhodesia and South Africa, see Neil R. McMillen, *The Citizens' Council: Organized Resistance to the Second Reconstruction, 1954–1964* (Urbana: University of Illinois Press, 1971), xiii.

34. *Mississippi Official and Statistical Register 1980–1984*, 454–55; "The District, County, and Precinct Coordinated Approach to the Recruitment of Black Voters for Thad Cochran in the U.S. Senate Race," Carmichael Papers, General Political, folder 215; Jo Ann Klein, "The GOP Sale," *Clarion-Ledger*, August 28, 1978.

35. Vern E. Smith, "A Different Campaign," *Atlanta Journal and Constitution Magazine*, November 5, 1978.

36. *Mississippi Official and Statistical Register, 1980–1984*, 458–59. Jasper was the one county Evers won that was not majority-black.

37. Lamis, *The Two-Party South*.

38. Harry S. Dent, *The Prodigal South Returns to Power* (New York: Wiley, 1978), 31–32; Jules Witcover, *Marathon: The Pursuit of the Presidency, 1972–1976* (New York: Outlet Book Publishers, 1980), 446.

39. Rowland Evans and Robert Novak, "The Incompetency Factor," *Washington Post*, July 31, 1975, clipping in Pottinger Papers, box 95, folder 270.

40. Witcover, *Marathon*, 446; Dent, *The Prodigal South Returns to Power*, 32; "Mississippi Republican Party 1976 Delegates and Alternate Delegates to the Republican National Convention Elected April 10, 1976," Dent Papers, box 26, folder 560.

41. Witcover, *Marathon*, 449–50; Dent, *The Prodigal South Returns to Power*, 47, 53; James Young, "GOP Looks to Blacks," undated newspaper clipping, Mississippi Republican Party Papers, box J-18, Charles Pickering folder.

42. Mounger and Maxwell, *Admidst the Fray*, 170–71, 197, 199–200; Trent Lott, *Herding Cats: A Life in Politics* (New York: William Morrow, 2005), 68–70; Bill Minor, "GOP Factional Quarrel Deepens," *Times-Picayune*, April 18, 1976; Carmichael to Richard Cheney, June 26, 1976, Carmichael Papers, General Political, folder 201; Charles Pickering to Carmichael, Carmichael Papers, General Political, folder 194; Lou Cannon, *Governor Reagan: His Rise to Power* (Washington, D.C.: Public Affairs Press, 2003), 395, 429; Crespino, *In Search of Another Country*, 236.

43. Telephone interview with Gil Carmichael, August 31, 2006; James Young, "GOP Looks to Blacks," undated newspaper clipping, Mississippi Republican Party Papers, box J-18, Charles Pickering folder; Mounger and Maxwell, 223–25; Crespino, *In Search of Another Country*; Lassiter, *The Silent Majority*; Kevin R. Kruse, *White Flight: Atlanta and the Making of Modern Conservatism* (Princeton: Princeton University Press, 2005).

44. Carmichael to Leon Bramlett, March 24, 1976, Carmichael Papers, 1975 Campaign Correspondence, folder 412.

45. *Mississippi Official and Statistical Register, 1980–1984*, 505; Carmichael Papers, 1979 Campaign, folder 261; "Carmichael Asks Black Support in Miss. Election," *New Orleans Times-Picayune*, October 15, 1979.

46. Dunbar Prewitt Jr. in *The Reporter*, September 20, 1979; "Carmichael Says Fuel Crisis May End Busing," *Northeast Mississippi Daily Journal*, July 20, 1979; Carmichael Papers, 1979 Campaign, folder 261; "Winter, Carmichael Outline Civil Rights Records to NAACP," *Northeast Mississippi Daily Journal*, October 29, 1979; "Blacks Back Carmichael,"

McComb Enterprise Journal, October 3, 1979; Carmichael Papers, 1979 campaign, folder 8; "Winter, Carmichael Outline Civil Rights Records to NAACP," *Northeast Mississippi Daily Journal*, October 29, 1979.

47. Dunbar Prewitt Jr., *The Reporter*, September 20, 1979; Deborah Lesure, "In Commemoration of a King," *Jackson Advocate*, January 10–16, 1980; John Howard, *Men Like That: A Southern Queer History* (Chicago: University of Chicago Press, 1999), 270.

48. David Bates, "Pickering Ads Claim Allain against Blacks," *Clarion-Ledger*, November 5, 1979; David Bates, "Allain Clings to 2 Percent Lead in Attorney General Election," *Clarion-Ledger*, November 7, 1979; *Mississippi Official and Statistical Register, 1980–1984*, 519.

49. Mounger and Maxwell, *Amidst the Fray*, 285–89; Dan T. Carter, *From George Wallace to New Gingrich: Race in the Conservative Counterrevolution, 1963–1994* (Baton Rouge: Louisiana State University Press, 1996); Dan T. Carter, *The Politics of Rage: George Wallace, the Origins of the New Conservatism, and the Transformation of American Politics* (New York: Simon and Schuster, 1995).

50. *Mississippi Official and Statistical Register, 1980–1984*, 47, 51, 517, 534

51. Wayne Weidie, "GOP Loses Ground in Municipal Elections," *The Carthaginian* (Carthage, Miss.), July 7, 1977; Winter interview, September 28, 2004; telephone interview with Gil Carmichael, August 31, 2006; Wayne Wiede, "Don't Pack Your Bags Yet," *Copiah County Courier*, August 15, 1979.

52. Jo Ann Klein, "GOP: Winter Building Patronage Machine," *Clarion-Ledger*, May 21, 1980; Gene Monteith, "Blacks Hope to Build GOP State Strength," *Clarion-Ledger*, September 27, 1980.

53. Cannon, *Governor Reagan*, 477–78; Lott, *Herding Cats*, 253; Toby Glen Bates, "The Reagan Rhetoric: History and Memory in 1980s America" (PhD diss., University of Mississippi, 2006), 23–25, 28–30; Manning Marable, *Race, Reform, and Rebellion: The Second Reconstruction in Black America, 1945–1990* (Jackson: University Press of Mississippi, 1991), 167–70. Cochran later called his opposition to the Neshoba speech "wrong," given the "great success" of the visit. Bates, "The Reagan Rhetoric," 37.

54. David Mould, "Black Group Urges More GOP Support," *Commercial Appeal*, September 27, 1980; Gene Monteith, *Clarion-Ledger*, September 27, 1980; Tom Bailey Jr., "Black Students Get Double Pitch for Reagan," *Commercial Appeal*, February 19, 1981; "Blacks Back Carmichael," *McComb Enterprise Journal*, October 3, 1979; Jo Ann Klein, "GOP Sale," *Clarion-Ledger*, August 28, 1978.

55. Mounger and Maxwell, *Amidst the Fray*, 262–63, 375; Lassiter, *The Silent Majority*, 14; Crespino, *In Search of Another Country*, 8.

56. Nash and Taggart, *Mississippi Politics*, 198; Black and Black, *Rise of Southern Republicans*, 4.

57. Frank R. Parker, "County Redistricting in Mississippi: Case Studies in Racial Gerrymandering," *Mississippi Law Journal* 44 (1973): 393–94, 399–400, 402–5; Lawson, *In Pursuit of Power*, 133, 160–61.

58. Raymond Wolters, *Right Turn: William Bradford Reynolds, the Reagan Administration, and Black Civil Rights* (Piscataway, N.J.: Transaction, 1996), 46–48.

59. Ibid., 63–64.

60. Lawson, *In Pursuit of Power*, 290–91; Bob Kyer, "Bolivar Remap Rejected," *Delta Democrat-Times*, June 15, 1983; Jane Egger, "Jackson Pushes in Delta," *Delta Democrat-Times*, June 5, 1983; "Dual Registration Should Go," *Delta Democrat-Times*, June 7, 1983; Rachel Brown, "Jackson Visits Cleveland, Urges Blacks to Vote," *Bolivar Commercial*, August 1, 1983.

61. "Civil-Rights 'Iceman' or Idealist?" *U.S. News and World Report*, June 17, 1985; "Reynolds's Inquisition," *National Review*, July 12, 1985; Michael S. Serrill, "Uncivil Times at 'Justless,'" *Time*, May 13, 1985; "A Public Disagreement about the Pursuit of Equality," *Black Enterprise*, January 1982; David M. Alpern, Ann McDaniel, and Margaret Garrard Warner, "A Roadblock for Reynolds," *Newsweek*, July 8, 1985.

62. "Civil Rights Lawyer Investigates Voting Charges," *Delta Democrat-Times*, June 14, 1983; "Registrars Coming to Delta to Sign Voters," *Delta Democrat-Times*, June 16, 1983; "Reynolds Takes a Ride in the 'Justice Buggy,'" *Newsweek*, June 27, 1983; Sandra Camphor, "Blacks' Voting Rights Complaints Heard," *Delta Democrat-Times*, June 15, 1983; Sandra Camphor, "Blacks Tell Justice Official of Problems," *Delta Democrat-Times*, June 15, 1983.

63. Sandra Camphor, "Blacks' Voting Rights Complaints Heard," *Delta Democrat-Times*, June 15, 1983; "Reynolds Takes a Ride in the 'Justice Buggy,'" *Newsweek*, June 27, 1983; "Registrars Coming to Delta to Sign Voters," *Delta Democrat-Times*, June 16, 1983; Lawson, *In Pursuit of Power*, 288–89; phone conversation with William Bradford Reynolds, August 14, 2006. The counties were Humphreys, Leflore, Madison, Quitman, and Sunflower. "Franklin Says Justice Visit Unfairly Convicts State," *Delta Democrat-Times*, June 17, 1983.

64. "Franklin Says Justice Visit Unfairly Convicts State," *Delta Democrat-Times*, June 17, 1983; "Blacks Hope Registrars Will Help Voter Turnout," *Delta Democrat-Times*, June 19, 1983; phone conversation with William Bradford Reynolds, August 14, 2006.

65. "Reynolds Takes a Ride in the 'Justice Buggy,'" *Newsweek*, June 27, 1983; Wolters, *Right Turn*, 70, 90–91; "Remarks at a Mississippi Republican Party Fundraiser Dinner in Jackson, June 20, 1983," Public Papers of the President: Ronald Reagan, 1981–1988, The Ronald Reagan Library, http://www.reagan.utexas.edu/resource/speeches/1983/62083b.htm.

66. Parker, *Black Votes Count*, 157–58; "No Serious Problems Seen by Poll Watchers," *Delta Democrat-Times*, August 4, 1983; "Franklin Blasts Federal Agency over Confusion," *Delta Democrat-Times*, August 2, 1983; *National Roster of Black Elected Officials*, vol. 12, 153–54; *National Roster of Black Elected Officials*, 15th ed., 229–31.

67. *National Roster of Black Elected Officials*, 15th ed., 229–31; Art Harris, "In Mississippi County, Blacks Dissect the Failure of a 'Revolution,'" *Washington Post*, August 18, 1983. The seven heavily black counties with no black supervisors were Sunflower, Washington, Carroll, Tallahatchie, Panola, Kemper, and Sharkey.

68. Jeremy D. Mayer, *Running on Race: Racial Politics in Presidential Campaigns, 1960–2000* (New York: Random House, 2002), 194; Abigail Thernstrom, *Whose Votes Count? Affirmative Action and Minoriy Voting Rights* (Cambridge: Harvard University Press, 1987), 234.

69. Mayer, *Running on Race*, 194.

70. Parker, *Black Votes Count*, 207–9.

71. Phone conversation with William Bradford Reynolds, August 14, 2006.

72. David M. Alpern, Ann McDaniel, and Margaret Garrard Warner, "A Roadblock for Reynolds," *Newsweek*, July 8, 1985; "Reynolds Wrap," *National Review*, July 26, 1985; George F. Will, "Battling the Racial Spoils System," *Newsweek*, June 10, 1985; Colleen O'Conner and Ann McDaniel, "The President's Angry Apostle," *Newsweek*, October 6, 1986. Much of the historical omission of Reynolds's Mississippi visit has carried over to historiography on Reagan's civil rights policies. One exception and defense of Reynolds is by the legal historian Raymond Wolters in his book *Right Turn*.

III

A Nation within a Nation?

6

Texas Philosophy, Nashville Agrarianism, Reagan Republicanism, and the Neo-Confederacy

The Influence of M. E. Bradford

FRED ARTHUR BAILEY

"In a Southern context the fight over the past is (and always has been) primarily a dispute concerning choices for the past and the future," proclaimed the Texas literary figure and political philosopher Melvin E. Bradford in 1987. Personally resistant to the profound social changes that swept over the American South after World War II, he emerged as an influential scholar whose interpretations of American history would at century's end help inspire a neo-Confederate resurgence. The author of scores of popular and professional articles, Bradford was also an accomplished orator who spoke with eloquence to crowds gathered in support of presidential candidate George Wallace or college and university assemblages throughout the world.[1]

Bold and consistent in his views, Bradford condemned faith in human equality while articulating the case for an ordered society premised upon the supposed innate inequality of mankind. He grounded his belief system in a grand historical paradigm that melded his comfortable conviction of white superiority with a distinctive interpretation of the ideological dynamics of both the American Revolution and the Confederate crusade.[2]

Bradford was a professor of English at the Jesuit University of Dallas from 1967 to 1993, and his forthright expression of his principles earned the respect of a certain cadre of southern intellectuals as well as those politicians fearful of a national government that might undermine the social customs they had long cherished. Although he proudly styled himself a conservative, in his candid moments he admitted to more radical and, to him, more virtuous inclinations. "'Reaction' is a necessary term in the intellectual context we inhabit late in the twentieth century," he reflected in 1990. "Merely to conserve is sometimes to perpetuate what is outrageous."[3]

The wholesale dismantling of the South's racist institutions seemed to Bradford a cultural catastrophe loosed upon the region by misguided reformers moved by dangerous egalitarian ideas. Influenced by conscience-driven northern liberals and long-restive southern blacks, a powerful national government had nullified laws that mandated racial segregation, denied blacks and large numbers of whites the elective franchise, and gerrymandered legislative districts that ensured patrician-driven rural counties' dominance over southern cities with significant minority populations. Bradford considered these alterations a crime against the natural order of mankind; he saw in civil rights and related democratic reforms the fundamental destruction of a southern civilization whose genius derived from a select, white, talented few. "The cult of equality," he wrote, "is the 'opiate of the masses' . . . part of the larger and older passion for uniformity or freedom from distinction. It flatters in us all that is worst."[4]

Although Bradford's admirers praised him as an original thinker, in reality he merely perpetuated a long tradition among southern white intellectuals that justified a cultural system in which race, class, and ethnic distinctions took precedence over leveling democracy. While a graduate student at Tennessee's Vanderbilt University during the height of the civil rights crusades, he partook of an academic environment that had long nurtured the South's distinctive race and class customs. During the 1930s it had been the special domain of the "Nashville Agrarians," a loose association of twelve intellectuals including the historian Frank W. Owsley, the poets Donald Davidson, Alan Tate, and Andrew Lytle, and the emerging literary giant Robert Penn Warren. Overwhelmingly elitist and racist in their social philosophy, they detested northern industrialism, criticized its impact upon the South, and condemned those southern reformers who, they maintained, gave aid and comfort to the Yankee colossus. Their works imagined an antebellum agricultural order in which aristocratic planters, white yeomen, and black slaves resided together in felicity with nature and in harmony with one another. In 1930 they produced the controversial anthology *I'll Take My Stand*. Dedicated to "a Southern way of life against . . . the American . . . way," it declared war on northern scholars and southern progressives alike.[5]

A sixth-generation Texan, Bradford grew up in a South where many whites, still bridling at the defeat of 1865, strove to preserve the essential trappings of the Old South. He moved in a carefully structured society that valued a southern version of Anglo-Saxon civilization as superior to all others and in which the relegation of blacks and Hispanics to a separate and inferior status was made normative. Born in Fort Worth on May 8, 1934, Bradford matured in a family proud of its Confederate heritage and moderate comfort from the income of ranch lands in Texas and Oklahoma. His progenitors had migrated from Tennessee and Alabama prior to the Civil War. "We were a storytelling people," Bradford explained in 1992. "I had three great-grandfathers who fought for the Confederacy." One lost a leg at Chickamauga "and suffered the rest of his life." Reconstructing the past, he reflected, "helped my family define who we were."[6]

Bradford excelled in a school system whose curriculum, long shaped by the Confederate patriotic societies, reinforced his perception of what it meant to be southern. As late as 1976, the historian of Fort Worth's Julia Jackson chapter of the United Daughters of the Confederacy praised its campaigns to "pressure . . . textbook publishers to give accurate accounts of the War Between the States" and to disapprove of "Northern teachers in the local schools who presented a view slanted." Looking back upon his youth, Bradford yearned for "that remembered Texas, which I like very much better than the one I now inherit."[7]

Reared in a closed intellectual environment, Bradford never broke free from the culture that so narrowed his ideological horizons. He viewed the Civil War as an unmitigated tragedy, one that destroyed a just southern civilization and whose cause could be traced to the malignant ambitions of a single individual—Abraham Lincoln. Bradford considered the sixteenth president an unprincipled scoundrel who, rather than allow the southern states a peaceful exit from the Union in 1861, launched a war that slaughtered six hundred thousand men, all for the benefit of his personal ambition and the prosperity of his northern industrial allies. He admitted a hatred for Lincoln so corrosive that whenever he spied his memorial in Washington, D.C., "a visceral wave of loathing rack[ed] his entire body." Pressed to explain Bradford's anti Lincoln bitterness, Harry Jaffa, who maintained with the Dallas professor a friendly debate over Lincoln's legacy, chuckled before responding: the Great Emancipator "stole Mel Bradford's great-grandfather's slaves."[8]

Graduating from high school in 1952, Bradford entered college with a love for the southern culture of his upbringing and with an acute awareness of the gathering pressures for civil rights reforms and other challenges to the traditional entitlements of the South's white elites. In the two decades from his freshman year at the University of Oklahoma until his doctorate in literature at Vanderbilt in 1968, Bradford witnessed profound, and for him troubling, alterations in the southern way of life. From *Brown's* seminal call to end public school segregation to the Civil Rights Act of 1964 and the Voting Rights Act of 1965, he imagined an aggressive national government forcing upon a righteously reluctant South a despised social leveling. This quest for equality was nothing more than "Old Liberalism hidden under a Union battle flag."[9] A Naval ROTC scholarship financed Bradford's bachelor's and master's degrees and plunged him into an intense period of military service critical to his intellectual development. Following brief deployment aboard a navy destroyer, he joined the teaching staff at Annapolis. There he enjoyed the fellowship of senior colleagues whose conservatism "of various kinds" helped him sort through his own ideological proclivities and apply them to his identity as a white southerner.[10]

Bradford's Annapolis friends also introduced him to the conservative quarterly *Modern Age*, edited by Russell Kirk. Years later, Bradford recalled that he eagerly awaited each of the publication's new issues, anticipating that its articles would serve as the basis of stimulating conversations with his fellow faculty. "In *Modern Age*," he reminisced, "I began to read . . . of a stream both broad and deep, coming down to us from antiquity in the multifaceted variety of European civilization. That there was a need to defend the West and that American intellectuals who understood the heritage would be in forefront of that defense was beyond dispute." Impressed that Donald Davidson, the last of the Nashville Agrarians at Vanderbilt, served as an editorial adviser of the journal, Bradford entered the university's English Department eager to earn his doctorate in a community famed as "a veritable nursery of intellectual conservatism."[11] A close friend and fellow graduate student remembered the school's English faculty as "utterly homogeneous . . . filled with Southern conservatives." Angered by assaults on Jim Crow, faculty defended the South in private and sometimes in public. "With such teachers, [Bradford] didn't have to waste time defending his convictions against the assaults of ideological adversaries."[12]

Bradford especially cherished his bonding with Davidson. As an undergraduate troubled by attacks on his native region's racial polity, he had devoured the Agrarians' anthology *I'll Take My Stand* and later reflected: "I said to myself [here] is a voice for the deepest sentiments of the people I have known best . . . [the] wisdom of the world 'where I was born and raised.'" While at Vanderbilt he sat at Davidson's feet, ingested his view on literary criticism, and absorbed his distaste for interpretations of American history contrary to those he believed. A powerful voice opposed to civil rights reforms, Davidson taught that the founding fathers never intended the phrase "all men are created equal" to apply to nonwhites, and he encouraged his students to see both the Declaration of Independence and the Constitution as conservative scriptures designed to shield society from the anarchy of democracy. "I have not changed my mind since I was a graduate student at Vanderbilt," Bradford reflected in 1986. "Not my mind, or my method."[13] He considered himself the intellectual heir to the Nashville Agrarians. Bradford admired their concept of southern community as "an informally hierarchical social organism in which all Southerners (including the Negro, insofar as the survival of that community permitted) had a sense of investment and participation." The South was a land where unequal men—white and black, privileged and impoverished—lived in harmony. The white and privileged Agrarians appreciated that reality and gloried in the critical "role of the gentleman . . . in cementing the bonds between unequal men." They feared an aggressive national government committed to wrongheaded egalitarianism. A corrupt national government almost destroyed southern order during the Civil War and Reconstruction, and in the 1930s it stood poised again as a threat to the rational order of men. Little wonder, Bradford mused, that the Agrarians entitled *I'll Take My Stand* as an affirmation "from the spirited anthem of their warlike forefathers."[14]

Although Bradford groomed himself for a quiet academic career, his love for politics would thrust him into the dynamic company of those who contested for control of the fundamental institutions of American intellectual life. He and those of similar persuasion wished to define the cultural creed by which all other Americans must manage their society. While in the end Bradford failed to achieve victory on a hoped-for scale, his legacy held a certain import. Across the South, a coterie of white academicians would hail Bradford's interpretations of America's past and present, dedicating themselves to the reversal of nearly fifty years of civil rights progress. Bradford taught briefly at Hardin-Simmons University in Abilene, Texas, and at Northwestern State in Natchitoches, Louisiana, before settling into his permanent post at the University of Dallas. A prolific writer, he produced engaging essays on southern literary themes. Emboldened by his faith in his own abilities as a rhetorical critic and driven by his intense distaste for central government intent upon dismantling southern institutions of inequality, in 1971 Bradford moved beyond the limited confines of literature to launch an attack on Abraham Lincoln. The brash assault upon this icon of American civil religion proved pivotal. It projected him into ideological circles beyond narrow academia and established him as an intellectual leader among those white southerners set on reversing the tide of civil rights reforms.[15]

Published in the magazine *Triumph*, Bradford's article "Lincoln's New Frontier: A Rhetoric for Continuing Revolution" branded the Great Emancipator a cultural heretic who misconstrued the phrase "all men are created equal," gave it a meaning never intended by the founding fathers, and then employed that faulty interpretation to make of the Union cause a holy crusade. In Bradford's paradigm, Lincoln's Gettysburg Address conjoined with Julia Ward Howe's "The Battle Hymn of the Republic" to whip the North into a religious fervor against the South. "To state my argument briefly," Bradford wrote, "what the Emancipator accomplished by confirming the nation in (or 'institutionalizing') an erroneous understanding of the Declaration of Independence made possible the ultimate elevation of that same error in Mrs. Howe's 'war song' and set us forever to 'trampling out the grapes of wrath.'"[16]

Bradford instead interpreted the Declaration of Independence as "a lawyer's answer to lawyers, a counterplea to the English government." The Declaration, he argued, defined the proper relationship between a prince and his subjects. Lincoln's rhetoric and Howe's anthem violated the intent of the Declaration, converted a single statement ("all men are created equal") into a sacred dictum, and loosed a religious crusade for "equality" that threatened to undermine fundamental institutions of social order more than a century beyond the Civil War. "With 'equality,'" Bradford proclaimed, we enter "the French Jacobin satrapy, where men are dignified by abstract 'proposition' and loud musketry."[17]

Bradford considered himself at war with a society moving rapidly toward anarchy worse than that of the French Revolution. The urban riots of the 1960s reinforced that conviction, stirring in him the urge to seek a strong leader capable of reversing what he saw as a trend toward social disintegration, and leading to his championing of George Wallace's 1972 presidential bid. Crusading throughout the Dallas area, Bradford organized Wallace followers, ushered them into the local presidential caucuses, and then led a solid pro-Wallace delegation to the Democratic state convention in San Antonio.[18]

The Wallace faithful elected Bradford to the Democratic state committee, where from 1972 to 1974 he proved an embarrassment to party centrists. Anxious to separate their movement from its segregationist past and to include Texas's ethnically diverse population, they held little brief for Bradford's open boast that he received his orders directly from Montgomery, Alabama—Wallace's home and once the Confederacy's capital. By 1975, Bradford moved into the Republican Party, and in 1980 he supported California governor Ronald Reagan over Texan George H. W. Bush in the presidential primary. When Reagan entered the White House, he nominated Bradford to head the National Endowment for the Humanities (NEH).[19] Although Bradford had served on Reagan's NEH transition team, his nomination surprised Washington pundits. On September 20, 1981, the *New York Times* leaked news of Bradford's impending appointment by quoting a "high-ranking Washington" official that the administration was pressed to this action "as a concession to conservative supporters" angered by Reagan's choice of Sandra Day O'Connor for the Supreme Court. Reactionary southern Republican senators John Tower of Texas and Jesse Helms and Bob East of North Carolina endorsed Bradford enthusiastically.[20]

Helms had for months resisted several recommended candidates on the grounds that they lacked sufficient ideological commitment to the cause. He bristled at the policies of current NEH director Joseph D. Duffey, the former president of the Americans for Democratic Action. Believing Duffey had unfairly favored the funding of "leftist" scholars from "effete" northeastern universities and associations dedicated to left-wing social agendas, Helms and like-thinking senators condemned such recent NEH grants as that to heighten the heritage awareness of female employees. Helms demanded that the new director reverse the trend and reward "scholarship from the conservative end of the spectrum as well as from the liberal."[21]

Sharing Helms's concerns, Bradford boldly articulated his vision of a reformed NEH. At Michigan's radically rightist Hillsdale College, he condemned the current NEH director's "talk of 'human values' and 'deep needs'" as little more than a cloak for "cultural populism" designed to serve "the political issues of the day." Under a Bradford administration, the NEH would focus on preserving the best of American society. "Americans of all backgrounds and levels of education know that something is wrong," he told his audience, "if we neglect in the cultural fields our role as leaders and preservers of Western civilization; wrong if we fail to preserve and promote the finest products of human reason and imagination and the best discussion of these books and artifacts . . . [and] such old fashioned activities." He would "avoid with all possible rigor" special programs "which reflect 'pop' sociology, social-scientific approaches to problem solving, and literary or historical themes which suggest a position on questions of public policy," and he would eliminate entirely all such efforts as "the 'Fellowship for College Teachers,'" a program he contemptuously termed "grants for second-rate scholars" because they amounted "to a hidden quota for minorities who have shown no academic promise but who have the right politics."[22]

Academicians, social activists, and newspaper publishers condemned Bradford's nomination, citing the professor's support for Wallace, his published condemnations of Lincoln, and his alleged racism. One of his strongest foes, the neoconservative godfather Irving Kristol, circulated among White House staffers a document sarcastically titled "Quotations from Chairman Mel." It revealed that Bradford had labeled Lincoln "a dangerous man" with a "very dark" and "indeed sinister" image. Bradford further held that slavery "was as good or as bad as the people who administered the regimen" and that it "seemed . . . both defensible . . . and civilized in its human results." As for the concept of equality of rights, Bradford dismissively commented that the subject belonged "to the post-Renaissance world of ideology—or political magic and the alchemical 'science' of politics. Envy is the basis for its broad appeal."[23]

Feeling himself unfairly maligned, Bradford called an impromptu press conference in the hallway of the Sam Rayburn Senate Office Building. His blunt way of talking, folksy style, and boisterous Texas humor served him well in private conversations with fellow ideologues and in public appearances before audiences predisposed to his views, but it failed to impress veteran journalists adept at unmasking the careful sophistry of government functionaries.[24]

Bradford's lack of political savvy lent to his comments an air of pettiness, vindictiveness, and insensitivity. How would Bradford change the NEH? "I'd stop washing money through the damn thing like Joseph Duffey has," he told the eager reporters. "I wouldn't give money to raise consciousness—for instance, that grant to the Ladies Garment Workers Union." Corrected, he repeated himself to properly reference the National Council of Working Women. Bradford then charged that the NEH had become far too partisan. "I wouldn't politicize it," he said. "I'd see that conservatives get a better shake than they did in Duffey's regime, not everything would go to Harvard, Yale, Princeton and Chicago." Even as the Dallas professor promised to shepherd more grants toward Texas and Oklahoma, he also pledged to restrict the NEH chair's personal prerogative to fund small projects. "I think chairman's grants ought to be stopped," he chuckled, but only "after I give out two or three. Don't quote me on that. But there really are two or three deserving conservatives." Several reporters pressed Bradford on his published critiques of Lincoln, leading one to ask the obvious: would Bradford have been a Confederate in 1861?[25]

Two days after the interview, an unnamed White House source revealed that Reagan was considering William Bennett to be NEH chair. His nomination easily passed Senate scrutiny, and Bennett was inaugurated to the prestigious post in the week before Christmas 1981. Although Reagan would later appoint Bradford to the Board of Foreign Scholarships, which administers the Fulbright Program, the Dallas professor largely faded from the national scene, but not from the consciousness of his conservative admirers, most of whom were white southern academicians. They saw in him a martyr sacrificed in their war against the forces of liberalism and cultural anarchy. "In the long run," reflected one of his staunchest supporters, "the political assassination of this immensely learned man may well have been the proverbial blessing in disguise for Bradford and a Pyrrhic victory for his tormentors; for the period between 1983 and 1993 proved to be the most productive of his career, highlighted by an outpouring of important books and essays that would not have been possible had he been tied down with administrative chores."[26]

A prolific scholar, Bradford employed the essay as his preferred mode of expression; throughout his career, he authored scores of tightly focused but abstrusely written papers whose themes had large cultural and intellectual applications. Although he never systematized his works, he customarily republished his more salient articles in book form, producing seven thick volumes.[27] He boldly asserted himself as an alternative voice to what he called the mandarins who teach in northern universities. Among those enamored of Bradford's insights was the conservative Dartmouth College scholar Jeffery Hart, who proclaimed Bradford an "American Plutarch" whose thoughts were "profoundly rooted in the tradition of Western civilization, Roman and biblical and regional. . . . [H]is work is both historical and deeply philosophical."[28]

Insofar as Bradford's sense of history and philosophy led him to articulate concepts "biblical and regional," his ideas were actually rooted in a cosmology influenced less from the New Testament and more from a sectarian belief encapsulated in the term "Reconstruction Theology." This dogma sprang largely from the thinking of the late-nineteenth-century southern Presbyterian theologian Robert L. Dabney and was carried forward by Richard M. Weaver, in common with Bradford a disciple of Donald Davidson and the Nashville Agrarians.[29]

Both Dabney and Weaver assumed that a decline of biblical morality in

America began with New England Unitarianism and its rejection of Jesus' divinity and gained momentum with northern intellectual enthusiasm for both the English Enlightenment's rational humanism and the French Revolution's egalitarian fervor. Dabney postulated that the antebellum South's defense of slavery and a stratified social order (which he grounded in his carefully selective interpretation of the Bible) enabled the region to retain its larger fidelity to the sanctity of Holy Scripture. Writing in the 1940s, Weaver espoused Dabney's essential themes, recasting them in light of the Agrarians' assertion that the antebellum South was a premodern society untainted by scientific rationalism. "The Southern people," he reflected, "reached the . . . Civil War one of the few religious peoples left in the Western World," and when the South went down in defeat in 1865, "the last barrier to the secular spirit of science, materialism, and pragmatism was swept away."[30]

Drawing his belief system from Dabney, Weaver, and like-minded southern chauvinists, Bradford presented the Civil War as a religious conflict, an American Armageddon that pitted the pious South against the secular North. He crafted a spiritual paradigm that contrasted a virtuous, Bible-based South of aristocracy and slavery with the less worthy, humanistic North of democracy and social leveling. Lincoln's Union, he proclaimed, personified "modern man," whose prototype was "the figure of Dr. Faustus, the omni-competent master of all the sciences, the alchemist who somehow summarizes the restless spirit of Western civilization." Bradford's imagined South, by contrast, had been largely unaffected by the scientific revolution, remained faithful to its traditions—especially its religious roots—and stood immune to secularism's soul-killing self-righteousness. The "Antebellum Southerner was not modern even though his adversary was," he lectured. "The Southerner could not believe that engineering, medicine, and the popular ballot could cure all the ills the flesh is heir to."[31]

Bradford worshipped reverent, gray-clad soldiers and the pious officers who led them. Referencing the Georgia historian E. Merton Coulter, he assured his audiences that "the Confederate Army was extraordinary among modern forces for its size—in this with no rival but Cromwell's host—in being free from vice." Just as the fervent Puritans of the English Civil War marched under the command of godly generals, so men of abiding faith similarly guided Johnny Reb. Bradford deemed Generals Thomas "Stonewall" Jackson and John Breckenridge and Admiral Raphael Semmes Christlike exemplars whose saintliness stimulated the faith-professions of Generals Braxton Bragg, Joseph E. Johnston, William Hardee, Dick Ewell, and

John B. Hood. He saved his strongest accolades for the southern clergy.[32] "Almost to a man," he sermonized, "the religious leaders of the Antebellum Southern society called for secession and led the way in reconciling the people of the South to all the hardships secession would cost them." These zealot divines proclaimed that "separation from the North was a 'holy enterprise,'" for they perceived something profoundly "wrong with Northern religion."[33]

The essential flaw with northern faith specifically and Yankee society in general was its failure to acknowledge the inerrant Word of God. Embracing the apostasy of science, northern intellectuals and clerics alike succumbed to the egalitarian heresies of the French Revolution, best illustrated in their antibiblical crusade against slavery. Clothing the institution of human bondage with the garb of divine sanction, Bradford declared that in "exalting their own religious sense above the historic witness of the Church, the abolitionist blasphemed." From this he argued that "if they behaved that way on one issue, using hieratic language to explore their own endless fresh revelations, they might well be expected to do the same in another context."[34]

Bradford preached that his own generation manifested that other context. For him the celebration of a spiritual South juxtaposed to a secular North meant far more than a mere exercise in antiquarian piety. If the infidel Yankee stood as the enemy in 1861, his spiritual descendants remained a threat more than a century later. "For all of the great issues fought out in the 1860s are with us still," he warned his listeners, "sometimes disguised, but in their fundamental character never changing." He sermonized that the post–World War II civil rights movement and the late-twentieth-century quest for multiculturalism emanated from the North's selfsame lack of biblical understanding and thus persisted as a threat to his native region's fundamental values. "The consequences of their admonitions are among us still, setting most Southerners aside from the primary delusions of our place and time," he averred. "Historians who wish to understand Southern persistence in character would do well to consider this . . . and be less concerned with explanations of Southern particularity which derive from slavery alone."[35]

Bradford's sense of religious and social righteousness rested upon his historical interpretations and underscored his essential faith in the virtues of human inequality. Widely read but never formally trained in the historian's craft, he approached the past as a dedicated ideologue rather than as a dispassionate observer of the human chronicle.[36] While a historian would, by his profession's canons, feel compelled to present documentary or other evidence to support his views of slavery's supposed efficacy or a biologist deem it essential to cite scientific research to substantiate any assertion of racial inferiority, no such compulsions moved the Texan. He issued his dicta grounded upon his personal proclivities and prejudices, feeling unobligated to justify his positions beyond this frame of reference. Bradford pleasured in his role as "a professor of literature" who was "free to range throughout the humanities and to combine insights from several disciplines with his particular skills as rhetor."[37] From his training as a student of language and its persuasive powers he assumed an intrinsic right to judge intuitively the worth of any document—poem, essay, political treatise, sermon, or history—and to determine which had the virtue of truth and which should be dismissed as polemic.

Bradford, of course, scaled the words of others with the measure of his predetermined sense of the past. Although the Dallas professor—in common with the Agrarians—disdained scientific analysis, he eagerly lent his imprimatur to Robert Fogel and Stanley Engerman's 1975 statistical study *Time on the Cross*, which concluded that enslaved antebellum blacks and independent subsistence farmers enjoyed almost equal levels of material comfort. "For those raised altogether inside" the "framework of Southern memory," Bradford declared, "there is no surprise at all." In his view, Fogel and Engerman validated the southern white tradition of benevolent slavery, a fact that should make it difficult—if not impossible—for liberal intellectuals to retain faith with their less-than-honest image of a malevolent slave system popularized in the "cult of Union, Father Abraham and the significance . . . of that great Gnostic fit that was our Civil War." Emboldened by *Time on the Cross*, he pledged his participation in future debates over the peculiar institution's merits—an effort he looked "forward to with warm anticipation."[38]

Given Bradford's sense of "Southern memory," he casually dismissed almost all of slavery's post-1950 historiography. "For reasons that have more to do with contemporary politics and the intellectual fashions of our times," he wrote in 1989, "we have experienced . . . a veritable explosion of commentary on the phenomenon of American Negro slavery." Those books were "so numerous and predictable" that they negated any "serious consideration of their subjects." Their only purpose, he complained, was "to give those who write . . . an opportunity to demonstrate their own moral refinement—as 'ethical proof' of their right to instruct those benighted conservatives" who do not "hate slavery to the point of distraction."[39]

To Bradford's disappointment, he felt that his would-be hero Robert Fogel succumbed to the liberals' blandishments. In a second edition of *Time on the Cross*, the author acknowledged that however good the material comforts provided slaves by the South's master class, they failed to make up for the slave's lack of human liberty. "Fogel has . . . to prevent neo-abolitionist hostility," surrendered to "the vituperative political context of contemporary American historiography." Unrepentant himself, Bradford assured his audience that the original publication, minus any apology, had "given the American intellectual community not only all it would wish to know about slavery, but . . . a good deal more than it was and is ready to digest."[40]

However flawed Bradford's historical methodology, the value of his work lies in its consistent interpretation of American history as a fundamental struggle between order and anarchy and in its influence upon other scholars who employ his views of the past to define their vision of the future. Bradford especially admired the American South and championed it as a society guided by a sagacious elite and dedicated to the preservation of fundamental white cultural values. A firm believer in virtuous aristocracy, he condemned all those he deemed social levelers, including French Jacobeans, Abraham Lincoln, and modern advocates of the civil rights movement. Bradford especially despised contemporary historians enamored with the concept of human equality. He airily dismissed these "gentlemen [as] greatly confused . . . about our early history" who "threaten what remains intact from an originally wholesome political inheritance."[41]

Bradford portrayed the past as a grandiose experiment peopled with high-principled champions and their foils. He imagined the seventeenth-century settlers who first constructed plantations upon southern soil as men "from landed families" dedicated to a culture premised upon patriarchy, "a social system more like old Scotland" or Anglo-Saxon Britain. Committed to the improvement of life for themselves and their progeny, they dreamed of the "acquisition and cultivation of land, 'real property.' . . . Theirs was a mind-set which presumed a culture of families, not atomistic individualism in the modern sense." Bradford held that long before slavery came to symbolize the South, these men's commitment to place and kin defined the region as they developed a sense of noblesse oblige, a dedication to the preservation of the communal weal. "The gentleman," Bradford claimed, "was no mere decorative creature; instead, he was an honored figure whose lofty status was matched by his function and large responsibility, encouraging the kind of deference which gives excellence to social unity." Born to privilege, the gentleman had a "heroic mission," the safeguarding "of civil life which gives meaning to the acts of the statesman, the warrior, the poet, and the priest." Aristocracy ensured social order and became the cement that shored up its "battlements within which all others found shelter."[42]

Bradford scoffed at the scholarship of those historians who would define the colonial South as a "debate over the merits and demerits of slavery as a social and economic system for half-wild Blacks and seventeenth-century Anglo-Saxons living uneasily together," or who would impose upon the region concepts of a white class struggle. Prior to the American Revolution, social stratification (class and slavery) was assumed to be normal and appropriate. "Egalitarianism got no foothold in the original South," he lectured, nor were there protests against an articulated society. "Bacon's Rebellion was . . . no outburst of democracy. Neither were the 'Regulators' of North Carolina. . . . These explosions were . . . 'against a governing class derelict in its duty,' not reductions of the idea of class."[43] For in the South, Bradford defined the struggle for independence from England as a conservative revolution, one designed "to preserve a familiar way of life." The region's oligarchy resented an all-powerful London government that threatened their local autonomy and prevented their "acting together against levellers, Indians, and the champions" of economic disorder. Thus to argue that the Declaration of Independence, written by a Virginia slave owner, was intended to affirm the equality of mankind sorely failed the test of logic. "This particular Declaration," Bradford reasoned, "makes it plain that Englishmen were in dispute with Englishmen . . . on English grounds." To Bradford, no modern-day "liberal, new or old, can make of that framework" a plea for universal equality.[44]

Bradford insisted that heresies associated with the Declaration threatened the destruction of American civilization. In the preface to his anthology *A Better Guide Than Reason* he explained that "presupposed in every chapter is the necessity to correct conventional misreadings of the Declaration of Independence: that is to say, the imperative to discourage compulsive filtering of our national beginnings through the first sentence of paragraph two in that instrument of separation." Jefferson, of course, was no egalitarian. Believing in the innate inferiority of the Negro race, he never intended that any non-Anglo-Saxon be included as citizens in the new American nation. "Jefferson," Bradford wrote, was "consistent with the ancients in maintaining that a republic should be racially homogeneous—in our case, Anglo-Saxon."[45]

Bradford believed that a later generation, one represented by Lincoln, would out of misguided humanitarianism forget the importance of homogeneity. "It is probable that Lincoln disliked slavery," Bradford reasoned, "just as it is obvious that most Southerners recognized slaves as human beings in that they hoped to see them accept Christianity." But while most white southerners never perceived the black as a potential citizen able to function on the same level with whites, Lincoln stretched the phrase "all men are created equal" beyond all reasonable interpretation and applied it to black men. This distortion of the Declaration became Lincoln's "lasting and terrible impact on the nation's destiny." His insistence that "the Negro was included in the promise" of the Declaration and that the "Declaration bound his countrymen to fulfill a pledge hidden in that document" moved the nation "toward a radical transformation of American society." While this application was to the issue of race, its larger implications involved the profound undermining of a properly articulated social structure. It was "the base and wheels of . . . the Trojan horse of our home-grown Jacobinism."[46]

Bradford emphasized that "the founders of the Southern Confederacy" saw themselves as emulating their ancestors who had earlier rebelled against George III. Southern statesmen considered secession "an attempt to preserve a precious heritage, a known and agreed upon social, cultural, and political arrangement developed in an unbroken continuum from reverenced antecedents." For too long, white southerners had endured the North's disparagement of their social order. They could no longer tolerate the "closing of territories to Southern settlers," the North's glorification of John Brown, and the threats implied in Lincoln's "House Divided" speech. "The dangers and the indignities of 1860–61," he reasoned, "were worse than those of 1774–1776." In the end, the Confederate fathers "felt no hesitation in pleading the example of that past to resist what they perceived as obnoxious alterations of its nature: unsanctioned changes, however high-sounding might be the terms employed to rationalize this introduction."[47]

The North, of course, won the Civil War and with that validated Lincoln's interpretation of the Declaration. To Bradford, the ultimate and tragic result was the formation of a polyglot society bent on the establishment of a "classless, raceless, sexless, and cultureless melting pot." America had lost sight of its vital essence, the fundamental heritage of Anglo-Saxon civilization. Schoolchildren mistakenly celebrated the "pietistic arrogance" enshrined "in the iconography of the Lincoln myth," praised the "civil disobedience" of Martin Luther King, and accepted as natural the invasion of their land by immigrants from south of the Rio Grande. "When our most refined moralists insist that . . . borders be ignored and distinctions of citizenship be set aside," Bradford warned, our "own institutions and identities" would be imperiled.[48]

As the twentieth century entered its last quarter, Bradford argued that the prospects of halting the American march toward cultural nihilism grew ever dimmer. In spite of the partial successes of George Wallace and the consequent faithfulness of many southern Republicans to the values of a racist South, the hope of achieving a national conservative majority seemed remote. "There is, however . . . an example which might be employed in achieving the end of a durable conservative majority," he postulated in 1974, "the example . . . of the Old South. And the clearest proof was in the organization of the armies by means of which that society almost achieved its independence." Certainly the Nashville Agrarians had yearned for white southern cultural autonomy, and Bradford reflected that "there are others—clergymen, lawyers, journalists, and politicians who hear the same music." Such a circle formed around Bradford, sharing with him a worship of the Old South and the Confederacy it spawned, and despising what they together perceived as an overbearing, malignant North.[49] To Bradford and his confidants, the late Confederacy represented far more than a nostalgic might-have-been; to them it stood as a political and social model, an ordered alternative to the anarchy they associated with the late twentieth century. This informal cadre assembled on numerous occasions—sometimes as friends, sometimes as academics celebrating the Agrarians' philosophical legacy, and sometimes as political ideologues questing for a white southern version of the conservative ideal.[50]

Bradford's circle embraced the Lost Cause's iconography, and the Texan often led them in its adoration. In 1974, Bradford and his friends convened with the North Carolina Conservative Society, where for entertainment they screened *Birth of a Nation*, the silent film classic that glorified a high-principled Old South, a courageous Confederate cause, and a heroic Ku Klux Klan. "There in the darkened hall," reminisced one participant, sat Mel Bradford "with scores of college students at his feet." He read "aloud each caption as it flashed upon the screen, and [did so] with no small gusto."[51] Bradford, the students, and the Tar Heel conservatives become one with the North Carolina native, the Reverend Thomas Dixon, his Negrophobic novels, and the movie that animated his themes.

Enveloped by the intellectual culture of the racist South, such men resented all criticism of their region, which by extension was also criticism of them. Believing that there were "almost no public voices raised in defense of the South and its traditions," in 1979 Thomas Fleming and Clyde

Wilson, two of Bradford's compatriots, published the inaugural issue of the *Southern Partisan*, a conservative magazine dedicated to reminding its readers "of all that was and is distinctively good about the South." Its editors promised to counteract the "barrage of [anti-South] propaganda from university lectures, magazines, movies and television programs" and to expose as well the traitorous "horde of intellectual Southerners—happily expatriate—who make their living ridiculing their homeland." Men of considerable academic clout themselves, Fleming, who possessed a doctorate in classics from Chapel Hill, and Wilson, a historian at the University of South Carolina, envisioned their new periodical as a means of bridging the gap between their vision of a South restored to the value system of the Nashville Agrarians and those "affluent and educated Southerners who are in danger of losing their birthright."[52]

From the *Southern Partisan*'s first issue, Bradford played a major role in its development. Wilson encouraged him, praising him in its opening pages as a spokesman for the South in the "tradition . . . of Patrick Henry and Jefferson, John Taylor and John Randolph, Calhoun and [Jefferson] Davis, [and] the . . . 20th century agrarians." Bradford donated an article to its initial publication and contributed regularly thereafter, served on its editorial board, and in 1990, "after years of persuasion," he became its principal editor. A magazine spokesman expressed delight to "have Mel Bradford officially installed at the helm of [the] journal," for, he reflected, Bradford had "always been our guardian of the tablets."[53]

These "tablets" projected an idealized image of the Confederacy and offered it, along with the Old South it protected, as a viable alternative to the Yankee-dominated South of their own era. With such regular features as the "CSA Today," the "Scalawag Award," and "Whistling Dixie," the *Southern Partisan*'s writers consistently ridiculed the political correctness they identified with civil rights, an economic culture homogenized by northern chain stores, and a wrongheaded, government-imposed spirit of egalitarianism. Contributors and readers alike saw themselves as champions of an unbroken thought process that stretched from John C. Calhoun and the antebellum fire-eaters to the regional chauvinism of the Nashville Agrarians. And, as true believers, they were hypersensitive to any and all who critiqued their beliefs.

When in 1992 an iconoclastic journalist for the Austin-based *Texas Monthly* disparaged Bradford, an editorialist for the *Southern Partisan* jumped to his defense. "What is one to make of an intellectual who despises Abraham Lincoln, believes that equality is a humbug, and compares the Klan . . . to the French resistance of World War II?" asked the perplexed journalist. The answer, responded the *Southern Partisan*'s writer, was that Bradford represented a legitimate trend in contemporary southern thought. "A good many people agree with" the Dallas professor, who "operates in a well-defined historical tradition . . . that is coming back into prominence after several decades of eclipse." Had the *Texas Monthly* journalist "driven a few miles west" he "might have spoken to Grady McWhiney at [Texas Christian University], whose views on eighteenth- and nineteenth-century America often coincided with Bradford's, as do those of Clyde Wilson (South Carolina), Forrest MacDonald (University of Alabama), Marion Montgomery (University of Georgia), and many others." These men were but a small portion of Bradford's intellectual circle, and they, along with many others, mourned his death in 1993.[54]

Inspired in large measure by Bradford's teachings, some prominent members of the history department at the University of Alabama—along with such cohorts as Fleming, Wilson, and McWhiney—met in Tuscaloosa in 1994 to organize the "League of the South" as a movement of southern thought-leaders dedicated to "secession [as] the best way to restore good government in the South" and preserve its "Christian, Anglo-Celtic" civilization. They acknowledged Bradford as their prophet, for his writings warned of the dangers to their view of society, of the challenges to it from without by a powerful national government dedicated to multiculturalism, and from within by liberal college professors and special-interest groups promoting minority rights. The league's membership grew to include professors of history, religion, political science, literature, journalism, and philosophy at such respected schools as Clemson, Emory, Baylor, and Virginia Commonwealth University and the universities of Virginia, South Carolina, Georgia, and Houston as well as smaller institutions across the South.[55]

To counteract what the league designated as the "anti-South" textbooks used in public schools and university classrooms, it sponsored summer institutes and weekend seminars, staffed them with scholars from among their membership, and indoctrinated high school teachers and homeschooling parents with a canted version of the past. The league recognized that in order to shape the next generation of white southerners it had to deal with the sensitive issue of race, but it pledged to do so "free of hatred and malice." This "does not mean," explained its president, that "we must subscribe to the flawed Jacobin notion of egalitarianism, nor does it mean that white Southerners should give control over their civilization and its institutions to another race, whether it be native blacks or Hispanic immigrants. Nowhere, outside of liberal dogma, is any nation called upon to commit cultural and ethnic suicide."[56] Bradford would have applauded the League of the South's goals, for he too longed for a South freed from oppressive forms of northern egalitarianism and bound once again by a glorious Anglo-Saxon order to the exclusion of all other races. Perhaps a clue to that desire exists in his presentation of his academic self. Like any good scholar, he carefully listed those organizations that defined his persona: the Modern Language Association, the American Political Science Association, the Southwestern American Literature Association, and, of course, the Sons of Confederate Veterans.[57]

Notes

1. "Melvin Eustace Bradford," *Contemporary Authors* (Detroit: Gale Research, 1984), 13:69–70.

2. M. E. Bradford, "All to Do Over: The Revolutionary Precedent and the Secession of 1861," in *A Better Guide Than Reason: Studies in the American Revolution* (Peru, Ill.: Sugden, 1979), 153–68; Thomas H. Landess, "Partisan Conversation with M. E. Bradford," *Southern Partisan* 5 (Spring 1985): 37–42.

3. "Melvin Eustace Bradford," *Contemporary Authors*, 69–70; M. E. Bradford, *The Reactionary Imperative: Essays Literary and Political* (Chicago: Open Court, 1999), viii (quotation).

4. M. E. Bradford, "On Remembering Who We Are: A Political Credo," in *Remembering Who We Are: Observations of a Southern Conservative* (Athens: University of Georgia Press, 1985), 11 (quotations); Landess, "Partisan Conversation," 37–42.

5. Twelve Southerners, *I'll Take My Stand: The South and the Agrarian Tradition* (New York: Harper and Brothers, 1930).

6. "Melvin Eustace Bradford," *Contemporary Authors*, 69–70; Gary Cartwright, "Mr. Right," *Texas Monthly*, March 1992, 60, 65 (quotations).

7. Dora Davenport Jones, *History of the Julia Jackson Chapter #141, United Daughters of the Confederacy, Fort Worth Texas, 1897–1976* (Fort Worth: "6333" Kwik-Kopy Printing Center, 1976), 34 (first quotation); M. E. Bradford quoted in Lee Cullum, "The Controversial Career of Professor Melvin E. Bradford," *Dallas Times-Herald*, September 2, 1990 (second quotation).

8. Cartwright, "Mr. Right," 65 (first quotation), 66 (second quotation). Although Jaffa and Bradford shared many values, for years they carried on a friendly disputation over the role Lincoln played in American history. Such was quite common for Jaffa. See M. E. Bradford, Harry V. Jaffa, and Jeffrey Hart, "Time on the Cross: Debate," *National Review*, March 28, 1974, 340–42, 359; Harry V. Jaffa, "In Abraham's Bosom: A Lifelong Dispute about Abraham Lincoln Has Been Remanded to a Higher Court," *National Review*, April 12, 1993, 50–51).

9. M. E. Bradford, "The Heresy of Equality: A Reply to Harry Jaffa," in *A Better Guide Than Reason*, 31 (quotation).

10. Cartwright, "Mr. Right," 65; M. E. Bradford, "Memories," *Modern Age* 26 (Summer/Fall 1982): 242 (quotations).

11. Bradford, "Memories," 242 (quotations).

12. "Melvin Eustace Bradford," *Contemporary Authors*, 69–70; Thomas H. Landess, "The Education of Mel Bradford: The Vanderbilt Years," in *A Defender of Southern Conservatism: M. E. Bradford and His Achievements*, ed. Clyde N. Wilson (Columbia: University of Missouri Press, 1999), 15–16 (quotations).

13. Landess, "The Education of Mel Bradford," 10–11; M. E. Bradford, "The Agrarian Tradition: An Affirmation," in *Remembering Who We Are*, 83 (first quotation); M. E. Bradford, "Rhetoric and Respectability: Conservatives and the Problem of Language," in *Reactionary Imperative*, 98 (second quotation). As early as 1939, Davidson condemned the emerging young historian C. Vann Woodward for suggesting that "class conflict" played a role in the Populist movement. "The problem with Woodward," he wrote, "is that 'the class approach' means, as it generally seems to mean nowadays, the obliteration of the color line in the South.... This alone is a solid and sufficient reason for the traditional Southern insistence that the Negro be put in a separate category and that his problems be treated separately.... In retrospect, it seems that it would have been a wise course, at the time of Negro emancipation, to remove the race question from politics by giving the Negro a status at least as special as that of the American Indian." Donald Davidson, "The Class Approach to Southern Problems," *Southern Review* 5 (1939): 272. Almost two decades later, Davidson wrote in a Canadian magazine that the "racial differences are simply too real for the South to accept an amalgamation of the Negro society with the white. The South's determined preference is to maintain white society as white. That preference cannot be removed by the decree of any court." Donald Davidson, "Integration Means a Cold Civil War," *Toronto Star Weekly Magazine*, November 9, 1957, 36.

14. Bradford, "The Agrarian Tradition," 85 (third quotation), 86 (first quotation), 87 (second quotation).

15. "Melvin Eustace Bradford," *Contemporary Authors*, 69–70. One of Bradford's biographers incorrectly lists him as teaching at Abilene Christian College instead of Hardin-Simmons University; both institutions are in Abilene, Texas. See Landess, "The Education of Mel Bradford," 16. The bulk of Bradford's early works were divided between essays that argued that liberal scholars largely misread and misinterpreted the Mississippi novelist and Nobel laureate William Faulkner and that touted the contributions to southern culture made by his mentor Donald Davidson and by Davidson's compatriots among the Nashville Agrarians. A bibliography of Bradford's works appears in Alan Cornett, "An M. E. Bradford Checklist," in Wilson, *A Defender of Southern Conservatism*, 152–85.

16. M. E. Bradford, "Lincoln's New Frontier: A Rhetoric for Continuing Revolution," *Triumph* 6 (1971), reprinted as M. E. Bradford, "Lincoln, the Declaration, and Secular Puritanism: A Rhetoric for Continuing Revolution," in *A Better Guide Than Reason*, 187.

17. Bradford, "Lincoln, the Declaration, and Secular Puritanism," 187 (first quotation), 191 (second quotation), 192, 196–99.

18. Lee Cullum, "The Controversial Career of Professor Melvin E. Bradford," *Dallas Times-Herald*, September 2, 1990; untitled newspaper clipping, September 23, 1984, in Melvin E. Bradford file, Texas/Dallas History and Archives Division, Dallas Public Library.

19. "Melvin Eustace Bradford," *Contemporary Authors*, 69-70; Lee Cullum, "The Controversial Career of Professor Melvin E. Bradford," *Dallas Times-Herald*, September 2, 1990; untitled newspaper clipping, September 23, 1984, in Melvin E. Bradford file, Texas/Dallas History and Archives Division, Dallas Public Library; Cartwright, "Mr. Right," 64.

20. *New York Times*, September 20, 1981 (quotation); N. Cider, "Report from the Capitols: Bradford for the Humanities," *Southern Partisan* 2 (Fall 1981): 4-6. One of Bradford's former students and a participant in various administrative functions in both the Reagan and George H. W. Bush administrations argued that "Bradford from the outset was President Reagan's favorite for the NEH post not so much for his learning, as for his charm as a conversationalist and storyteller." Benjamin B. Alexander, "The Man of Letters and the Faithful Heart," in Wilson, *A Defender of Southern Conservatism*, 31.

21. *New York Times*, September 20, 1981 (first quotation), December 27, 1981 (second quotation); *Dallas Morning News*, September 21, 1981; *Washington Post*, September 3, 1980, September 11 and 12, 1981.

22. M. E. Bradford, "Culture and Anarchy: Federal Support for the Arts and Humanities," in *Remembering Who We Are*, 95 (first quotation), 97 (second quotation), 99-100 (third, fourth, fifth quotations). For later examples of Bradford's critiques of the NEH see M. E. Bradford, "Subsidizing the Muses," in *Remembering Who We Are*, 102-9; M. E. Bradford, "The Form and Pressure of Our Time: The Social Role of Modern Drama," in *Reactionary Imperative*, 15-26.

23. *New York Times*, September 24, 1981; *Washington Post*, October 14, 15, 20, 22, 1981 (quotations); M. E. Bradford, "A Southern Candidate Recalls His Struggle," *Humanities in the South* 56 (Fall 1982): 1, 12-13; Marshall L. DeRosa, "M. E. Bradford's Constitutional Theory: A Southern Reactionary's Affirmation of the Rule of Law," in Wilson, *A Defender of Southern Conservatism*, 123.

24. *New York Times*, October 27, 1981; *Washington Post*, October 28, 1981.

25. "Well," he responded, "who's to know what one would have done?" *New York Times*, October 27, 1981; *Washington Post*, October 28, 1981 (quotations).

26. *Washington Post*, October 31, 1981; *New York Times*, November 14, December 27, 1981; James McClellan, "Walking the Levee with Mel Bradford," in Wilson, *A Defender of Southern Conservatism*, 41 (quotation).

27. Bradford, *A Better Guide Than Reason*; M. E. Bradford, *A Worthy Company: Brief Lives of the Framers of the United States Constitution* (Marlborough, N.H.: Plymouth Rock Foundation, 1982); M. E. Bradford, *Generations of the Faithful Heart: On the Literature of the South* (La Salle, Ill.: Sugden, 1983); Bradford, *Remembering Who We Are*; Bradford, *Reactionary Imperative*; M. E. Bradford, *Against the Barbarians, and Other Reflections on Familiar Themes* (Columbia: University of Missouri Press, 1992); M. E. Bradford, *Original Intentions: On the Making and Ratification of the United States Constitution* (Athens: University of Georgia Press, 1993).

28. M. E. Bradford, "Artists at Home: Froster and Faulkner," in *Reactionary Imperative*, 1 (first quotation); Jeffery Hart, introduction, in *A Better Guide Than Reason*, xiii (second quotation).

29. Edward H. Sebesta and Euan Hague, "The US Civil War as a Theological War: Confederate Christian Nationalism and the League of the South," *Canadian Review of*

American Studies 32 (2002): 257–64. For a lengthy exposition on Dabney's theological ideas, see his *A Defense of Virginia and the South (And Through Her, Of the South) in Recent and Pending Contests against the Sectional Party* (1867; repr., Harrisonburg, Va: Sprinkle, 1999).

30. Sebesta and Hague, "The US Civil War as a Theological War," 258–59; Richard M. Weaver, "The Older Religiousness of the South," *Sewanee Review* 51 (Spring 1943); 248 (quotation). Weaver's article is reprinted in George M. Curtis III and James J. Thompson Jr., eds., *The Southern Essays of Richard M. Weaver* (Indianapolis: Liberty Press, 1987), 134–46.

31. M. E. Bradford, "The Theology of Secession," *Southern Partisan* 11 (Fourth Quarter 1991): 21.

32. Ibid., 20, 22 (first quotation). Although Coulter and Bradford shared similar views about the righteousness of the Confederate cause and the spiritual virtues of the army that fought for it, Bradford broadened the historian's observation beyond its original context. Writing about the camp-meeting revivals that broke out among the Rebel armies during the winter of 1863–64, Coulter reflected that for "a time vice among the soldiers was routed, and the Confederate army took on the nature of Cromwell's Ironsides." E. Merton Coulter, *The Confederate States of America, 1861–1865* (Baton Rouge: Louisiana State University Press, 1950), 526–27.

33. Bradford, "Theology of Secession," 23 (quotations), 25.

34. Ibid., 21.

35. Ibid., 24 (first quotation), 25 (second quotation).

36. "Piety, or better pietas, runs through M. E. Bradford's work," wrote Elizabeth Fox-Genovese and Eugene D. Genovese in their analysis of his historical vision. "Bradford considered himself, and faithfully assumed the responsibilities of, a steward—a custodian of the collective memory of the South and, beyond the South, of the essence of what it means to be an American." Elizabeth Fox-Genovese and Eugene Genovese, "M. E. Bradford's Historical Vision," in Wilson, *A Defender of Southern Conservatism*, 78.

37. Bradford, "Memories," 243.

38. M. E. Bradford, "Just as We Were Told," *National Review,* March 28, 1974, 340 (first quotation), 341 (second, third, fourth quotations).

39. M. E. Bradford, "The Ambiguous Muse," *National Review,* February 24, 1989, 50.

40. M. E. Bradford, "All We Would Want to Know," *National Review,* December 31, 1989, 39 (second quotation), 40 (first quotation).

41. M. E. Bradford, "And God Defend the Right: The American Revolution and the Limits of Christian Obedience," in *Remembering Who We Are*, 39.

42. M. E. Bradford, "First Fathers: The Colonial Origins of the Southern Tradition," in *A Better Guide Than Reason*, 177 (fourth and fifth quotations), 179 (first quotation); M. E. Bradford, "Where We Were Born and Raised: The Southern Conservative Tradition," in *Reactionary Imperative*, 118, 120 (second quotation); M. E. Bradford, "Is the American Experience Conservative?" in *Reactionary Imperative*, 136 (third quotation).

43. Bradford, "First Fathers," 174 (first quotation), 178 (second, third quotations); M. E. Bradford, "Word from the Forks of the Creek: The Revolution and the Populist Heritage," in *A Better Guide Than Reason*, 61; Bradford, "Where We Were Born and Raised," 118.

44. Bradford, "Where We Were Born and Raised," 121 (first quotation); Bradford, "The Heresy of Equality," 36, 37 (second quotation), 39 (third quotation).

45. M. E. Bradford, preface to *A Better Guide Than Reason*, xi (first quotation); M. E. Bradford, "Franklin and Jefferson: The Making and Binding of Self," ibid., 143 (second quotation).

46. M. E. Bradford, "Against Lincoln: A Speech at Gettysburg," in *Reactionary Imperative*, 223 (first quotation); Bradford, "The Heresy of Equality," 32 (second quotation); M. E. Bradford, "The Lincoln Legacy: A Long View," in *Remembering Who We Are*, 144 (third quotation); M. E. Bradford, "A Fire Bell in the Night," in *Remembering Who We Are*, 48 (fourth quotation).

47. M. E. Bradford, "All to Do Over: The Revolutionary Precedent and the Secession of 1861," in *A Better Guide Than Reason*, 154 (first, second, fourth quotations), 159 (third quotation).

48. Bradford, "A Fire Bell in the Night," 52 (first quotation); Bradford, "The Heresy of Equality," 46 (second quotation); Bradford, "The Lincoln Legacy," 155 (third quotation); Bradford, "Rhetoric and Respectability," 97–98 (fourth quotation); M. E. Bradford, "Sentiment or Survival: The Case against Amnesty," in *Remembering Who We Are*, 114 (fifth quotation).

49. M. E. Bradford, "The Lasting Lesson of Southern Politics," in *Remembering Who We Are*, 56 (first quotation); Bradford, "The Agrarian Tradition," 89 (quotation).

50. Marion Montgomery, "Remembering Who M. E. Bradford Is," *Modern Age* 41 (Spring 1999): 115–16. In the preface to Bradford's discussion of the "Theology of Secession," the *Southern Partisan*'s editor noted that that paper had originally been presented before the "annual assembly of Southerners at Willie Pie's Store in Crozier, Virginia. Bradford, "Theology of Secession," 20.

51. T. Kenneth Cribb Jr., "M. E. Bradford: An Appreciation," *Southern Partisan* 12 (Fourth Quarter 1992 [1993]): 8 (quotation); Norman Stewart, "'Galloping Tintypes,' the Birth of the Movies: The Legacy of D. W. Griffith," *Southern Partisan* 13 (Fourth Quarter 1993 [1994]): 45. Volumes 12 and 13 of the *Southern Partisan* were dated incorrectly. I have indicated the actual years of publication in brackets.

52. "Forward," *Southern Partisan* 1 (1979): n.p.

53. Clyde N. Wilson, review of *A Better Guide Than Reason* by M. E. Bradford, *Southern Partisan* 1 (1979): 35 (first quotation); "At the Helm," *Southern Partisan* 10 (Fourth Quarter 1990), 10 (second, third, fourth quotations). In addition to "Theology of Secession," Bradford's contributions to the periodical include "William Henry Drayton, a Neglected Founding Father," *Southern Partisan* 1 (1979): 7–17; "The Beast in Todd County," *Southern Partisan* 2 (Fall 1982): 20–24; "Window on the West," *Southern Partisan* 3 (Fall 1983): 22–23; "The Dark Side of Abraham Lincoln," *Southern Partisan* 5 (Fall 1985): 18–22; "Samuel Chase," *Southern Partisan* 6 (Summer 1986), 40–44; "The 'Gamecock' of South Carolina," *Southern Partisan* 6–7 (Fall 1986–Winter 1987): 41–43, 46; "With No Love of Innovation: The Prophetic Politics of Rawlins Lowndes," *Southern Partisan* 7 (Spring 1987): 33, 35–37; "The Nabob as Anti-Federalist: Benjamin Harrison of Virginia," *Southern Partisan* 7 (Summer 1987): 38–39; "The Trumpet Voice of Freedom: Patrick Henry and the Southern Political Tradition," *Southern Partisan* 8 (Summer 1988): 16–19, 22; "Steady Hand

at the Wheel: Thomas Johnson of Maryland," *Southern Partisan* 10 (Second Quarter 1990): 37–39; Bradford, "Theology of Secession," 20–25.

54. Cartwright, "Mr. Right," 60 (first quotation); Matthew Sandel, "Triium," *Southern Partisan* 12 (First Quarter 1992): 7 (second, third, fourth, fifth quotations).

55. *Rome (Ga.) News-Tribune*, January 7, 1996, quoted in "The League of the South in the News, 1996," www.dixienet.org/_vti_bin/shtml.exc/press_quotes/1996news.html/mrpl; "The Right of Secession: A League of the South Position Paper," www.dixienet.org/positions/secede.htm (quotation).

56. "League of the South Institute for the Study of Southern Culture and History," www.dixienet.org/ls-institute/los-institute.htm; Michael J. Hill, "The Issue of Race in the Southern Independence Debate: A Call for Proportionality, Honesty, Integrity, Morality, and an End to Demagoguery," www.dixienet.org/positions/race.htm (quotations).

57. "Melvin Eustace Bradford," *Contemporary Authors*, 70.

7

The Evil Empire Within

Southern Nationalism and the Washington Problem

DAVID R. JANSSON

The South has truly had a conflicted relationship with the national government in Washington for most of its history, and this applies not only to white southerners but also to black southerners and the region's Native Americans. The latter experienced time and again betrayal and oppression, as one treaty after another with the federal government was unilaterally broken by Washington. From the perspective of African Americans in the South, it is worth remembering that the U.S. Constitution defined the enslaved as less than fully human. After the abolition of slavery, the story of Reconstruction in the eyes of black southerners is ultimately one of abandonment, the betrayal of lofty promises. In the twentieth century, having mobilized to fight for their basic civil rights in the region, black southerners often turned to Washington for assistance in solidifying their achievements and breaking new ground. Not infrequently, they faced considerable ambivalence from federal authorities, in contrast to the typically heroic role federal officials (such as the FBI) play in Hollywood renderings of southern history.[1] For southern whites, "the North" represented an important market for the products of the region's fields and factories, but it also signified a power center in Washington, D.C., that was often outside the control of the region's politicians. The tensions between the North and the white South may have culminated in the violent orgy of the Civil War, but they have continued ever since, through Reconstruction, through the major upheavals of the twentieth century, and into the era of a culturalized politics in the 1990s and early twenty-first century.

The white South in particular continues to have an ambivalent relationship with Washington; many parts of the South depend heavily on federal spending for their economic vitality, while Washington seems to increasingly represent the epicenter of overbearing, centralized, unaccountable, and undemocratic power. At issue in this chapter is the contribution of these tensions to the (re)production of a vision of (white) southern identity, and in particular the southern identity subscribed to by southern nationalists. I mean the term as analytic rather than judgmental, and I define "southern nationalists" as those individuals and groups who believe that the entity of the "southern people" make up a separate nation, distinct from the rest of the "American" nation. Quoting historian Clyde Wilson, the Southern National Congress argues that "we Southerners are a separate and distinct people, rooted in kinship and place, with a common culture and history. In other words, we are a nation. We respect the rights of other national and ethnic communities to self-preservation and self-determination, and we demand the same."[2] This interest in the self-determination of the "southern nation" is a defining attribute of southern nationalism.

Southern identity and southern nationalism have been created not within the South but through the interactions between the South and the North (understanding "the North" here as the rest of the country outside the South). Human geographers are keen to emphasize that place identity is produced through interactions between places and at different scales;[3] without these interactions, there is simply no need for a place identity. In the context of regionalism in the United States, historians have noted that the "sectional conflict" forged a coherent regional identity for southern whites and provided the foundation for southern nationalism. (It did the same for northern nationalism, even if this side of the equation is rather neglected compared to its southern counterpart.) In the words of historian John Hope Franklin:

> During these years [the 1840s] the pressures of sectional conflict were causing Southerners to minimize the physiographic variations within their section, the differences in the economic and social status of the people, and the several disagreements in political allegiances and philosophies. Committed to perpetuating a system of servitude increasingly condemned by the rest of the western world, southern whites began to think of themselves as having a set of common values, common problems, common dangers, and common aspirations that set them apart from other Americans. Inevitably they came to believe also that they had a common and distinctive history.[4]

As we know, these "pressures of sectional conflict" would not subside even after the Civil War but would be destined to live on in various forms. Southern nationalism is one expression of the continuation of the sectional conflict.

The purpose of this chapter, then, is to analyze the role of representations of Washington (as a synecdoche for the federal government) in the (re)production of a particular vision of southern identity and southern destiny among southern nationalists. The chapter will focus on two organizations: the League of the South and the Southern National Congress. The data comprise recent communications by these groups, in the form of sixty-three e-mails sent to subscribers to their various listservs between May 9, 2006, and January 9, 2012.

First, some background on these groups. The League of the South was established in June 1994 when a group of forty white southerners met in Tuscaloosa, Alabama, to discuss the formation of an organization that would strive to improve "the public understanding and appreciation of the South's history, and to increase reverence and respect for the region's culture and symbols."[5] By 2002 the League claimed a membership of "upward of fifteen thousand people."[6] The Southern Poverty Law Center has classified the League as a "hate group" because it says the League is "dominated by racism."[7]

Professor Clyde Wilson, a historian at the University of South Carolina and one of the League's leaders, writes that the founding members "unembarrassedly and unfashionably embraced a mission to preserve and celebrate Southern distinctiveness and to that end to promote devolution of power in the United States." He describes the social context of the League's founding in this way:

> There was an urgent sense that distinctive but still viable features of the South were rapidly succumbing to the relentless centralization and standardization of thought, manners, attitudes, and habits of living that characterize modern society. On the other hand, much of the world seemed to be in a devolving mood, with flourishing movements of regional self-assertion such as the Lega Nord in Italy, the Parti Quebecois in Canada, and the Scottish National Party, not to mention the breakup of the Soviet Union. Further, for the first time in its history since the seventeenth century, the South was free of the racial institutions that had drawn condemnation from the outside

world. Thus, there seemed to be a new window of opportunity to celebrate Southern history and culture for its own sake, despite the unpopularity with which such an effort would certainly be received in many quarters.[8]

In the League's eyes, devolution of power to the southern states would be one step on the road to the re-secession of the South and the re-formation of the Confederate States of America. It is clear from the League's website (dixienet.org) and the e-mails discussed below that secession is ultimately seen to be the only way to secure true sovereignty for the South and thus allow the "southern nation" to control its own affairs without interference from the North.

The Southern National Congress (SNC), created in 2008 at the First Southern National Congress in Hendersonville, North Carolina, is also keen for the southern states to minimize their bonds to the federal government. The SNC describes itself as "a representative assembly of citizens of the Southern States, providing an alternative, legitimate forum to express Southern grievances and advance Southern interests in a way that is no longer possible through today's political process or the major political parties." Thomas Moore, chairman of the SNC Committee, explains:

> We believe the courts and especially the U.S. Congress no longer provide the necessary checks on the growth of the centralised state and its threat to our liberty and prosperity. The U.S. Congress no longer represents the people's interests; it represents the interests of the highest bidder, the big corporations and money power. Through oppression, greed, corruption, incompetence, and imperial folly, the centralised state in Washington has forfeited its moral authority. The result is increasingly harsh measures against the people as the Regime loses control. Decent, honourable people of the South who still love liberty and justice, and who seek to preserve their livelihoods, their identity, and their heritage have no choice but to withdraw their consent from this corrupt and criminal Regime. But withdrawing our consent by itself is not enough. We must have alternative, legitimate institutions to which we can transfer our consent. This is the principle behind the SNC.[9]

(Note the British spelling; this represents a conscious effort by groups like the League and the SNC to resist the "Americanization" of the South and reclaim their roots in British culture.) Both the League and the SNC clearly find "southern culture" to be threatened by the South's ties to the rest of the country, particularly to the seat of national political power, Washington. In the following section we will review the themes and arguments presented in the groups' communications.

"Rome on the Potomac": The Washington Empire and the Southern Solution

Significant differences in the perspectives of the two groups are difficult to discern. The League of the South and the Southern National Congress have similar diagnoses of what ails the South, and the culprit is clearly identified as Washington, D.C. One of the primary themes threading through the groups' communications is the notion that the United States has become an ungovernable, unaccountable, and immoral empire that plagues not only the South but distant lands as well. One difference between the groups is that the League pushes the idea of secession much more vigorously and openly than the SNC. The SNC's focus appears to be, at least at this point, on establishing an alternative institutional structure in the South that does not necessarily require secession but which could at some future point be put in the service of that goal.

This section will explore the major themes of the e-mails with regard to their portrayals of the federal government. The underlying theme that provides the foundation for the groups' conceptualization of Washington is that of empire. Specifically, the argument is that the federal government has become an empire—in the military, economic, cultural, and political senses—and that the southern states are suffering under the rule of this empire. The American empire, according to this analysis, pays no heed to the Constitution and ignores the wishes of the population by striking down legislation passed in the states that responds to local needs and desires. Immigration is a subject that is a particular thorn in the sides of the southern nationalists, as it illustrates two key aspects of the problem with Washington: an abuse of power by preventing states from policing their borders to prevent illegal immigration, and the cultural "annihilation" of the South by facilitating an "invasion" of people with a "foreign" culture.

Washington as a Military Empire

Considering both the ancient association of the white South with a militaristic culture and the pro-military views that southerners are said to have in the present, the assertion that the federal government (and by association the armed forces) constitutes a military empire is fairly striking. This theme is highlighted by the League more (at least in these communications) than by the SNC. It should be noted that the majority of the e-mails sent by the League are signed by League president Michael Hill. Hill, a former academic with a Ph.D. in history, is certainly the most prominent voice in the organization and appears to be the most important source of leadership. He is uncompromising in his assault on the federal government, and he does not allow his professional interest in military history to blunt his attack on the United States' military engagements in the international arena. Hill is fond of referring to the U.S. government as an "organized criminal enterprise," and he sees no difference between Republicans and Democrats in terms of the management of the empire:

> Finally, the mainstream Republican Party has no interest whatsoever in curbing the insatiable appetite of the United States government to occupy and control other nations. Irrational fear of the Islamic terror threat has prompted far too many Americans to endorse a perpetual military occupation of Iraq and Afghanistan, with the prospect of war with Iran and possibly Pakistan on the horizon as well. The magnitude of resources consumed by the war machine that is the US military will continue to drag down our economy; yet among all the outrage within the Tea Party and its supporters about government spending, we hear very little about reducing the US military presence in foreign lands.
>
> We at the League of the South believe all peoples are entitled to the right of self-determination, even those who do not share our Southern cultural values. The people of Iraq and Afghanistan should be free to decide for themselves what government they will have, just as the people in Dixie have the same God-given right. This is why we advocate peaceful separation from the United States government.[10]

A few of the themes of this passage are worth highlighting. First, the notion that there is no meaningful difference between the Republican and Democratic Parties is a common one among southern nationalists and is shared by the SNC. Indeed, if the Republican Party were seen as a viable alternative to the Democratic Party, the strategies of self-determination and secession would have less justification. Second, the concern with the economic drain of military spending connects with the feeling (discussed below) that the U.S. economy is hurtling toward collapse. And finally, Hill is very careful to place his interest in the self-determination of the southern nation beside the right of other nations to determine their own fates without external interference. In the cases of (for example) Afghanistan, Iraq, and the South, the external interference is provided by the U.S. government—the difference, of course, being that the South is contained by the territory and rests under the sovereignty of the United States. This difference complicates the League's push for self-determination for the South.

The complication rests in the national patriotism historically exhibited by many white southerners, and this emotional attachment to "America" can make the League's argument a tough sell. Consider the following, from the Florida League of the South's newsletter, distributed by e-mail by Hill:

> Wars start when empires wish to expand. That was the cause of the Spanish-American War, World War I and World War II. The Korean and Vietnam wars were civil wars in which our politicians involved us. The wars against Afghanistan and Iraq are again wars of an empire trying to expand. In these cases, we are the empire, and you might as well face the ugly truth that our invasions of both countries were no different from the Nazi invasions that led to World War II. Neither Afghanistan nor Iraq had attacked us or were even capable of attacking us.[11]

The comparison of the U.S. invasions of Afghanistan and Iraq with the actions of Nazi Germany may be difficult to swallow for southerners who, though they may be frustrated with the federal government, still have an emotional investment in their American national identity. Hill recognizes that his comparison is an "*ugly* truth," in that it is likely to sound offensive to many of his fellow southerners, but he considers it a truth nonetheless. And the ugly truths do not stop with attacks on U.S. foreign policy, but continue through a critique of the tyranny of the federal government's actions at home.

The Domestic Imperial Tyranny of Washington

Both the League of the South and the SNC are emphatic in their accusation that the U.S. government brazenly violates the Constitution at will while simultaneously depriving the residents of individual states the right to enact legislation reflecting the will of the local electorate. Writing under the title "The Harsh Reality of Federal Supremacy," James Ronald Kennedy (half of the writer-duo the "Kennedy Twins") argues:

We the people of the once sovereign states live in the shadow of Federal tyranny. For example; when the people of California expressed their sovereign will in an open plebiscite a Federal judge nullified the will of the people; when the elected legislature of Arizona passed a law to defend the people of that once sovereign state against armed criminal invasion originating from a foreign country, the Federal President filed a suit in the Federal court to prevent Arizona from executing its inalienable right of self-defense; and when the elected governor of Louisiana attempted to protect his state from a man-made disaster in the Gulf of Mexico the Federal bureaucracy stepped in and halted his efforts—the central theme of all of these examples is the fact of the harsh, oppressive, and unconstitutional reality of America's current system of Federal supremacy.[12]

Kennedy signals the Federalist interpretation of the Constitution that the southern nationalists argue is the only legitimate and historically accurate interpretation, that is, that the federal government is beholden to the individual states and not the other way around, that sovereignty resides in fact with the states and not the federal government, the latter being an instrument created by the states to serve the interests of the peoples of the states. The preference is to refer to the country as "these United States," as a plural form, rather than as a singular—"*the* United States." It is the loss of the ability of the states to serve as a check on federal power that is seen as a betrayal of the original intentions of the founders. The League puts it this way:

A majority of Americans agree that we are losing our Founding Principles at an increasing rate. . . . The federal government is out of control because the system of checks and balances established by our Founding Fathers was eliminated. The balances—the three branches of the federal government was intended to keep one branch from totally dominating the other two. More or less this is still in place and works to some extent.

But the checks on the federal government were eliminated at Appomattox, destroyed by the war that Lincoln forced upon the country. Our Founding Fathers considered the States to be the check on the federal government, to force it to abide by the Constitution. But the ability of the States to restrain or be a check on the federal government was the loser in the War of Southern Independence.[13]

Thus one of the things the Civil War accomplished, according to this analysis, was to eliminate the states as a check on the federal government, thereby facilitating the concentration of power in Washington at the expense of the states. The struggle to hold the federal government accountable and ensure that its actions are consistent with the Constitution is thus seen, in a sense, as a continuation of the Civil War. This has the effect of simultaneously legitimizing that historic conflict and the present battle against the perceived domestic tyranny of the federal government.

The matter of interpreting the intentions of the founders is of central importance to both groups; history lessons are a common element in their communications. For example, the SNC e-mailed a series of essays titled "What Is States' Rights?" by Mike Crane, who is a member of both the SNC and the League. In these essays, Crane discusses the idea of states' rights and how the concept was intended to work by the founders. He goes into extensive detail and supports his argument with quotes from the original sources. Crane's essays can be seen in the context of the desire of southern nationalists to educate southerners about their "true" history, a task made necessary by the fact (from the perspective of southern nationalists) that what they refer to as the "government" (or public) schools do not teach the truth about southern history. This was a repeated theme in my interviews with members of the League. When asked his opinion on what the most important goal for the League is, one respondent replied: "At the moment I think the most important goal is education. Because the amount of ignorance out there about why the [Civil] War was fought is boundless, I'm sorry to say. You know, unless all of them are replaced with truth, not much can be accomplished in terms of reestablishing a proper relationship between the states and Washington, which is one of the goals of a lot of members of the League, which right now is completely hopeless."[14] As this respondent suggests, one of the primary purposes of the League's educational mission is to pave the way for a return to the days when the states served as effective checks on Washington's power. This goal cannot be achieved, however, and southerners will not be motivated to act, if the general population is unaware of the historical role that states played—and were meant to play—according to early interpretations of the Constitution.

That said, one of the challenges facing the South, from the perspective of southern nationalists, is that the region is oppressed by Washington in more than just the political sphere. In fact, the e-mails argue that "the

North" as a whole (not just the federal government) promotes a kind of cultural imperialism that threatens to eliminate "true" southern culture.

Cultural Imperialism and the Threat to Southern Culture

In addition to being a military and political empire, southern nationalists find the federal government to be responsible for a cultural imperialism that threatens the integrity and future of southern culture. As the League has argued, "Living under the yoke of the Yankee empire has already damaged our Southern culture. Will we be able to leave any of it to our children and grandchildren? Not if the Yankee empire has its way."[15] The following statement, called the "Declaration of Southern Cultural Independence," was originally issued by the League on March 4, 2000, and is worth quoting at length on this subject:

> [W]e exhort all Southerners to abjure the realm of the American Empire that now threatens the liberties of our families and communities, and of the corrupt and sterile national culture that pervades this land. The national culture of the United States is violent and profane, coarse and rude, cynical and deviant, and repugnant to the Southern people and to every people with authentic Christian sensibilities. Purveyors of the national culture have everywhere lowered standards of morality and debased human dignity. They have appealed to mankind's worst impulses through profanity and obscenity in the arts and literature; they have depicted decadence and debauchery as normal and desirable; they have distorted Southern symbols and denied our right to interpret or display those symbols; they have assumed the authority of parents in the areas of religion and education; they thus have driven a wedge between the generations; they have prostituted all areas of thought and learning for market share; they have demonised Southern heroes and canonised tyrants and war criminals; they have distorted Southern history to advance their ideas of social justice; they thus have driven a wedge between the races and regions; they have destroyed hope; they have spread despair; they have called good evil and evil good; they have everywhere substituted the opinions of men for the decrees of God.
>
> We, as Southerners, will, as far as possible, decline to participate in this alien, national culture. Rather, we shall seek to defend and perpetuate our noble heritage and be of service to our people.[16]

Thus the cultural forces that are felt to be undesirable are given an origin outside the boundaries of the South and defined as national (that is, non-southern) in character. The League is essentially describing a binary moral geography where "America" represents cultural degradation and "the South" stands for a pure, dignified, moral, and especially Christian culture. Importantly, this southern culture constitutes its own *national* culture, distinct from the other culture(s) in the United States:

> I believe we Southerners are a distinct People, with our own particular folkways, traditions, customs, music, speech, and a common history lived out in a shared space. In essence, we are an authentic nation. In fact, I believe we are the last authentic Western civilization in the historic sense of the word "civilization," especially in contrast to today's America, with its militant secularism, tawdry commercialism, and infantile celebrity worship that pass for civilization. One thing that distinguishes us in today's America is that we Southerners understand the truth that we are what we remember. We are a people rich in memory.[17]

As suggested above, one challenge to the southern nationalist movement is that one cannot "remember" something that one has neither participated in nor heard about. Thus in order for southerners to embrace the truths of what they are, which are strongly grounded in their collective past, they need to know the truths of that past. Once again, this signals the important educational role of groups like the League and the SNC.

As we have seen, southern nationalists argue that southern culture is inherently Christian, and furthermore that the South is the only part of the United States that tries to remain faithful to the country's founding Christian vision: "Southern culture is founded on the enduring and permanent: trust in God, family, tradition, manners, property, community, loyalty, courage, and honour. We know that free and just government cannot derive from laws, regulations, bureaucracies, and ideologies. It springs only from the soil of faith and love, watered by struggle and sacrifice, and the harvest of which is liberty, justice, prosperity, and peace."[18] It is thus not surprising that the communications of both groups are often replete with biblical references and Christian metaphors. For example, the SNC adopted a "Southern National Covenant" at its second congress:

> In mutual support of one another as Christian Southerners, we covenant together

To renounce the evils of corrupt government that our forebears warned against, and to resist by all honourable means acts of federal tyranny, as our circumstances permit and as the Lord leads.

To seek to revive our local economies, working together to promote every man's prosperity as our own and toward freeing ourselves from the snare the Empire's worthless money and perpetual debt which are the lifeblood of tyranny, and seeking a return to honest public money in daily use—gold and silver coin or currency backed by gold and silver.

To support every measure which restores the sovereignty of our State and local governments, and the sovereignty of the Southern people.

To resist any Federal statute or Presidential directive that threatens our fundamental freedoms of speech, press, assembly, exercise of religion, and petition for redress, freedom from illegal search and seizure, and the right of due process under law.

Never to allow ourselves willingly to be disarmed nor submit to the confiscation of our means of lawful self defence; nor comply with any firearms registration scheme, which is the certain precursor to confiscation.

We declare before God and men that we earnestly desire to restore a Godly order in our respective States by peaceful means. We seek only that which may turn to the honour of God and the increase of peace and justice in our States and communities. Yet the growing evils of the time may not grant us the choice of peaceful means of redress. In such a pass, when criminal violence may be directed against one of us by the state, our fortunes shall be as their fortunes, their wives or husbands as our wives and husbands, their children as our children, their losses as our losses, and injuries done them as injuries to our own persons; and we shall not rest till they be delivered.[19]

It us thus clear that for southern nationalists, the term "Christian Southerner" is redundant.[20]

We have now discussed the ways in which southern nationalists consider Washington to represent a political and cultural empire within the borders of the United States. As the above excerpt suggests, there is also an important economic element to Washington's empire, and this is something southern nationalists are keen to resist.

Economic Imperialism

According to the analysis presented in the e-mails, the federal government is the primary culprit behind the North's economic imperialism. One of the tools of this economic oppression is the federal treasury: "At bottom, Washington's power is economic. The feds rely for control on taxing money from the states and giving some of it back in exchange for obedience. They cannot arrest Wyoming, but they can deny it federal highway funds. This technique provides de facto control over everything from kindergarten to MIT."[21] There is a sense in which federal funding chains not just southern states but also individual southerners to the federal government in a relationship of dependency: "On a personal level it is time for Southerners to wean themselves from dependence on federal largesse. Since the New Deal, Washington has funneled more tax dollars into the South than it has taken out, and this has caused the region to be bound tightly by the attached strings. If Southerners are ever to be free from federal dictates, we must learn to provide for our own needs without depending on government wealth transfers."[22] It is not the money itself that is the crux of the problem; rather, it is the *strings* to which the money is attached that constitute the destructiveness of the act of receiving federal money. The strings mean that the acceptance of the money comes at a high cost, that of the gradual dissolving of "southern culture" and the weakening of the "southern economy."

In a speech at the 2003 annual meeting of the League of the South, Robert W. Watson—head of the English Department at a Christian school, graduate of Bob Jones University, and frequent lecturer to the Sons of Confederate Veterans and home-school conventions, as well as the League—exhorted League members to take a range of steps to resist the subordination of the South. In addition to getting guns for the family and taking the kids out of "government" schools, Watson offers a couple of suggestions that relate to resisting economic subordination. One is to start one's own business. The idea behind this recommendation is that small businesses are seen as less beholden to the national capitalist machine and thus would help to free the South and southerners from external economic domination. By running one's own "southern" business rather than working for a "foreign" multinational corporation, the southerner contributes to the region's economic secession from the United States and simultaneously gains control over the family's economy. The logic is similar behind the exhortation to start an intensive organic garden. The garden provides food for the family, and because it is organic it reduces one's dependence on the multinational chemical companies that produce fertilizers and pesticides.[23] The problematic nature of these corporations underscores the fact that Washington is not the sole economic problem facing the South, according to the southern nationalists.

In fact, the potential importance of the garden in feeding one's family is highlighted by the argument that the U.S. empire is doomed to collapse in the not-so-distant future. The League has encouraged its members to make preparations for the possibility of the serious instability within the United States in the near future; as Michael Hill puts it, it is time to "man the lifeboats."[24] In fact, the theme of the League's annual meeting in 2008 was "Surviving the Empire's Collapse." As the League put it in promotional information for its 2008 conference e-mailed by Michael Hill:

> As inflation soars and the dollar falls, resulting in higher and higher prices for energy, food, and many other necessities, life becomes more difficult for the average, hard-working families of the South. Indeed, because of these factors coupled with continuing wars and the subprime mortgage crisis and the potential meltdown of the credit markets, it is, we believe, imperative that folks learn how to provide for the basic necessities themselves or at least within their local communities. Not since the Great Depression of the 1930s has it been more important for local communities to be able to help themselves instead of depending on a fragile system of money, credit, supply, and transportation. The speeches at our 2008 conference will help you understand the crisis and prepare practically to withstand it. If we are to be there to "pick up the pieces" after the collapse and restore ordered liberty to our communities and States, then we had better start getting ready now.
>
> Among the things you will learn: How to help develop a local agricultural economy; How to become a freeholder and wean yourself from dependence on the corporate system; How gold and silver can free you from a corrupt inflationary money system; How to implement the ideas of the Nashville Agrarians and the English Distributists in our own day; How to organize a political movement based on "localism;" Short- and long-term strategies for self-sufficient households; the Biblical foundations for self-sufficiency and localism, among others.[25]

It is by now clear that these are not just solutions to the expected crisis; they are specifically *southern* solutions that provide continuity with the past experiences, practices, and philosophies of the South.

To summarize the previous three sections, from the perspective of southern nationalists, the social coherence, cultural integrity, economic health, and political viability of the South is threatened by the American empire, based in Washington, D.C. An example of a contemporary issue that brings together all of these concerns is that of border policing and immigration.

Immigration and Washington's Betrayal of the South

The League has been particularly vocal about the subject of "illegal immigration," and this section will focus primarily on the League's views as expressed in their e-mail communications. (The SNC has similar views on this issue, as expressed on their website, but immigration was not mentioned in the e-mails under consideration.) The League has forcefully opposed the federal government's challenges to immigration legislation in Alabama, Georgia, and Arizona. In Alabama, the state legislature passed a bill in 2011 that was intended to deny undocumented immigrants the ability to buy or rent a home, to work or to travel, and to enter contracts. The Justice Department challenged this legislation as unconstitutional, to the chagrin of the League.

> The League of the South, the oldest and most prominent Southern nationalist organization, deplores the federal government's attempt to thwart the will of the people of the Sovereign State of Alabama....
>
> We in the League encourage the people of Alabama to contact their Governor and State legislators to let them know that the feds must be resisted to the point of nullification, interposition and secession, if necessary. This is a hostile act against Alabama. If enough illegal aliens come here, it will change the cultural and demographic make-up of our State to the point that it will become a Third World entity. I don't think most Alabamians would want that to happen.[26]

For Hill and the League, the federal government's actions constitute a suppression of local democracy, or the ability of the residents of Alabama to enact legislation that reflects their will. From the League's perspective, legislation such as Alabama's is necessary to address the inability or unwillingness of the federal government to prevent undocumented migrants from crossing the border from Mexico into the United States. Thus, if Alabama does not take charge of the situation, the cultural integrity of the state will be mortally threatened. There is a clear racialized imagined geography at work here, as these Spanish-speaking immigrants are associated with the "Third World" and are presented as being fundamentally out of place in Alabama.

A similar anti-immigration bill was passed in Georgia in April 2011. A federal judge later halted two sections of the law while upholding other parts of the bill. The problematic sections involved one that would have given police the ability to check the immigration status of suspects who do not produce identification, and one that would punish people who knowingly harbored or transported undocumented immigrants in the act of committing a crime.[27] In response to the judge's decision, the League issued this statement:

> "By striking down these measures, the federal government has literally ripped the guts out of Georgia's anti-immigration law," said League President Michael Hill. "The majority of Georgians support their State's attempt to end the scourge of illegal immigration," Hill continued. "They don't want federal judges telling them that they can't defend the borders of their sovereign territory. Moreover, in this terrible economy there are undoubtedly plenty of native Georgians who would like to have one of the many jobs that are currently held by someone here illegally."[28]

If the response to the Alabama legislation focused on cultural and political issues, here we see the addition of explicitly economic concerns. Thus do federal judges not only violate the South's cultural integrity and political autonomy but also hamper the economic prospects of native southerners.

In an attack on yet another federal court ruling on immigration legislation, this one targeting a bill passed in Arizona, the League argued that "the federal government has shown itself to be an organized, criminal enterprise that defines the extent of its own power and rules for the benefit of the elite."[29] According to the League, the motivating factor behind the federal government's desire to strike down anti-immigration legislation is the philosophy it calls multiculturalism, or "MC." In a 2006 essay titled "The Poison of Multiculturalism," Hill wrote that multiculturalism is

> the poison that will ultimately prove fatal to Western Christian civilization unless an antidote is quickly administered. At present, the

main method by which the poison is being pumped into the West's veins is Third World immigration.... MC is really not about ushering in equality among all races, religions, and cultures; rather, it is about destroying Western Christian civilization, the world's premier unmitigated evil. And because the South is the strongest enclave of this civilization, it finds itself square in the crosshairs of the MC crowd. Why do you think the Feds are not willing to lift a hand to stop our dispossession by a floodtide of illegal immigrants? It is the continuation of Reconstruction to the ultimate degree....

All indications point to the success of the MC agenda of paralyzing the West through guilt manipulation. Though we never had any sort of debate about whether we wanted to be a MC nation, it has been forced upon us anyway. Anyone who protests is silenced by the usual epithets. Even opposition to illegal immigration is enough to get you called a "racist" or a "xenophobe."

If the scenario of the South (and the rest of America) being overrun by hordes of non-white immigrants does not appeal to you, then how is this disaster to be averted? By the people who oppose it rising up against their traitorous elite masters and their misanthropic rule. But to do this we must first rid ourselves of the fear of being called "racists" and the other meaningless epithets they use against us. What is really meant by the MC advocates when they peg us as "racists" is that we adhere to ethnocentrism, which is a natural affection for one's own kind. This is both healthy and Biblical. I am not ashamed to say that I prefer my own kind and my own culture. Others can have theirs; I have mine. No group can survive for long if its members do not prefer their own over others.[30]

Hill does several things here. First, he suggests that multiculturalism is being advanced by the federal government not ultimately for the sake of diversity but rather in the service of reconstructing the South, which is in turn motivated by some irrational hatred of Western Christian values. Presumably, "Western Christian civilization" has been either eradicated or at least neutered in the rest of the country, necessitating a final push to conquer its bastion in the South. These rulings by U.S. District Court judges are thus really salvos in the continuing war between the Confederacy and *the* United States (aka the federal government).

Second, Hill reproduces the essentialized binary of the imagined spaces of "America" and "the South" by positing these spaces as fundamentally different and existing in opposition. Each end of this binary is thus homogenized and totalized, suggesting that it would be somehow "un-Southern" to oppose the legislation passed in Alabama and Georgia. Finally, Hill tries to defuse the issue of racism by questioning the validity of the term and contesting its application to people who oppose "being overrun by hordes of non-white immigrants." The League is no stranger to charges of racism, and much of this can be traced to the group's stance on immigration and comments such as these about the invading hordes. This comment also reveals the extent to which the League racializes the imagined space of the South. That these "hordes" are "non-white" suggests that the only racial classification that is "in place" in the South is white; the presence of black southerners in the region is quietly erased, as is that of the Native Americans who still call the South home. The preference for one's own "race" is naturalized, and even "biblicized"—the assertion that "ethnocentrism" is biblical is meant to help ameliorate potential concerns the reader might have about being called a racist; Hill wants to stress that ethnocentric white Christian southerners have God on their side.

That the southern god is a Christian god means that other religions are as out of place in the region as are non-whites. Islam, for example, is an unwelcome addition to the South's cultural landscape, in the eyes of the League. After a U.S. Army officer, a Muslim, shot and killed thirteen people at the U.S. Army base at Fort Hood, Texas, in November 2009, the League issued this statement:

> The League of the South, the premier State Sovereignty and Secessionist organization, deplores not only the recent shootings at Fort Hood, Texas, by Muslim jihadists, but the cowering, politically correct reaction of the mainstream media and the US government.
>
> The murders point to the fact that the multicultural US military (and the larger society in general) is not working. The reaction from the media and various organs of the US government demonstrates that maintaining the correct multicultural attitudes is more important than the lives of US servicemen and citizens. For proof, we quote General George Casey: "What happened at Fort Hood was a tragedy, but I believe it would be an even greater tragedy if our diversity becomes a casualty here. It's not just about Muslims, we have a very diverse army, we have very diverse society and that gives us all strength."

League President Dr. Michael Hill noted that "Diversity, in this sense, does not make us stronger; it makes us weaker, and it gives the DC government more power to run its empire by displacing the descendants of the European, Christian founding stock with compliant and dependent immigrants from the Third World. The only antidote to this insanity is the reassertion of State sovereignty and secession. That is the only way to save our liberty and prosperity, and we ought to make it happen as soon as possible. Procrastination only allows the ruling elite to forge our chains even stronger than they are at present."[31]

If Washington multiculturalism, as the League might call it, is the enemy, then once again the solution is state sovereignty and secession. The federal government is beyond reform, the powers behind it too strong for southerners to have any hope at taming the beast.

A consideration of the League's stance on undocumented immigration illustrates that in order to fully understand the southern nationalist position it is important to be aware of their interpretation of the U.S. government as empire, at home and abroad. This is an empire that is bent on using the cover of multiculturalism to destroy Western civilization generally, and southern culture specifically. Southern nationalism, then, is the most relevant, promising, and urgent solution to this problem.

Conclusion

Ronald Reagan famously referred to the Soviet Union as an "evil empire." It will be clear by now that the title of this chapter, "The Evil Empire Within," is a reference to the idea that southern nationalists consider the federal government a domestic empire as much as an international one, as the government operates within the borders of the United States. However, in another crucially important respect, this evil empire is actually foreign to the South, and thus in a way not *truly* within. This is because the imagined geographies of southern nationalism posit "the South" and "America" (as represented by Washington, D.C.) as fundamentally different, occupying opposite poles of an essentialist binary that homogenizes and totalizes both ends. While the southern states are legally part of the United States of America, from the perspective of southern nationalists, the (white) South constitutes a fundamentally different culture from the rest of the country, one that is (somewhat ironically) true to the founding ideals of the United States, even while these ideals may have been forgotten elsewhere in the fifty states. Thus this particular evil empire oppresses southerners in their homeland while it simultaneously oppresses other nations in their homelands.

I hope it is obvious that the views I have been presenting are those of the southern nationalists themselves, even when I have not explicitly qualified them as such (as in the previous sentence). However, I find myself in the interesting situation of agreeing with some of the southern nationalist critique of the federal government. It is striking that the critiques of the U.S. wars quoted above could have been written by just about any commentator from the left. Few would confuse the southern nationalists with leftists, but elements of their anti-imperial, anti-multinational corporation critique are consistent with the views of those who occupy the other side of the ideological aisle. Especially in light of the recent Occupy movement, one is tempted to consider the possibilities for potential cooperation between southern nationalists and activist groups on the left.

The ability to envision concrete alliances between such groups is, however, beyond the powers of this author. An obvious stumbling block is the mental association that many (if not most) in the United States make between southern nationalism and racism, which is grounded partly in the words of southern nationalists and partly in prejudices that many outside the South have against white southerners (at least in the abstract). Southern nationalist movements might gain credibility if they were able to cultivate links with activists on the left, but that in itself would be enough of a reason for many of these activists to shun such potential alliances, in spite of any similarities in parts of their critiques of the U.S. government. (Interestingly, Michael Hill claims that the League had been asked to participate in some of the Occupy protests throughout the South, but he declined because the League prefers abandoning Wall Street, rather than trying to reform it, by forming a southern republic.)[32]

Notes

1. See David R. Jansson, "'A Geography of Racism': Internal Orientalism and the Construction of American National Identity in the Film *Mississippi Burning*," *National Identities* 7, no. 3 (2005): 265–85.

2. See www.southernnationalcongress.org/2ndcallfordelegatesprint.html (accessed January 25, 2012).

3. See, e.g., Doreen Massey, *Space, Place, and Gender* (Minneapolis: University of

Minnesota Press, 1994); and John A. Agnew, *Place and Politics: The Geographical Mediation of Society* (Boston: Allen & Unwin, 1987).

4. John Hope Franklin, "As for Our History . . . ," in *The Southerner as American*, ed. Charles Grier Sellers Jr. (Chapel Hill: University of North Carolina Press, 1960), 5.

5. Gerald R. Webster, "If at First You Don't Secede, Try, Try, Again," in *Spaces of Hate: Geographies of Discrimination and Intolerance in the U.S.A.*, ed. Colin Flint (New York: Routledge, 2004), 137. According to League president Michael Hill (interview with the author, July 10, 2003), twenty-eight out of the forty attendees stayed until the end of the meeting to become part of the new organization.

6. Clyde N. Wilson, "The Greatness of Southern Literature," in *Dictionary of Literary Biography, Yearbook: 2002*, ed. Matthew J. Bruccoli and Georbe Garrett (Detroit: Gale, 2002), 469–72.

7. Webster, "If at First You Don't Secede," 138.

8. Wilson, "The Greatness of Southern Literature," 469.

9. All quotes are from http://spofga.org/flag/2008/august/southern_national_congress.php (accessed November 3, 2013).

10. Michael Hill, "League of the South Statement," October 2010, http://www.freetennessee.org/ (accessed October 27, 2013).

11. Florida League of the South newsletter, e-mailed by M. Hill, November 25, 2007.

12. Southern National Congress newsletter, September 7, 2010, quoting James Ronald Kennedy.

13. League of the South weekly update, December 27, 2007.

14. Jansson, "'A Geography of Racism'"; Mike Crane, "What Is States' Rights?," http://dixienet.org/rights/2013/what_is_states_rights_part1.php (accessed October 25, 2013).

15. League of the South update, November 23, 2009.

16. Ibid.

17. Southern National Congress, June 1, 2010, by Thomas Moore.

18. Southern National Congress, January 3, 2010.

19. Ibid., excerpt from the Southern National Covenant, adopted by the second Southern National Congress, September 12, 2009.

20. For more on the religious views of League of the South members, see David Jansson, "What Would Lee Do? Religion and the Moral Landscapes of Southern Nationalism in the United States," in *Mapping the End Times: American Evangelical Geopolitics and Apocalyptic Visions*, ed. Jason Dittmer and Tristan Sturm (Farnham, Surrey, UK: Ashgate, 2010), 27–47.

21. Southern National Congress, April 13, 2010, by Fred Reed.

22. League of the South, February 4, 2011, quoting from the New Dixie Manifesto, published in the *Washington Post* on October 29, 1995.

23. Information for this paragraph comes from David Robert Jansson, "Voices of the Other(s): Internal Orientalism and the Construction of Southern Identities in the U.S." (Ph.D. diss., Pennsylvania State University, 2005).

24. League of the South, "Southern Patriot," January–February 2009, e-mailed February 24, 2009.

25. Michael Hill, League of the South News and Updates, August 16, 2008, e-mailed August 18, 2008.

26. League of the South News and Updates, August 12, 2011, League of the South statement.

27. See Jeremy Redmon, "Judge Halts Parts of Anti-Illegal Immigration Law," *Atlanta Journal-Constitution*, June 27, 2011, http://www.ajc.com/news/news/local-govt-politics/judge-halts-parts-of-anti-illegal-immigration-law/nQwnX.

28. League of the South News and Updates, July 1, 2011, League of the South statement.

29. League of the South statement on lawsuit, July 28, 2010.

30. League of the South update, May 9, 2006.

31. League of the South press release, November 9, 2009.

32. From the e-mail "Statements on current events, October 19, 2011" from the League of the South.

IV

Economic Development and Reform

8

Getting Farmers—and Tourists— "Out of the Mud"

Alabama's Nineteenth-Century Experience with Public Projects and Its Response to the Federal Road Aid Acts of 1916 and 1921

MARTIN T. OLLIFF

Alabama has a well-deserved reputation as a consistent opponent of the federal government, especially when it "intrudes" on the prerogatives of the state's powerful elite and their populist allies. From the secessionist rhetoric of "fire-eaters" like William Lowndes Yancy to the "late unpleasantness" of Civil War, from political Redemption during Reconstruction to the Dixiecrat movement of 1948 and beyond, from Governors John Patterson's and George Wallace's resistance to racial desegregation to Governor Fob James's quixotic insistence that the Fourteenth Amendment does not apply to states, Alabamians have presented themselves as a caricature of anti-federal mossbackism. This stereotype sometimes portrays Alabama as pridefully willing to reject any assistance from the federal government—particularly in the form of grants with strings attached.[1]

Of course, however much truth it contains, this stereotype obscures the far more nuanced history of relations between Alabama and the federal government. Even a cursory glance reveals that Alabama has readily accepted exceptional levels of targeted federal largesse: the Tennessee Valley Authority and Marshall Space Flight Center in northern Alabama; thriving or recently decommissioned military bases in Anniston, Montgomery, Mobile, and the Wiregrass; federal assistance to keep Mobile Bay open for shipping; VA hospitals; and the social safety net that allows consumers to buy goods and services in poor communities or retirement destinations.

Inspecting the state map reveals a more concrete example of Alabama's eagerness to accept federal intervention—paved roads. America's—and

Alabama's—modern highway system began in earnest toward the end of the Progressive Era specifically because the federal government provided financing and required systematic management as well as technical expertise. Alabama's response to the Federal Road Aid Acts of 1916 and 1921 demonstrates that the state was not only content to accept federal funds (even with strings attached) but also actively sought such funds and direction.

Alabama was incapable of improving its transportation infrastructure, but it was not alone in its predicament; very few states had the constitutional authorization or political machinery required to raise the enormous amounts of capital needed to build and maintain highways capable of supporting automobile and truck traffic. Nor did more than a handful of states have the managerial or engineering ability to create a workable system of roadways regardless of the kind of traffic they served. Alabama is far from unique concerning road building. It is, rather, a case study.

Some background is in order to show how Alabama had hobbled its ability to carry out projects for the public good, making the state and its citizens long for the deep pockets of Progressive Era Washington, D.C. Alabama roads began poor and deteriorated over the nineteenth century for multiple reasons. In his 1935 master's thesis, Leonard C. Cooke followed H. B. Meyer and U. B. Phillips to locate the original causes for Alabama's poor roads in the character, economy, and needs of the people. Cooke maintained that Alabamians were individualistic and conservative, which inhibited joint projects for the common good. This reluctance came from more practical concerns as well. For many years before and after statehood, Alabama's population was scattered lightly across the state. The less prosperous engaged in subsistence agriculture, which meant they carried few crops to market and so needed few roads beyond walking or mule trails. The more prosperous cotton planters, though they were part of the market economy, needed roads only from plantation to steamboat landing. Because planters used roads for little more than transporting their cotton harvest during the lay-by when time delays were unimportant, poor roads that slowed travel or required multiple lightly laden teams were not a concern.[2]

Economic historian Gavin Wright supplies a different perspective that also explains Alabamians' reluctance to invest in transportation infrastructure of any kind. Planters, he writes, were not landlords tied to a home place that they nourished and improved with an eye to maximizing long-term profits from the land. Rather, they were labor lords highly invested in slaves instead of land. Planters used slaves to raise as many crops of King Cotton as possible; then, when they wore out the soil, they moved on.[3] Planters, therefore, were not likely to commit their own labor resources—slaves—to building roads that lasted beyond their own limited needs. As mobile as planters though less likely to be lords of the lash, subsistence farmers also discounted improving roads and other physical infrastructure that they themselves might use only occasionally and then only for a few years.

Beyond farmers' disinterest in improving overland transportation systems, Alabama's political structure impeded road building by making it the province of underfunded county governments. Beginning with the territorial acts of 1818, Alabama law specified that four-member courts of county commissioners and probate judges were responsible for building and maintaining roads, bridges, and ferries in their counties. Two years later, "An Act to Reduce into One the Several Acts Concerning Roads, Bridges, Ferries, and Highways" further strengthened the counties' control over roads, allowing the courts of commissioners to divide each electoral precinct into road sections and appoint overseers. This 1820 law also empaneled "juries of seven freeholders" to advise the courts of commissioners on routes for new roads. These juries were oath-bound to "lay the road out to the greatest advantage to the public"; this stands in marked contrast to neighboring Mississippi, where the law allowed any ten freeholders along a trail to demand the county establish a road for their benefit.[4] Such an administrative infrastructure, though more functional and compact than that of its western neighbor, was neither fiscally nor politically robust enough to finance roads programmatically. Furthermore, it established a barrier to creating road systems or using then-advanced techniques of road construction such as macadam surfaces. A majority on each jury and court of commissioners had to vote in favor of cooperating with other jurisdictions to link roads into a system or use new building methods, both of which required large organizations and much tax money to implement effectively.

Such expense and organizational scale themselves were problematic in nineteenth- and early-twentieth-century Alabama. Many ordinary Alabamians dogmatically resisted increasing taxes for any reason and distrusted large economic entities; on the other hand, the planters who dominated the state's political elite favored the emerging market economy with its requirements for capital and organizational intensity, and those who put down roots in the state were expert at equating their desires with conceptions of the public interest. The resulting struggle between planters and ordinary citizens rendered the state as a whole ambivalent about the role of governmental support of public projects. Alabama's early constitutions allowed the state to expend public funds to gather information on navigable waterways and roads, but it did not address the emerging issue of public funding for internal improvements or corporate aid. As the nineteenth century progressed, the state's political elite secured public funding for banks and nascent railroads. Ultimately, their success split the state over providing support for large general projects, expanding the public debt, and using public credit to support corporate indebtedness. Railroads provided the model for how Alabamians thought about public support for improving transportation infrastructure throughout the nineteenth century and into the twentieth, but the collapse of the Bank of Alabama in the 1840s laid the foundation for Alabamians' ongoing distrust of private or public corporate power.

During the cotton boom that occurred from the end of the War of 1812 until the Panic of 1837, Alabama's economy grew so quickly that the state created the Bank of Alabama in 1825 to exploit loose money policies and the wealth such policies entailed. Lax oversight and the Jacksonian apotheosis of the "man on the make" led the state's political structure to ignore the concentrated power and corruption of two of the bank's branches. But the Panic of 1837 changed that. Tales of illegal loans, bad practices, and overall malfeasance dominated reports in the state press for eight years between the beginning of the panic and the final liquidation of the state bank in 1843. One legislative investigation demonstrated that the Decatur branch held in specie only 1 percent of its outstanding notes, and the Mobile branch only 4 percent. All branches trafficked in sweetheart loans to directors (illegal), directors' friends (immoral), and well-placed legislators (out-and-out bribery). Bank reform became a central issue in the 1841 gubernatorial and legislative campaigns. One reform legislator's investigation led to shocking revelations of excessive uncollectable loans and to a reinvigorated call to close the Bank of Alabama altogether. Proceeding slowly for fear of doing more damage to the struggling economy, the legislature liquidated the Decatur and Mobile branches. Vindictive friends of those branches allied with the east Alabama hard-money foes of banking to wreck the entire system. These allies were able to pass an act that required any operating branch to redeem in specie any other branch's notes, making the frugal but strapped, semi-autonomous branches liable for the profligacy and malfeasance of the Mobile and Decatur branches. This poison pill killed the Bank of Alabama and left citizens with a withered private banking sector, a shrunken currency supply, and a mountain of bonded indebtedness. Citizens remembered the pain and humiliation of these events for a long time, and it shaped their perception of large public investments of any kind.[5]

In addition to their repulsion at the level of corruption and the unsavory political maneuvering of closing the bank, Alabamians must have been profoundly disappointed at the failed promise that bank profits alone could fund state government. In their own version of "irrational exuberance," Alabamians acted as though the cotton boom and ensuing bank profits would last forever; the state actually stopped direct taxation in 1835. In the wake of the bank's failure, however, Alabama resumed collecting internal taxes, which were much more onerous than if they had grown over time.[6]

The sides that squared off in the Bank of Alabama fiasco resumed their battle on the question of public financing of railroads. As they had with banks during the boom times, antebellum planters and merchants touted railroads as both a panacea for the ills confronting river transport and a requirement for improving the overall economy. But railroads were expensive, and private corporations had difficulty raising enough capital to build and operate them effectively. Merchants and planters wanted the state government to aid railroads by backing bonds and providing subsidies. Smallholders and subsistence farmers, on the other hand, stood against public funding of internal improvements. Some considered such funding as a raid on the treasury by the well-connected who should fund their own transport system, since they were the only ones likely to use it. Other smallholders opposed public funding of railroads because of the sectional jealousies at play in the state since its founding or because of their strict construction of the state constitution. Because the need for railroads and the question of state funding emerged in the 1850s, just after the state bank failed, many opponents simply did not trust the state to manage fiscal affairs properly. Regardless, these sides hammered away as they usually did—in electoral politics and through the partisan press.[7]

The central issue of the gubernatorial campaigns of 1853 and 1855 was state subsidies for railroads. Conservative Democrat John Winston ran successfully in both contests as an opponent of public support for internal improvements. He received 60 percent of the vote in his second campaign, almost entirely from yeomen who opposed public funding of railroads, but faced legislators who supported such assistance. Reflecting the concerns of those who voted him into office just a decade after the bank closure, he feared placing more debt onto the state's books; he also believed that private corporations should be privately funded. The legislature was equally strong-minded and overrode central Winston vetoes, thus providing a $400,000 loan to the Mobile and Ohio Railroad (which paled in comparison to the City of Mobile's subsidy of $1.1 million). These subsidies and the resistance to them demonstrate the ambivalence of Alabama's political system concerning the public funding of both internal improvements and private ventures, but the continued wrangling over such support slowed the growth of railroads as well as industrialization in Alabama. By 1860 Alabama had only 743 miles of track, and the Mobile and Ohio relied on English capital for its completion in 1861.[8]

Prosecuting the Civil War led Alabama's body politic to postpone consideration of antebellum questions, and the war's conclusion changed the political and economic calculus that underpinned those older questions. The Reconstruction legislature took a different tack from Winston's defensive parsimony, and was extraordinarily generous to private railroad companies. The results were predictable. In 1867 the Democratic legislature provided direct support of $12,000 per mile to railroads that had completed twenty miles of track. The following year the new Radical Republican legislature expanded the terms, and the Constitution of 1868 even enshrined the right of the legislature to do so; this was the first time an Alabama constitution made it the state's responsibility to advance and support internal improvements. In these wild days, fraud prevailed in state funding of railroads just as it did at the national level. The Alabama and Chattanooga Railroad is the most prominent of such frauds, but not the only one. This road built 240 miles of track, of which 154 were actually in Alabama. According to law, it was entitled to $768,000 of state subsidy, but the legislature had endorsed $4.2 million in Alabama and Chattanooga bonds and issued $2 million in state bonds using the railroad's property as collateral. Unsurprisingly, after being pumped so full of cash, the Alabama and Chattanooga defaulted and went into bankruptcy, the state paid interest on all the bonds, then bought at auction the company property that it already owned for $312,000 (state and federal courts later vacated this action). Eventually, Alabama paid bondholders more than $1 million. Similar antics occurred with the South and North Railroad, the East Alabama and Cincinnati Railroad, the Selma and Gulf Railroad, the Mobile and Alabama Railroad, the Eufaula and Montgomery line, and others.[9]

Like the failure of the Bank of Alabama just thirty years earlier, the failure of the railroads left the state almost bankrupt. Even after renegotiating the debt in 1873, Alabama owed $8.85 million. This was not the end of the red ink. An 1876 debt commission reported total state debt at $25.63

million of which $14.74 million (59.7 per cent of the total) was related to railroad bonds and debt.[10]

By the time the Redeemers reestablished Conservative rule in 1875, all state-aid railroads in Alabama were bankrupt, some because of fraud, others because of the economic depression that enveloped the United States after 1873. The Bourbon constitution of 1875 retrenched state government. Gone was its responsibility to aid education; gone were its subsidies for internal improvements. But the people remained ambivalent concerning state aid to transportation. As historian James Doster wrote, "there was seething antagonism yet a great desire for more railroads" to improve the state's economy and foster industrialization. This ambivalence opened the door to an ongoing battle between powerful national railroads and their allies in the state on one side and their commercial customers on the other. This dispute went on through the prosperous 1880s, the politically volatile 1890s, and the emerging progressive 1900s. A battle between railroad boosters and regulators became one of the touchstones of the progressive movement in Alabama. This was played out on a backdrop of tight restrictions on public debt even at the local level. The latter ensured that few internal improvements would find public financial support without loud, boisterous campaigns in their favor.[11]

Loud, boisterous campaigns alone did not secure roads and highways between 1890 and 1920, the heroic era of the Good Roads Movement in Alabama and the nation, nor did local and state agencies. Serious attention to building a network of roads and highways had to await the deep pockets and guiding hand of the federal government in 1916 and 1921. Although "the late unpleasantness," bitterness over Reconstruction, and the heavy dead hand of tradition might have mitigated Alabamians' zeal to accept federal funds and directives, their zeal for improved roads and the sheer magnitude of funds involved led the state to develop a working highway department, pass constitutional amendments, and conform to the strictures laid out by the U.S. Department of Agriculture's Bureau of Public Roads. In fact, Alabama's chief highway engineer, W. S. Keller, reported that the state was one of the few that sought and received its full appropriation from the 1916 Federal Road Aid Act.[12] Regardless of the past, regardless of the federal requirements, Alabamians happily did what they had to do—which was considerable—to secure federal funds.

One of the most important issues confronting early road-builders was deciding to create farm-to-market roads ("Get the Farmers Out of the Mud") or long-distance "trunk" roads for automobile tourists and, after

World War I, cargo-hauling trucks. Private individuals, organizations, railroads, counties, states, and even the federal government discussed this over the course of thirty years, making the fight between advocates of these different systems part of the reform impulse of Populism and Progressivism. On one side were farmers, farm supporters, and railroads—which did all long-distance hauling until motor trucks developed in World War I—who favored short-run farm-to-market roads. The U.S. Post Office did as well, for market roads played right into its mid-1890s designs to construct rural free delivery roads as a service to postal patrons. Bicycle clubs, especially the League of American Wheelmen, who were the leading edge of the 1890s Good Roads Movement, also supported market roads. On the other side after 1907 were "automobilists," often tourists, who began seriously promoting trunk routes when automobile technology and availability improved. A complete road system required serving both farmers and long-distance tourists, which Alabama attempted to do by securing federal funds for trunk routes that released state and county monies for market roads.

Regardless of what kind of road system emerged, financial considerations occupied a central place in every highway conversation. Building any kind of properly engineered permanent road, much less a system of all-weather roads, required more capital than states or counties could raise, especially as most jurisdictions used "antiquated methods of taxation" to finance roads.[13]

This was certainly true in Alabama. The most notorious of these "antiquated methods" was the so-called statute labor tax. Since territorial days, citizens paid their road taxes by physically laboring on the roads in their neighborhood. With a few exceptions—ministers, teachers, and students—all able-bodied men between ages eighteen and forty-five (and prior to emancipation all male slaves eighteen to fifty) were required to work the roads up to ten days per year. Road overseers "called out" rural residents to work roads near their homes during the lay-by or rainy season, giving three days' notice.[14] This system was not unique to Alabama. Maurice Eldridge reported in 1904 that as of 1889 "no cash or property taxes were levied for road purposes in Kentucky, South Carolina, Georgia, Alabama, Mississippi, Louisiana, New Mexico, or Utah, the roads being built and maintained exclusively by statute labor," and that in 1902, even after Alabama laws allowed cash payments, only thirty-four of sixty-seven counties accepted money.[15]

By the twentieth century, critics universally decried statute labor as worthless in constructing passable roads. Some of this criticism was driven by Progressive Era attitudes that privileged "scientific" (meaning "modern technological") methods and professional expertise over time-honored (or time-worn) ways of doing things. Some criticism came from urban writers bewailing the benighted life of rural folk, even when the author felt paternalistic rather than wrathful. For example, Eban Rexford wrote in the travel magazine *Outing* in 1908 that "year after year the roads remained a disgrace and a danger to the localities through which they ran. . . . Road building was not done in a businesslike manner. The man who had it in charge knew no more about the science of road making than the men who were at work under him." In 1916, even as he acknowledged that counties in his home state of Maryland had built some automobile-worthy roads and bridges, H. M. Clark complained that statute labor and roads that stopped at the county line led to "no system at all, but a haphazard, go-as-you-please, catch-as-catch-can affair" in which "many miles of roads . . . seem to have merely happened."[16]

Critics who had worked the roads knew that one of the problems was workforce motivation. That is, because statute laborers had neither a vested interest in the roadway nor the mechanical ability to build it beyond their or their draft animals' strength, they did as little as they possibly could. N. S. Shaler wrote in 1889 that workers gathered at the call-out point, gossiped until "slow-acting conscience" provoked them to fill some holes, dig out the drainage ditches, use the ditch muck to resurface the roadway, then smooth it with a mule-drawn drag.[17] Alabama congressman Fred Blackmon, speaking to the Alabama Good Roads Association meeting in Selma in 1911, reiterated Shaler's critique. He said, obviously ending on a sarcastic—but all too understandable—note, "I have often thought that the hard work I did as a road-hand was partly the cause of my failing to develop as I should have developed, physically. I feel that I would have grown up to be a full-size man but for the overwork and fatigue occasioned by the hard work of carrying a hoe along the road and talking with the other boys about the neighborhood gossip."[18]

Some criticism was driven by real issues, such as the lack of weatherproofing that left roads prone to develop potholes or turn into extensive bogs of muddy "gumbo" that reduced the hauling weight of agricultural wagons and impeded motorized traffic. Reformers called this the "mud tax," the cost difference between transporting farm goods on poor roads and on even modestly improved roads.[19] Although the dearth of road-surfacing materials and heavy road-making machinery contributed to the mud tax, the lack of engineering expertise was the greatest problem. Colleges in the South began teaching highway engineering courses only in 1913, and even by 1916 there were few requirements for employment as a county or state road engineer anywhere in America. Critics cried out for engineers to raise their professional standards as automobiles and trucks—faster and heavier than horse-drawn wagons—demanded smoother surfaces, lower grades, shallower turns, wider roads, and protected ditches to prevent accidents and property damage.[20] Properly applied engineering expertise not only saved lives and property but reduced the mud tax as well as the cost of maintaining the road.

Building and maintaining roads was expensive. Estimates for a twenty-foot-wide road ranged from more than $26,000 per mile for brick pavement to less than $1,200 per mile for sand-clay. Gravel, chert, or shell surfacing cost approximately $3,500 per mile, and waterbound macadam, which required a bed of layered rock topped by a surface of gravel sealed with a paste of dust and water, cost approximately $8,200 per mile. If the road required excavation to reduce grade or straighten curves, the cost jumped significantly. Transporting surfacing material outside the areas where they naturally occurred added almost insurmountable costs, so engineers used the surfacing that was readily at hand.[21]

Raising funds to construct and maintain more than a few miles of road proved politically difficult as well. Some counties in the nation used "pay-as-you-go" financing funded by taxes on property, but that was a slow way to improve roads. Charles M. Upham, secretary of the American Roadbuilders Association, gave a hypothetical example of the defects of "pay-as-you-go" in 1929. He posited that a $100,000 road project financed at $10,000 per annum would leave the county debt-free but take ten years to complete, an unacceptably long time. Upham's real argument was that bonded indebtedness cost the county more, of course, but the hypothetical road project would be completed in one-tenth the time and enjoy over 50 percent more use than the same road built by "pay-as-you-go" financing.[22]

Alabama counties often let bonds after the state followed New Jersey's 1889 lead in allowing counties to take on road debt. Their fate demonstrates the ambiguity Alabamians felt about spending public money on improved roads. Some counties did well—Montgomery County built the first improved roadway in Alabama in 1895, and by 1912 it enjoyed 532 miles of gravel road as well as a number of steel or concrete bridges.[23] Further north, travelers in 1911 reported that once they entered Jefferson County they motored over fourteen miles of excellent roadway into Birmingham. But most roads were not so well made.[24]

Urban areas often had reasonable roads, but rural counties fared poorly for quite a while. In February 1920, one correspondent to the *Montgomery Advertiser* wrote that "if Barbour County didn't need good roads, I don't want to live in a place that does," while another wrote that in rural Elmore County after recent heavy rains "no car, not even a Tin Lizzie, could negotiate those fearful roads." The *Advertiser* editor blamed county commissioners who were not technical experts in road building. Even though they had spent considerable sums of county bond money, commissioners seldom hired competent engineers or understood the difference between well-made and poorly made roads.[25]

Regardless of a few counties' ability to supply their own roads, it became increasingly obvious that the state should take a role in modernizing its transportation infrastructure. It took its first tentative steps in 1907, when voters passed Amendment 1 to the Constitution of 1901 authorizing the legislature to appropriate up to $400,000 from the state convict fund to pay for public road improvements.[26]

Alabama took its second major step toward building a modern road system with the creation of the State Highway Commission in April 1911. This was the direct result of agitation by the Good Roads Movement, which was also instrumental in securing federal road improvement aid to states.[27] The commission initially consisted of three citizens appointed by the governor to four-year terms plus the state geologist and the professor of civil engineering at the Alabama Polytechnic Institute (later Auburn University).[28]

The real backbone of the commission was its tiny staff: Chief Engineer W. S. Keller (who was paid $4,000 per year), an assistant engineer, and a stenographer. Their initial job was to prepare a report concerning road statistics, map a trunk-line system for the state, and establish standards for construction. Within a year, the commission had divided the state into regions and expanded the staff to nine resident engineers (paid $5 per day) augmented by ten county engineers who agreed to serve as resident engineers in their areas.[29]

The 1911 Highway Commission law authorized annual appropriation from the state convict fund of $154,000 to fund its operations and provide matching grants up to $2,000 to counties. The law also allowed counties to retain one year's grant money to finance a more expensive project the following year. To be considered for state grants, counties had to agree to build roads according to commission regulations. The surface had to be sand-clay, gravel (also chert or shell), or waterbound macadam at least ten feet wide on a roadbed twenty feet between ditches, all on a right-of-way of fifty feet. State-funded county roads also had to be part of a main road.

Road work could be done by county workers or county convicts, or it could be subcontracted to private firms.[30]

Even with state funds, counties felt too penurious to participate. In 1924, Loraine Bedsole Bush, noted reformer and first director of the Alabama Department of Child Welfare, wrote exasperatedly that in the first years of its existence the highway commission had "begged" counties to apply for grant funds and secure their match, but many did not because they were, she claimed, "small minded."[31] As the Great War in Europe harmed Alabama's cotton economy and pinched its resources, participant numbers shrank. In 1915 only nine counties received $2,308 each in matching grants, though Chief Engineer W. S. Keller reported to Governor Charles Henderson that the commission made grants to forty-one counties since 1912 for a total of $157,115.[32] Most county roads were farm-to-market, intracounty roads, and even with state aid very few were well made. As of March 1, 1913, only 10 percent of the state's roads were "improved," that is, surfaced with topsoil or more, though by late 1916 that proportion rose to almost 17 percent.[33]

Eventually, it was the federal government that provided Alabama with the capital and managerial framework to build a system of paved roads. Federal intervention in the form of the Federal Road Aid Acts of 1916 and 1921 took more than two decades and a significant shift in Americans' conception of the role of government to come to fruition. Beginning in the 1890s, the federal government sought to insert itself into supporting the emerging transportation sector by staying thoroughly within the accepted bounds of constitutional law and precedent.

Article 1, section 8, paragraph 7 of the Constitution opened one door for such federal intervention: the right of the central government to build post roads. In 1893, the Post Office Authorization Bill contained an appropriation to build an experimental rural free delivery (RFD) postal road between Charleston and Uvilla, West Virginia, and by 1897 there were forty-four operating RFD routes. In 1900 the Post Office decreed it would approve RFD only along "reasonably good roads" (as reported by mail carriers), thus pressuring localities to improve roads and connect them to those of its neighbors. That same year, the Post Office and the Office of Road Inquiry (ORI) joined forces to promote good roads at conventions and support local RFD route building with inspection and construction guidance from ORI engineers.[34]

The ORI received $8,000 per year until 1900, when its annual appropriation climbed to $14,000. Congress seemed not to relish directly funding or controlling a national system of highways, but it did recognize that no road transportation system had ever been constructed without some guidance and financing from the central government.[35]

Although the Office of Public Roads could investigate, report, and educate, it could not constitutionally build new roads or maintain existing operational ones. Nevertheless, it skirted such constitutional issues during World War I by extending its educational mission with the Washington–Atlanta Maintenance Demonstration Road. Covering 1,039 miles through forty-nine counties in four states, it was designed to show the advantage of permanent surfacing and was a proof-of-concept trial for getting counties to cooperate under federal supervision. Counties along the route received engineering assistance from the OPR if they agreed to maintain two surfaced roads. Counties in the program linked more than 870 miles of paved roads by 1916, of which none had been closed due to weather—a remarkable feat at the time.[36]

With the advent of the motorcar, paved roads became essential, but neither states nor counties could satisfy the rising demand by themselves. Congress understood the need for federal largesse and from 1900 to 1916 entertained multiple bills proposing federal aid for road construction. Only with the senatorial leadership of John Hollis Bankhead of Alabama, however, did the federal government reenter the internal improvement field it had abandoned with the 1830 Maysville Road veto.

Bankhead entered the U.S. House of Representatives in 1886, serving on the House Rivers and Harbors Committee, among others. He introduced his first road improvement bill in 1906, but lost his House seat later that same year. The Alabama legislature appointed him to the U.S. Senate in 1907, and he introduced road improvement bills in 1908 and 1910. Senator Bankhead had a kindred spirit in Missouri representative Dorsey Shackleford, who became the most prominent congressional proponent of federal road aid to states. In 1912 Shackleford introduced the backbone of what became the 1916 Federal Road Aid Bill, but it failed because its funding mechanism was too complex and because long-distance automobilists objected to its narrow focus on farm to market roads. Bankhead, chairman of the Senate Post Office and Post Road Committee, introduced a funding bill in 1913, worked with Shackleford to introduce another in 1914, and introduced yet another in December 1915. This latest bill bundled most of the suggestions from past critics, created a partnership between the federal government and the states, and satisfied both market road and trunk-line supporters. On July 11, 1916, President Wilson signed it into law.[37]

The Federal Road Aid Act of 1916 provided funds to build and maintain interconnected roads and highways on a national scale. It appropriated $25 million annually for grants that required states to match dollar-for-dollar. Each state could receive at least $6,000, with the OPR apportioning the remainder based on a formula that combined a state's postal and star route mileage, total area, and total population. Alabama's share for 1917 was $104,149, and its total original appropriation through 1921 was $1,211,683. For Alabama, this was a substantial amount of money.[38]

Yet accessing these funds seemed impossible. Besides Alabama's traditional reluctance to raise large amounts of public capital, its tax- and debt-aversion, and its troubled relationship with the federal government, its legislature met only quadrennially. In 1917, the first year road aid appropriations became available, the legislature was two years away from meeting. Yet the Road Aid Act required the legislature to pass laws accepting funding. How could Alabama access its sorely needed appropriation and put it to legitimate use?

State Highway Commission chairman Robert Spragins and U.S. secretary of agriculture D. F. Houston presented an answer. Because Alabama's legislature met in 1915, before the act passed, and so could not have appropriated sufficient funds to match federal grants for 1917 through 1921, Governor Charles Henderson could pledge the good faith of the state to make up the shortfall when the legislature met again in 1919. Henderson wrote Houston to "assent to the provisions of the Federal Aid Road Act passed July 11th, 1916, and accept the conditions imposed in said act, and assure you that the State will undertake to comply with the provisions contained therein until the final adjournment of the next legislature."[39] This statement opened the door for federal road aid funds for Alabama.

Politically, securing federal money was one thing, but accepting federal limitations on Alabama's traditional distribution of power was another. The 1916 act required states receiving funds to have a highway commission of some sort. This provided a state-level agency to funnel money to Federal Aid Projects (FAPs) and prevented the OPR from having to deal directly with individual counties or state legislatures. Furthermore, although counties initiated FAPs by applying to the highway commission, which forwarded those it approved to the OPR, Secretary Houston told Governor Henderson that a state could neither appropriate matching funds nor accept federal funds until it had designated a system of trunk roads the building of which superseded any county-initiated project.[40] Finally, federal engineers oversaw and approved contracts, engineering specifications, and rights-of-way to ensure uniform quality and economy. Henderson did not balk, and Houston accepted his pledge for Alabama on March 26, 1917.[41]

In addition to Henderson's acquiescence, the Alabama Highway Commission accepted the Federal Road Aid Act and adapted to the OPR administrative regulations. This was complicated by the makeup and small size of the commission—three volunteers, two professors, and a small staff of engineers who administered the already-existing state road aid program as well as the new, distinct federal program. It was further complicated by everyone's inexperience and by the anxious maneuvering of counties to get their share of the new money as quickly as possible.

Only a week after President Wilson signed the act, Jefferson County's Board of Revenue president R. F. Lovelady proposed applying for a $50,000 "pro rata" share of the $1,608,000 of federal money the highway commission was to distribute between 1917 and 1921. Lovelady wanted to improve the "Warrior Road" from Birmingham to Nichols Fish Trap and Taylor's Ferry on the Warrior River and argued it might appeal to the state and federal engineers because named road advocate groups had included it on the Atlanta-Birmingham-Memphis route, which was part of the proposed Bankhead Highway. Jefferson County engineer George Clark recommended that the county could claim the cost of its use of convict labor on the roads as the state's full match. The entire project failed when a resident successfully sued to stop the county from pursuing it. Lovelady and Clark were ill-informed and did not understand how federal road aid worked. They also were overconfident that their proposal was self-evidently acceptable and that they had figured all the angles. Even though they never made a proposal before the highway commission, the way they conceived of the requirements to access federal money demonstrates how little the state or federal government had formulated FAP procedures. It also underscored the murky, changing relationship between county and state when it came to controlling road projects. The federal government's intervention through the "carrot" of funding altered that relationship and tended to centralize control over road building projects while strengthening its and the state's power vis-à-vis counties.[42]

Thus strengthened, the commission struggled to conduct the business of building roads professionally. At first it met once every month or two, scheduling county applications as agenda items, but this was a time-consuming process that required multiple contacts between county representatives and the understaffed Commission. As more counties proposed road projects for federal aid, the Commission streamlined the process by adopting standard application forms and authorizing the State Highway Engineer to sign approvals subject to ratification at subsequent Commission meetings.[43]

In their applications, counties had to produce a route "profile" that included a survey by a competent engineer, a cost estimate, and a construction plan conforming to commission specifications (sent from the OPR, ratified by the commission). Even after the commission authorized the state highway engineer to approve these profiles, the process was too slow. By April 1, 1917, only seventeen counties had applied and the commission had approved only FAP No. 1, a sand-clay road between Union Springs and Bruceville, Bullock County, for OPR consideration. By July, though sixteen more counties had applied, only ten had completed their profiles.[44]

Further slowing progress was the OPR's requirement that the state submit a map showing a system of trunk roads.[45] Fixing this misunderstanding required redrawing the map which the engineering staff completed by October 1917, designating trunk roads with colored lines. More importantly, it also required reconsidering the various county proposals already submitted and reconfiguring the commission standards to include the trunk road limitation.

The Alabama Highway Commission resolved its problems with the OPR by conforming to the centralizing thrust of the OPR's administrative mandates even as it attempted to accommodate the desires of the counties to route the roads as they saw fit. The OPR's insistence on trunk roads was not capricious but was rooted in the constitutional limitations on federal funding of internal improvements.[46]

Such conformity benefited the state. Alabama was one of only ten states to claim its entire 1917 federal allotment; this put the highway commission in the unusual position of having more money than it could spend. At first unsure of how far to commit itself to spending unprecedented federal aid for which it had uncertain matching funds, the commission planned for counties to claim only $10,000 in federal funds, but soon raised that limit to $12,000, and raised it again to $13,536 as 1918 funds began to appear. Anticipating even more funding for 1919, the commission raised the per-county limit to $17,000. In addition, it allowed counties already in the system to apply for the new maximum each time the limit was raised and created a mechanism to distribute unclaimed federal funds to other participating counties.[47]

Federal largesse required a dollar-for-dollar match, which posed a significant problem to the state. The Alabama Highway Commission used its appropriation from the convict fund, but that supplied no more than $154,000 per year to support the commission staff and offices as well as build and maintain roads. In 1918, the legislature reduced that to $97,000 for state aid, and Governor Thomas Kilby's 1919 budget called for an appropriation of only $100,000. This meager sum could not keep pace with the available federal monies, and the state stood to lose both the 1917 federal funds (which had to be spent within two years) and the 1918–21 funds, which state highway engineer W. S. Keller estimated to total more than $5,776,000. This was far more than Alabama's original appropriation, largely because Congress amended the law in 1919 to supply more funds.[48]

The Alabama Highway Commission desperately sought state funds to make up its shortfall. In 1918 it asked to receive a larger appropriation from the convict fund and, more important, to have all the receipts from the automobile, truck, and taxi license fees appropriated for road improvement. Success would have quadrupled the commission's operating budget in a single year; in 1919 Alabama had approximately 60,000 cars, trucks, taxis, and motorcycles registered, for total vehicle license revenue of $541,349. Although it was a gamble at the time, for no one accurately predicted the exceptional increase in registrations that actually occurred, by 1923 the number of registrations doubled, generating almost $3.9 million in revenue.[49]

The 1919 legislature passed a new highway law taking that gamble and modernizing the commission in line with Alabama's postwar progressive *mentalité*. The law reorganized the commission, raising it from three at-large commissioners to one commissioner per congressional district, and retained the state geologist and Auburn's civil engineering professor. It also changed the name of the commission to the Alabama Highway Department, assigned the department more specific and robust duties, and earmarked the motor vehicle license fees for the State Highway Fund to maintain roads and pay interest and principal on future bonded indebtedness.[50]

Still, it was not apparent in 1919 that the motor vehicle tax receipts would suffice to match the proffered federal road aid. The legislature therefore considered S. 218, a state issue of $25 million in 5 percent forty-year bonds to match federal road aid. The Alabama Highway Improvement Association, a leading advocate of all good roads measures, petitioned the legislature and bought newspaper advertising. The North South National Bee Line Highway Association, another advocate with a high profile but tiny treasury, had a resolution of support for S. 218 read into the journal of the Alabama House. Such support was successful, and after receiving the original bill back from Governor Kilby with a small change, the legislature passed the so-called Road Bond bill on the last day of the session.[51] Alabama's 1901 Constitution, like its predecessors, required bond measures to be passed only as constitutional amendments, so Governor Kilby set February 16, 1920, as the election date, and voters favored the amendment by 83,607 to 12,026.[52]

That kind of one-sided vote indicated significant support and excitement for the bond issue and road improvement. Indeed, agitation for good roads had been part of Alabama life for almost a quarter century, though it had become particularly vigorous after 1909, with newspaper editorial offices serving as hotbeds of publicity. Whether favoring improved roads or fearing possible boondoggles, editors simply could not leave good road stories alone. Edward Doty of the *Andalusia Star* was a proponent of the Atlanta–to–New Orleans Highway as early as 1911, and he reported avidly on path-finding tours and the Alabama Good Roads Association meeting of that year.[53] In 1911 and 1912 the *Birmingham Ledger* sponsored six path-finding trips around the state and reported on all meetings of the Alabama Good Roads Association, the Jackson Highway Association, and the Bee Line Highway Association throughout the decade. The other major papers in the state were similarly active, notably the *Birmingham Age-Herald* and the *Montgomery Advertiser*, as well as smaller sheets in Selma, Huntsville, Dothan, and elsewhere. The campaign over ratification of the amendment was loud as a consequence of newspaper interest.

Between January 9 and February 16, 1920, the *Dothan Eagle* ran thirteen letters, articles, editorials, and comments about the upcoming road bond election. Twelve of these were laudatory, if a bit sarcastic, and argued in favor of passage. Speaking for the *Eagle*, the editor's only concern about the amendment was that the "periphery counties" like those in southeast Alabama were treated as well as those nearer the capital of Montgomery.[54]

Twenty-five miles north of Dothan on the Bee Line Highway, Ozark's weekly *Southern Star* wholeheartedly supported the bond issue. Beginning in August 1919, the newspaper ran multiple editorials in favor, noting on August 6 that the bond issue was designed to provide the state's required match and so would leverage double its amount in usable funds. It ran four editorials in the three weeks prior to the February 16, 1920, election, sometimes asserting that great benefits would flow to Ozark, sometimes arguing against naysayers, sometimes breathlessly propagandizing for passage. Although the paper reported in its February 18 issue that turnout was light, it also reported the amendment's passage across the state. In Dale County, early returns reported 817 in favor to 339 against—not the eight-to-one drubbing reported elsewhere, but still a significant majority.[55]

In the capital, the *Montgomery Advertiser* ran its own campaign in support of a positive vote. Besides editorials every few days calling for a favorable vote, the *Advertiser* ran at least a dozen obvious and even ham-handed editorial cartoons between January 29 and February 15 about the bond issue, and after February 11 it changed its masthead motto from "Alabama's Greatest Newspaper" to "Pull Alabama Out of the Mud. Boost Good Roads." The paper published a number of letters objecting to the amendment, each one accompanied by a point-by-point refutation. On the other hand, no comment of any kind accompanied pro-amendment letters. The *Advertiser* was joyful in reporting the victory on February 17 in the headline and story, "Alabama Has Been 'Pulled Out of the Mud!'" Reporting more solid vote tallies the next day under the headline "54,170 Majority for $25,000,000 Highway Bond Issue Proposal," the paper noted that of the counties reporting, only Geneva County polled against the amendment, but a recount showed even that opposition to be in error, though only slightly.[56]

Once citizens ratified the amendment, state officials sought to ensure they sold the bonds legally. At a cost of $2,000, the governor authorized the Boston law firm of Storey, Thorndike, Palmer, and Dodge to examine the law for constitutional deficiencies, and it found enough problems that it advised the state to get a case before the Alabama Supreme Court to prevent an illegal bond sale. During that same period, A. M. Johnson, a car dealer in Montgomery, brought a friendly suit against the highway commission in Montgomery County Circuit Court, challenging the law on the same deficiencies Storey and company had discovered. Judge Walter B. Jones dismissed *Johnson v. Craft*, but Johnson appealed and the case wound its way to the Alabama Supreme Court later in the year.[57] Storey's concern and Johnson's complaint held that the road bond amendment contained five technical deficiencies, but neither commented upon the size or kind of indebtedness. In fact, both assumed that they were making the sale of $25 million in bonds for road work legal.[58]

Associate Justice Thomas C. McClellan delivered the court's split decision, which found the amendment unconstitutional on February 3, 1921, and declared additional deficiencies, one technical. A second, though, struck at the very nature of the road bond amendment—amendment section 7 that laid out the $25 million bond issue specifically for roadwork was outside the limits on type and amount of public debt allowed under the constitution's section 213.⁵⁹ That the court went beyond the technical problems brought before it by plaintiff Johnson to address the size and type of indebtedness, and that it split 4–3 over its decision, demonstrates anew the profound ambiguity the state's political machinery felt toward support for internal improvements. The state supreme court was the bellwether of elite opinion, even more so than the state senate. The split in this elite body, however, is instructive. Justices William H. Thomas, Ormond Summerville, and Lucien D. Gardner critiqued the majority as perverting the intention of the constitution to allow the people to pass amendments. Gardner added that the overwhelming passage of the amendment in both legislative houses and by vote of the people, as well as the activities of the state government in restructuring its highway commission and preparing to sell bonds, indicated acceptance of the gist of the amendment that the court should not have thwarted.⁶⁰

Amendment supporters raised a storm of criticism against the court immediately after its decision severe enough to draw a rebuke from Justice McClellan when he rejected a rehearing of *Johnson v. Craft* on February 24. He complained in a long, defensive passage, that,

> Ignorance, and nothing more, accounts for . . . this . . . publicity, ignorance of the distinction between anarchy and constitutional government; ignorance of the imperative necessity to . . . preserve the independence of the judiciary . . . ignorance . . . that judges are bound by oath . . . to enforce the constitution . . . ignorance . . . that no power . . . is conferred on this court or its judges to forgive, condone, or heal violations of plain mandates . . . of the Constitution, even if the violation results in the greatest good.⁶¹

Until the legislature could meet again and the people ratify another amendment, the state had only a small and uncertain fund to match federal road aid grants. The highway commission had finagled a match for the 1917 grants by the July 1919 deadline, but without secure funding—from the bond issue—it could not guarantee matching the 1918–21 grants. Alabama's 1919 highway bill not only modernized the highway commission and earmarked license taxes for the commission but also guaranteed reimbursements to any county that provided monies to build roads on the state trunk system that were eligible for federal aid. The state and counties split the match to secure federal funds, with counties putting 25 percent of the cost into a highway commission account. The commission supplied another 25 percent and used the combined funds to leverage federal aid.⁶²

By this mechanism counties made it possible for Alabama to secure its full allotment. George G. Clark of the Bureau of Public Roads reported in 1921 that counties had pledged $1.045 million for FAPs completed since 1917 and another $717,000 for FAPs contracted but not completed by the time of his report.[63] The commission reported expenditures that tell the same story. Between 1916 and 1921, Alabama completed forty-nine road projects totaling 318 miles, with counties paying $1.16 million, federal road aid paying $1.46 million, and the state paying $486,000. Individual project reports emphasize the contrast more starkly. Barbour County's FAP 48, for example, was 8.66 miles of sand-clay road, twenty-four feet wide, from Clayton to Eufaula, constructed between January 1920 and September 1921. The county paid $13,300, the federal government paid $18,200, and the state provided $4,900. A Jefferson County project, FAP 57, was an eight-foot-wide, six-mile-long asphalt road from Bessemer to Birmingham that cost the county $129,000, the federal government $113,000, and the state a mere $1,000.[64]

Uncertainty, the mounting nationwide depression, and general unfamiliarity with how to make the system function meant counties struggled with securing promised reimbursements. This was particularly painful for counties that had contracted for roadwork while the road bond amendment was under judicial review.[65]

By condemning the road bond amendment on a narrow technicality, the Alabama Supreme Court had created an emergency, said Governor Thomas Kilby, in that Alabama could not secure federal matching funds without bonded indebtedness. But there was a remedy. The court had left the door open for the legislature to rewrite the amendment. Governor Kilby called for another special session of the Alabama legislature for October 4–29, 1921. In his opening speech, Kilby was so sure the need was self-evident that he told legislators, "argument addressed to you on the subject of better highways would be superfluous, and hence I recommend without further comment that you again submit to the qualified electors of the State an amendment to the Constitution providing for the issuance of bonds not to exceed the sum of $25,000,000."[66] There were seventeen other items on the special session agenda, but none so important as this. The legislature dutifully reported a much improved amendment and set the election date for January 30, 1922.

As the legislature and electorate dealt with financial issues, the reorganized Alabama Highway Department dealt with the newly passed 1921 Federal Road Aid Act, which provided more funds and more federal oversight.

Designed to privilege the federal-state cooperative model enshrined in its 1916 predecessor, the 1921 act incorporated greater federal direction over state road systems in order to thwart the bill introduced in 1920 by Senator Charles E. Townsend of Michigan to centralize road routing under a Federal Highway Commission.[67]

The Alabama Highway Department and its supporters fought the Townsend Bill directly and behind the scenes. The commissioners officially resolved their support for the "present plan of co-operation between the Federal Government and the states in the building of roads under the operating agencies . . . [and deemed] it unwise . . . to inaugurate any radical departure . . . such as is contemplated by the Townsend Bill providing for a Federal System of highways built, maintained, and controlled solely by a Federal highway Commission."[68] Chief highway officer W. S. Keller was more candid. He wrote to newly appointed senator B. B. Comer that the Townsend Bill would act only "for the benefit of those who are able to tour, and for the automobile interest of Michigan and other northern states." Mostly, Keller fretted over the financial impact—that the $3 billion total appropriation proposed by Townsend would dry up all other federal road funds, leaving Alabama with only its own resources.[69] Even erstwhile friends and good roads allies chose opposing sides. Highway Commissioner John Craft wrote to newly elected senator Tom Heflin that Asa Roundtree, Craft's longtime associate in the Alabama Good Roads Association, was working for the Townsend Bill through Roundtree's other organizations—the United State Good Roads Association and the Bankhead Highway Association—and voted against supporting it. Like Keller, Craft thought the Townsend Bill was the brainchild of northerners in the American Automobile Association and would benefit no one but "the joy riding leisure class."[70]

Senator Townsend compromised when the Federal Road Aid Act required grant recipients to designate 7 percent of their total road mileage as interstate trunk lines, called Primary Roads, and intercity or intercounty roads, called Secondary Roads. Once the Bureau of Public Roads approved its 7 percent system map, the state could spend three-sevenths of its federal allotment on primary roads and four-sevenths on secondary roads. The act further required states to build and maintain Federal Aid roads to uniform national standards. If a state failed to maintain its primary roads, the law allowed the federal government to do so directly, paying for maintenance with the unspent portion of that state's appropriation and refusing to fund any more building projects. Congress sweetened the deal by continuing the

1919 amendment that provided surplus war materiel suitable for road work to the states, centralizing power over highways in the state highway departments, and allowing states whose constitutions did not permit funding for road improvement three years to modernize their laws while receiving funds. The act made $75 million available nationwide by June 1922.[71]

To access those federal funds, Alabama had to pass, again, its road bond amendment. An all-out campaign by good roads advocates, particularly Fred Cramton's Alabama Highway Improvement Association and its county-level affiliates, the state highway commission, and all state newspapers except an occasional "reactionary backwoods journal preaching the gospel of mud and causeways rather than hard and permanent paths," succeeded.[72] Few new arguments for or against the amendment were advanced, and newspapers used almost exactly the same tactics as in 1920. The vote was small, hampered by disinterest and bad weather, but decisive: almost ten-to-one in favor. Cramton reported that newly enfranchised women "unanimously" supported the amendment across the state. Geneva County was the only jurisdiction where the amendment failed.[73]

The Alabama Highway Commission made its peace with the 1921 Federal Aid Highways Act quickly, for the law reinforced the federal-state partnership rather than centralizing road administration. Furthermore, the required 7 percent system was just an extension of the Bureau of Public Roads' administrative regulations for the 1916 Federal Road Aid Act and fell within the commission's original mandate. But securing the maximum appropriation by getting the BPR to agree with Alabama's determination of what constituted the state's total road mileage was problematic.

The final adjustment was a contretemps that arose in the spring of 1923, when the BPR determined the total mileage of Alabama roads eligible for federal funding based on the map the highway commission submitted in 1916. This total, 3,872 miles, was 87 miles less than Alabama wanted. Scraping for every penny, the commission resolved in April to present its case by visiting the BPR in Washington. Tempers cooled by June, so the commission decided to have the governor present a new 7 percent map to the bureau, then in July it invited Montgomery-based BPR district engineer A. E. Loder to discuss the dispute. The following October, the commission's annual report included a resolution to the dispute: the BPR recognized 3,872 miles as the total Alabama 7 percent system. The commission gave in, and Alabama built a road system with federal money and oversight.[74]

Why were Alabamians so willing to do what they had to do to secure federal funding—from reorganizing their highway department to erecting a makeshift, temporary funding formula to holding two elections to amend their constitution? The answer is pretty simple and harkens back to the same malaise that led them to rely on bank profits to fund state government in the 1830s and 1840s: they refused to tax themselves to pay for the services they demanded.

Two studies by Hastings Hart of the Russell Sage Foundation are illustrative. In 1918, Governor Henderson commissioned Hart to investigate why the U.S. Army rejected so many Alabama draftees for medical reasons. Hart's report looked at a broad array of social ills and agencies in the state and concluded that one overarching reason for Alabama's problems was its low level of property tax collection. Property taxes were the single largest source of state income, and the Constitution of 1901 allowed assessment on "60 per cent of fair and reasonable cash value" of the property. Actual assessments, he estimated, were only 22 percent of market value in 1918. Four years later he returned at the behest of Governor Kilby and discovered the state doing much better, though it still assessed property at only 24 percent of its market value. Alabamians successfully maintained their low-tax status, ranking thirty-seventh among the forty-eight states in state tax burden.[75]

Resentment toward paying federal taxes, too, lurked just beneath the surface in the state. Tariff policy had discriminated against southern and western agricultural economies for almost a century, and few Alabamians seemed to appreciate the income tax legalized by the Sixteenth Amendment passed in 1913. Even though Alabama contributed only 0.5 percent of the total federal income tax in 1918 and was slated to contribute only 4 percent the following year, John A. Rogers used that resentment to campaign for the road bond amendment. A state senator and member of the highway commission, Rogers told the Birmingham Rotary Club on January 25, 1922, that the only way to recover "any of the $20,000,000 that [Alabama] paid into the federal treasury for income tax" was to pass the bond issue to ensure the federal government had to provide $25,000,000 to the state. Perversely, when Alabamians were unable to control their tax burden, they jumped at the chance to recapture what they thought of as their fair share, even if that meant going into significant long-term debt.[76]

Passing the road bond amendment did everything its proponents hoped. The state sold $4.25 million in road bonds in fiscal year 1922, which provided a state match for federal funds for 1921 and 1922 and released the counties from contributing any further to FAPs. The Alabama Highway Department reported on September 30, 1923, that for the four road and two bridge projects started, completed, and paid for in fiscal year 1921, the federal government paid $261,000, the state paid $288,000, and the counties paid nothing. Counties did not stop paying for roads, however. They continued to let bonds, but they deliberately spent the money on roads not included on the state trunk-line system.[77]

Alabama before and during the Progressive Era lacked the fiscal or managerial resources to develop a modern road system to connect its farmers to market towns, its county seats and major cities to one another, or the state to the rest of the nation, leaving farmers and tourists stuck in the mud on roads that did not go anywhere. Some Alabamians wanted the benefits of a good road system and tried to concoct mechanisms to attain one. They created the state highway commission in 1911 and reorganized it in 1919 to oversee road-building projects; counties passed bond issues, often by slim majorities; the Good Roads Movement combined with state newspapers to educate and propagandize Alabamians to favor good roads; and the state earmarked a significant source of revenue specifically to building and maintaining good roads. Nevertheless, too few Alabamians comprehended the enormous scale of building even short, all-weather roads, much less erecting a unified road system. Such public infrastructure demanded long-term investments of extraordinary amounts of money, a large-scale programmatic managerial infrastructure, a significant corps of technical experts, and unified political will.

Political will was the greatest obstacle. For its entire history, save for a few years after the Civil War that Alabama political mythmaking considered a horrible aberration, the state was mired in a corrosive individualism that tended to reject any large-scale public cooperation. There are many good reasons for this. During the state's early years, the population was both scattered sparsely across the state and did not stay for many years in any one area, so long-term investments in public projects benefited few. The graft and corruption surrounding the failure of the Bank of Alabama in the 1840s—as well as the disappointment that followed resumption of high taxes when the promised bank profits failed to support government—soured Alabamians on government run public projects. After the Civil War, more corruption that attended the failure of state-subsidized railroads strengthened the distaste for large projects. Furthermore, the state's economy recovered very sluggishly in the so-called Gilded Age while an economic and political alliance between the Big Mules and Big Planters siphoned money and power from the people to the "interests." All this, combined with long-term issues such as rigid racial segregation, uneven economic development, brutal industrialism, and other civic events that fall outside the scope of this chapter, led the state to be tax-, debt-, and public-project-averse. The political will was not strong enough to change that culture until an outside mechanism galvanized Alabamians' belief in success. That outside mechanism was, of course, the Federal Road Aid Acts of 1916 and 1921.

The federal government had tried to fund state and local road improvement since 1893, with the Agricultural Appropriations Act that established the Office of Public Road Inquiry. The Post Office's creation of Rural Free Delivery at that same time spurred greater federal intervention in local-level internal improvements. But this was slow and awkward. Congress took up the challenge as representatives and senators introduced many bills every year after 1900 advancing schemes to move money from the federal treasury to the states. A few leaders emerged, notably Representative Dorsey Shackleford of Missouri and Senator John Hollis Bankhead of Alabama. After years of wrangling, Shackleford and Bankhead succeeded in appeasing both the long-haul trunk-line faction and the farm-to-market faction, overcame constitutional objections, and presented a funding scheme that was neither too complex nor too centralized. The result was the Federal Road Aid Act of 1916, which set aside federal money to match state contributions toward building well-planned and well-executed roads.

Alabamians jumped at the opportunity to secure federal money, putting themselves through significant contortions to make their match. The state's appropriations from the convict fund to the state highway commission were too small to match available federal money, so the legislature passed a constitutional amendment to allow the state to go into deep debt through forty-year bonds as well as earmarking all receipts from the motor vehicle license tax to pay interest and principal. That making this kind of commitment required a constitutional amendment demonstrates how tax- and debt-averse the culture of Alabama was. That the amendment passed in 1920 by an eight-to-one margin demonstrates how much Alabamians were willing to cooperate with the federal government when sufficient largesse was at stake. The state demonstrated its cooperative spirit a second time, in 1922, when it voted by even larger margins for a revised version of that amendment after the Alabama Supreme Court declared the first one void on a constitutional technicality.

Alabamians did not balk when the Federal Road Aid Act of 1921 required the state highway department to designate 7 percent of its total road mileage as a "system" and to spend three-sevenths of its state and federal matching funds on interstate roads in that system and four-sevenths on intercounty ("courthouse-to-courthouse") roads. The highway department's only complaint was that the federal government used an old map that contained fewer miles of roadways—and so gave Alabama a smaller appropriation—than the department thought was fair. Once all the pieces were in place—the law was settled, bonds were to be sold, roads were being mapped—counties immediately asked for promised reimbursements and to know which roads the state was designating as "Seven Percent Roads" so they could spend their money on their own farm-to-market roads.

So it is true that Alabamians fuss and fume over perceived interference from the federal government. But it is equally true that when that same government offers vitally needed or deeply desired funds, Alabamians will throw their resentment to the winds and get into line, hat in hand.

Notes

1. William Warren Rogers et al., *Alabama: The History of a Deep South State*, 2nd ed. (Tuscaloosa: University of Alabama Press, 2010), chapters 9–13, 31–32; Wayne Flynt, *Alabama in the Twentieth Century* (Tuscaloosa: University of Alabama Press, 2004), chapters 2 and 7; Harvey H. Jackson, *Inside Alabama: A Personal History of My State* (Tuscaloosa: University of Alabama Press, 2004); Gene Howard, *Patterson for Alabama: The Life and Career of John Patterson* (Tuscaloosa: University of Alabama Press, 2008); Warren A. Trest, *Nobody but the People* (Montgomery: NewSouth Books, 2008); Dan T. Carter, *The Politics of Rage: George Wallace, the Origins of the New Conservatism, and the Transformation of American Politics* (New York: Simon and Schuster, 1995); Sandra Baxley Taylor, *Fob: The Incredible Story of Fob James Jr.* (Mobile: Greenberry Publishing, 1990), 337–52; Christina Nifong, "Alabama Governor to Courts: 'En Garde,'" *Christian Science Monitor*, September 10, 1997, http://www.csmonitor.com/1997/0910/091097.us.us.4.html.

2. Leonard Calvert Cooke, "The Development of the Road System of Alabama" (M.A. thesis, University of Alabama, 1935), 115–16.

3. Gavin Wright, *Old South, New South: Revolutions in the Southern Economy since the Civil War* (Baton Rouge: Louisiana State University Press, 1996), 17–31.

4. Cooke, "The Development of the Road System of Alabama," 72–74; William Elejius Martin, *Internal Improvements in Alabama* (Baltimore: Johns Hopkins University Press, 1902), 29, http://www.archive.org/details/internalimprovem00martrich; C. Dallas Sands, *A Study of Alabama Highway Laws* (Montgomery: Alabama State Highway Department, 1965), 190; Corey T. Lesseig, *Automobility: Social Change in the American South, 1909–1939* (New York: Routledge, 2001), 57.

5. Albert Burton Moore, *History of Alabama* (University, Ala.: University Supply Store, 1934), 223–30, 236; Rogers et al., *Alabama*, 141–45; William H. Brantley, *Banking in Alabama, 1816–1860*, 2 vols. ([Birmingham, Ala.]: Privately published, 1967), 1:319, 2:194–97, 233–35, 277.

6. Brantley, *Banking in Alabama*, 2:235; Moore, *History of Alabama*, 236.

7. Martin, *Internal Improvements in Alabama*, 74.

8. Rogers et al., *Alabama*, 166, 177–79; Martin, *Internal Improvements in Alabama*, 75.

9. Rogers et al., *Alabama*, 252–53; Martin, *Internal Improvements in Alabama*, 80–81, 87; James F. Doster, *Railroads in Alabama Politics, 1875–1914* (Tuscaloosa: University of Alabama Press, 1957), 4; Allen Johnston Going, *Bourbon Democracy in Alabama, 1874–1890* (Tuscaloosa: University of Alabama Press, 1992), 63, 126–27.

10. Going, *Bourbon Democracy in Alabama*, 63–65; W. T. Callahan, "Mr. Callahan's Final Word," *Montgomery Advertiser*, January 30, 1920.

11. Doster, *Railroads in Alabama Politics*, 8; Going, *Bourbon Democracy in Alabama*, 73–74, 140–44.

12. Minutes, April 18, 1918, Alabama Highway Commission Minutes, vol. 1, 1915–September 1923, Alabama Department of Transportation, Montgomery, Alabama [hereafter ALDOT].

13. Wayne E. Fuller, "Good Roads and Rural Free Delivery of Mail," *Mississippi Valley Historical Review* 42, no. 1 (June 1955): 67.

14. Sands, *A Study of Alabama Highway Laws*, 215–18; Martin, *Internal Improvements in Alabama*, 29; Cooke, "The Development of the Road System of Alabama," 72–75; "Notice to Those Subject to Road Work," *Southern Star* (Ozark, Ala.), August 6, 1919.

15. Maurice O. Eldridge, *Public-Road Mileage, Revenues, and Expenditures in the United States in 1904* (Washington, D.C.: U.S. Department of Agriculture, Office of Public Roads, 1907), 20, 22.

16. Eben E. Rexford, "The Country Home: How to Get Good Roads," *Outing*, June 1908, 382; H. M. Clark, "System of County Road Management," *American City (Town and County Edition)*, May 1916, 443, 445.

17. N. S. Shaler, "The Common Roads," *Scribner's Magazine*, October 1889, 477, quoted in Howard Lawrence Preston, *Dirt Roads to Dixie: Accessibility and Modernization in the South, 1885–1935* (Knoxville: University of Tennessee Press, 1991), 21–22.

18. "Congressman F. L. Blackmon's Able Address on Good Roads," *Selma Times*, October 4, 1911.

19. United States Federal Highway Administration, *America's Highways, 1776–1976: A History of the Federal-Aid Program.* ([Washington, D.C.]: U.S. Department of Transportation, Federal Highway Administration, 1977), 84.

20. Preston, *Dirt Roads to Dixie*, 25–26; Edwin A. Stevens, "The Future of Good Roads in State and Nation," *Scribner's Magazine*, February 1916, 187.

21. W. W. Crosby, "Types of Road Crusts or Pavements Suitable for Use in Southern States," *American City*, February 1914, 170–75; American Association for Highway Improvement, *The Official Good Roads Yearbook of the United States* (Washington, D.C.: American Association for Highway Improvement, 1912), 282–83; Stevens, "Future of Good Roads in State and Nation," 189; Robert Platt Boyd, "Alabama Highway Department History, Part 1: 1911–1923," *Alabama Roadbuilder*, February 1958, 20. To determine the cost in 2010 dollars, multiply each number by 17.5. Costs determined using the GDP Deflator attached to Samuel H. Williamson, "Seven Ways to Compute the Relative Value of a U.S. Dollar Amount, 1774 to present," MeasuringWorth, March 2011, www.measuringworth.com/uscompare (accessed January 20, 2012).

22. Charles M. Upham, "A Study of Highway Finance," *Alabama Highways*, May 1929, 7–8.

23. Preston, *Dirt Roads to Dixie*, 24.

24. "Scouts Reach Decatur after Very Hard Day," *Pensacola Journal*, September 7, 1911.

25. Winston Thompson, "Barbour County's Special Needs," *Montgomery Advertiser*, February 6, 1920; Henry C. Jones, "Concrete Example of the Need for Good Roads," *Montgomery Advertiser*, February 10, 1920; "Progress," *Montgomery Advertiser*, February 2, 1920.

26. *Constitution of Alabama, 1901*; Margaret Shirley Koster, "The Congressional Career of John Hollis Bankhead" (M.A. thesis, University of Alabama, 1931), 109; Cooke, "The Development of the Road System of Alabama," 128.

27. Rogers et al., *Alabama*, 429.

28. Cooke, "The Development of the Road System of Alabama," 128–30; Rogers et al., *Alabama*, 429.

29. Cooke, "The Development of the Road System of Alabama," 128–30; Boyd, "Alabama Highway Department History," 11.

30. A. E. Johnson, *Published on the Occasion of the Golden Anniversary of American Association of State Highway Officials: A Story of the Beginning, Purposes, Growth, Activities, and Achievements of AASHO* (Washington, D.C.: The Association, 1965), 211; Boyd, "Alabama Highway Department History," 10–11; Cooke, "The Development of the Road System of Alabama," 130–31.

31. Mrs. L. B. Bush, "A Decade of Progress in Alabama," *Journal of Social Forces* 2, no. 4 (May 1924): 542–43; Thomas Owen, *History of Alabama and Dictionary of Alabama Biography*, 4 vols. (Spartanburg, S.C.: The Reprint Company, 1978), 3:271.

32. W. Keller, State Highway Engineer, to Gov. Charles Henderson, November 9, 1915, Good Roads (Subject File) Folder 21, 1916, Alabama Governor (1911–1915: O'Neal) Administrative Files, SG029236, Reel 6, Alabama Department of Archives and History [hereafter ADAH], Montgomery.

33. Boyd, "Alabama Highway Department History," 10, 18.

34. Fuller, "Good Roads and Rural Free Delivery of Mail," 70–72; United States Federal Highway Administration, *America's Highways, 1776–1976*, 80; Preston, *Dirt Roads to Dixie*, 19.

35. United States Federal Highway Administration, *America's Highways, 1776–1976*, 44–45, 50; Martin Dodge, "The Government and Good Roads," *Forum*, November 1901, 294.

36. United States Federal Highway Administration, *America's Highways, 1776–1976*, 72–73.

37. Fuller, "Good Roads and Rural Free Delivery of Mail," 78–82; Rogers et al., *Alabama*, 429; Preston, *Dirt Roads to Dixie*, 33–36; Johnson, *Published on the Occasion of the Golden Anniversary*, 53; Koster, "The Congressional Career of John Hollis Bankhead," 108–9, 130, 135, 172 n. 1, 180–83; Cooke, "The Development of the Road System of Alabama," 134.

38. Johnson, *Published on the Occasion of the Golden Anniversary*, 53, 152; "Federal Road Aid Act" pamphlet, Box 95b, John Hollis Bankhead Papers, LPR 49, ADAH; United States Federal Highway Administration, *America's Highways, 1776–1976*, 85–86; John Bell Rae, *The Road and the Car in American Life* (Cambridge: MIT Press, 1971) 36–37; W. S. Keller, "Special Report of W. S. Keller, State Highway Engineer, to His Excellency The

Honorable Thomas E. Kilby, Governor of Alabama, concerning the Operations of the State Highway Department" [September 3, 1921], SG031372, Reel 18, Alabama Governor (1919–1923: Kilby), Administrative Files, SG22119-22146, ADAH."

39. Charles Henderson to D. F. Houston, January 30, 1917, Good Roads (Subject File) Folder 22, SG029236, Reel 6, Alabama Governor (1911–1915: O'Neal), Administrative files, SG029235-29236, ADAH.

40. D. F. Houston to Charles Henderson, February 27, 1917, ibid.

41. D. F. Houston to Charles Henderson, March 26, 1917, ibid.

42. "Board of Revenue Plans to Get Slice of Federal Money For Warrior Road," *Birmingham Ledger*, July 20, 1916; "Will Seek Federal Aid to Construct Warrior Highway," *Birmingham Age-Herald*, July 21, 1916; "County Ought to Get Federal Fund, Declares Clark," *Birmingham News*, August 3, 1916.

43. Minutes, October 9, 1916, and March 6, 1917, Alabama Highway Commission Minutes, ALDOT.

44. Minutes, February 24, March 6, April 1, and July 9, 1917, ibid.

45. Minutes, April 18, 1917, ibid.

46. Minutes, October 11, 1917, ibid.

47. Minutes, April 18, July 25, 1917, April 15, May 14, 1918, ibid.

48. Thomas Erby Kilby, *Message of Thos. E. Kilby, Governor, to the Legislature of Alabama, October 4, 1921* (Montgomery: Brown Printing Co., 1921), 44–45; *Acts of the General Assembly of the State of Alabama* (Printed by J. Boardman, 1919), xxvi; Keller, "Special Report of W. S. Keller, State Hwy Engineer," ADAH."

49. National Automobile Chamber of Commerce, "Facts and Figures of the Automobile Industry, 1920," 26–27; *Twelfth Annual Report of the State Highway Commission of Alabama from Oct. 1, 1922 to Oct. 1, 1923* (Montgomery: Brown Printing Co., State Printers and Binders, 1924), 24; *Seventh Annual Report of the State Highway Commission of Alabama from April 1, 1917 to April 1, 1918* (Montgomery: Brown Printing Co., State Printers and Binders, 1918), 4.

50. *Eleventh Annual Report of the State Highway Commission of Alabama from Oct. 1, 1921 to Oct. 1, 1922* (Montgomery: Brown Printing Co., State Printers and Binders, 1922), 53; *Acts of the General Assembly of the State of Alabama*, 893–94. Henceforth I will refer to the policy-making group as the commission and the expanded staff as the department, as is consistent with the functional division established in the 1919 law.

51. *Acts of the General Assembly of the State of Alabama*, 787–91.

52. American Automobile Association, *Highways Green Book* (Washington, D.C.: American Automobile Association, 1922), 67; Lawrence H. Lee, *Report of Cases Argued and Determined in the Supreme Court of Alabama during the October Term, 1920–1921*, vol. 205 (St. Paul, Minn.: West Publishing Company, 1921), 412.

53. "From Pensacola to Chicago in Scout Car," *Pensacola Journal*, August 20, 1911; "Good Roads Meeting a Big Success," *Andalusia Star*, August 24, 1911; "Gulf to Lakes Scout Trip Is Bright Subject," *Pensacola Journal*, August 26, 1911.

54. [Editorial Quip], *Dothan Eagle*, January 9, 1920; "Bond Issue Sentiment," *Dothan Eagle*, January 9, 1920; "Who Should Pay for State Roads," *Dothan Eagle*, January 10, 1920; "Suckers!," *Dothan Eagle*, January 17, 1920; "The Road Bonds," *Dothan Eagle*, January 22, 1920; editorial, *Dothan Eagle*, January 28, 1920; "Voters Reminded of Road Election,"

Dothan Eagle, February 2, 1920; "Sen. Bankhead Favors Road Bond Issue," *Dothan Eagle*, February 5, 1920; "Farmers [sic] Golden Opportunity," *Dothan Eagle*, February 7, 1920; "Why He Likes Good Roads," *Dothan Eagle*, February 7, 1920; "Great Increase in Motor Vehicle Tax a Certainty," *Dothan Eagle*, February 12, 1920; [Editorial Quips], *Dothan Eagle*, February 16, 1920; editorial, *Dothan Eagle*, February 21, 1920.

55. "$25,000,000 for Roads," *Southern Star* (Ozark, Ala.), August 6, 1919; [Editorial Quip], *Southern Star*, January 21, 1920; "Our People Favor the Bond Issue," *Southern Star*, January 28, 1920; "Good Roads Bond Issue," *Southern Star*, February 4, 1920; "State News Indicates Bond Issue Will Carry by Big Majority," *Southern Star*, February 11, 1920; "The Bond Election," *Southern Star*, February 18, 1920.

56. "Alabama Has Been 'Pulled Out of the Mud'!" *Montgomery Advertiser*, February 17, 1920; "54,170 Majority for $25,000,000 Highway Bond Issue Proposal," *Montgomery Advertiser*, February 18, 1920.

57. Storey, Thorndike, Palmer, and Dodge of Boston to John B. Weakley, Birmingham, November 16, 1920, SG031372, MF Reel 18, Alabama Governor (1919–1923: Kilby), Administrative Files, SG22119-22146, ADAH; Lee, *Report of Cases Argued and Determined*, 386–87, 399.

58. Lee, *Report of Cases Argued and Determined*, 388–89.

59. Ibid., 391–97.

60. Ibid., 405–18.

61. Ibid., 398.

62. *Acts of the General Assembly of the State of Alabama*, 894; Minutes, November 10, 1919, Alabama Highway Commission Minutes, ALDOT; *Tenth Annual Report of the State Highway Commission of Alabama from Oct. 1, 1920 to Oct. 1, 1921* (Montgomery: Brown Printing Co., State Printers and Binders, 1921), 3.

63. George G. Clark, "Review of State Highway Work in Alabama," 1921, 16–19, reel 18, SG031372, Alabama Governor (1919–1923: Kilby), Administrative Files, SG22119-22146, ADAH.

64. *Tenth Annual Report of the State Highway Commission of Alabama from Oct. 1, 1920 to Oct. 1, 1921*, 12, 27–28, 53–55.

65. Telegram, B. A. Rogers, Florence, to John A. Rogers, Montgomery, May 17, 1921, Alabama Governor (1919–1923: Kilby), Administrative Files, SG22119-22146, ADAH; Charles McCall to Thos. E. Kilby, Montgomery, June 13, 1921, ibid.; telegram, J. F. Koonce, Florence, to Gov. Emmett O'Neal, January 9, 1913, Good Roads: Post Roads (Subject File) Folder 40, SG029236, Reel 7, Alabama Governor (1911–1915: O'Neal) Administrative Files, SG029235-29236, ADAH; Governor Emmett O'Neal to Postmaster General Frank N. Hitchcock and Sec. of Agriculture James Wilson, Washington, D.C., January 10, 1913, ibid.; Postmaster General Frank H. Hitchcock to Governor Emmett O'Neal, March 3, 1913, ibid.

66. Kilby, *Message of Thos. E. Kilby*, 6.

67. United States Federal Highway Administration, *America's Highways, 1776–1976*, 102, 107–8; Minutes, February 25, 1920, Alabama Highway Commission Minutes, ALDOT; W. S. Keller to Senator B. B. Comer, May 15, 1920, Folder 1, SG22127, Alabama Governor (1919–1923: Kilby), Administrative files, SG031372-31374, ADAH.

68. Minutes, February 25, 1920, Alabama Highway Commission Minutes, ALDOT.

69. W. S. Keller to Senator B. B. Comer, May 15, 1920.

70. John Craft to Thomas Heflin, May 30, 1921, SG031372, Reel 18, Alabama Governor (1919–1923: Kilby), Administrative Files, SG22119-22146, ADAH.

71. Federal Aid Highway Act, 1921, *Statutes of the United States of America* (Washington, D.C.: Government Printing Office, 1921), 212–19; John Williamson, "Federal Aid to Roads and Highways since the 18th Century: A Legislative History" (Congressional Research Service, January 6, 2012), 6, http://www.fas.org/sgp/crs/misc/R42140.pdf (accessed March 20, 2012); United States Federal Highway Administration, *America's Highways, 1776–1976*, 108.

72. "Alabamians Accept the Amendments with Substantial and Gratifying Majorities," *Birmingham News*, January 31, 1922.

73. "Amendments to Carry in State Election, Belief," *Birmingham News*, January 30, 1922; "Reports Indicate Light Vote, with Quick Count Seen," *Birmingham News*, January 30, 1922; "Bond Issue Carries in Houston County," *Dothan Eagle*, January 31, 1922; "County Measures Carry Handily as Amendment Wins," *Birmingham News*, January 31, 1922; "Vote 10 to 1 for Amendments in State, Belief," *Birmingham News*, January 31, 1922.

74. Minutes, April 25, June 26, July 24–25, 1923, Alabama Highway Commission Minutes, ALDOT; *Eleventh Annual Report of the State Highway Commission of Alabama from Oct. 1, 1921 to Oct. 1, 1922*, 3; *Twelfth Annual Report of the State Highway Commission of Alabama from Oct. 1, 1922 to Oct. 1, 1923*, 37.

75. Hastings H. Hart, *Social Problems of Alabama: A Study of the Social Institutions and Agencies of the State of Alabama as Related to Its War Activities* (Montgomery, 1918), 5–9, http://www.archives.state.al.us/reorganization/1918.pdf (accessed March 20, 2012); Hastings H. Hart, *Social Progress of Alabama: A Second Study of the Social Institutions and Agencies of the State of Alabama* (Montgomery: Russell Sage Foundation, 1922), 58–59, http://www.archives.state.al.us/reorganization/1922.pdf (accessed March 20, 2012).

76. Hart, *Social Problems of Alabama*, 7–8; "Vote Road Bond and Put Thousands to Work, Is Plea of Senator Rogers," *Birmingham News*, January 25, 1922.

77. *Twelfth Annual Report of the State Highway Commission of Alabama from Oct. 1, 1922 to Oct. 1, 1923*, 15, 24; Minutes, May 25, 1922, and July 25, 1923, Alabama Highway Commission Minutes, ALDOT.

9

"From Nothin' to Somethin'"

The Tennessee Valley Authority and Federal-Local Cooperation in the Sun Belt South, 1940–1960

MATTHEW L. DOWNS

In late 1949, Barrett Shelton, the editor of Decatur, Alabama's daily newspaper, spoke to the United Nations Scientific Conference on the Conservation and Utilization of Resources. To representatives of the Tennessee Valley Authority, on whose behalf Shelton addressed the assembled delegates, Shelton's community represented an economic development success story, an account of how close cooperation with the federal government, and particularly the TVA, transformed Decatur, in Shelton's words, "from nothin' to somethin'" in their fifteen-year partnership. In relating "The Decatur Story," as his speech was entitled, the editor exemplified the larger victory that TVA won over dreadful economic conditions in the South. In the process, Shelton captured perfectly the development ethos of the Sun Belt South.

Shelton began by painting a dire picture of Depression-era North Alabama, a region that, by 1929, had already suffered years of declining agricultural profits and lackluster industrialization. When the city's last major industry, a railroad shop employing two thousand, closed in the face of the Depression, Decatur languished. As Shelton noted, "Lands were selling for taxes, the people were ill-housed, ill-clothed and out of hope."[1] Initially, city leaders scoffed at TVA's plan to use hydroelectricity produced at nearby dams to attract industry, believing that cheap power would do little to address the region's larger economic problems: "[We] were not interested in saving a dollar or so on our power bill." Yet when Shelton and other "progressive" leaders tried their own solutions, they failed to provide any "lasting good." Finally, the editor and several fellow business and civic leaders agreed to meet with David Lilienthal, a member of TVA's board of directors and the chief proponent of economic development within the agency. At first, Shelton was hostile to Lilienthal's suggestions; he remembered telling the former lawyer, "You're here, you were not invited, but you're here. You are in command, now what are you going to do?" His reply shocked the men: "I'm not going to do anything. You're going to do it."[2]

Lilienthal provided a quick primer of his vision for economic recovery in the Valley, centered on directed development. TVA provided "tools of opportunity" such as advice, assistance, and cheap power, but Decatur's citizens would need to use those "tools" to, in Shelton's words, "[grow] our own industry based upon the resources of the land." Soon, Shelton and his fellow citizens brought in new and relocated industries and created a permanent civic and regional economic leadership dedicated to the principle of industrial development. Yet, for Shelton, the greatest change was the new mind-set of the people of his city, who had become more confident and who now possessed a better "spirit" that would "go far" in attracting more industries.[3] As he later wrote in a guest editorial for the nearby *Huntsville Times*, "We are no longer afraid. We are confident. We know what we can do." Shelton praised TVA for "a vigorous and intelligent effort," but the editor equally credited the region's population: "TVA is not a magic wand. TVA would be helpless to activate community progress without the brains and energies of a free people."[4] He ended his address on a note of confidence in the Valley's economic future: "[Our] people are constantly at work on new plans to perfect a soundly begun economic system so that our people might have opportunities to earn [the] better things of life."[5]

On the surface at least, Shelton's praise for TVA recalled the agency's extensive work in the Tennessee River watershed. The TVA had long targeted poverty in the agricultural region, hit hard by the Great Depression, and agency officials consistently promised to include the communities of the Valley in their plans for economic growth. Yet Shelton's Decatur differed from TVA's original vision in important ways. Instead of semi-rural communities of small producers and craft-based industries, the Valley city moved decidedly in the direction of industrialization. By the 1950s, TVA and civic leaders throughout the region, including Shelton, saw industrial and commercial growth as providing the surest route to prosperity. The "Decatur Story," then, was not simply a testimonial to the success of a New Deal planning agency; it was an enunciation of the prevailing economic development ethos of the postwar TVA and the region in which it operated.

And Shelton, whose work pushed the agency toward industrial growth, and whose cooperation ensured the participation of a number of Valley leaders and organizations in that program, was the perfect spokesman for the emerging Sun Belt South.

* * *

Created in 1933 during President Franklin Roosevelt's flurry of initial New Deal legislation, the Tennessee Valley Authority proved as radical as any piece of legislation passed during the "Hundred Days." The TVA Act targeted the watershed of the Tennessee Valley, providing for the construction of a series of hydroelectric dams on the Tennessee River to control seasonal flooding and provide power for farms, homes, and factories in a massive region that included parts of seven southern states. TVA representatives spread throughout the Valley, training farmers in intelligent agricultural practices, setting up schools and clinics, staffing community education and recreational programs for workers and their families, and employing thousands. And, at the heart of Roosevelt's goals for the Valley was local initiative—once TVA set reform in motion, the people of the region would become important partners in their own betterment. As Roosevelt explained, his administration "has realized that the value and permanence of the effects of its work will be increased if the local people and local institutions cooperate in the development rather than merely permit the development to be imposed upon them." Expansive in its scope and in its prescription for economic recovery, TVA captured Roosevelt's enthusiasm for real social and economic change in the South; in asking Congress to approve the creation of the TVA, the president called it "a laboratory for the Nation to learn how to make the most out of its vast resources for the lasting benefit of the average man and woman."[6] As he told reporters at a November 1934 press conference, "What we are doing there is taking a watershed with about three and a half million people in it, almost all of them rural, and we are trying to make a different type of citizen out of them."[7]

The first chairman of TVA's Board of Directors, Arthur Morgan, attempted to implement that idealistic vision by fostering a series of self-sufficient communities across the Valley. As president of Antioch College, located outside Dayton, Ohio, Morgan created what one scholar called an "educational utopia," where students balanced study with work in local farms and factories. The school was an early example of the community he hoped to build in the Tennessee Valley, improving society through education and agricultural and small-scale industrial labor while working to return the benefits of employment to the larger community.[8] This spirit of reform brought Morgan to the attention of President Roosevelt and propelled him to the leadership of the New Deal agency. Morgan criticized the South's "rugged individualism," a single-minded pursuit of profits that led southerners to depend on cotton monoculture and low-wage and low-skill factory jobs. In the chairman's vision for the Valley, hydroelectric generation, flood control, and improved navigation were simply smaller aspects of a much larger program in which TVA would "teach the American people in the rural communities how to live."[9]

Morgan's TVA would bring economic development by growing small, localized industries that would allow farmers to work on their farms in the summer and in factories during winter. Representatives of the agency would teach southerners, both longtime rural residents and new arrivals, to abandon profit-driven, self-serving individualism in favor of small, self-sufficient, mutualistic communities. In Morgan's estimation, the culture of the people was integral to the project's success, and to change the economy of the Valley was to change its inherent culture. He hoped TVA would "distribute the sense of social responsibility among the people."[10] His son Ernst recalled that Morgan realized that "technical engineering and physical engineering without human engineering" precluded real change. TVA provided an opportunity for him to prove this maxim. As Ernst recalled, Morgan understood that "You need a lot more than just dams and dredging to [make] a culture."[11]

Yet even as Morgan set in motion TVA's program, he faced increasing opposition from fellow board member David Lilienthal, a midwestern lawyer with experience handling utilities cases. When the board decided to divide responsibilities, Lilienthal took charge of electricity production and distribution, which he came to see as the most important aspect of the agency's program for the Valley. Lilienthal argued that the spread of cheap electricity would not only ease domestic burdens but also allow larger industries to locate in the region. Those industries would then employ those southerners no longer able to turn a profit in agriculture or trapped in low-wage manufacturing. In TVA's first year, Lilienthal organized an Industrial Development Division to locate businesses that might "find a way to absorb the vast supply of power we are creating."[12] Specifically rebuking Morgan's communalism, Lilienthal promised that the Valley would be the "scene of an expansion of industry which in the course of the coming decade will change the economic life of the South."[13]

Through most of its first decade, TVA's program seemed expansive enough to accommodate the dueling visions of its board. Yet even as Morgan oversaw dam construction and training and education programs, and as Lilienthal negotiated power contracts and challenged existing utilities, the two men failed to come to a consensus and the boardroom fight became public. Lilienthal's aggressive pursuit of industrial contracts, combined with his increasing notoriety as TVA's most strident public defender, irked Morgan, who appealed to Roosevelt. The president, however, sided with Lilienthal. Lilienthal was the face of TVA's struggle to delineate territory once covered by a number of private utilities, and he understood Roosevelt's desire for evidence that the South was recovering economically from the effects of the Depression. When Morgan attempted to block Lilienthal's reappointment to the board, Roosevelt warned him that "he must be ready to take responsibility for delaying and perhaps disrupting not only TVA but the whole future."[14] Morgan continued to obstruct Roosevelt's plan for the TVA, and in 1938 the president removed him from office. H. A. Morgan, the third board member who oversaw TVA's agricultural program, became the nominal chairman, but Lilienthal emerged as the driving force behind the agency's plan for the Valley.

* * *

Even as Roosevelt removed Arthur Morgan from the chairmanship, his concern for the reconstruction of the southern economy gained national attention. On August 6, 1938, the National Emergency Council, an agency concerned with coordinating and releasing information on New Deal recovery efforts, printed 100,000 copies of *The Report on Economic Conditions of the South*.[15] In his introductory letter, Roosevelt set the tone for the report's critique of the southern economy: "It is my conviction that the South presents right now the Nation's No. 1 economic problem—the Nation's problem, not merely the South's. For we have an economic unbalance in the Nation as a whole, due to this very condition of the South."[16] What followed was a litany of economic and social failings. The South had a wealth of physical and human resources, but decades of mismanagement and exploitation rendered those advantages moot—a region "blessed by Nature" boasted the "poorest [people] in the country."[17] The final section of the report suggested a solution: "purchasing power."[18] As the authors noted, "[The South's] growing population, with vast needs and desires, now largely unfilled, could keep a large part of the rest of the country busy supplying them." With money to spend and the confidence to spend it, "the Nation's greatest untapped market and the market in which American business can expand most easily" would bring the region, as well as the rest of the country, out of the Great Depression.[19]

In Knoxville, Tennessee, TVA's board replied to the report with its own account of progress in the Valley, highlighting the agency's work to address each economic problem described by the presidential committee. Farmers replenished their soil with TVA fertilizer. Reforestation, wildlife protection, and careful planning kept southern resources from being wasted. Dams on the Tennessee prevented destructive flooding and provided the power that electrified homes, farms, and businesses at affordable rates below those imagined by private industry. TVA created thousands of jobs on its construction projects and clearance crews, and its self-described policy of nondiscrimination set a standard for treatment of southern blacks for other regional businesses. Workers fought the spread of malaria and educated communities on proper nutrition. The response also provided Lilienthal with an opportunity to highlight development work, and specifically, his efforts to address southern "underconsumption" by locating industries in the region that would employ former farmers and mill hands, boost paychecks, and encourage southerners to spend money on the products being produced in the South and around the country. TVA, the reply noted, actively developed new industries in the Tennessee Valley, providing new sources of income that would give southerners a larger share of the national economy.[20]

Interestingly, Valley leaders also responded to the National Emergency Council's report, highlighting their own work to improve the southern economy. And, just as importantly, their reply signaled a growing convergence between their point of view and that of TVA's leadership. The *Decatur Daily* boasted that *Fortune* magazine had named the South the "nation's number 1 opportunity," with data offsetting the National Emergency Council's report. Editor Barrett Shelton promised that the region was on the verge of unprecedented development. In fact, he argued, the coming prosperity would cause "painful readjustments in certain Northern industries" as factories decided to relocate where cheap power, transportation, and available labor provided a better business climate. The paper promised that the tendency of some southern leaders to "grovel in ashes strewn by the Emergency Council" did not represent the majority of southerners.[21] Shelton conceded that the South was the poorest section of the country, but, he suggested, in pointing out the problem, Roosevelt's council provided an opportunity to bring in better schools, more industry, and diversified farming. The area needed the "substantial payrolls that come from industry," and that industry would only come with improved stewardship of Valley resources.[22] Like TVA officials, Valley leaders acknowledged their economic inequality with the rest of the nation but resented the implication that the region had become an economic "problem." Instead, as an economic "opportunity," the region was ready to welcome development, and by the time the *Report on Economic Conditions of the South* was published, leaders in TVA's boardroom and in communities across the Valley were prepared to cooperate in pursuit of an improved economy.

* * *

On the eve of the 1940s, as the U.S. economy geared for wartime production, southern leaders and TVA officials found the perfect opportunity to accelerate the development of the region. Lilienthal encouraged government defense plants and private contractors to consider locating (or relocating) in the Valley. He worked with community leaders to facilitate industrialization. He noted, "Growth of industry in the South ... has been inevitable. The change has been coming gradually, and it was right that it should, but national defense needs have accelerated the pace. Now the South is ready."[23] Lilienthal used cheap electricity as the region's chief selling point, and he saw real dividends as manufacturers, armories, arsenals, and depots chose to set up shop in the Tennessee Valley.

No defense industry in North Alabama received as much wartime attention from TVA as the Reynolds Metals Company. When the Virginia business announced its decision to locate in the Valley in 1940, locals praised TVA officials and congressional leaders for their work in negotiating with company president Richard R. Reynolds. In particular, Senator Lister Hill formed a personal relationship with the aluminum manufacturer, making daily calls and petitioning the Reconstruction Finance Corporation for loans and TVA for a favorable power contract.[24] Florence's T. M. Rogers, a longtime proponent of Valley development, and Allen J. Roulhac of Sheffield worked to convince Hill and fellow senator John J. Sparkman to help bring the facility to Sheffield. Roulhac captured perfectly the allure of a TVA-covered Valley, which was "located in the territory served by public power, in an area which certainly needs industrial development of high order badly [and] should be a most desirable location for any kind of national defense or peace time industry." Cheap, available electricity was a crucial determinant in the decision, making negotiations with TVA especially important. Sparkman set up meetings with Reynolds and TVA representatives, who promised to make an "equitable" contract with the company. Rogers agreed to pay all of the expenses of local leaders who helped show Reynolds officials the site at Sheffield. He saw the initial financial outlay as an investment in the district's future: "The best thing I see about the Reynolds Metal Company is the fact that it will make available aluminum for other industries, both large and small, who would be interested in locating here due not only to cheap power but local materials."[25] Local and federal leaders cooperated in their attempt to influence the decision. Sparkman worked with TVA to formalize power contracts, and when he realized that Reynolds was concerned with transportation and material availability, he contacted Rogers and Roulhac, asking the businessmen to find "anyone competent" to advertise the area.[26]

In mid-September, Sparkman's secretary informed Rogers and Roulhac that a tentative contract had been signed to locate the plant at Sheffield, and on October 7, 1940, the news became public. Reynolds Metal Company began construction on a facility two miles from Wilson Dam, producing aluminum for the Army Air Corps. The factory replaced "fields of lespedeza, turnips, potatoes and cotton," consumed $1 million in TVA power, and, except for "key men," employed local labor.[27] Reynolds's decision to locate in North Alabama demonstrated a number of benefits the Valley possessed. The personal and political pressure exerted by Hill and Sparkman helped to convince Reynolds's leadership to locate in the Tennessee Valley in general and in Sheffield in particular. The senators also used their influence to ensure that TVA provided ample electricity for aluminum production, even as other communities in TVA's coverage area increased their demands for power. As Sparkman and Hill traipsed through the halls of Congress, civic leaders in the Valley provided the groundwork for Reynolds's decision. Rogers, Roulhac, and a host of business-minded citizens housed representatives of the company, scouted sites, led tours, and kept pressure on state and national leaders to come to an agreement. The location of Reynolds Aluminum in Sheffield exemplified the multifaceted approach that TVA and southern civic leaders took to attract industry to the Valley, and throughout the war effort, similar negotiations occurred across the region.

In fact, even TVA encouraged defense investment in the region, Lilienthal and other agency officials built important relationships with groups across the Valley. In 1940, TVA set up a cooperative exchange with the Alabama State Planning Board (ASPB), providing its vast regional research mechanism in the hopes that the ASPB could more closely oversee and manage the local development groups that put its plans into action.[28] In 1943 the cooperation became even more formalized when the two signed a seven-year contract. TVA provided a full-time planning technician to the state agency and reimbursed all expenses, and together the agencies prepared zoning legislation, organized and funded local economic development groups, provided services and amenities in cities across the state, and worked to improve the regional infrastructure.[29] As officials with TVA noted, the relationship with ASPB helped both agencies address the "serious community development problems associated with the current intensive national-defense expansions."[30]

In its relationship with the ASPB, TVA insisted on an approach that encouraged local initiative. In 1944, TVA's director of the Department of Regional Studies, Howard K. Menhinick, drafted a formal program of operation for the ASPB, hoping to guide the state board into the postwar years. At the heart of the TVA's instructions was a provision to stimulate local planning, encouraging the ASPB to guide local agencies, particularly area chambers of commerce, by fostering multi-county cooperation and cataloging regional resources.[31] Menhinick stressed the larger picture: "When many people are thinking and working on the same problems and all are pulling together in the same direction, there is created a wealth of manpower, ingenuity, and ideas which could never be supplied by a limited number of federal or state personnel."[32] TVA hoped to streamline industrial recruitment, encouraging communities to cooperate with each other instead of undercutting bids or stealing prospects. Lilienthal stressed that economic revitalization would only come when communities used their resources to bring in industries, increasing the purchasing power of Valley residents and pumping money into the area that could be used for needed improvements. In this environment, civic leaders across the Tennessee Valley looked to both state and federal officials for assistance in facilitating industrial development. In Decatur this combination of active community leadership and federal, state, and regional support revitalized a devastated economy, and the city's story came to represent the possibilities inherent in a program of federal-local cooperation.

* * *

In 1930, Decatur was the largest city in North Alabama, counting nearly 15,600 residents.[33] The town and its surrounding area had a fairly well established economy based on cotton cultivation and processing, but the Great Depression crippled Decatur and the rest of the Valley. The town still claimed thirty-three manufacturers in the 1930 census, but by 1932 only one major industry remained viable, the Louisville and Nashville Railroad machine shop, and nearly every resident relied on the company's paychecks, either directly or indirectly.[34] The next year, the Depression claimed the machine shop as well, creating an economic crisis on the eve of TVA's entrance into the Valley. The town's inhabitants struggled to make ends meet in a region that was, by 1933, "severely depressed," "broke, sick [and] discouraged."[35]

As one resident noted, TVA "put the spark back in the growth of Decatur."[36] The city immediately began using low power rates to sell itself to industrial prospects, and in 1935, local leaders worked with TVA officials and the state government to attract a Chicago aluminum plant.[37] That same year, thanks in part to recruiting by Decatur's chamber of commerce, the Ingalls Iron Works purchased eight acres of riverfront property to build boats and barges in expectation of increased navigation on the river. The plant praised the city's efforts to create a "successfully planned community of activity and progress."[38]

The driving force behind Decatur's growth was Barrett Shelton, editor of the *Decatur Daily*. As his city pushed for industrial prospects, Shelton cultivated relationships with Alabama's congressional delegation and with TVA's David Lilienthal, whom Shelton knew to be very receptive to plans for industrial growth and economic development. The editor made sure that Lilienthal understood the importance of Decatur's economic success, noting that "So long as Decatur remains in her present position, one of unsoundness and one of comparative poverty, she will be no advertisement for the effectiveness of TVA. A down-at-the-heel town cannot prove good advertising." As Decatur's economic fortunes rose, Shelton promised, TVA's image would follow suit.[39]

At first the editor found Lilienthal and other TVA officials hesitant to act, afraid that providing specific assistance to Decatur would violate TVA's mandate to ensure regional growth. Shelton suggested that TVA might convince the government to locate a defense plant in the city, but officials at the agency reminded him that it had to remain "regional" and impartial in dealings with Valley residents. Instead, TVA's general manager, Gordon Clapp, hoped to convince Shelton and his colleagues in Decatur's business community to take the initiative. They refused to relent, and as TVA began its work to locate defense-minded plants in the Valley in the late 1930s and early 1940s, Shelton increased pressure on both TVA and Alabama's congressional representatives. In late 1939, the editor told Hill that his city needed industries that would "[belong] to the Tennessee Valley section of Alabama"; in fact, Shelton argued, Decatur "[had] these things coming to us."[40] A few months later he made a similar appeal to TVA chairman H. A. Morgan, relating that Decatur was "in a most uncomfortable industrial position" and asking for any information on relocation requests made by industries that Decatur or the state board might use to contact interested businesses.[41]

Even as Shelton made inquiries, he also led city leaders to act, aggressively pursuing plants and businesses that could take advantage of the region's resources. In October 1940, the Nebraska Consolidated Mills announced the construction of an eight-hundred-barrel-per-day flour-processing plant along the Tennessee River in Decatur.[42] In 1941, in cooperation with TVA, Shelton and Decatur Chamber of Commerce president John M. Nelson led a campaign that won the Southern Aviation Training School for the city, located on a site just north of the city across the Tennessee River, and hoped to make the school the foundation for even further defense investment.[43] Such active leadership made Decatur the ideal example of Lilienthal's plans for the Valley. Traveling through North Alabama at the outset of World War II, Lilienthal called the city a "grand experiment." Just four years earlier, he remembered, Decatur was "in admittedly bad shape," looking for industry to revitalize the area economy.[44] Yet by 1940 the city had a population of over 16,000 with nearly 5,500 wage earners, more than double the number in 1930, though Decatur added only 1,000 new residents.[45] The city also boasted a veritable catalog of items manufactured and processed in the vicinity: "flour, brick, tile, meats, furniture, boxes, baskets, structural and ornamental iron products, tanks, skids, septic and grease traps, poultry processing, felt hats, crude cotton seed and oil, steel ships and barges, dairy products, aluminum fabricating, steel nuts and screws, concrete pipe, copper tubing fabrication, [and] cotton and rayon tire fabric." Even taking into account the decline from peak numbers from World War II defense production, in 1948 Decatur counted 87 firms employing 5,204 workers with a total payroll of over $12.5 million.[46] In summing up the transformation of the city, Lilienthal reserved specific praise for Shelton, who had the "brains and spirit" to bring in industry.[47]

But simply locating industries in Decatur could not create a lasting foundation for growth, and even as Lilienthal praised Shelton and Decatur's civic leaders for their work, TVA collaborated with the city to address the problems that emerged with industrialization. New facilities and the expansion of existing industries forced leaders to consider the quality of economic growth. Shelton regularly editorialized on the subject. He quoted a McComb County, Mississippi, newspaper on the growth of "boom towns" marked by economic speculation, immorality, and crowded conditions. Shelton warned that only "slow and methodical" growth would save Decatur from a similar fate. He praised the confidence of local workers, who wanted not only employment and steady income but also a better city, and worked toward that goal.[48] Decatur launched an $820,000 public improvement program to build four new school buildings, pave twelve city blocks, and locate a new marine park on an island in the Tennessee River.[49] In 1941 the city organized an official planning commission, designed to cooperate with both TVA and the various federal war agencies directing defense funds across the country, even as the federal agency formed its own relationship with Alabama's state board. Decatur's commission prepared zoning ordinances and looked into the use of the Tennessee River waterfront, including land owned by TVA, for planned growth.[50] Ingalls Shipbuilding expanded onto adjacent TVA property, but rising employment and waterfront industries put a strain on the city's outdated sewer system. In conjunction with federal agencies such as the Public Housing Authority, the commission worked to update the municipal water supply and extend utilities to industrial and residential developments.[51]

In 1943, Shelton proudly boasted of his city's growth. On the occasion of TVA's tenth anniversary, he quoted an unnamed Decatur businessman who told Lilienthal, "We are building a city here, not necessarily a bigger city, but a better city, a city that will live, that will not blow down in the face of ill economic winds."[52] The story may have been apocryphal, but its sentiments undoubtedly pleased TVA. In fact, Lilienthal appreciated the editor's leadership not just for his successful work to bring industry to the region but also for his careful understanding of the means by which communities might follow in Decatur's footsteps. Shelton embraced the long-term perspective that Lilienthal and TVA's leadership cadre wanted for its local leaders. The editor looked to TVA and state and national leaders for assistance, but he also mentored locals, whose initiative brought new industries to the city. Shelton also refused to rest on his laurels, encouraging the city to prepare its infrastructure for further expansion even as civic leaders approached potential business clients. The city was quickly becoming an example of the way TVA hoped to operate in the region.

* * *

In fact, the cooperation between communities, state and national leaders, and the TVA was so important to Lilienthal's vision for the Valley that he took active steps to entrench the policies in the agency's program. In December 1945, TVA held a conference with representatives of the state planning commissions within its borders. In the first session, the agency's Commerce Department director, John Ferris, told the assembled planners that their objective should be "a rising standard of living for the people of the region resulting from their direct participation in conserving and making use of the resources of national wealth of the region as a whole," and he promised that TVA would be a "technical partner" in that growth.[53] TVA staff and their colleagues at the region's research institutions offered assistance, and Ferris reminded the audience that, as an impartial government agency, TVA would serve only as an information center, working with state and community development groups looking to attract different companies—local cooperation was essential for real, lasting success. When the planning agencies met with TVA again in 1947, Ferris captured TVA's vision for local development work in the postwar South: "The planning of the Valley's future must be the democratic labor of many agencies and many individuals, and final success is as much a matter of general initiative as of general consent."[54]

The director of Alabama's State Planning Board, W. O. Dobbins, actively participated in TVA's development conferences. In the years following World War II the state agency worked feverishly to preserve the advantages that defense investment introduced in the state. Embracing its role as a source of information for local efforts, Dobbins's group produced a massive ten-volume study of the state's industrial resources, titled *Alabama's Industrial Opportunities*. Each volume cataloged manufacturers in a given industrial sector, from agricultural products to electrical machinery. The publication presented the wide variety of resources the state offered industrialists while embracing an optimistic vision of the state's future. In an introduction reprinted in each volume, Dobbins wrote, "The foundations of the future rest upon the development of industries which will utilize the resources, labor, and capital of the state."[55] In an accompanying summary, Dobbins boasted that his state had "many attractions for industrial leaders," particularly mineral resources; cheap labor, fuel, and electricity; and a strong regional market.[56] TVA's influence is apparent. Like fellow leaders of state industrial groups across the South, Dobbins created a database of industrial information, a reference readily available for any community interested in recruiting industry.

In fact, Dobbins's work in Alabama reflected the growing popularity of state-based development programs in the South after the war. By the 1940s a third of southern states produced specific industrial directories like Alabama's, and many state agencies moved toward a more active industrial recruitment policy, particularly as competition increased.[57] The best-documented program emerged in Mississippi. There, the Balance Agriculture with Industry (BAWI) program supported legislation allowing municipalities to issue bonds that could be used to purchase land and buildings for incoming factories.[58] In South Carolina the government advertised through chambers of commerce, provided tax exemptions to interested clients, and financed the expansion of community services.[59] Like many other state leaders, South Carolina's governor, Fritz Hollings, encouraged "safaris" to New York City in which political and business leaders "sold" the state to companies interested in relocating.[60] Across the region, development efforts matured into active, organized efforts to bring business to the Southeast.

Alabama also moved to create a more favorable environment for the recruitment of industries. In 1949 the state legislature passed the Cater Act, authorizing the formation of municipal industrial development boards and empowering them to acquire and furnish land, sell and lease property, and issue bonds. The Wallace Act followed in 1951, allowing municipal governments to finance the construction and outfitting of facilities for incoming businesses, as well as any other improvements needed on manufacturing and commercial projects.[61] The State Planning Board even changed its name to reflect the increased emphasis, becoming the State Planning and Industrial Board, though its actions changed little. The Cater and Wallace Acts mobilized community groups and civic clubs to sponsor industrial parks and to prepare factory sites for potential industrial clients. In fact, the laws specifically encouraged facility and site planning in industrial recruitment, and TVA's developers wholeheartedly embraced the practice, which allowed TVA to use its substantial regional landholdings, left over from dam planning and construction, as an incentive for economic growth.

* * *

By the 1950s, TVA's New Deal–era construction program was a distant memory, especially in North Alabama, where more than a decade had passed since TVA finished work on the dam at Guntersville. From time to time the agency renovated its facilities, adding new steam plants to dam sites in order to meet wartime and postwar residential and industrial demand, but for the most part TVA no longer needed its acres of unimproved waterfront property as insurance against an untamed flood or as potential dam sites. Instead, the land had become valuable as the setting for industrial development. Located alongside a main navigation artery, in a zone of cheap power and labor, TVA's waterfront sites proved the perfect asset for the region's economic recruiters. By 1955, TVA counted 107 waterfront establishments, including 56 manufacturing plants accounting for three-quarters of the $2.3 billion invested on the waterfront.[62] The agency also claimed 63 additional sites, consisting of 74,500 acres suitable for industrial use. Despite the number of locations, the "choice" spots were limited, so careful planning was needed to match industrial requirements with the specifics of each site. As TVA's planning staff warned, "Many waterfront communities will find it in their self-interest to reserve, plan, and develop much of their remaining waterfront land exclusively for industries."[63] In particular, TVA recommended industries such as pulp and paper mills, inorganic chemical plants, synthetic fiber manufacturers, and electro-metallurgical producers, all of which made use of the water supply for cooling and transportation.[64] The agency acknowledged that unbounded industrial development might adversely affect the diverse uses that Valley citizens and communities made of its landholdings. Waterfront sites promised profitable returns when used by industry, but they also met recreational, residential, and even irrigational needs. The key to planning for waterfront industrial sites was "a well integrated program using the resources of all responsible agencies to achieve sound development."[65]

Planning necessitated the inclusion of state and local agencies already working with TVA for development. TVA's Aelred J. Gray met with the Alabama state board to discuss land along the shores of TVA reservoirs, valuable as both industrial sites and recreational areas. Gray admitted that the studies of waterfront industrial areas were still in need of "broad planning" and coordination and that utilization depended largely on the activities of local groups. Dobbins was optimistic that since "industrialization and urbanization of the South in general and north Alabama in particular was almost certain to occur . . . lands along the reservoir represented a major resource in this development."[66] Gray also held discussions with civic groups in Florence interested in attracting industries to locate along Wilson Reservoir, despite the "high land values" of lakefront lots. TVA convinced Lawrence and Colbert Counties to create planning commissions to advertise their sites, and in Decatur, where city planners were already creating a land-use survey, agency officials helped zone industrial land on the river.[67]

TVA determined to play an active role in helping communities to understand the full implications of locating industry on waterfront property. Agency staff instructed state and local developers on the most successful strategies in preparing sites for industrial clients, relating a number of "modern" development techniques, including community planning, zoning, subdivision control, highway access, taxation, local transportation, and parking regulation. TVA expected community groups to clear and grade land, provide access to highways and railroads, prepare utilities, and even clear local legislation needed by potential businesses.[68] In North Alabama, TVA counted a number of successful usage programs. In Huntsville, a private development group raised funds to purchase TVA land, creating an industrial park that would house a number of firms expanding on valuable defense contracts. In Guntersville, the city's development group purchased a large tract for both industrial sites and residential plots on Lake Guntersville, which was quickly becoming a regional tourist draw.[69]

Perhaps the greatest success of TVA's land-use policies came in Decatur. Much of the city's industrial growth during the war occurred along the Tennessee River, including Ingalls Shipbuilding, Alabama Flour Mill, and several oil companies. With the end of the war, however, Decatur faced the challenge of expanding its industrial sector, and city leaders looked to TVA for assistance. Ferris's Commerce Department recommended a careful preparation of new sites, extending road, water, and city utilities to waterfront land outside current municipal boundaries. The agency even provided Shelton with preliminary data on eight specific sites, complete with the estimated cost of getting each ready for industrial use.[70] Informative studies were important, but in the spirit of the agency's more aggressive embrace of economic development after World War II, TVA officials wanted to go further to "insure the future availability of waterfront sites for the industrial growth of the Valley." Director J. Ed Campbell of TVA's Reservoir Properties Division suggested that Decatur create a checklist of available land, clearing titles and rescinding surplus declarations that made land harder to transfer to private control while actively matching industries to particular sites.[71]

As a "regional" entity, TVA only made recommendations. Yet encouraged by the agency and in cooperation with the State Planning Board, Decatur's City Planning Commission delved even further into the possibilities of waterfront land. Its report recommended contacting manufacturers in need of riverside resources (such as lumber or fresh water), as well as factories dependent on waterborne transportation (such as agricultural processers, lumber mills, and watercraft manufacturers). The group expanded road and rail connections, built conveyors down to the Tennessee River, and dredged shallow areas, all in an attempt to expand the city's water frontage.[72] Soon, outsiders referred to Decatur's waterfront as Alabama's "Gold Coast," with investments totaling $65 million and companies employing more than five thousand local residents on waterfront industrial tracts.[73]

By the late 1960s, the city boasted a number of success stories. One sixty-six-acre waterfront site sold in conjunction with adjoining private land to the Worthington Air Conditioning Plant. The company was so sure of its purchase that it began improving the site two months before the public auction, a sign that city leaders worked carefully with potential clients to ensure an easy transition. Worthington officials praised the city: "[Our] selection of Decatur as a manufacturing site was an excellent choice. In fact, we do not know how we could have done better."[74] The city's chamber of commerce purchased several land tracts, financed by a combination of public subscription and mortgage loans. The city sold two "sizable" sites to industries, including a 357-acre tract to a manufacturing plant. On another plot, Decatur officials removed buildings, graded land, and held a public subscription drive, all in an effort to bring in an industrial client.[75] In addition to Worthington, postwar investment in the city included Monsanto's Chemstrand, 3M, Wolverine Tube, Expanded Foam Products, Valley Steel Construction, and a number of smaller concerns.[76] Wolverine's leadership specifically cited the waterfront location as a prime consideration in its decision to move operations to Decatur, which overcame competition from 274 communities in eleven different states to win the plant.[77]

The economic success of Decatur's "Gold Coast" highlighted the remarkable revitalization of the city after the devastation of the Great Depression. By 1950 the city had a population of 19,974, with 7,500 residents gainfully employed (up 2,000 from 1940). According to census records, male workers were predominantly operatives or craftsmen and foreman, positions associated with industrial employment.[78] By 1960, as the population approached 30,000, the city boasted 10,700 workers, still dominated by craftsmen, operatives, managers, and an increasing number of professionals.[79] Whereas in 1950 surrounding Morgan County still claimed a plurality of farmers and farm laborers, in 1960 manufacturing outpaced agriculture in the county 6,000 to 1,800 workers, respectively.[80] Such success spoke highly of Shelton's and his fellow civic leaders' work to bring industry to the city and surrounding region. The editor clearly grasped the ways and means of economic development, both in his relationship with the various business leaders who decided to locate in Decatur as well as in his relationship with the leadership of TVA. In citing Shelton as representative of the best of the civic leaders in the Valley, Lilienthal certainly understood his potential for success and its reflection on TVA's success.

Yet, just as important, Lilienthal knew that Shelton's value lay in more than employment numbers and dollar amounts. As much as Shelton grasped the ways and means of industrial attraction, he also understood the underlying development ethos. The editor's embrace of regional cooperation in pursuance of economic growth best illustrated the vision that both Valley leaders and TVA had for the southern economy. This work, as much as the statistical proof of Decatur's revitalization, made the city's story valuable to Lilienthal and other agency leaders, and it was Shelton's encouragement of regional cooperation that made his experience a perfect stand-in for the success of TVA's program in the Valley.

* * *

In late 1948, Shelton pitched the idea of a regional development group to Gordon Clapp, who became chairman of the TVA board after Lilienthal's departure for the Atomic Energy Commission. Chairman Clapp happily encouraged Shelton, proposing financial cooperation with municipal and county power boards. He suggested that Shelton contact "qualified professionals" versed in the needs of industries yet objective enough to spread prosperity across North Alabama.[81] Clapp then provided an outline of a "North Alabama Development Council" tasked with industrial recruitment for member communities across the region. The council, later named North Alabama Associates (NAA), served as an intermediary between TVA, the Alabama State Planning Board, and civic and community development groups. Its members gathered and disseminated information on available resources, encouraged further local organization, and contacted prospective companies.[82] TVA asked its power distributors to make a minimum investment in the organization, based on their industrial and commercial receipts (the more business a distributor had, the greater responsibility it had to help its neighbors grow), and Decatur joined Huntsville as one of the two largest initial investors. Giving their approval to Shelton's organization, agency officials recommended he put a "good man on the job."[83] Shelton found that man in T. D. "Tom" Johnson, the former director of Alabama Power's Industrial Development Division and twenty-year veteran of industrial recruiting.[84]

At NAA, Johnson divided his time between research and promotion, carefully documenting the advantages of the Valley, making personal contacts, and releasing publicity pieces. TVA enthusiastically supported the formation of the organization; as Johnson noted after a visit with officials at headquarters: "I came away with the deep feeling that . . . [the] Tennessee Valley Authority had a wealth of information that would be most useful in our work [and] that we would receive their wholehearted cooperation in our efforts to develop new industry in the Valley."[85] Johnson almost immediately found himself fighting to keep defense money flowing to North Alabama. He helped reactivate the Army's Redstone Arsenal in Huntsville and offered his services to Senator John Sparkman, Senator Lister Hill, and Representative Bob Jones in their (ultimately unsuccessful) attempt to locate a hydrogen bomb production facility in the Valley. Sparkman related his confidence in Johnson to the Atomic Energy Commission's general manager, Carroll L. Wilson, calling the developer a "good man" who "will do a good job if called upon."[86]

Johnson's persistence certainly paid dividends. The revitalization of the arsenal alone cemented his legacy as an architect of the postwar boom, and in Decatur, Johnson helped Shelton and other leaders to preserve their postwar gains. NAA worked with Shelton and other civic leaders as they approached Monsanto, which opened with two hundred jobs in 1952 and expanded dramatically throughout the 1950s and 1960s, and Worthington Air Conditioners, whose sales grew rapidly in the suburban economy of the postwar Sun Belt. In 1959 Johnson and Shelton landed Minnesota Mining and Manufacturing Company, better known as 3M, which announced plans to construct a $4.5 million plant west of Decatur to produce the water- and stain-repellent chemical Scotchguard.[87] As part of the waterfront "boom" in the city, many of the companies NAA attracted bought sites along the Tennessee River, utilizing the water for industrial processes, the river for navigation, and contracting with municipalities for large amounts of cheap TVA electricity. Johnson relied on TVA for assistance in conducting research on the Valley's offerings and on locals like Shelton and his colleagues to prepare sites and the community as a whole for economic growth.

Decatur's leadership, and particularly Barrett Shelton, grasped the potential inherent in TVA's program, and the creation of NAA demonstrated just how fully the Valley's leaders had adopted the development ethos. Shelton kept in constant contact with TVA, asked for information, petitioned for funds for city improvement, used the agency's influence to spur the

Decatur Chamber of Commerce to action, and aided in the creation of a regional development organization to further streamline efforts. TVA's leaders encouraged Shelton's work; it provided a great advertisement for the agency's ability to use resource development and cheap power to revitalize the economy. In fact, in using Shelton and Decatur as representative of the agency's success in the Valley, TVA placed local initiative and regional cooperation at the center of its plan for continued economic growth. If community, regional, and state leaders acted as Shelton, Johnson, and Alabama officials had, then cities and towns across the Tennessee Valley might reliably expect to see the same kind of success.

* * *

It would be easy to conclude that Decatur's leadership wholeheartedly accepted cooperation with the federal government in hopes of bringing about industrial development that might improve the city's economic fortunes. In his relationship with David Lilienthal and later leaders of the Tennessee Valley Authority, Barrett Shelton certainly relied on the representatives of the federal agency to understand, catalog, and "sell" Decatur and the surrounding region's resources, and both Shelton and TVA's leadership routinely gave high praise to each other's efforts. However, it is also true that Decatur embraced a kind of federal assistance that was itself premised on the idea that national leaders would allow locals to direct and control their own program of development. This laissez-faire style of encouragement provided the region with just enough support to help Decatur plan for and control the contingencies of economic growth while the city's business and civic leadership chose what kinds of development to approach, as well as how to entice interested companies to the area. In its relationship with TVA, then, Decatur's leadership received the benefits of growth without worrying about qualifications or conditions placed on the city by the federal representatives working to make that growth possible.

In many ways, Decatur's story was the story of the southern Sun Belt. While investment by the federal government prepared the region for growth, and while federal agencies played a major role in encouraging development, civic leaders shouldered the burden of attracting industry and maintaining prosperity. With its economy devastated by poor farming practices, extractive industry, and the Great Depression, the Valley needed help, and TVA stepped in to provide such assistance. Yet relatively quickly, the agency's initial plans for a socioeconomic transformation shifted decidedly in the direction of disinterested industrialization, a process both supported by and encouraged by the people of the region. TVA found local leaders eager to cooperate in plans for economic development, and the success that some communities experienced convinced the agency that industrial attraction would revitalize the Valley's depressed, misguided economy. The end goal, for TVA and for the Valley, was growth, and in the minds of both federal representatives and local leaders, that growth meant progress.

Barrett Shelton concluded his address to the UN conference with a comment that he "routinely" received from visitors to his city. After viewing the remarkable economic rebound in the Valley, outsiders asked, "Wouldn't this all have happened without a TVA?" Shelton always answered, "It didn't."[88] Had David Lilienthal or any other development-minded TVA official been asked a similar question about Shelton or any other active civic leader in the Tennessee Valley, their answer likely would have been the same. When officials asked Shelton to give the "Decatur Story" before the United Nations, they understood that the editor was a perfect example of TVA's success in the region. They also knew that in relating the city's story, Shelton would encourage his neighbors, in the Valley and across the South, to embrace economic development along the same lines. Shelton's testimonial embodied the rapid emergence of the Sun Belt in postwar America—an economy supported by federal assistance and built by southerners themselves.

Notes

1. Barett Shelton, "The Decatur Story," December 1949, box 152, folder 2528, Bob Jones Papers, University of Alabama at Huntsville. Shelton's speech was printed by TVA as well. See Barrett Shelton, *The Decatur Story* (Knoxville: Tennessee Valley Authority, 1950). For the venue of Shelton's speech, see G. H. Aull, L. P. Gabbard, and John F. Timmons, "United Nations Scientific Conference on the Conservation and Utilization of Resources," *Journal of Farm Economics* 32, no. 1 (February 1950): 95–111.

2. Shelton, "The Decatur Story."

3. Ibid.

4. Barrett Shelton, "Unity in the Valley," *Huntsville Times*, August 4, 1950, 4; Shelton, "The Decatur Story."

5. Shelton, "The Decatur Story."

6. Franklin D. Roosevelt, "A Suggestion for Legislation to Create the Tennessee Valley Authority," April 10, 1933, in *The Public Papers and Addresses of Franklin D. Roosevelt, Vol. 2: The Year of Crisis, 1933* (New York: Random House, 1938), 127, 129.

7. "Press Conference #160," November 23, 1934, 214, in *Roosevelt, Complete Presidential Press Conferences of Franklin D. Roosevelt, Volumes 3–4, 1934* (New York: Da Capo Press, 1972).

8. Amity Shlaes, *The Forgotten Man: A New History of the Great Depression* (New York: Harper Perennial, 2007), 177, 179.

9. "Morgan Visits Muscle Shoals," *Florence Times*, May 26, 1933, 1, 6.

10. "Authority Moves on Power," *Florence Times*, July 25, 1933, 1, 3.

11. Mark Winter, interview with Ernst Morgan, April 6, 1983, p. 4, box 7, "Morgan, Ernst A.," Oral History Records, 1965–1993 (Oral History Records), TVA Records, National Archives and Records Administration, Southeastern Branch (Morrow, Georgia) [hereafter NARASE].

12. David Lilienthal, "Project: Industrial Development Division," May 11, 1934, 1, in box 218, "901.02 Industrial (surveys, statistics, studies, etc.)," Tennessee Valley Authority, Office of the General Manager, Records of the Board of Directors, Harry Curtis, Arthur Morgan, and Harcourt Morgan Papers [hereafter Curtis-Morgan-Morgan Papers], NARASE.

13. David Lilienthal, "The Future of Industry in the Tennessee Valley Region," April 21, 1934, in *Congressional Record* (Senate), 73rd Cong., 2nd sess., 1934, 78, pt. 7:7110–12.

14. David E. Lilienthal, *The Journals of David E. Lilienthal*, vol. 1, *The TVA Years, 1929–1945* (New York: Harper and Row, 1964), 62 (May 12, 1936).

15. David L. Carlton and Peter A. Coclanis, eds., *Confronting Southern Poverty in the Great Depression: The Report on Economic Conditions of the South with Related Documents* (New York: Bedford/St. Martin's, 1996), 15, 21.

16. Ibid., 42.

17. Ibid., 47.

18. Ibid., 78.

19. Ibid.

20. "Summary Statement, TVA Cognizance of the Economic Conditions of the South and Its Contribution toward Their Improvement," [1938], box 111, "901.04 thru 1948," Tennessee Valley Authority, Records of the Chairman and the Members of the Board of Directors, 1939–1957, James P. Pope and Raymond R. Paty Papers [hereafter Pope-Paty Papers], NARASE.

21. "Number 1 Opportunity," *Decatur Daily*, October 31, 1938, 4.

22. "Definite Objectives," *Decatur Daily*, September 11, 1939, 4.

23. "Valley Future," *Decatur Daily*, June 21, 1940, 4; Don Whitehead, "World at War Rapidly Is Reshaping Economic Scenery in Tennessee Valley," *Decatur Daily*, August 14, 1940, 3.

24. "Aluminum Plant to Be Built in North Alabama by Virginia Firm," August 2, 1940, *Decatur Daily*, 1; Allen J. Roulhac to Lister Hill, June 30, 1940, box 162, folder 3, Lister Hill Papers, W. S. Hoole Special Collections Library, The University of Alabama, Tuscaloosa.

25. T. M. Rogers to John Sparkman, August 5, 1940; Roulhac to Sparkman, August 12, 1940; Rogers to Sparkman, August 17, 1940; Harold T. Pounders, Secretary, to Rogers, August 19, 1940; Rogers to Sparkman, August 27, 1940; Rogers to Sparkman, September 3, 1940; all in box 22, "House Miscellaneous: Reynolds Aluminum," John J. Sparkman House of Representatives Papers [hereafter Sparkman House Papers], W. S. Hoole Special Collections Library, The University of Alabama, Tuscaloosa.

26. Sparkman to Rogers, September 2, 1940, ibid.

27. Pounders to Rogers, September 20, 1940, ibid.; "Valley Gets Huge Plant," *Decatur Daily*, October 7, 1940, 1; "Aluminum Plant Is Expected to Be Completed within Next Six Months," *Decatur Daily*, October 17, 1940, 1.

28. "Alabama Planning and Local Planning in Six North Alabama Towns, Part I, Alabama Planning," [1940s], 12, box 38, "092, Alabama (A–Z)," David E. Lilienthal Correspondence Files, TVA Records, NARASE.

29. Menhinick to Clapp, September 9, 1943, box 110, "092 Alabama, Folder 1," Curtis-Morgan-Morgan Papers.

30. Lilienthal to Dixon, September 25, 1941, box 110, "092 Alabama, A–Z," Curtis-Morgan-Morgan Papers.

31. Howard K. Menhinick, "A Suggested Program for the Alabama State Planning Board: A Statement Prepared at the Request of the Governor of Alabama," August 10, 1944, 1–3, box 59, "092 Alabama A–Z," Pope-Paty Papers.

32. Ibid., 9.

33. U.S. Census Bureau, *Fifteenth Census of the United States, Manufactures: 1929, Volume I: General Report, Statistics by Subjects* (Washington, D.C.: Government Printing Office, 1933), 292.

34. Ibid.; Shirley McCrary, interview with John Caddell, February 27, 1989, SPR 521, Tape AC-54, Side A, Colonial Dames Oral History Collection, Alabama Department of Archives and History, Montgomery [hereafter ADAH].

35. McCrary, interview with John Caddell.

36. Shirley McCrary, interview with Rutledge Thomas, February 23, 1989, SPR 521, Tape AC-54, Side A, Colonial Dames Oral History Collection.

37. "Aluminum Plant for Decatur Looms with Signing of Act," *Decatur Daily*, July 11, 1935, 1, 2.

38. "Ingalls Iron Works to Put Permanent Plant in Decatur," *Decatur Daily*, November 12, 1935, 1; "Varied Industry," *Decatur Daily*, December 5, 1935, 4.

39. Shelton to Lilienthal, September 15, 1937; J. Haden Aldridge, Principal Transportation Economist, to Lilienthal, September 23, 1937; and Shelton to Lilienthal, September 23, 1937; all in box 58, "095, Decatur, Alabama, thru 1937," Lilienthal Correspondence Files.

40. Shelton to Hill, September 20, 1939, and Hill to Shelton, September 23, 1939, box 162, folder 9, Hill Papers.

41. Shelton to Morgan, May 13, 1940, and Shelton to Morgan, May 18, 1940, box 33, "095 Shelton, Barrett," Pope-Paty Papers.

42. "Nebraska Consolidated Mills to Put Big Flour Plant Here," *Decatur Daily*, August 28, 1940, 1.

43. Nelson to Sparkman, July 9, 1941, box 11, "Morgan County: Decatur Projects, 1940–1," Sparkman House Papers.

44. Lilienthal, *Journals*, 1:215 (September 15, 1940).

45. U.S. Census Bureau, *Sixteenth Census of the United States: 1940, Population, Volume II, Characteristics of the Population, Part 1: United States Summary and Alabama–District of Columbia* (Washington, D.C.: Government Printing Office, 1943), 321; and *Fifteenth Census of the United States, Manufactures: 1929, Volume I: General Report, Statistics by Subjects* (Washington, D.C.: Government Printing Office, 1933), 292.

46. Shelton, "The Decatur Story."

47. Lilienthal, *Journals*, 1:215 (September 15, 1940).

48. "Boom Towns," *Decatur Daily*, December 2, 1940, 4; "Building Facts," *Decatur Daily*, September 30, 1940, 4.

49. "Triple City-Building Plan Begun," *Decatur Daily*, August 8, 1940, 1.

50. Alabama State Planning Commission, Annual Report, "Alabama Planning," December 14, 1942, 2, box 1, "095 Alabama A–Z," Pope-Paty Papers.

51. Alabama State Planning Board, "Progress Report on Local Planning in North Alabama, July 1, 1942–June 30, 1943," August 1943, 17–21, box 110, "092 Alabama, A–Z," Curtis-Morgan-Morgan Papers.

52. "Ten Year Appraisal," *Decatur Daily*, May 18, 1943, reprinted in *Congressional Record* (Appendix), 78th Cong., 1st sess., 1943, 89, pt. 10:A2619.

53. "Report of Conference between Representatives of State Planning Commissions and the TVA," Knoxville, December 12–13, 1945, 2–3, box 112, "913 Regional Planning, Social Planning, Economic Planning, National Planning, Etc.," Pope-Paty Papers.

54. John Ferris, "Industrial-Business Development in the Tennessee Valley Region," Meeting of Directors of Valley States Planning and Development Agencies and Other Organizations Interested in Industrial-Business Development, July 9, 1947, 11, box 218, "901.02 Industrial 1944–1957," Curtis-Morgan-Morgan Papers.

55. The volumes are scattered throughout the ADAH collection. For pertinent examples, see *Alabama's Industrial Opportunities, Volume 7: Stone, Clay, and Glass Products* (Montgomery, 1947), box SG 13419, folder 4(4), Alabama, Governor (1947–1951: Folsom), Administration Files [hereafter First Folsom Administration Papers]; and *Alabama's Industrial Opportunities, Volume 9: Electrical Machinery* and *Volume 10: Automobiles and Automobile Equipment* (Montgomery, 1947), box SG 13437, folder 13, First Folsom Administration Papers.

56. W. O. Dobbins, "Summary Industrial Opportunities in Alabama (Preliminary Draft), 4, 12, box SG 13437, folder 15, First Folsom Administration Papers.

57. See Peter K. Eisinger, *The Rise of the Entrepreneurial State: State and Local Economic Development Policy in the United States* (Madison: University of Wisconsin Press, 1988), 25–26.

58. Albert Lepawsky, *State Planning and Economic Development in the South* (Kingsport, Tenn.: Kingsport Press, 1949), 72. See also James C. Cobb, *The Selling of the South: The Southern Crusade for Industrial Development, 1936–1980* (Baton Rouge: Louisiana State University, 1982); and Connie L. Lester, "Balancing Agriculture with Industry: Capital, Labor, and the Public Good in Mississippi's Home-Grown New Deal," *Journal of Mississippi History* 70 (Fall 2008): 235–63.

59. Lepawsky, *State Planning and Economic Development in the South*, 62–77.

60. Lacy K. Ford and R. Phillip Stone, "Economic Development and Globalization in South Carolina," *Southern Cultures* 13 (Spring 2007): 24–25.

61. Charles M. Stephenson, *Industrial Sites: A Community Problem* (Bureau of Public Administration, University of Tennessee, 1961), 6–7, box 48, loose, Division of Navigation Development Volume Files, 1954–1968 [hereafter Navigation Files], Office of the General Manager, TVA Records, NARASE.

62. Government Relations and Economics Staff, "Industrial Development on the Tennessee River," January 1955, 3, box 15, "901.2 Industrial, 1955," Office of the General

Manager, Government Relations and Economic Staff Papers, General Correspondence, 1953–57 [hereafter GRES Papers], TVA Records, NARASE.

63. Ibid., 6–8, 17–18.

64. Ibid., 20.

65. Ibid., 28–29.

66. Gray, untitled memo, April 29, 1955, box 7, "092: Alabama A–Z," GRES Papers.

67. Gray to Robert B. Nichols, Navigation Engineering Section, March 2, 1956, box 15, "902.2 Industrial, 1956–57," GRES Papers; and Gray, untitled memo, December 30, 1955, box 8, "092.1 Counties A–L," GRES Papers.

68. Stephenson, *Industrial Sites*, 1–2.

69. Ibid., 16–17.

70. Commerce Department, "Physical Problems Relating to Industrial Waterfront Development at Decatur, Alabama," January 1948, box 57, loose, Navigation Files.

71. Campbell to General Manager John Oliver, May 27, 1954, box 15, "901.2 Industrial, 1955," GRES Papers.

72. Decatur City Planning Commission and Alabama State Planning Board, "Preliminary Decatur Waterfront Development Report," June 1948, 14–18, box SG 13438, folder 1, First Folsom Administration Papers.

73. "Industrial Variety Makes Decatur Grow," *Huntsville Times*, August 18, 1959, 15.

74. Richard J. Ricard, Manager, Guntersville-Wheeler Branch, Division of Reservoir Properties, to Director Raymond Paty, July 16, 1953, and E. J. Schwanhausser, Executive Vice President, Worthington, to Paty, July 29, 1953, both in box 12, "095 Decatur, Alabama," Pope-Paty Papers. See also "New Plant to Be Operating by December 1," *Decatur Daily*, July 24, 1953, n.p., clipping courtesy of North Alabama Industrial Development Agency (NAIDA; North Alabama Associates changed its name to NAIDA in the early 1960s).

75. Stephenson, *Industrial Sites*, 15.

76. Listing of Morgan County Industries, 1947–1961, from Alabama Manufacturing Directory, courtesy NAIDA.

77. "Wolverine Picked Decatur Because of River Location," *Huntsville Times*, July 16, 1959, 8.

78. U.S. Census Bureau, *Census of Population: 1950, Volume II: Characteristics of the Population, Part 2: Alabama* (Washington, D.C.: Government Printing Office, 1952), 8.

79. U.S. Census Bureau, *Census of Population: 1960, Volume I: Characteristics of the Population, Part 2: Alabama* (Washington, D.C.: Government Printing Office, 1961), 157.

80. U.S. Census Bureau, *Census of Population: 1950, Volume II: Characteristics of the Population, Part 2: Alabama*, 95; and *Census of Population: 1960, Volume I: Characteristics of the Population, Part 2: Alabama*, 206, 212.

81. Clapp to Shelton, December 10, 1948, box 111, "901.04 1949," Pope-Paty Papers.

82. "Organization of a North Alabama Development Council," December 1948, ibid.

83. Ferris to Gant, January 10, 1949, ibid.

84. Johnson, Meeting of Cullman Rotary Club, August 8, 1950, 2–3, courtesy NAIDA.

85. Johnson, untitled speech, [ca. January–February 1952], 3, courtesy NAIDA.

86. Johnson to Sparkman, July 17, 1950, box 119, "A, Reactivation, Retention, or Expansion of Army Facilities, #1"; and Sparkman to Wilson, July 24, 1950, box 119, "4G,

Hydrogen Bomb Site"; both in John J. Sparkman Papers, Senate, W. S. Hoole Special Collections Library, The University of Alabama, Tuscaloosa.

87. John Washburn, Executive Director, NAIDA, "'Success Story' Chronicles Industrial Growth," *Decatur Daily*, June 20, 1976, B1; "New Plant to Be Operating by December 1," *Decatur Daily*, July 24, 1953, n.p.; and "3M Announces New 4½ Million Plant in Decatur," *Hartselle Enquirer*, July 23, 1959, 1 (clippings courtesy NAIDA).

88. Shelton, "The Decatur Story."

10

Lighting the "Dark and Evil World"

Judge J. Smith Henley, Arkansas, and
the Federal Judiciary's Reform of the Southern Prison

GREGORY L. RICHARD

Southern prisons after Reconstruction quickly became one of the most dangerous and mysterious places in the nation. Very few southerners could comprehend what took place within the prison walls, and even fewer cared. Penitentiaries served their purpose, for prisoners needed to be segregated from law-abiding society and punished for their crimes. It represented the perfect "see no evil, hear no evil" scenario.

But changes within American society, beginning in the middle of the twentieth century, began removing the blinders of not only southerners but those outside Dixie as well. The civil rights movement began to cast light on the particularly brutal conditions of southern prisons. And while prisons throughout the nation were barbaric, it was the peculiar nature of southern prisons that made them particularly heinous in the eyes of many. Southern prison systems after the Civil War reeked too much of slavery for most to handle.

Fortunately, the work of a few courageous federal court judges helped bring some of the cruelty of southern prisons to a halt. Judge J. Smith Henley was one such jurist. His years of involvement with the reform of Arkansas's prison system left a lasting mark on prisons not only in the South but throughout the nation, producing the spark that would ignite the judicial review of many state prison systems in the decades that followed.

The Birth and Evolution of the Penitentiary

Understanding the roots of the penitentiary, its growth and evolution in colonial America, and its divergent history in the growingly schismatic

United States approaching the Civil War creates the proper context within which to study the reform of southern state prison systems. At the very core of the prison rested the relationship between those in power and the powerless. Power, though, is different from physical force, violence, or that which causes pain to the body. It is created by the position of relationships, especially that which could make an otherwise free subject do something he or she did not want to do—in other words, altering the will of others.

Early in the classical period the state chose physical punishment to display power to the populace, arranging public executions as state celebrations and events. Theaters of execution became a visceral means to demonstrate the reins of power. The body became something regulated, arranged, and supervised. Eventually, the focus shifted from pure physical punishment to reformation and rehabilitation, as did concepts of individuality, the delinquent, and reforming the soul. Transforming the prisoner to delinquent followed; someone who should be set apart from society. The working of the carceral system with the growth of the human sciences spawned the creation of the delinquent.

Evolutions of discipline and power maintained that similar structures could control not only those within the prison walls but those outside as well. Thus the modern penal system evolved to turn the structure of criminal justice on its head. The once physically punished body, a show for all, now became the delinquent, hidden yet capable of reform.

Adam Jay Hirsch studied early Massachusetts to reveal that America, by the 1820s, had become disillusioned with Cesare Beccaria's deterrent approach to handling criminals through the drafting of criminal statutes.[1] Thus, Jacksonians, in what Hirsch questionably calls a "novel—and distinctly American" idea, set out to rehabilitate criminals and return them to the community as reformed citizens. Other European nations followed similar trajectories to identify "the root cause of crime . . . in the social environment, rather than in misconceived criminal codes." Toward the end of the nineteenth century, the United States, along with England and France, began to realize that rehabilitation and healing of the soul represented sounder criminal punishment rather than physical punishment to the body.[2]

Rationalism took root in the eighteenth century, during which theorists began rejecting scripture in favor of logic and reason. The harm crime caused to others in society was its worst effect, thus the prevention of future harm represented the most rational purpose of punishment. Rationalists such as John Locke claimed that environmental stimuli, not innate characteristics or moral principles, guided human behavior—an idea Cesare Beccaria built upon by postulating that the *certainty* of punishment contributed far more to the inhibition of crime than mere deterrence. These ideas guided Beccaria to reject the death penalty and suggest "perpetual servitude" as its replacement.[3]

Beccaria's ideas eventually fell out of favor with American reformers in the late eighteenth century, as more began to accept Bentham's placement of blame upon the social environment as the primary producer of crime, and his ideas of the panopticon and the penitentiary. Hard labor, in the form of the English workhouse, became the precursor of the penitentiary system in the United States, the seedling of the modern penal system. Thus, the blending of these European ideals of servitude and penal punishment became the sea from which the American penitentiary system flowed. America, however, had a number of other problems to face when it came to penal servitude and imprisonment, most notably slavery.[4]

Comparisons between chattel slavery in the United States and the penitentiary system had an impact on the development of the American penitentiary. Both prison inmates and southern slaves followed daily routines; both were dependent upon masters for basic human needs. Both slave and prisoner suffered from isolation from a general population of free humans, and both worked longer hours for very little or no compensation. Southern artisans and laborers complained that slaves took a number of their jobs, an argument that northern mechanics and workers made against the prison industry. The imprisonment of classes of criminals and their placement into deviant communities shared a number of characteristics with African slaves. Arguments for the continuation of slavery in the South and for the imprisonment of lawbreakers in the North both had a "ridding society of criminal masses" component. It is curious that, despite these similarities, the nation accepted penal servitude even as it abolished slavery.[5]

During the nineteenth century, Americans began to associate the idea of penal servitude with ideals of republican liberty—ideals that made the South more accepting of slavery. Political leaders such as Benjamin Rush justified the penitentiary and the forced servitude of prison. The argument that the ends justified the means also helped northern Americans justify the penitentiary system while criticizing slavery in the South. Criminals committed crimes that justified the state's taking of their liberties and freedoms, while African slaves on southern plantations did no such thing.

Locke's arguments of natural rights to life and liberty helped fortify this position. Thus, many northerners had no issue sustaining prisons while at the same time degrading chattel slavery in the South.[6]

Studying the development of the penitentiary in a northern state alongside the growth of slavery in a southern state during the nineteenth century reveals a number of interesting issues that enhance the study of punishment in the United States and Arkansas in particular. Michael Hindus's work on Massachusetts and South Carolina revealed that Yankee law gravitated toward bureaucratic methods in order to guarantee efficiency, which meant control and social order.[7] Urban and industrial, the emerging commercial society of Massachusetts required a bureaucratic administration of justice, with the traditional restraints of church and family proving inadequate. South Carolina, on the other hand, did not experience this movement toward formal structures of legal authority. Law in South Carolina became characterized by "highly personalized, ad hominem justice," unstructured, rural, and upheld through custom and deference. Thus South Carolina continued to accept extralegal techniques of social control, such as dueling and vigilantism. Slavery disfigured and contoured South Carolina's view of criminal justice. In the Palmetto State, as in most of the South, whites became more concerned with race domination rather than crime control. Corporal and capital punishment offered the best opportunity to control slaves, according to white southerners. Thus, northern states' financial and intellectual investment in developing a penitentiary system was not necessary in Dixie. Class control became most important in Massachusetts, while race domination did in South Carolina.[8]

The "disfigured" nature of southern prisons continued through the late 1800s, fueled mostly by the society and economy of the post-Reconstruction South. After the destruction caused by the Civil War, many southern states began replacing their wrecked and nonexistent prison systems with ones modeled after the antebellum slave plantation. This system served a twofold purpose for the white planter classes. Not only did it reentrench older notions of white control over African Americans in a postslavery world, but the plantation-style penitentiary also brought much-needed state revenue. The new prison farms not only generated self-sustaining revenue but also brought in profit to near empty southern state coffers. For these reasons, southern prisons and the way they were run, while perfectly acceptable to most southerners, appeared especially heinous to those outside the South.

The Penitentiary of the South: Arkansas

Arkansas offers a prime example of the rebirth of the southern prison system. Its experiment with a postwar convict lease system put to death fully one-fourth of its prisoners from 1873 to 1893. State actors, feeling this excessive brutality had to be limited, ended the private lease system and purchased former plantation farmland. Here, they created the Cummins Prison Farm in 1902 and the Tucker Farm in 1912. State officials ushered in a new era of the Arkansas prison system. After the demise of slavery, this fertile farmland had been uncultivated for years, presenting the perfect opportunity for the state to create a new self-sustaining system. The prisoners built their own quarters and produced their own food. They even guarded each other, which meant that the hiring of outside guards—and with that, the bottom line—could be kept to a minimum. And not only did these prisons bring in self-sustaining revenue, but the sale of farm products often raised more revenue than necessary, which meant these prisons were not only self-sustaining but profitable.

Interestingly enough, when state troopers and other state officials would later investigate the prison farms, prisoner-guards made them leave their weapons at the front gate. Throughout these early years, the prison established its own internal hierarchy of control, from prison "line riders" controlling groups of workers on down to guards who would monitor prison camps. More often than not, these prisoner-guards attempted to solve their interpersonal prison matters via their clout as guard. The trusty guards, as they became known, also used a number of other methods of control and abuse to keep prisoners in line, such as not allowing certain prisoners to eat their meals. A prisoner's chance of surviving the brutality at Arkansas's prison farms increased when their families bribed these trusty guards to ensure the survival of their kin. Up until the 1950s, this system worked for Arkansas's state officials. As long as this invisible, self-sufficient system produced enough profit to pay for itself, government officials were happy. And as long as the state of Arkansas was happy, the courts accepted the system as well.[9]

For years, U.S. federal courts claimed that no mechanism existed for their intervention into state prison matters. Scholars labeled the period of non-interference the "hands-off" period. According to the courts, the federal government "has no power to control or regulate the internal discipline of the penal institutions of its constituent states. All such powers are reserved to the states, and the Fourteenth Amendment does not authorize

Congress to legislate such matters."[10] This statement eliminated the option of prisoners utilizing habeas corpus to secure their release due to the issues raised having nothing to do with the underlying conviction. Consequently, prisoners had few opportunities to challenge their confinement conditions.[11]

The era of federal court silence ended in 1965, when Judge J. Smith Henley of the U.S. District Court for the Eastern District of Arkansas declared that certain conditions and practices at two Arkansas prison farms were unconstitutionally cruel and unusual. The Eighth Amendment now became relevant to cases concerning prison condition, forming the basis of federal judicial jurisdiction. Now, courts could look at the conditions of imprisonment without evaluating the conviction itself, which took away the chief reason courts refused to investigate prison conditions utilizing habeas corpus. Over the next few decades, courts would interpret the Eighth Amendment and create for themselves boundaries within which they could exercise their authority. Within a decade of the 1965 Arkansas decision *Talley v. Stephens*, prisons within twenty-five states and the entire prison systems of five other states had been placed under comprehensive federal court orders. By 1995, forty-one states, as well as the District of Columbia, Puerto Rico, and the Virgin Islands, would have their prison systems fall under intense judicial scrutiny.[12]

None of this watchfulness, however, would have been possible had it not been for the initial litigation in Arkansas and the efforts of J. Smith Henley to spearhead such reform. Jesse Smith Henley, born on May 18, 1917, hailed from St. Joe, Arkansas, a mining town of around three hundred people. Henley stated that the only thing his family did not own in the town was the then recently constructed Missouri and Arkansas Railroad depot. And by owning "everything" in the town, Henley meant that they owned "a general store, a cotton gin," and "a grist mill." His paternal grandfather, Benjamin Harrison Henley, was a former Union soldier, who came from the Kentucky side of the Cumberland River on the border of Kentucky and Tennessee.[13]

Henley hailed from a family of mostly Republicans, except for the few circumstances where a change in presidential administration necessitated the need for a Democrat to hold the position of postmaster. Members of his family "were Republicans . . . all along." In his words, "all of them, yes. Except for the one or two in-laws . . . so we'd have somebody to be postmaster," stated Henley. He earned his law degree from the University of Arkansas in Fayetteville in 1941 and practiced law in Harrison till the mid-1950s. Early in his legal career he served for a few years as a federal referee in bankruptcy for the Western District of Arkansas. From 1954 onward, Henley served in a number of positions within the federal government at the appointment of President Dwight Eisenhower, beginning with associate general counsel of the Federal Communications Commission and then head of the Office of Administrative Procedure for the Justice Department. In January 1958 he was appointed to his first federal judgeship, that of district judge of the Eastern District of Arkansas. Although he managed to sit on the bench by recess appointments, his confirmation was delayed until September 1959. Senator John McClellan of Arkansas wrongly accused him of participating in writing an opinion that gave the president authority to send troops to Little Rock during the battle over the desegregation of Central High School. Henley later became chief judge of the Eastern District from 1959 to 1975, which allowed him to participate in a number of desegregation cases. But it was the litigation concerning the Cummins and Tucker Prison Farms in Arkansas that placed Henley's lasting mark on his home state.[14]

During Henley's earliest times on the federal bench in Arkansas, the mere fact that a prisoners' petition would ever reach his office was something of a miracle. According to Henley, had a prisoner written a letter to a judge in the late 1950s, "a warden would have beaten the hell out of him and he would have been thrown in the hole or chased over the levy and shot as an escapee. We just didn't get the mail." Prisoners' complaints remained unheard until Governor Orval Faubus appointed Dan Stephens commissioner of Cummins Prison Farm. "Dan was the first warden I could ever remember down there," stated Henley, "who ever undertook, there may have been some exceptions, but who undertook to do a little bit of something humane for the prisoners." One thing he provided the inmates with was hot plates so they could cook their eggs. Before the prisoners had their own hot plates, they would have to fry eggs the night before in the kitchen. And, even Judge Henley admits, "a cold fried egg is not very good." While this improvement might not sound like much, it meant a great deal to prisoners and to Judge Henley to see positive, changes take place at the farms.[15]

Henley never hashed words when it came to the brutality of Arkansas prison farms in the 1950s and 1960s. Sitting on the bench during this litigation allowed him to hear firsthand the accounts of brutality that made these prison farms sound less like penal institutions and more like medieval torture chambers. One implement frequently used at Cummins and Tucker Prison Farms, known as the teeter, was comprised of a simple plank placed on the ground with a round device forming a pivot. Though this implement resembled the teeter-totter of one's childhood past, there was nothing innocent about this contrivance. The prisoner balanced himself while standing on the device, a leg on each side of the pivot. Prison officials forced the prisoner to maintain his balance and prevent either side of the board from hitting the ground. Sounds simple enough, but trying to maintain one's balance for minutes, even hours, became quite a chore. The punishment for allowing one side of the board to touch the ground: lashes with the strap. The strap consisted of a heavy piece of leather about five feet long, four inches wide, and about an inch thick attached to a six-inch wooden handle. The strap quickly became the most notorious torture device used by guards at the farms.[16]

Henley listened to hours of testimony describing other torture devices. These implements provided not only physical but psychological punishment. The "Texas TV," for example, taken from a practice used in a nearby state prison, provided a way for prison officials to manage larger crowds or lines of inmates. Trusty guards required prisoners to stand facing a wall with their hands clasped behind their backs, their feet roughly two feet from the wall. Finally, the guards forced prisoners to place their foreheads on the wall. Guards found this particular practice useful when prisoners were waiting in line for a meal or a disciplinary hearing. This would go on for half an hour to an hour at a time. As prisoners moved down the line, they merely continued the previous position. When a prisoner's head stopped touching the wall, he did not have to wait long to feel the strap. The plank and the Texas TV provided the psychological and physical pain the guards needed to subdue and control the prison population.[17]

The "Tucker Telephone," however, advanced far beyond the other torture implements used at the prison in terms of brutality. Guards placed these boxes, which resembled older pay telephones, at regular positions throughout both prison farms. It had a crank that when turned produced electric voltage, which was then transmitted through cables with clamps at the end. These clamps would be placed on various body parts of the prisoner, with the fingers and the genitalia being most popular. As the prison guard would turn the crank on the device, the voltage would generate throughout the cables and electrocute the clamped body parts. These devices were often used as punishment for prisoners who wrote writs and petitioned the courts. Even today, it is customary for anyone visiting the warden of Arkansas Penitentiary to ask whether or not the phone on his desk is in fact a "Tucker Telephone." If any worthwhile reforms were to take place at the prison farms in Arkansas, these punishments, especially the shooting of complaining prisoners as escapees, had to be stopped. The voices of these prisoners must be heard, according to Judge Henley, and he would do what he could to make sure their petitions reached his desk.[18]

Consequently, the most significant change Dan Stephens brought to the prison farms involved allowing prisoners to petition and write the courts. Judge Henley spoke of Stephens having issues with letters that were "saucy" or "impudent or impertinent." Stephens even went so far as to prevent the letters from being sent, and later he approached Henley about the matter personally. The judge, however, told Stephens not to censor the letters except for security reasons. And although Stephens did not agree with this outright disrespect of the court from the prisoners, he allowed the letters to continue. Shortly thereafter, writs started pouring into Henley's court, and the state government finally had to face the harsh realities of the Cummins and Tucker Prison Farm.[19]

Other actions of violence toward inmates from trusties and administrators of the prison further convinced Henley that prisoners definitely needed the protection of the U.S. Constitution. Shortly after hearing testimony from petitioning prisoner plaintiffs regarding their treatment at the prison farms, Judge Henley learned that Mose Harmon Jr., a thirty-eight-year-old field warden trusty, whipped one of the petitioners, Winston Talley, on October 14, 1965, the day after Talley had testified in Judge Henley's court. Talley stated that in the past three years he was probably whipped around seventy-five times, while Harmon placed that number at around seven or eight. The whippings took place around thirty minutes after the workday began. Harmon called Talley in from the field and administered eight or nine lashings. While Talley quoted Harmon as stating that the whippings were "for lying yesterday" in court, Harmon claimed that the lashings served a disciplinary purpose: attempting to correct Talley "for agitating work-stopping and insolence." What seriously led Judge Henley to believe that more protections were necessary for prisoners came from Harmon's continued invective: Henley would have a chance to address the issue of corporal punishment given without any sort of procedural protections once he issued his opinion.[20]

Lighting the Darkness: Reform in Arkansas

In Judge Henley's opinion, as evidenced by both his oral biography and his role in the litigation, matters of prison reform rested beyond political ideologies and party affiliation. And he would demonstrate this philosophy in the first case that questioned the constitutionality of prisons in Arkansas, *Talley v. Stephens*. Henley credits governors and politicians from both the Republican and the Democratic Parties for helping reveal the atrocities and unconstitutional conditions in Arkansas prisons, stating that he was "immensely pleased with the response of the state and of every administration to the needs for prison reform. This [was] true whether it was Republican or Democrat in office." Although most scholars have a negative view of Orval Faubus owing to his demagoguery over the desegregation at Little Rock, Henley praised the governor for attempting to bring light to the dark conditions at the Arkansas prison farms. Politicians such as Faubus saw beyond the public rhetoric on prisons and the treatment of prisoners in general, for "the public at large has no idea what goes on in there," stated Henley. He continued, "They don't pay much attention to what's being done to the prisoner, and they don't realize or stop to think that a person is put in prison as punishment not for punishment." Henley would most probably credit the governor and legislature with utilizing the "running room" to clean up the prisons.[21]

The idea of "running room" represented one theme of Henley's view of prison reform at the state level. More precisely, the phrase exemplified Henley's views of the relationship between the federal and state governments. His conception of federalism reflected his position on the role of judges within the system. In response to criticism that judges make law rather than interpret it, Henley realized that it was true but that there was nothing inherently wrong with it. Judges merely filled in the void left by legislators, who drafted bills that could in no way serve all the needs of society at large. "Those" spaces, claimed Henley, "can only be filled in by judges who, in that sense, make law as they try to adapt the basic constitutional and statutory provisions to circumstances that are new." If the plain language of the Constitution can guide a law pertaining to modern telephone communication, for example, then it must prevail and guide. As long as judges embrace the middle ground of an issue and make reasonable interpretations, they can and must certainly "make law."[22]

While Henley believed judges made law by their mere interpretation and application of the Constitution to current situations, he envisioned his role in prison litigation as more of an administrator. Henley believed there were two ways to approach institutional reform guided by judges: either say "you must do this" and appoint an administrator to make sure it gets done, or say "look, this is wrong, you've got to stop it and fix it, now you tell me how you want to fix it." As evidenced by his opinion in the *Talley* case and the court proceedings that ensued, Henley favored the latter approach. The first almost always brought resentment from the state government due to their not being allowed to offer alternative methods of fixing the problem. Henley largely felt that taking this second approach as "administrator from above" contributed to the successes that followed in Arkansas. He also thought that this was a better way to approach reform of institutions outside prison as well, such as schools and hospitals. This train of thought formed the foundation for the reform of the "dark and evil world" known as the Cummins and Tucker Prison Farms and made them not only constitutional but also safe for prisoner and guard alike.[23]

Judge Henley wrote the first of many opinions concerning the constitutionality of Arkansas's prisons on November 15, 1965. In the case of *Talley v. Stephens*, the petitioning prisoners stated that they had suffered a number of abuses at the hands of prison officials, including severe corporal punishment at the hands of both official guards and trusty guards. The petitioners also claimed that prison officials denied them medical attention when requested and access to the courts for relief. Early in the opinion, Henley wrote that it was not within the power of the federal courts to undertake complete management of the prison system, nor was it the task of the court to review every complaint made by a prisoner. It was under this cautious pretext that Henley began sifting through the individual prisoner complaints.[24]

Henley began by establishing the basis for an Eighth Amendment violation of cruel and unusual punishment in the prison setting, writing that "the Court has no difficulty with the proposition that for prison officials knowingly to compel convicts to perform physical labor which is beyond their strength, or which constitutes a danger to their lives or health, or which is unduly painful constitutes an infliction of cruel and unusual punishment." The lack of established guidelines for the procedure and administration of corporal punishment most alarmed Henley. The punishment's being summarily applied, within the sole discretion of the official administering the lashings, did not hold up to constitutional scrutiny. An informal requirement of a punishment not exceeding ten blows was not sufficient.[25]

Henley stopped short, however, at declaring the use of corporal punishment per se unconstitutional. Corporal punishment remained constitutionally permissible if it was not excessive, if responsible people gave it dispassionately, and if it was applied according to established standards. This way, the prisoner could know what conduct would bring about such a punishment and would also know which punishment to expect for a particular type of behavior. Those safeguards did not exist in Arkansas's prisons at the time. Therefore, Henley declared the use of the strap in the prison farms unconstitutional. From this particular ruling, Henley did not dictate the particular methods the state should use in creating a constitutional regime of corporal punishment. He did, however, create broad principles that the state would have to follow if it wanted to continue using corporal punishment on its prisoners.[26]

Henley now had the opportunity to address the lashings administered by Mose Harmon Jr. to Winston Talley. While Harmon stated for the record that the lashings had a disciplinary nature, one of quelling insolence and the promotion of work stoppage, Talley testified that the whipping came directly from his "lying in court." Once Talley reported this new instance of punishment to Judge Henley, the judge procured new testimony from Talley, Harmon, and other prisoners who might have witnessed the punishment. Talley further stated that in addition to receiving nine lashings for lying, Harmon stated that he still owed Talley about twenty-five more strokes and that he might as well "get started right now." Harmon stated that the punishment came for Talley's "agitating work-stoppage and insolence." He further indicated that Talley was urging fellow inmates to slow down and refuse to work, stating that "the 'people in Little Rock' were on his side and none of them would be punished because the Institution Officials were afraid to do anything." More alarming to Henley was Harmon's concession that "at the time of the punishment I also remarked to him that perhaps it would teach him not to lie in court."[27] Henley admonished Harmon, stating that it was not his function to determine the truthfulness of the testimony given by Talley or any other prisoner. Henley went on to criticize the prison farm administration, opining that prison administrators should have been aware of the situation following the days of testimony. It should have been foreseeable not only that Talley and his fellow prisoners would be boastful but also that Harmon and other trusties might seek revenge. "Although both risks were foreseeable," wrote Henley, prison officials "apparently took no steps to prevent the occurrence of either." This, along with other factors and conditions at the prison farms, left Henley with no choice but to issue injunctive relief to further protect the constitutional rights—and the safety and health—of the prisoners.[28]

Prison officials also had to further define the amount of work prisoners were expected to complete, in order to give prisoners a tangible goal to be reached. The standard of "sufficient work" would not be acceptable unless it was defined. Reprisals came from prison officials and "line riders" not simply from lack of work. Physical mistreatment came down upon many prisoners who chose to petition or write the courts to ask for relief. In one instance, a prison official meted out punishment on one of the petitioner prisoners due to the official's own personal declaration of perjury. Whether the prisoner's testimony was truthful or otherwise, stated Henley, "it was certainly not the function" of prison officials "to punish [the prisoner] for perjury, if any was committed."[29]

Thus, in the opening volley of litigation that would continue for more than a decade, Judge J. Smith Henley declared the unregulated, capricious use of the strap as a form of corporal punishment in Arkansas's prison farms to be a violation of the cruel and unusual punishment prohibition of the Eighth Amendment. He also opined that prison officials, whether paid workers or trusties, must not prevent prisoners from petitioning and gaining access to the courts. The days of "escapees" being shot while fleeing were gone. Henley's insistence on prisoners' voices being heard gave prisoners from other states, both within and outside the South, the ability to utilize their courts more fully. This massive intervention of the federal courts all began with Henley's insistence on prisoners' voices being heard in Arkansas. And, according to his philosophy on the role of judges and the courts, there was nothing wrong with that. Going against popular notions of the way prisoners should be treated, Henley helped forge a distinctly personal and southern approach to prison reform.

Notes

1. Adam Jay Hirsch, *The Rise of the Penitentiary: Prisons and Punishment in Early America* (New Haven: Yale University Press, 1992).

2. Ibid., xiii–xv.

3. Ibid., 21–22.

4. Ibid., 23–25.

5. Ibid., 74–76.

6. Ibid., 77–78.

7. Michael Stephen Hindus, *Prison and Plantation: Crime, Justice, and Authority in Massachusetts and South Carolina, 1767–1878* (Chapel Hill: University of North Carolina Press, 1980).

8. Ibid., 121, 124; Mark Tushnet, "Review of *Prison and Plantation: Crime, Justice, and Authority in Massachusetts and South Carolina, 1767–1878* by Michael Stephen Hindus," *Journal of Interdisciplinary History* 12, no. 4 (Spring 1982): 727–28.

9. Malcolm M. Feeley and Edward L. Rubin, *Judicial Policy Making and the Modern State: How the Courts Reformed America's Prisons* (New York: Cambridge University Press, 1998), 51–53.

10. U.S. v. Jones, 207 F.2d 785 (5th Cir. 1953), 786.

11. Feeley and Rubin, *Judicial Policy Making*, 30–31.

12. Ibid., 14.

13. "Henley, Jesse Smith," *The Encyclopedia of Arkansas History and Culture*, n.d., http://www.encyclopediaofarkansas.net/encyclopedia/entry-detail.aspx?entryID=417 (accessed March 12, 2011); and J. Smith Henley, "Interviews with Honorable J. Smith Henley," Transcript, March 23, 1987, Eighth Circuit U.S. Court of Appeals Library (St. Louis), 1, 3–4.

14. "Henley, Jesse Smith."

15. Henley, "Interviews," 57–58.

16. Ibid.

17. Ibid., 12–14.

18. Ibid., 59–60; Feeley and Rubin, *Judicial Policy Making*, 56.

19. Henley, "Interviews," 60.

20. "Rules Ordered on Use of Whip at Penitentiary," *Arkansas-Gazette*, November 16, 1965.

21. Henley, "Interviews," 142–43.

22. Ibid., 119–20.

23. Ibid., 145–46.

24. Talley v. Stephens, 247 F. Supp. 683, 685–86 (E. D. Ark. 1965).

25. Ibid., 686–88.

26. Ibid., 689–90.

27. Ibid., 691.

28. Ibid.

29. Ibid., 247, 690–91.

V

Tax Fury and the Tea Party

11

The Tea Party in the South

Populism Revisited?

ALLAN B. MCBRIDE

In 1785 Thomas Jefferson wrote of the differences between southerners and northerners in a letter written to the Marquis de Chastellux. Jefferson characterizes northerners as "cool; sober; laborious; independent; jealous of their own liberties and just to those of others," among other qualities. Of southerners he wrote that they were "fiery; voluptuary; indolent; unsteady; zealous for their own liberties, but trampling on those of others" plus a few other traits.[1] Perhaps the differences identified by Jefferson were the result of immigration patterns, or perhaps they were the result of Jefferson's own cultural biases, though he was a southerner as well.

The distinguishing characteristics reported by Jefferson have been embellished upon in the ensuing centuries by a multitude of southerners and northerners, some academically trained and others not. For example, Ben Robertson, a North Carolinian, writes of his family that they were southern Stoics who "believe in self-reliance, self-improvement, in progress as the theory of history, in loyalty, in total abstinence, in total immersion, faithfulness, righteousness, justice, in honoring our parents, in living without disgrace. We have chosen asceticism because all our lives we have had to fight an inclination to license. . . . [W]e have set for ourselves one of the strictest, sternest codes in existence, but our country is Southern and we are Southern and frequently we fail."[2]

Northerners thought southerners were unusual, and southerners thought the same. Whether it was the climate, immigration patterns, slavery, the difficulty of eking out an existence in much of the region, or some combination of all that and more, at the end of the Civil War attempts began to be made to reintroduce the South into mainstream American life. Race relations retarded those efforts throughout the twentieth century, fueling the thoughts of many non-southerners that Dixie would never be reconciled with the rest of the nation, but the effort continued nonetheless.

John Egerton has argued that not only has the South become more Americanized, but the rest of the nation has been strongly affected by southern culture, including its literature (from Faulkner to John Grisham), its music (including country and western, jazz, and the blues), its religion (the Southern Baptist Church), and its pastimes (stock car racing).[3]

Earl and Merle Black, who have made careers by the study of southern politics, report that in many, but not all, ways the South has become similar to the rest of the nation. One of the distinguishing features of the South (and some western states) politically has been its devotion to the principle of states' rights coupled with an antagonism toward the national government, a remnant of the Civil War and Reconstruction. Initially, these ideals were connected in the minds of many, southerners and non-southerners alike, with the presumed right of the southern states to retain slavery, extend its practice to new states, and to later deal with the black population in the manner that the South felt was most appropriate.[4]

The current economic and political environment provides a setting to test the distinctiveness hypothesis. Two parallel historical occurrences, one economic and one political, have combined to create that opportunity. The failed economy, which many blame on a relaxed economic regulatory regime, is the first; the second is the passage of the Patient Protection and Affordable Health Care Act. A political movement developed as a result of these two occurrences which seemed to share the political beliefs that are often associated with the South: an anti-government mentality, veiled racism under the cover of "deservingness," and a determination to keep federal regulation of the economy restricted and to reduce American reliance upon welfare.

The edited volume of which this essay is a part seeks to evaluate the South's relationship with the federal government from the perspective of its citizenry. It is the purpose of this essay to examine the South within the context of the recent economic and political turmoil with some reference to the Tea Party which arose as a result of those events coinciding with election of Barack Obama. Michael Thompson, Richard Ellis, and Aaron Wildavsky's *Cultural Theory* will be invoked to provide a cultural framework with which to analyze the movement in the South using survey data collected on behalf of the Associated Press and the *Washington Post* in April 2010, at one height of interest in the Tea Party.[5] Additionally, using a less intrusive method, Tea Party websites in four states will be examined for motivational and cultural themes. The first section provides an introduction to cultural theory and hypothesis development. The next section will examine the organizational structure of the party, before turning to the analysis of the poll data and the discussion and conclusion.

Cultural Theory (and Hypotheses)

Exceptionalism is a term used to describe the United States in comparison to other nations, particularly in reference to its lack of a landed aristocracy, a fact that has been thought to contribute to the weakness of the socialist movement in this country. Exceptionalism is a qualifier that could also be used to describe the American South in relation to the rest of the nation. The exceptional character of the South is certainly related to its "peculiar institution" (slavery) and the Civil War, which many believe was caused by the South's dogged attachment to slavery. Slavery also contributed to the "traditionalistic" character of southern culture, or what has been called its hierarchic cultural bias.[6]

Traditionalistic cultures, one of three cultural types used by Daniel Elazar to create a cultural topography of the United States, exist primarily in the South and have the following characteristics: a well-defined political and cultural elite; a view of the marketplace as a mixed blessing; a limited role for government; and a conservative approach to change tempered by tradition and the expectation that any change should benefit the elite.[7] The cultural model developed by Thompson, Ellis, and Wildavsky uses a four-part typology that includes a category they call "hierarchy," resembling Elazar's traditionalism. In their model, hierarchies have the following characteristics: extensive rules about who may interact with whom and the manner of the interactions; strong boundaries that limit entrance and exit from the culture and also restrict movement between classes; an inclination toward the view that human nature is flawed, requiring substantial external controls; resistance to unmanaged risks; and wealth creation that benefits not only the elite but also the community, among other things.[8]

Although Elazar mapped the South as largely traditionalistic/hierarchic, a perceptive observer may also detect prominent elements of individualism in the region, at least partially a result of the religious preferences of many of its inhabitants. Thompson, Ellis, and Wildavsky report that August Comte argues that "religion functions to fulfill the 'two great ends of human existence,' i.e., 'to regulate and combine' members of a social unit.... establish(ing) the requisite conditions for social order."[9] Southern

Baptists, among Christian denominations, place great emphasis upon the role of the individual and the congregation in their relations with God and heaven and, more importantly here, concerning the issue of control. According to the precepts of the Southern Baptist Church, the Bible is interpretable by the individual congregant and church members are empowered with direct communication with God, without intercession on the part of the church clergy, leading to greater independence for the individual church member. It would be foolish to ignore southern hierarchic/traditionalistic characteristics, but that does not preclude the coexistence of these two cultures, hierarchy and individualism, in the same region. In fact, in a hierarchic/traditionalistic culture, such as Elazar reported for the American South, it is to the advantage of the elite to allow the controlled development of disciplined individualism (e.g., in the form of classical liberalism or Baptism) among its lower-echelon members to create wealth (and independence) and to ensure that the lower classes learn to restrain themselves. Of course, the danger is that they will become so independent and so focused on wealth creation that they will seek to usurp the elite (a problem not just for the South).

While Elazar is silent on the issue of the virtue of pluralistic cultures (he recognizes this possibility, however, in versions of his widely reproduced maps), for Thompson, Ellis, and Wildavsky cultural purity is a recipe for disaster, a postulate that they call the "requisite variety condition."[10] The most stable societies are those in which permanent or temporary alliances exist between the adherents of several of the cultures. For example, egalitarianism would have trouble existing in a system that neither created nor supported inequalities against which to define itself and to oppose. Similarly, individualists in contemporary America need established authority in the form of government (hierarchy) to protect the rights of property, while individualists and egalitarians will combine in opposition to a government that desires to intrude into their private affairs. In the United States evidence of all four cultures can be found, but, according to the authors, the low-grid cultures (individualism and egalitarianism) have cooperated to weaken hierarchy.

The four cultures are inductively created from a two-by-two matrix derived from two variables—group and grid. The original group/grid theorist, British anthropologist Mary Douglas, defines *group* "as the experience of a bounded social unit."[11] Boundaries may be physical (walls, fences, etc.) or they may be psychological/legal or a combination. Boundaries/borders are more rigid in high-group cultures (hierarchy and egalitarianism) and more permeable in low-group cultures (individualism and fatalism). *Grid* refers to the nature and type of prescriptions that determine the manner of relationships that members of a culture may have with each other. In low-grid cultures (individualism and egalitarianism) individuals are freer to negotiate their own relationships than they are in high-grid cultures (hierarchy and fatalism).

Cultural types are distinguishable partially by what may be called "cultural indicators." For example, equality is an example of a cultural indicator; egalitarians are dedicated to as much equality of outcome as possible, while individualists are willing to concede only "equality of opportunity." Hierarchists entertain support for a more limited "equality before law," and fatalists accept whatever level of equality drops into their collective laps. Attitudes toward authority and the manner in which authority is conferred also provide clues about the way of life: hierarchists support authority and imagine that it may be conferred according to lineage, race, or gender, or some other ascriptive characteristic; individualists are ambivalent about authority ("What have you done for me lately?") but willingly follow those who are competent and achievement oriented; egalitarians are distrustful of authority because it generates inequality, but they may be convinced to support a leader who has a vision of a new tomorrow with greater equality for all. Fatalists are the least-well-defined of the four cultures, but they probably would be obsequious toward authority with the slim hope that something good might result.

Cultural expectations regarding policy preferences lead to specific cultural hypotheses for the South. If the South remains distinctive, and traditionalistic, we should find evidence that its residents will be more critical of Democratic president Obama; that because traditionalism/hierarchy are more suspicious of the market, southerners should be more supportive of an economic regulatory regime than are non-southerners; that they should express more support for big government; and that they would strongly oppose *Roe v. Wade*.

Regarding the Tea Party; organizationally, because hierarchy has high boundaries and high prescriptions, if the Tea Party is hierarchic the following should ensue: difficulty in joining, a well-defined leadership structure, a culture of deference, and limited devotion to democratic decision making. Further, because hierarchs are rule-oriented and distrustful of markets, they might support regulation of the economy; they are willing to impose a moral structure on members who are unable to control their baser urges; and they shed blame or blame dissidents/outsiders for mis-performance of the economy, for example. Generally they prefer closed borders, because immigrants do not have a well-defined status either legally or socially. Politically, in the United States, they adhere to democratic principles, though they might distinguish between the "masses and the classes," believing that the former need to be regulated and controlled. Their preferred form of representation would be trustee.

If the Tea Party is largely individualistic, it will have the following characteristics: membership in the Tea Party should be voluntary with an ad hoc structure; member attitudes toward leaders and leadership are probably ambivalent (approving, if the leader achieves what the membership desires, distrustful otherwise); decision making is also probably based upon majority rule, but leaders may function authoritatively. American individualists favor the free-market model with minimal regulation (just enough to provide equality of opportunity); they oppose any moral code imposed from above; they argue that the recent economic failure was caused by individuals and that individuals should have to bear the responsibility for that failure (including homeowners and stockholders); if immigration is the issue, then individualists in the United States favor a more open immigration policy to provide the market access to workers, while providing workers opportunities to improve their economic standing. Politically, individualists are majoritiarian democrats who probably adhere to the political ideal of representation.

Egalitarian-style organizations are driven by the issue of equality. They would favor a more closed organizational structure, with membership determined by the level of individual support for greater equality; oppose leadership in general because leaders are by their nature not equal to other members; evidence strong support for democratic values, including support for the delegate model of representation (wherein representatives closely follow the desires of their constituents) and consensual decision making. In terms of policy preferences, egalitarians distrust the market, because it tends to create great inequalities and prefer economic regulation to level the playing field and to ensure greater equality; oppose the imposition of moral codes, because any imposed rules imply inequality; blame the system for economic failure and favor widespread systemic change; and finally, they might be conflicted about American borders, favoring national borders that ensured greater equality while opposing those that created greater economic and political oppression.

Divisive Issues in the South and Non-South

For many Americans the Declaration of Independence is the salient founding document, as it maintains that citizens have "unalienable rights" to "life, liberty, and the pursuit of happiness." When government imposes taxes, regulations, and laws it is impeding that free pursuit. Markets are responsive to the impersonal forces of supply and demand and are, according to classical economics, not subject to the abuses associated with governments (why state governments are thought to be more trustworthy remains to be satisfactorily explained). Social Darwinism is the guiding moral principle of the market, as benefits and risks are equally shared by market participants, and presumably the most fit get more of the former. This, of course, is the ideal; in practice, in the current economy, for those at the top of the market the risks have been effectively reduced and even eliminated, while the benefits have become even more substantial than has historically been true. Critics of the market argue that the cost of reducing risk in the market is that of paying taxes.

The following subsection explores the attitudes of southerners and non-southerners on a variety of issues, most of which address economic regulation, while one survey item is designed to probe beliefs about the social/political world. The data were collected on behalf of the Associated Press and the *Washington Post* between April 22 and April 25, 2010, from a national sample of the adult population via telephone (land lines and cell phones). The total number of respondents is 1,001; however, because they used "split half" methodology for some items, the number of respondents varies considerably.

Economic Issues

The first series of items in the AP/*Washington Post* poll queried respondents about Obama's overall performance as well as his performance in economic terms. Approval levels for Obama's performance in April 2010 were mixed; he had majority approval in three of four Census Bureau regions (Northeast, Midwest, and West) and nearly majority support in the fourth (South). More specifically, the ABC/*Washington Post* poll also queried respondents about Obama's performance regarding the economy, the budget deficit, health care, and regulation of the financial industry. Additionally, respondents were to assess Obama compared to congressional Republicans in dealing with the same four issues.

Generally, respondents were divided relatively evenly between those who approved and disapproved of the president's performance in these issue areas. However, across all four regions and across the four issues, "strong disapprovers" were more common than "strong approvers." In other words, approvers were relatively evenly divided between those who approved strongly and those who approved "somewhat," while among disapprovers, strong disapproval was more common. In one instance the "strong disapprovers" were more than twice as common as those who indicated "strong disapproval," in percentage terms. Obama's disapproval ratings were slightly elevated in the South, but the regional differences, while consistent, were not strong (Cramer's V for all of these associations never exceeded .12). For example, 40.23 percent of southerners ($n = 353$) reported strong disapproval of Obama's overall handling of his job, while only 35.93 percent ($n = 615$) of non-southerners gave similar responses.[12]

Southerners were more critical and disapproving of Obama across the board, registering strong disapproval rates between 42 and 52 percent, depending on the issue. Non-southerners' strong disapproval levels ranged from 35 to 45 percent. The highest level of criticism was in response to Obama's handling of the federal budget deficit for both regions. Among non-southerners he received nearly 50 percent approval for his handling of the economy, health care, and financial industry regulation, while southerners expressed approval of those issues at a lower level (table 11.1).

Respondents were also asked whether they felt that President Obama or President Bush was more responsible for the current economic crisis and for the record budget deficits. Bush received blame most often from both geographic areas of the country, though again southerners were slightly more likely to blame Obama. Virtually 60 percent of non-southerners blamed Bush for the current state of the economy, while 58 percent blamed him for the budget deficit. Fifty-two percent of southerners blamed Bush for the economy, and 58 percent blamed him for the deficit (table 11.2).

When respondents were asked whom they trusted more to handle the economy, Obama or congressional Republicans, the president fared somewhat better, suggesting that the southern bias may be against the national government. For this series of items, respondents were given two response categories ("trust Obama"; "trust Congressional Republicans"); a significant number also volunteered "trust neither" or "trust both." Comparisons are made on the same four issues (the economy, regulation of the financial industry, health care, and the budget deficit), again according to whether respondents were southerners or non-southerners (see table 11.3). The

Table 11.1. Obama approval levels among Tea Party supporters

	Region		NS-S		
Tea Party supporters	Non-South	South	Difference	Total	n=
Approval for Obama	12.36	10.72	1.64	11.73	290
Obama handling economy	10.59	5.77	4.82	8.76	137
Obama handling health care	11.9	11.54	0.36	11.77	136
Obama handling budget	8.24	6.67	1.57	7.64	157
Obama handling regulation	14.61	10.72	3.89	13.11	145

Table 11.2. Blame Obama (or Bush) for weak economy by region, controlled for Tea Party support (positive support reported)

	Region		NS-S		
Tea Party supporters	Non-South	South	Difference	Total	n=
Blame Obama for economy	57.45	51.72	5.73	55.26	152
Blame Obama for deficit	55.17	51.02	4.15	53.68	131

Table 11.3. Trust for Obama (or congressional Republicans) on economic issues by region, controlled for Tea Party support (positive support reported)

	Region		NS-S		
Tea Party supporters' trust for Obama	Non-South	South	Difference	Total	n=
Handling the economy	9.44	9.01	0.43	9.28	291
Handling financial regulation	10.61	11.93	-1.32	11.11	288
Handling budget deficit	9.34	7.21	2.13	8.53	293
Handling health care reform	9.39	9.91	-0.52	9.59	292

average percentage of non-southerners who reported trust for Obama was 50.46 (range = 47.6–52.56). Non-southerners trusted him least to handle the budget deficit. Southerners reported trusting Obama on average about 44 percent of the time, a virtually identical percentage to those who reported trusting congressional Republicans (43.3). On three of the four issues (the economy, financial regulation, and health care), southerners were more trusting of Obama than they were of Republicans. Respondents who answered that they trusted neither or trusted both were also recorded; the percentages who trusted neither ranged from 10.5 to 14.38 percent for non-southerners and from 10.8 to 12.18 percent for southerners. The fact that 10–15 percent of respondents in the South and elsewhere *volunteered* that they trusted neither the president nor congressional Republicans suggests a solid core of discontent with the federal government. No more than 2 percent of respondents indicated that they trusted both, regardless of region.

Finally, regarding the role of regulation of the economy, respondents were asked whether they favored or opposed stricter regulation of the financial industry, whether they thought it appropriate to regulate derivatives, whether they supported a new banking insurance fund underwritten by the industry to finance failed banks, and, lastly, whether they would support increased regulation of consumer lending (table 11.4).

As observed above, the South generally takes a more "conservative" view of the economic situation: southern respondents were more likely to oppose stricter banking regulations, regulation of derivatives, the banking insurance idea, and regulation of consumer lending, though in every instance except one (regulation of derivatives) a majority were in favor of greater regulation. For non-southerners, between 54 and 73 percent supported greater regulation of the economy (mean = 62 percent), with the strongest support for regulating banks and weakest support for the regulation of derivatives. Between 50 and 68 percent of southern respondents supported more financial regulations (mean = 57 percent), with the strongest support coming for bank regulation. In both regions respondents seemed to be less sure about the regulation of derivatives, both in terms of supporting further regulations and in terms of non-responses. Seventeen percent of respondents did not respond to that item compared to 3–5 percent for the other three items, indicating less familiarity with the derivatives issue.

The four items just reported speak more directly to the notion of the political culture issue, since they are presented as "preferences" or value statements about the most desirable nature of the relationship between the public and private sectors. It is apparent that, on average, Americans favored more-extensive regulation and backstop programs to protect the economy, though a solid minority opposes many of the ideas. Generally, those who opposed one type of regulation tended to oppose others (as a rough indicator, the r^2s between these items ranged between .17 and .32).

Although southerners in the aggregate were consistently more likely to oppose regulation and to give Obama lower ratings than non-southerners, the differences were small across the board. Cramer's V, a measure of

Table 11.4. Support for economic regulation by region, controlled for Tea Party support (positive support reported)

Tea Party supporters	Region		NS-S		
	Non-South	South	Difference	Total	n=
Stricter regulation on banks	47.96	50.5	-2.54	48.89	270
Derivatives	28.21	34.69	-6.48	30.68	251
Bank insurance fund	35.43	27.27	8.16	32.28	285
Federal oversight of consumer lending	35.17	41.12	-5.95	37.37	289

Table 11.5. Support for smaller government and *Roe v. Wade* by region, controlled for Tea Party support (positive support reported)

Tea Party supporters	Region		NS-S		
	Non-South	South	Difference	Total	n=
Smaller government	88.2	89.19	-0.99	88.58	289
Roe v. Wade	40.00	39.81	0.19	39.93	289

association for data at the nominal level of measurement, for these associations never exceeded .09, indicating little to no association.

Culturally, the willingness of the respondents, regardless of region, to support greater regulation suggests that Americans are leaning toward a more restricted market (less likely to favor unfettered individualism). Whether that makes them egalitarians or hierarchists is less clear (fatalists would probably reckon that regulation would have little positive personal effect). Given the presumption that the South is more likely to oppose big government and therefore to support the Tea Party, it is appropriate, first, to examine the level of support for the Tea Party regionally, and second, to evaluate the impact of regional effects on Obama's performance and general support for economic regulation, while controlling for Tea Party support. Such an analysis will provide evidence of the effects of region on Obama's approval and support for regulation independent of the effects of Tea Party support.

The Tea Party, as a political movement, is one of the latest representatives in a line of popular movements extending to at least the Jacksonian era in the early 1800s. One of the best known of those movements was the eponymous Populist movement of the late 1800s, which sought relief especially for farmers in the form of fiat money and government ownership of the railroads.[13] Populist-style movements in the twentieth century included a strong socialist movement, the civil rights movement, an anti–civil rights movement (though the latter was not defined as such), and the Red scares of the 1920s and 1950s.

Although it is not easy to separate out the issues that have motivated these movements, some seem to have been more about economics and others more about social and political issues. For example, Populism and socialism were largely focused on economics, while the civil rights movement was largely about human dignity, with economics as an essential ancillary issue. In some instances the movements targeted actions of the government as needing redress, while in others the movement sought the government's assistance in seeking the resolution of grievances. In many instances popular movements have defined themselves ("us") as in opposition to others ("them"). The "us" side of the equation has included producers (farmers and workers), the 99 percent, wage earners, citizens, and religious adherents. The "them" has alternately referenced variously defined elites, government officials, bankers, corporate leaders, as well as liberals and socialists, depending upon the movement. Populists and Tea Party supporters have raised the issue of "deservingness" as a way of delineating the "us" from the "them." For Populists it was producers, especially farmers. Williamson, Skocpol, and Coggin report that Tea Party supporters are not opposed to all government largesse—many Tea Partiers receive Social Security and Medicare, among other programs. It is the view of the party supporters that they "deserve" these programs because they have paid for them with their taxes. The Tea Partiers interviewed by Williamson and her colleagues stressed the importance of working and of the work ethic, what social scientists have referred to as the liberal Protestant ethic, a self-disciplined version of individualism.[14]

Southerners in the AP/*Washington Post* poll were slightly more likely to support the Tea Party than non-southerners, 33 percent to 30 percent, respectively, though the differences were not statistically significant (chi-square = 1.5, df [2], p = .473, n = 956). The size of the regional differences in Tea Party support are also reflected in the respondents' evaluations of Obama and the economy, as will be observed in the ensuing. On the other hand, the differences between Tea Party supporters and opponents are strong and as might be predicted (Tea party supporters in 2010 were markedly anti-Obama and anti-regulation). For example, when Tea Party supporters were asked to evaluate Obama's overall performance, as well as his handling of the economy, health care, the budget deficit, and regulation of the economy, only about one in ten approved of his performance. Although non-southerners were consistently more likely to approve, the regional differences were uniformly small (average difference on the five measures was only 2.5 percent) (see tables 11.1–11.3)

When queried about whether they trusted Obama or congressional Republicans to better handle economic and budget issues, the results were nearly the same; about one in ten Tea Party supporters trusted Obama more regardless of region. Tellingly, slightly more than half of Tea Party supporters (range 51–57 percent) blamed Obama for the state of the economy (spring 2010), in both the South and non-South. For the purposes of comparison, 85–89 percent of Tea Party opponents blamed George W. Bush for the state of the economy.

When Obama's name was not invoked as part of the questions, Tea Party responses were less extreme. For example, when Tea Party supporters were asked their views about regulating the financial and banking sectors, support levels increased, ranging from 27 to 50 percent. The websites we investigated in South Carolina, Mississippi, Minnesota, and Massachusetts also illustrate the importance of the economy to the Tea Party membership. Bloggers frequently remark upon the Tea Party's desire to reduce the amount of economic regulation and the size of the government. One Tea Partier expressed her disdain through a humorous blog post entitled "Free Market? What Free Market?" She continues her frustration in the commentary: "There's just one problem. Our government is so thoughtful and compassionate that they insist on 'protecting' us from everything imaginable, including ourselves. It is that concept that inspired my favorite Tea Party sign, 'Please Don't Help Me Anymore, I Can't Afford It.'"[15]

According to these websites, fiscal responsibility is the overwhelming battle cry of Tea Partiers: "From the beginning a cornerstone of the Tea Party Movement has been a focus of the lack of Fiscal Responsibility on the part of our elected officials." "Our country is bleeding red ink. Tea Party members have been screaming that we cannot sustain this lifestyle. As individuals we know that if we spend more than we make for an extended period of time, the debt crushes our households, devastates our families and endangers our children."[16] Yet the data from the AP/*Washington Post* poll finds that Tea Party supporters favor some regulations.

Non-Economic Issues

Comparisons of southerners with non-southerners can also be fruitfully conducted on a few additional, non-economic issues raised in the 2010 AP poll, which included measures of attitudes toward *Roe v. Wade* and the advisability of having a large, engaged government. If Elazar is correct and the South is largely traditionalistic, then we should find greater support for *Roe v. Wade*; if individualism is strong in the South, then opposition to *Roe* may be in line with the rest of the nation. Finally, regarding opposition to big government, the South has been one of the regions of the country that has embraced states' rights, thus southerners might indicate a preference for smaller government; if Elazar is correct, then opposition to big government should be weaker than elsewhere. However, given the level of southern support for economic regulation that has been observed in the preceding, southerners may prefer a stronger, more active government. The evidence follows.

The differences between respondents in the South and non-South on the non-economic issues outlined above are small. Sixty-four percent of non-southerners ($n = 607$) and 62 percent of southerners ($n = 342$) report that they support upholding the *Roe v. Wade* decision, a finding that is virtually identical between regions. Sixty percent of Tea Party supporters in both regions indicate that their preference is to overturn *Roe*, while 85 to 88 percent of Tea Party opponents (South and non-South) indicate support for *Roe* (see table 11.5). From the Massachusetts and Charleston, South Carolina, Tea Party websites we also find evidence of a willingness for the federal government to impose moral standards, especially regarding gays in the military and abortion. One Massachusetts blogger, disturbed by the repeal of "Don't Ask, Don't Tell," suggests that allowing gays into the military is a threat to the country: "One by one our traditional American institutions have become prey to the liberal Socialist Agenda to weaken our country. The Obama administration took aim at our military and knowingly at our national defense."[17] Anti-abortion sentiments were also expressed on blogs: "Democrat [sic] House Minority Leader, Nancy Pelosi said, 'There is a war on women,' which is silly. If women want to have an abortion they can pay for themselves rather than require those of us who find abortions both evil and repugnant to pay for them."[18]

We would expect individualists and egalitarians, both low-grid ways of life in the "cultural theory" scheme, to oppose undue restrictions upon their personal conduct. Hierarchists, on the other hand, would be comfortable with government action to enforce "necessary" rules on the lower classes (i.e., those who are not "capable" of restraining themselves).[19]

Southern and non-southern respondents were equally likely to prefer "smaller government with fewer services"; about 63 percent of respondents in both regions agreed with this ideal. Though this survey does not delve into which services should be targeted for saving and which are best jettisoned, Americans have expressed a variety of viewpoints on the topic. A small number of Americans take the extreme position that any government above the county sheriff position is superfluous, while others implicitly or explicitly apply the "deservingness" criteria and still others are willing to use government to achieve social and economic goals. For Tea Party supporters, 88 and 89 percent, non-South and South, respectively, support the "ideal," if not the practice, of smaller government.

The structure of the "Party" reinforces the importance of individual action. American political parties are famously weak, lacking disciplinary tools common in parliamentary systems (restricted access to the party label for election purposes, for example). Nonetheless, American parties, at the national level, have a loosely defined structure and rules for primaries and nominations, with fund-raising facilities that provide a level of continuity. The Tea Party lacks even these fundamentals, with numerous web pages proclaiming themselves (or at least so-identified by Google) as official websites.

Zachary Courser makes several observations about the movement: lack of coordination among its constituent parts; no control over membership or over the use of the movement's name; 42 percent of the Tea Party groups reported being unaffiliated; a local resistance to organization; an unwillingness to campaign for candidates; a CBS News/*New York Times* poll from April 5–12, 2010, found that only 7 percent of Tea Party voters supported electing their own candidates; and its leaderless and spontaneous nature. Courser says that FreedomWorks and the Tea Party Express, two umbrella national Tea Party organizations, have actively encouraged "the disorganized nature of the movement.[20] (One is tempted to conclude that the lack of organization makes the movement more subject to impermanence and to manipulation.)

As a first pass at the organizational structure of what appears to be a movement that was incubated on the Internet, we reviewed Tea Party websites from four states for content and activity levels: South Carolina, Mississippi, Minnesota, and Massachusetts. The websites in the winter of 2012 varied noticeably in their levels of activity. For example, the number of posts on the Spartanburg, South Carolina, web page reached 1,650 in 2011, while others show very little evidence of activity.[21] Many links to local organizations are now defunct, even though their links are still displayed on neighboring Tea Party websites and on statewide blog rolls listed by the Patriot Action Network. Sites that were once owned and managed have since been abandoned or are relatively inactive and poorly maintained. And there is also little evidence of ongoing or substantive interchanges between posters. Comments, when they do appear, are often along the lines of "I truly wanted to send a small remark so as to say thanks to you for the magnificent facts you are sharing on this site."[22]

Because the Tea Party movement formed at the local grassroots level, it is difficult to find an official spokesperson or even website. Potential spokespersons include Ron and Rand Paul, Sarah Palin (who spoke at the national Tea Party convention), Michelle Bachman, and conservative media opinion leader and comedian Glenn Beck. Additionally, a search for an "official" website turns up several candidates: "Re Tea Party" (reteaparty.com), the "Tea Party Platform" (teaparty-platform.com), Tea Party Patriots (teapartypatriots.bing.com), TeaParty.org, Patriot Action Network (Patriotstoactionnetwork.com), Tea Party Express (teapartyexpress.org), and The Tea Party (theteaparty.net). No apparent linkage exists among these sites, except for the common name.

Discussion

The American South and its inhabitants have been thought to be distinctive components of the United States since the Revolutionary War era, as indicated by no less a personage than Thomas Jefferson, who enumerated the differences between southerners and northerners. The devotion that vocal southerners exhibited to slavery exacerbated those sorts of thoughts on the part of both southerners and non-southerners, while the loss of the Civil War and the resulting Reconstruction era solidified the feelings.

It has been the intention of the current work to explore the evidence in support of the distinctiveness thesis, especially as it related to the South's relationship with the national government. In this essay two types of arguments have been made. First, it has been hypothesized that political culture might provide some clues as to the nature of the regional differences. Two cultural models, with overlapping categories, were presented. The first, developed by Daniel Elazar, presented the South as a largely traditionalistic region with a well-developed elite that protected its own status. Using the second, informed by the model of culture elaborated by Thompson, Ellis, and Wildavsky, we hypothesized that the South, a region in which many if not most residents are low-grid Southern Baptists, is likely a combination of individualism and hierarchy/traditionalism. Second, the Tea Party, as a recent manifestation of conservative populism, was offered as an examplar of southern-style anti-government mentality.

Using a data set collected in April 2010, the following results were reported: southerners were more critical of President Obama across the board, though the differences between the residents of the South and non-South were not large (on the order of 2–7 percent); though southerners were less likely to trust Obama than were non-southerners, they generally trusted him more than they trusted congressional Republicans across four policy issues; both southern and non-southern respondents were substantially more likely to blame George W. Bush than Obama for the economic downturn and the large budget deficit—again, southerners were slightly more likely to blame Obama; on the final set of economic items, respondents across all regions indicated a preference for a more heavily regulated market, especially the banking sector. The differences between South and non-South were generally weak to non-existent (Cramer's V ranged between .04 and .11).

Finally, evidence was presented on two additional issues: support for *Roe v. Wade* and for a small versus a large government. In both instances, the regional differences were small. A significant majority of southerners (62 percent) favored upholding *Roe* (compared to 64 percent of non-southerners). Sixty-three percent in both regions favored a small government.

Culturally, the South's differences from the non-South are a matter of degree. A majority of southerners and non-southerners reject an unfettered economy, preferring to err on the side of the consumer. Support for regulation would come from hierarchists, who display little affection for an uncontrolled market, or from egalitarians, who prefer to control the market in order to reduce inequalities. The data from the AP/*Washington Post* poll provide no evidence to test for that distinction. If the South has a tradition of hierarchy, as suggested by Elazar and the history of the plantation economy, the support for regulation probably results from that source, rather than from egalitarianism, though one might suspect that southern African Americans might favor egalitarian solutions. For instance, 75 percent of southern blacks favored federal regulation of banks, compared to 67 percent of southern whites, though the number of southern blacks was only in the range of 50, making that conclusion tenuous at best.

The level of support for *Roe*, regardless of region, suggests a low-grid cultural bias, reinforced by the strong support seen in the poll for small government. The conflicting evidence reported herein (support for regulation and opposition to large government coupled with support for *Roe v. Wade*) is consistent with the "requisite variety condition" of cultural theory, which stipulates that the most stable cultures are those that blend cultural values.

Turning to the role of the Tea Party; southerners are only marginally more likely to be supportive than non-southerners. Tea Party supporters and opponents take decidedly different positions on most of the issues discussed in the foregoing, from opposition to Obama and regulation of the economy to support for *Roe*.

The "deservingness" issue is one that resonates back to the nineteenth-century Populists, who viewed bankers and others as non-producers who lived off the sweat of honest farmers/workers. It is an indication of how successfully the financial community has redefined itself that they are no longer considered part of the non-producing class. Deservingness was an issue that George Wallace also capitalized upon in his presidential campaigns of 1968 and 1972 when he targeted "welfare cheats" as a national problem. Contemporary Tea Party supporters, based on the evidence from Williamson, Skocpol, and Coggins, are themselves recipients of government services but worry about others who they believe make no contributions but still receive benefits.

Although many Americans in both regions pledge their support to smaller government with fewer services, at least in principle, a large proportion of both regions favor additional regulations, especially on the financial sector. It might be argued that these seemingly contradictory findings can be resolved by reference to the deservingness issue. Americans are willing to support programs that benefit producers and to support regulations that have the effect of leveling the playing field. Where they seem to draw the line is at expanded programs (such the 2010 Affordable Health Care Act) that benefit what they believe to be the undeserving. However, the Affordable Care Act targets not the undeserving (unemployed) poor (who are covered by Medicaid) but the working poor, who are presumably deserving. One is left with the conclusion that for Tea Partiers some other factor explains their opposition to government programs from which they do not benefit.

Does the South retain its distinctive character? In some ways, yes—southerners are more likely to be poor than their non-Southern counterparts and to register lower levels of educational attainment. Regarding the federal government, however, the differences seem to be evaporating. Changes in southern demographics suggest not only that the South is becoming more like the non-South but also that the non-South is becoming more southern. The growth of the Southern Baptist Church outside the South has contributed to the latter. Migration into and out of the South over the past century has also created pressure toward homogenization (Louisiana and Mississippi remain as the most "home-grown" states as more residents of those two states report that they were born there than any other American states). The widespread availability of television programming as a medium of mass communication may have contributed to the process as well.

V. O. Key and Earl and Merle Black argue, from different historical vantage points, that the South was adapting to the ways of the non-South. Even in the late 1940s Key was able to observe that the South was not uniform in its political beliefs and that the "black belt" regions were distinctive from the areas where the black population was a smaller proportion of the overall population. He observed about the latter that white residents in these regions had been less supportive of the Civil War and had been more likely to support the Republican Party and Populism and to express "coolness toward schemes to restrict the suffrage." Furthermore, civil rights decisions were less likely to be resisted. Among the areas of the South that Key singles out for mention were Texas, Arkansas, Tennessee, Virginia, North Carolina, and Florida (i.e., none of the so-called Deep South, though even in the Deep South, pockets of resistance to the Civil War have been reported in northern Louisiana and southern Mississippi, among other places).[23]

Black and Black reported evidence of an "entrepreneurial individualism" in the late twentieth century that challenged the existing social and economic order and sought to expand the economic pie, with the potential for greater shared prosperity. Industry began to move into the South, lured by the uniformity of low wages and "right to work" laws, though industrial development in the South occurred more often in rural areas instead of according to the northern pattern of urban industrialization. Wages lagged behind those of the North as well. The forces of hierarchy and tradition have not been totally routed, however: "the opposition of both traditionalists and urban entrepreneurs to public policies explicitly aiding the region's have-littles and have-nots constitutes a profound continuity in elite political orientations."[24]

Conclusion

The Democratic Party in the South has been the party of Jim Crow, segregation, racial inequality, and hierarchy (the planter elite). It has also been the party that has opposed big government (except in the defense field), has been anti-welfare, and pro–law and order (in 2011 Alabama enacted HB 56, the nation's most restrictive immigration law, partially invalidated in 2012 by the Eleventh U.S. Circuit Court of Appeals, but one that in cultural theory terms is resplendent with boundary implications). The Tea Party is an active force in the region as well, injecting an element of individualism into the cultural mix. From individualism comes the anti-welfare attitude that is prominent in the South. On the other hand, the South remains the home of many African Americans as well as the civil rights movement, which sought legal rights for blacks, a form of equality (before the law) that even hierarchy can eventually come around to supporting.[25]

The contemporary distrust of the federal government that is ascribed to the South has a lot to do with the passage of the 1964 Civil Rights Act and the 1965 Voting Rights Act. Lyndon Johnson is reputed to have said when he signed the 1965 act, that he just signed the South over to the Republican Party. Voting, especially in presidential elections, has essentially proven him correct. The South has, since before the Civil War, been dedicated to the idea of states' rights and a weaker central government, which has provided them with the cover to address slavery and the black population in a manner that maintained power for whites. Limited government is an idea that was a cornerstone for the American Constitution and has appeal well beyond the South, even as many Americans call upon the national government to take on new responsibilities, ranging from social programs to defense.

Some Tea Party ideals, while less southern in provenance though consistent with the precepts of limited government, call for a freer marketplace, with reduced government regulation, at least as indicated by the data presented here. Coupled with the Tea Party call for "deserved" social programs, campaign rhetoric of which George Wallace and Richard Nixon would have approved in 1968, these Tea Party ideals have a very southern tenor. Two Tea Party–style websites call for eliminating the national debt and deficit spending, for tax reform, and for support for a literal translation of the Constitution.[26] And in one way or another, both favor reducing government, either by ending "pork," eliminating the 2010 health care bill, or reducing the size of government. The Tea Party platform specifically calls for redefining the influence of "big money" and special interests while the Contract singles out "cap and trade"(and the 2010 health care plan) for elimination. A general reading of these two sets of proposals leads to the conclusion that they seek to empower the individual and the states.

If Americans, southern and non-southern, are concerned with the growth of government, some are probably equally concerned about growth in the corporate sector, especially in the area of finance (Populism, which was an important movement in the South, targeted banking as one of the non-productive economic sectors) as evidenced by the Occupy movement of late 2011. The solution is to balance them against each other in the form of "countervailing power," an ideal that the founders would have approved of. It has puzzled party leaders in the United States for several decades as they have observed voters consistently electing a president from one political party and a Congress controlled by the other. Southerners and other Americans, in a manner that is not entirely fathomable, have found a way to ensure countervailing power at the national level.

Notes

1. James L. Golden and Alan L. Golden, *Thomas Jefferson and the Rhetoric of Virtue* (Lanham, Md.: Rowman & Littlefield, 2002), 63 (quotation); Fred C. Hobson, *Tell about the South: The Southern Rage to Explain* (Baton Rouge: Louisiana State University Press, 1983), 20 (quotation also found). See also Darnell Felix Harkins, ed., *Violent Crimes: Assessing Race and Ethnic Differences* (New York: Cambridge University Press, 2003).

2. Ben Robertson, *Red Hills and Cotton: An Upcountry Memory* (New York: Knopf, 1942), 6.

3. John Egerton, *The Americanization of Dixie: The Southernization of America* (New York: Harper's Magazine Press, 1974).

4. Earl Black and Merle Black, *Politics and Society in the South* (Cambridge: Harvard University Press, 1987).

5. Michael Thompson, Richard Ellis, and Aaron Wildavsky, *Cultural Theory* (Boulder: Westview Press, 1990).

6. Ibid.; see also Daniel Elazar, *American Federalism: A View from the States*, 3rd ed. (New York: Harper and Row, 1984).

7. Elazar, *American Federalism*, 118–22.

8. Thompson, Ellis, and Wildavsky, *Cultural Theory*, introduction and chapter 3.

9. Ibid., 115.

10. Ibid., 4.

11. Ibid., 11.

12. N-sizes vary significantly for some of the data reported here, since the survey used a split-half methodology for some questionnaire items.

13. See, e.g., Lawrence Goodwyn, *Democratic Promise: The Populist Movement in America* (New York: Oxford University Press, 1976); and Michael Kazin, *The Populist Persuasion: An American History* (New York: Basic Books, 1995).

14. Vanessa Williams, Theda Skocpol, and John Coggins, "The Tea Party and the Remaking of Republican Conservatism," *Perspectives on Politics* 9 (February 2010): 32.

15. See http://greaterbostonteaparty.com/?p=264#comments (accessed January 15, 2012).

16. Both quotes are from http://www.meridianteaparty.com/march-madness-u-s-govt-spent-more-than-eight-times-its-monthly-revenue (accessed January 12, 2012).

17. See http://massteaparty.org/2011/navy-first-same-sex-couple-share-first-homecoming-kiss (accessed January 12, 2012).

18. See http://charlestonteaparty.org/for-america%e2%80%99s-sake-take-it-away-from-democrats-by-colonel-bob-pappas-usmc-retired (accessed January 7, 2012).

19. For an interesting discussion of an American hierarchic-style political party, see Daniel Walker Howe's *The Political Culture of the American* Whigs (Chicago: University of Chicago Press, 1979).

20. Zachary Courser, "The Tea Party at the Election," *Forum* 8, no. 4 (2011): 7 (quotation), 9, 11.

21. See http://www.spartanburgteaparty.org (accessed January 6, 2012).

22. See http://greaterbostonteaparty.com/?p=566#comment-1010 (accessed January 15, 2012).

23. V. O. Key Jr., *Southern Politics in State and Nation* (New York: Knopf, 1949), 668.

24. Earl Black and Merle Black, *The Rise of Southern Republicans* (Cambridge: The Belknap Press of Harvard University, 2002), 49.

25. Michael Schwarz and Michael Thompson, *Divided We Stand: Redefining Politics, Technology, and Social Choice* (New York: Harvester Wheatsheaf, 1990), 66–67.

26. See http://thecontract.org/the-contract-from-america; and http://tea party-platform.com (accessed August 16, 2011).

12

Deal or No Deal

Taxes, Government Spending, and Alabamians Having Their Cake and Eating It Too

NATALIE MOTISE DAVIS

Whether a legacy of early debates between Federalists and anti-Federalists, the Civil War, a backlash against Reconstruction, or a rejection of the civil rights movement, the South has always been a defender of states' rights and a critic of an expansionist federal government. George Wallace epitomized this pushback. In a speech delivered on July 4, 1964, just two days after the Civil Rights Act of 1964 was signed into law by Lyndon Johnson, Wallace railed against the new law, the Congress, and the federal judiciary:

> Never before in the history of this Nation have so many human and property rights been destroyed by a single act of the Congress. It is an act of tyranny. It is the assassin's knife stuck in the back of liberty. With this assassin's knife and a blackjack in the hand of the federal force-cult, the left wing liberals will try to force us back into bondage. Bondage to a tyranny more brutal than that imposed by the British monarchy which claimed power to rule over the lives of our forefathers under sanction of the Divine Right of Kings. . . . They assert more power than claimed by King George III, more power than Hitler, Mussolini, or Khrushchev ever had.[1]

Today we hear much the same from Tea Party advocates, though their focus is not the Civil Rights Acts of the 1960s nor busing. Wallace's candidacy for president was based on taking the same kinds of arguments about an encroaching federal government that were rhetorically effective in Alabama and using them to advance his candidacy nationally. He took his case to the rest of the nation and was able to garner 13.5 percent of the popular vote and forty-six electors in the 1968 presidential contest.

The modern Republican Party has devoted significant energies to warning Americans about the evils of an overreaching federal government that taxes too heavily, delivers too little, and seeks control over their lives. The Wallace tradition of shaking one's fist at the federal government lives on in Alabama. In a 2010 *Washington Post* op-ed piece, Senator Jeff Sessions of Alabama wrote: "The breathtaking expansion of government—highlighted by record federal spending and a dramatic new federal role in healthcare system—is a source of deep concern across the political spectrum. People are increasingly worried that Washington is exceeding the limits set by the Constitution, asserting too large a role in American life."[2] The southernization of political rhetoric has gone viral. The speeches of 2012 Republican presidential candidates echoed the southern perspective. Over and again, candidates condemned President Obama and the federal government:

Michele Bachmann: I want my candidacy for the presidency to stand for the moment when "we the people" reclaimed our independence from a government that has gotten too big, spends too much and has taken away too much of our liberty. . . . Americans have always confronted challenges. Ours is a history marked by struggles as well as prosperity. . . . Americans still have that same spirit. But government keeps trying to erase it because government thinks it knows better—that government can create jobs, and make a better life for all of us, even make us healthier! But that's NOT the case. We have to recapture our founders' vision of a constitutionally conservative government if we are to secure the promise of the future.[3]

Rick Santorum: We have a group of people in Washington and in other places around this country who believe that the elites in Washington are the ones who should be making the decisions for all of us, and they have systematically gone and grown the size and scale of government to beyond where it's—well, it's just unrecognizable. We are running deficits, where we're borrowing 40 cents of every dollar.[4]

Mitt Romney: We know that this election is about the kind of America we will live in and the kind of America we will leave to future generations. When it comes to the character of America, President Obama and I have very different visions. Government is at the center of his vision. It dispenses the benefits, borrows what it cannot take, and consumes a greater and greater share of the economy.

With Obamacare fully installed, government will come to control half the economy, and we will have effectively ceased to be a free enterprise society. This President is putting us on a path where our lives will be ruled by bureaucrats and boards, commissions and czars. He's asking us to accept that Washington knows best—and can provide all. We've already seen where this path leads. It erodes freedom.[5]

Regardless of the claims of Republican politicians, for the South this comes down to a "reality check." Those attentive to public-policy issues are well aware that federal dollars are not distributed equitably by state. That is, federal dollars returned to states are typically not equal to the amount of tax dollars contributed by their respective taxpayers. In fact, the states most likely to benefit the most from this redistribution are the original eleven states of the Confederacy (table 12.1).

Note that with the exceptions of Florida and Texas, which receive nearly the same amounts of federal dollars contributed by their citizens, southern states have a good thing going. Mississippi ranks first among these southern states, in that it gets back double what it puts in. Alabama's allotment, which ranks sixth nationally, is $1.66 (for every $1.00 paid by taxpayers). By most calculations, this is a pretty good deal. It is not surprising that the redistribution of federal dollars comes from wealthier states to poorer states such that New Jersey, Connecticut, and New York in the Northeast carry more of the federal tax burden when compared to southern states. Given the economic problems it has experienced during the recession that began in 2008, the unanticipated state that bears the heaviest burden is Nevada, which receives only 65 cents for every dollar it sends to Washington. Are southerners less happy with the federal government than other Americans, and are non-southerners more resentful? Interestingly enough, data from the 2004 National Election Study reveal that the South actually gives the "government in Washington" higher ratings than do other regions. In fact, Alabama's ratings are higher than the South as a whole (fig. 12.1).

This is not to say that Alabamians are entirely satisfied with the performance of government. In a 2012 statewide survey, the federal government, especially when compared to state government, is not given high marks. One-fourth say the national government does not do as good a job as state government; 76 percent believe it does too much. Yet, 64 percent want the national government to do more—an example of voters wanting it both

Table 12.1. Number of dollars states received for every dollar paid in federal income taxes, 2010

State	Dollars returned
ORIGINAL ELEVEN STATES OF CONFEDERACY	
Mississippi	$2.02
Louisiana	1.78
Alabama	1.66
Virginia	1.51
Arkansas	1.41
South Carolina	1.35
Tennessee	1.27
North Carolina	1.08
Georgia	1.01
Florida	0.97
Texas	0.94
OTHER STATES RECEIVING "HIGH DOLLAR" RETURN	
West Virginia	$1.76
Kentucky	1.51
Oklahoma	1.36
BOTTOM TEN STATES	
New Jersey	$0.61
Nevada	0.65
Connecticut	0.69
New Hampshire	0.71
Minnesota	0.72
Illinois	0.75
Delaware	0.77
California	0.78
New York	0.79
Colorado	0.81
Average for all states:	$1.17

Source: taxfoundation.org.

ways. Figure 12.2 also makes clear that state government is not doing as good a job as it should.

How do we sort out these incongruities? Certainly, lack of awareness concerning federal tax redistribution is one factor, but even if southerners were knowledgeable about federal spending, it is doubtful that the federal government would be held in higher esteem. What else can explain southerners' animus toward the federal government, especially when federal spending privileges them over residents of other states?

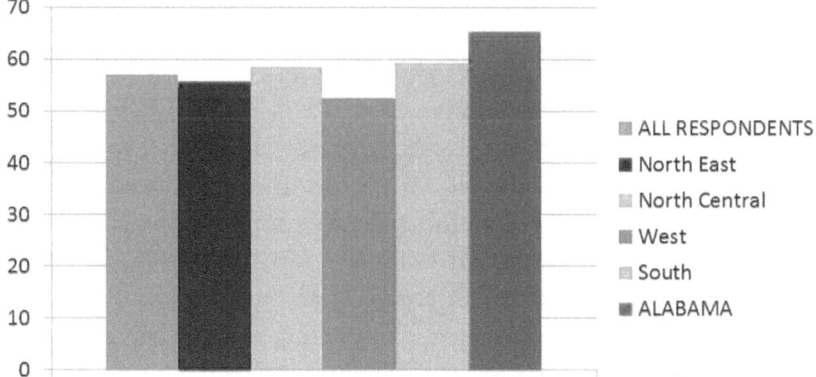

Figure 12.1. Is the South different from the rest of the country? (Source: 2004 National Election Study)

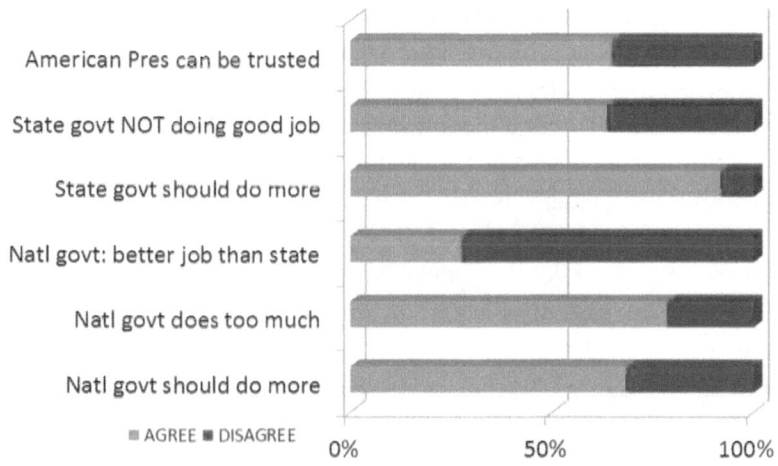

Figure 12.2. Confidence in federal and state government (Source: Annual Survey of Alabama Voters, Birmingham-Southern College, 2012)

Paying One's Fair Share?

In *The Submerged State*, Suzanne Mettler examines awareness of the impact of federal programs and policies on individual citizens.[6] In a 2008 national survey conducted by the Cornell Survey Institute, respondents were asked whether they paid their "fair share" or "more than their fair share" of federal income taxes. Responses revealed considerable variation: Over half (56 percent) reported that they paid their "fair share," in contrast to 42 percent who said they paid "more than their fair share."[7] Mettler and Julianne Koch queried respondents on specific federal programs which were divided into three groups: "visible," "partly visible," or "submerged."[8] The definition of these categories is somewhat intuitive. Policies such as food stamps or public housing fall into the "visible" category; "partly visible" are programs like veterans benefits and student aid for college. The "submerged" category is the most interesting, because this category covers tax policies less perceived to be federal benefits. For example, mortgage interest deductions or tax-deferred employee benefit programs are benefits least likely to be acknowledged by recipients. What is interesting is that when actual dollars are compared, the three largest "submerged" policies (home mortgage interest deduction, deductions for employer health insurance benefits, and tax-deferred retirement benefits) totaled close to $400 billion in 2007.[9] This dwarfs total expenditures for food stamps, unemployment insurance, and Section 8 housing vouchers, which totaled roughly $100 billion in the same period. Not surprisingly, Mettler found that receiving "submerged" benefits was unrelated to attitudes about taxes or whether one had been paying his or her "fair share" of federal income taxes.[10]

Why this disconnect? Why did over 40 percent of those receiving submerged and other federal benefits not acknowledge that they paid their fair share? Koch and Mettler deal directly with this question. Their specific answer comes under the general rubric of "deniability." They find, for example, that 40 percent of Medicare recipients say they "have not used a government social program." Twenty-seven percent of those receiving government-subsidized housing claim they had never used a government "social" program; 60 percent of those who benefit from the home mortgage deduction say they had never used a government "social program."[11] Mettler's work has received some criticism. The fact that Americans who receive these "submerged" benefits and claim never to have used a government "social program" may be more a semantics and measurement issue than a key finding. The use of the term "social program" might be construed as something of a "gotcha" question, in that by using the term "social program," there is a suggestion that these policies are welfare programs, not likely to be acknowledged; this would be especially true of high income earners. If this is deniability, is it deliberate on the part of the respondent? One critic took issue with the concept of the submerged state itself and argued that these are not programmatic benefits at all, but tax exemptions, which are qualitatively different. Jim Saxton, a former Republican Member of Congress, made the argument that the submerged state thesis implies that the government is somehow "owed" this money.[12] A conservative view might claim that the submerged state thesis assumes that tax exemptions are somewhat equivalent to tax evasions, and therefore, tax dollars, which should accrue to the federal treasury absent these exemptions, become tax expenditures, and as such, are benefits.

The gnawing question "How come those who receive federal benefits refuse to acknowledge them?" takes us back to the South, perhaps the Old South.

Elsewhere in this volume, political scientist Allan McBride makes the case that southern culture not only involves a response to the Civil War, Reconstruction, and the civil rights movement but also has much to do with the values of self-reliance and individualism. McBride is not alone. Historian Wayne Flynt, in *Poor but Proud*, talks of the skepticism among early settlers in North Alabama on the question of public education. They so distrusted the large landholders who controlled state government that they believed that public education could not be in their best interests; they were willing to sacrifice the public education of their children in service to a belief about the evils of state government. There was also a distrust of market capitalism. According to Eugene Genovese, market capitalism created a new social order that would inevitably disturb the ability of individuals to become what God intended. As a market-driven economy took root, the romanticism and poetry of the Old South would be jettisoned in favor of a materialist, anti-Christian world. Capitalism was denounced as being "brutal, immoral, irresponsible wage-slavery in which the masters of capital exploited and impoverished their workers without assuming personal responsibility for them."[13]

In addition to the culture of the South being described as individualistic, self-reliant, and dedicated to self-improvement, religion and a sense of social order are underscored. Disproportionately, southerners are more likely to say they are "born-again" Christians; they typically adhere to a belief in a literal reading of the Bible, a respect for authority and obedience, and a rejection of the concept of separation of church and state. There is a certain irony here. On one hand, southern culture emphasizes independence, but child-rearing practices focus on respect for authority. When Alabamians were offered juxtaposed terms related to child-rearing, respect is valued over independence, as are good manners over curiosity, and obedience over self-reliance. Equal numbers of Alabamians attach importance to being considerate as to being well behaved (table 12.2). Moreover, there are clear differences between southerners and non-southerners. These values

Table 12.2. Alabamians on religion and child rearing (percentages only)

	Alabama	U.S.
RELIGIOUS VALUES		
BORN-AGAIN CHRISTIAN	78	44
Believes		
"The Bible is the actual Word of God to be taken literally, word for word."	56	36
"Not everything in the Bible should be taken word for word."	27	47
"The Bible [was] written by men inspired by God but not necessarily the word of God."	15	16
CHILD-REARING VALUES		
MORE IMPORTANT FOR A CHILD TO HAVE/LEARN		
Independence	15	17
OR		
Respect for elders	81	73
Curiosity	18	29
OR		
Good manners	76	59
Obedience	64	49
OR		
Self-reliance	29	38
Being considerate	43	58
OR		
Being well behaved	43	26

Table 12.3. Perceptions of tax fairness, percentages only

	Alabama (2010)	U.S. (2010)
WHEN IT COMES TO FEDERAL INCOME TAXES, DO YOU BELIEVE YOU PAY		
Your fair share	52	50
More than your fair share	40	43
Less than your fair share	4	5

Source: Pew Research Center for the People and the Press, 2010.

combined with fundamentalist faith paint a picture of an authoritarian South that honors tradition and history over change and modernism; it is responsible for itself and expects to be left alone. The federal government is an outsider, an intruder.

If it is conventional to be distrustful of the federal government, it is equally reasonable not to believe that Alabama benefits disproportionately when it comes to federal spending. Consequently, it is not surprising that 40 percent of Alabamians believe that they pay more in federal taxes than they should, though there is little difference between Alabama and the rest of the nation on the question of "paying one's fair share" in federal taxes (table 12.3). Roughly half the samples believe that they pay their fair share; not surprisingly, very few across the country believe they pay "less than their fair share" of income taxes. If fair share is connected to return on taxes, those who live outside the South are probably justified in believing that they pay more than their fair share.

The concept of right-wing authoritarianism has been used to predict fundamentalist religious views along with racial prejudice.[14] The definition of right-wing authoritarianism relies on three attitudinal clusters: submission to authority, aggression toward those who challenge prevailing norms and values, and conventionalism.[15] Moreover, right-wing authoritarianism is associated with political cognition—those who score high in right-wing authoritarianism typically score low in political knowledge.[16] When asked about the redistribution issue, 29 percent of respondents stated their belief that Alabama gets back "less than it puts in." Another 36 percent answer that Alabama gets back "about what it puts in." Only 20 percent were correct in answering that Alabama gets back "more than it puts in."

Alabamians and Federal Benefits

Respondents in the Alabama survey were given a list of federal benefits and asked whether they or someone in their household had ever received any of the twelve benefits offered (tables 12.4 and 12.5). When presented with a list of specific benefits, the results reveal the largest group of recipients to be seniors who make use of Medicare (48 percent); coming in second were those who benefited from student aid programs (42 percent). Federal programs typically associated with social welfare—Medicaid, Food Stamps (SNAP), Head Start, and public housing—are reported by less than 20 percent of the sample. Only seven percent claimed not to have received a single one of the twelve benefits offered. The mean number of benefits was 3.15.

Table 12.4. Types of federal benefits reported

Benefit	(percent)
Medicare	48
Work study, student loan or grants	43
Tax-deferred employee retirement benefits	35
Disability or survivor benefits under Social Security	29
Child or dependent care tax credit	29
Unemployment insurance	29
Veteran's benefits	26
Home mortgage interest deduction	25
Medicaid	19
Food stamps	16
Head Start	9
Government housing	9

Table 12.5. Number of federal benefits reported

Number	(percent)
0	7
1	14
2	19
3	21
4	16
5	8
6	6
7	2
8	3
9	1
10	1
Mean = 3.15 benefits	

Note: Twelve different benefits were offered to respondents.

The question remains: with 93 percent of Alabamians claiming to receive federal benefits, why are they unaware that the federal government spends more money on Alabama than their own taxpayers contribute to the federal treasury?

To avoid the criticism leveled at Mettler, the "social program" question was not asked in the Alabama survey. Instead, we examined the relationship between opinions on tax fairness with perceptions of return of federal tax dollars to Alabama (table 12.6). Here we find that 45 percent of those who believe they pay more than their fair share in federal taxes are most

Table 12.6. Perceptions of return of federal taxes to Alabama by respondent's belief about tax fairness (percentages only)

	Pays more than fair share	Pays less than fair share	Pays fair share	All
ALABAMA...				
gets *less* back than puts in	45	28	27	34
gets *more* back than puts in	21	39	24	23
gets back *about* what it puts in	34	33	49	42
gamma = .257; p<.001	[40]	[4]	[52]	[100]

likely to say that Alabama gets back less than it puts in. For those who answer that they pay their fair share, 27 percent believe the state gets back less. Overall, only 4 percent believe that they pay less than their fair share; this small segment is the one group most likely to believe Alabama gets more than it pays in (39 percent).

The fact that nearly half of those who say they pay more and believe Alabama gets less should be of concern to public officials. Clearly, Alabamians do not believe they are getting their money's worth. Why don't they understand this better? Is it just a matter of continued exposure to the political rhetoric of campaigns and elections where politicians make clear that the federal government does not work in one's interest, federal dollars are wasted, and good money is thrown after bad? If in election after election that kind of rhetoric is a set piece for political speeches, is it not unreasonable to believe that perceptions of waste, fraud, and abuse make it less likely that Alabamians (or Americans in general) would think that their return on investment was positive?

Table 12.7 lends additional support to much of this argument by demonstrating that "fair share" beliefs are related to the number of benefits received. On average, respondents reported receiving 3.15 benefits of the

Table 12.7. Number of benefits received by perceptions of tax fairness

	Average number of benefits
Pays more than fair share	3.35
Pays less than fair share	3.32
Pays fair share	2.86
All respondents	3.15

eta = .104; p<.05

twelve offered in the survey. However, among those who claim to pay "more than their fair share," the average was 3.35 federal benefits. For those who say they pay "their fair share," the average drops to 2.86 benefits. The small percentage who answer that they pay "less" reports receiving 3.32 benefits.

If we divide benefits into the three groupings developed by Mettler—visible, partly visible, and submerged—the submerged category is most worthy of note. As we have already pointed out, there is considerable debate about whether these policies—"tax expenditures"—are actually government outlays. What makes them less visible is the fact that they come in the form of tax deductions that can be claimed as part of the filing of income taxes. In our list, submerged benefits include the home mortgage interest deduction, the child/dependent care tax credit, and tax-deferred employee retirement benefits. They involve considerable dollars that would be deposited in the federal treasury if the tax code did not provide for these deductions or exemptions. It is clear that the taxpayer pays less in federal taxes if the benefit is able to be claimed, but is it a "social program"? In asking about whether one has ever received benefits under a government social program, recall that Mettler found that 60 percent of those who claim the home mortgage interest deduction said they had never ever used a government social program. Apparently, taxpayers do not see the deduction as a program from which they benefit. Notwithstanding whether the taxpayer makes a distinction between a direct payment or a reduction in taxes, without question, if the taxpayer is eligible for the deduction, there can be significant savings in taxes to be paid. In fact, as has been pointed out, nationally, submerged benefits are worth substantially more in dollars than are the more visible social programs that serve low-income segments of the population.

Who is most likely to believe that the tax system treats them unfairly? Paradoxically, 42 percent of those who say they pay "more than their fair share" are receiving one or more of the four "visible" benefits. With respect to the five "partly visible" benefits, 38 percent of Alabamians, who receive one or more of these, say they pay more than their fair share. These are statistically significant findings (table 12.8). What about those recipients of submerged benefits? They fit the pattern for the survey as a whole, with just over 40 percent claiming to pay more than their fair share. In terms of specific benefits, only three are statistically significant, and all are contained in the "partly visible" category: Medicare and Social Security disability and/or survivor benefit recipients are less likely to say they pay more than their fair share. Those who have received unemployment benefits in the past

Table 12.8. Benefits received by perceptions of tax fairness (percentages only)

	Pays more than fair share	Pays less than fair share	Pays fair share
VISIBLE			
Public housing	49	5	46
Head Start	40	2	58
Food stamps	42	6	52
Medicaid	38	10	52
Total	42	7	52[a]
PARTLY VISIBLE			
Veterans benefits	38	4	57
Medicare	30	6	64[a]
Student aid	39	4	58
Disability/survivor benefits under Social Security	36	5	59[a]
Unemployment insurance	41	4	54[a]
Total	38	5	57[a]
SUBMERGED			
Home mortgage interest deduction	37	3	59
Child/dependent care tax credit	44	6	50
Tax-deferred employer retirement benefits	38	3	59
Total	41	4	55
All respondents	40	4	52

Note: a. Statistically significant.

differ from others in the "partly visible" grouping and respond more like the survey as a whole—41 percent say they pay more than their fair share.

Recipients who have ever been enrolled in visible programs are primarily disadvantaged individuals and families. Why would they be more likely to say they pay more than their fair share? They may believe that while it is true that they receive these benefits, it does not mean they are not paying for them themselves. Perhaps, hearing political talk of the "1 percent" causes them to believe that the tax system is unfair and regressive. Medicare is an interesting area, because fewer respondents claim to be paying more than their fair share for that program. This can be explained by the simple fact that most Medicare recipients pay little or no taxes.

In the Alabama survey, we found that over one-third of respondents

Table 12.9. Benefits received by perceptions of return of federal taxes to Alabama (percentages only)

Alabama	Gets back less than it pays in	Gets back about what it pays in	Gets back more than it pays in
VISIBLE			
Public housing	52	41	6[a]
Head Start	32	55	12
Food stamps	39	44	17
Medicaid	37	39	24
Total	36	46	19
PARTLY VISIBLE			
Veteran's benefits	41	29	30[a]
Medicare	34	40	26
Student aid	38	41	21
Disability/survivor benefits under Social Security	38	40	22
Unemployment insurance	32	46	22
Total	34	42	24
SUBMERGED			
Home mortgage interest deduction	31	36	33[a]
Child/dependent care tax credit	41	42	17[a]
Tax-deferred employer retirement benefits	31	36	34[a]
Total	36	40	24
All respondents	36	46	19

Note: a. Statistically significant.

believe that the return of taxes to Alabama in the form of federal expenditures is *less* than the contributions they make as taxpayers. Using the same classifications that were used by Mettler, we see in table 12.9 that those most likely to "get it right" (get back *more*) are those who receive submerged benefits. In particular, those who are able to deduct home mortgage interest and defer taxes on retirement benefits are about 15 percent more likely to be aware that Alabama gets back more than it pays in comparison to the sample as a whole. In contrast, those more likely to be incorrect are those who have lived in public housing or have received veterans benefits or make use of the child or dependent care tax credit; they are 10 to 15 percent more likely to get it wrong.

What we have learned so far is that Alabamians are not very different from the rest of the country when it comes to their opinions about the

Table 12.10. Regression model: predictors of perceptions of return of federal taxes to Alabama

Model	B	Std. Error	Beta	t	Sig.
(Constant)	1.516	.390		3.886	.000
RWA	-.023	.010	-.151	-2.292	.023
FAIRTAX2	.173	.074	.134	2.329	.021
BORN	-.124	.100	-.072	-1.232	.219
PARTYID	.029	.029	.067	.998	.319
IDEOLOGY	-.013	.045	-.019	-.278	.781
AGE	.008	.003	.174	3.068	.002
EDUC × INC	.020	.005	.225	3.696	.000

Above the B/Std.Error/Beta columns: Unstandardized Coefficients

Note: Dependent Variable: PERCEPTIONS OF RETURN OF FEDERAL TAXES TO ALABAMA; RWA = Right Wing Authoritarianism; EDUC × INC = interaction term (EDUCATION WITH INCOME); $R = .356$; $R^2 = .127$.

performance of the federal government. They are mostly not aware that the state is privileged when it comes to the redistribution of federal tax dollars in the form of program benefits. Few—4 percent—believe that they pay less than their fair share in federal taxes. The variables that explain their perceptions on the question of whether Alabama gets back more or less than it pays in are summarized in a regression analysis (table 12.10). The model takes into account many of the concepts that have already been discussed. We found that the best predictors of perceptions on the question of return of federal taxes to Alabama are the interaction of education and income, age, right-wing authoritarianism, and beliefs about paying one's fair share. The interaction of education with income suggests that those who are better educated and more affluent are most likely to understand that Alabama gets back more than it pays in. The older the respondent, the more likely he or she is to be equally aware. Those with authoritarian attitudes are more likely to be incorrect in their perceptions of return of federal taxes to Alabama. Finally, those who believe they pay more than their fair share are likely to believe that Alabama gets back less than it pays in.

The implication of the submerged state thesis is that somehow recipients of submerged benefits are in denial that they receive such benefits. That was not borne out in this analysis for Alabama. What we did find is that those who make use of submerged benefits are by and large aware that they are receiving them. They are also most likely to understand that the state of Alabama has a good deal when it comes to federal taxation. The other significant finding is that less-affluent and less-educated citizens are not only less aware that Alabama is advantaged when it comes to federal taxation but are also the most likely to have received visible benefits such as public housing and food stamps. Moreover, higher levels of right-wing authoritarianism predict lower levels of awareness. We did not find a racial component in any of this research. Rather, we found a consistency that is reflective more of the culture and values of the deep South—values that have migrated to the rest of the country. Southernization has led to regular and routine negative messages on the ability of government to govern. Consistent reinforcement of the idea that government does not work, that citizens are taxed too much, and that there is corruption and waste in the system is hard to turn around absent education. When it comes to campaigns and elections, it is not in the interest of candidates to make the case that government can play a positive role in the lives of its citizens. Arguing such a case does not bolster electability in the short run. In the long run, indicting the efficacy of government damages the political system in an egregious way. We have the South to thank for this.

Notes

1. George C. Wallace, "The Civil Rights Movement: Fraud, Sham, and Hoax," speech from *The American Experience; LBJ; Primary Resources: A Segregationalist's View of the Civil Rights Movement, 1964* (PBS, February 14, 2006).

2. Jeff Sessions, "Americans Look for Supreme Court to Restrain Federal Power, Not Expand It," *Washington Post*, May 7, 2010, http://www.washingtonpost.com/wp-dyn/content/article/2010/05/06/AR2010050605016.html.

3. Michele Bachmann, "Announcement of Candidacy for President," *Huffington Post*, August 27, 2011, http://www.huffingtonpost.com/2011/06/27/michele-bachmann-2012-president_n_860215.html.

4. Amanda Zamora (full text of a speech given by Rick Santorum), "Rick Santorum's Super Tuesday Speech," *Washington Post*, March 6, 2012, http://www.washingtonpost.com/blogs/election-2012/post/rick-santorums-michigan-primary-speech-full-text-and-video/2012/02/28/gIQAtFsJhR_blog.html.

5. Charlie Spiering, "Full Text: Mitt Romney's Victory Speech," *Washington Examiner*, April 24, 2012 http://campaign2012.washingtonexaminer.com/blogs/beltway-confidential/full-text-mitt-romneys-victory-speech/500426.

6. Suzanne Mettler, *The Submerged State* (Chicago: University of Chicago Press, 2011).

7. Suzanne Mettler, "Reconstituting the Submerged State: The Challenges of Social Policy Reform in the Obama Era," *Perspectives on Politics* 8 (September 2010): 808.

8. Julianne Koch and Suzanne Mettler, "Who Perceives Government's Role in Their Lives? Assessing the Impact of Social Policy on Visibility" (2012, unpublished paper in possession of the author).

9. Leonard Burman, Eric Toder and Christopher Geissler, "How Big Are Total Individual Income Tax Expenditures, and Who Benefits from Them?" (paper presented at the American Social Science Association annual meeting, New Orleans, January 5, 2008), 7.

10. Mettler, *The Submerged State*, 808.

11. Koch and Mettler, "Who Perceives Government's Role in Their Lives?" 38.

12. Jim Saxton, "Tax Expenditures: A Review and Analysis" (Washington, D.C.: Joint Economic Committee, 1999), 1–2, http://www.house.gov/jec/tiscal/tax/expend.pdf.

13. Wayne Flynt, *Poor but Proud: Alabama's Poor Whites* (Tuscaloosa: University of Alabama Press, 1989); Eugene D. Genovese, *The Southern Tradition: The Achievement and Limitations of an American Conservatism* (Cambridge: Harvard University Press, 1994), 31.

14. Bob Altemeyer, *Right-Wing Authoritarianism* (Winnipeg: University of Manitoba Press, 1981); and Bob Altmeyer, *Enemies of Freedom: Understanding Right-Wing Authoritarianism* (San Francisco: Jossey-Bass, 1988).

15. Brian Laythe, Deborah Finkel, and Lee A. Kirkpatrick, "Predicting Prejudice from Religious Fundamentalism and Right-Wing Authoritarianism: A Multiple-Regression Approach," *Journal for the Scientific Study of Religion* 40, no. 1 (2001): 2.

16. Bill E. Peterson, Lauren E. Duncan, and Joyce S. Paang, "Authoritarianism and Political Impoverishment: Deficits in Knowledge and Civic Disinterest," *Political Psychology* 23 (2002): 105.

Contributors

Fred Arthur Bailey is professor emeritus and former head of the Department of History at Abilene Christian University. He is the author of *William Edward Dodd: The South's Yeoman Scholar* and also *Class and Tennessee's Confederate Generation*.

Chris Danielson is assistant professor of history at Montana Tech of the University of Montana. He is the author of *After Freedom Summer: How Race Realigned Mississippi Politics, 1965–1986*.

Natalie Motise Davis is Howell T. Heflin Professor of American Politics at Birmingham-Southern College, where she has taught for four decades. She is a nationally recognized public-opinion expert who conducts political polls throughout Dixie. Davis was a candidate for the U.S. Senate in 1996.

Rebecca Miller Davis is lecturer in American history at the University of Missouri–Kansas City. Her work has appeared in several journals such as the *Journal of Mississippi History* and *South Carolina Historical Magazine*.

Matthew L. Downs is assistant professor of history at the University of Mobile. His current work focuses on the effects of the Tennessee Valley Authority on the Sun Belt South.

Glenn Feldman (1962–2015) was professor of history at the University of Alabama at Birmingham. He was the author or editor of a number of books on American and southern politics, religion, race relations, economics, and historiography.

David R. Jansson is researcher in the Department of Social and Economic

Geography at Uppsala University in Sweden. He is the editor of the forthcoming book *From Åland to America: The Immigrant Experience and the Art of Warner Sallman, Haddon Sundblom, and Phil Fagerholm.*

Allan B. McBride is associate professor and chair of the Department of Political Science, International Development, and International Affairs at the University of Southern Mississippi. He is the author of numerous journal articles.

Martin T. Olliff is associate professor of history and director of the Archives of Wiregrass History and Culture at Troy State University–Dothan. He is the editor of *The Great War in the Heart of Dixie: Alabama during World War I.*

Gregory L. Richard is assistant professor of history at Winona State University. His work has appeared in *Louisiana History*.

Thomas F. Schaller is professor of political science at the University of Maryland–Baltimore County and a columnist for the *Baltimore Sun* and several other newspapers. He is the author of the best-selling *Whistling Past Dixie: How Democrats Can Win without the South.*

Zachary C. Smith is a Ph.D. candidate in history at the University of Georgia. He has published in the *Journal of Southern History* and other journals.

Jason Morgan Ward is assistant professor of history at Mississippi State University. He is the author of *Defending White Democracy: The Making of a Segregationist Movement and the Remaking of Racial Politics, 1936–1965.*

Index

Abortion, 21, 316, 320. See also *Roe v. Wade*
Adams, John Quincy, 27; and "Corrupt Bargain," 59n10
Affordable Care Act, 320–23
Agriculture. *See* Cotton; Farmers
Alabama, 10–12, 120n29; and the 1960 election, 146n41; and the 1964 election, 148n52; benefits from federal government and, 325–41; and the Dixiecrat Revolt, 128, 129, 144n23; economic development in, 261–86; immigration to, 219–20; last state to abolish convict lease, 61n34; Latinos in, 219–20; meeting in Tuscaloosa, 207; military installations in, 229; opposition to military draft in, 86, 87; road and highway construction in, 229–60; taxes and, 325–41. *See also* Birmingham; Bradford, Melvin E.; Collins, Charles Wallace; Graves, John Temple; Wallace, George C.
Allain, Bill, 163
American Revolution, 24–25. *See also* Tories
Anti-Catholicism, 4, 21, 69
Anti-Semitism, 4, 69, 74, 77; and Tom Watson, 94n3. *See also* Frank, Leo; Weinberger, Harry
Arizona, 220; and the 1964 election, 148n52
Arkansas, 12–13, 287–300, 328; and desegregation, 33; opposition to military draft in, 86, 87; penal reform in, 287–300. *See also* Eisenhower, Dwight D.; Little Rock
Arminianism, 14
Atwater, H. Lee, 8, 21
Auburn University, 245
Austrian School, 2

Bachmann, Michele, 318, 326
Bailey, Fred Arthur, 9
Bailey, Josiah, 104
Ball, William Watts, 109–10, 113
Bankhead, John Hollis, 241
Barbour, Haley, 149
Barnes, Roy, 50
Barnett, Ross, 7, 133–36, 150; and Mississippi GOP, 153
Barnwell, John, 30
Bass, Jack, 173nn17,19
Beasley, David, 21; and decision to remove Confederate Battle Flag, 49–50
Beccaria, Cesare, 288–89
Beck, Glenn, 318
Bilbo, Theodore, 123
Bill of Rights, 26, 59n8
Birmingham, 86
Black, Earl, 150, 304, 321
Black, Merle, 150, 304, 321
Black Codes, 2
Blease, Cole, 36–37, 39, 53, 58
Bledsoe, Oscar, 111
Bob Jones University, 4, 21, 217
Bradford, Melvin E., 9, 181–204; and

admiration for George Wallace, 9, 186–87; admired by Ronald Reagan, 9, 187–89, 201n20; attacks Martin Luther King, 195; and attacks on Abraham Lincoln, 9, 183, 185–86, 194–96; and attacks on egalitarianism, 9, 181–82, 193–95, 198–99; on the Declaration of Independence, 186; defense of aristocracy, 193–94; defense of extremism, 181–82; and defense of slavery, 9, 192–93; and nomination to NEH, 187–89; praise for the Klan, 197–98; racism of, 182, 192, 195; and "Reconstruction Theology," 189–92; ties to Neo-Confederacy, 196–99. *See also* Nashville Agrarians; Vanderbilt University

Brannon, Hazel, 125, 133, 136
Briggs v. Elliott, 42
British aristocracy, 193–94
British East India Company, 3
British Parliament, 3
Brooks, Preston, 20, 53
Brown, J. J., 80–81, 98n50
Brown v. Board of Education, 4, 131, 140; and South Carolina, 21, 42–43
Burke, Edmund, 3, 15n2
Burleson, Albert Sydney, 89
Burt, Armistead: and refuge for Jeff Davis, 57
Burton, Orville Vernon, 15n1
Bush, George H. W., 21
Bush, George W., 49, 310–11, 319; and smearing of John McCain in South Carolina, 52
Business, 2; and pro-business climate, 2
Byrd, Harry F., 45, 120n29
Byrnes, James F. "Jimmy," 38, 39, 105; and reaction to *Brown v. Board*, 42; turns on New Deal, 116

Calhoun, John C., 1, 4–5, 44, 53, 58; and "nullification," 20, 27–30; and slavery, 30–31
Calvinism, 14, 119n16; and the "deservedness" of aid recipients, 14, 314, 317;

ties to race, 109–10, 113, 114. *See also* Business; Capitalism; "Profitarianism"; Religion

Capitalism, 4, 119n16; alleged suspicion of market values, 14; anti-capitalism in Georgia, 67–101; free markets and, 308–9, 315, 319; hostility toward New Deal, 102–21; racialized versions of, 6; suspicion toward, 4, 14; unfettered, 151
Carmichael, Gil, 8, 153–64, 171, 173n17
Carpetbaggers, 5, 6
Carter, Dan T., 163
Carter, Hodding, Jr., 129, 135, 138
Carter, Hodding, III, 138–39
Carter, Jimmy, 48–49, 140n1, 164
Cash, W. J., 9; and "nation within a nation," 9
Catholics, 4. *See also* Anti-Catholicism
Chicago School, 2
Citizens Councils. *See* White Citizens' Councils
Civil rights, 1, 6, 7, 8, 10, 117, 185, 193; and alienation of white South, 46, 122; and Mississippi, 126–30. *See also* Bradford, Melvin E.; Civil Rights Act of 1964; Democratic Party; Dixiecrat Revolt; New Deal; Republican Party; States' Rights; Voting Rights Act of 1965
Civil Rights Act of 1964, 6, 7, 8; and alienation of white Democrats, 46. *See also* Johnson, Lyndon; Kennedy, John F.
Civil War, 1, 11, 213, 290–91, 318, 325; and prisons, 290–91; romanticized, 183–85; and South Carolina, 20, 30–32, 57–58. *See also* Bradford, Melvin E.
Clay, Henry, 1, 27; and "Corrupt Bargain," 59n10
Cleveland, Grover, 20, 34
Clifford, Clark: memo on race, 127
Clinton, Bill, 140n1
Cochran, Thad, 154–55, 159–63, 165, 173n19
Collins, Charles Wallace, 116–17
Colmer, William, 111, 124–25

Colom, Wilbur, 165
Communism, 6; the New Deal characterized as, 102–21
Compromise of 1850, 30–31, 60n17
Compromise of 1877, 34, 60nn23,24
Comte, Auguste: on religion, 305
Confederacy, 4. *See also* Bradford, Melvin E.; Confederate Memorial Day; Civil War; Neo-Confederacy; United Daughters of the Confederacy
Confederate Battle Flag, 49–50, 102
Confederate Memorial Day, 4
Conner, Mike S., 114
Conservatism, 2, 139–40, 181–204; of Edmund Burke, 3; and extremism, 181–82; racial conservatism, 5–6, 7, 8, 13; religious conservatism, 2, 14. *See also* Bradford, Melvin E.; Neo-Confederacy
Conservative Manifesto, 104
Convict lease, 2, 36, 61n34
Cotton, 79–81, 92, 93, 230–33, 240
Coulter, E. Merton, 190–91, 202n32
Crespino, Joseph, 15n1, 151, 162; work reviewed, 15n1
Cruse, Kevin, 162
"Cultural Theory," 304–8
Culture. *See* South: culture and
Cummins Prison Farm, 12, 291–300

Dabney, Robert L., 189–90
Danielson, Chris, 4, 7–9
Davidson, Donald, 184–85, 200n15; criticism of C. Vann Woodward, 200n13
Davis, Jefferson, 57
Davis, John W., 42–43
Davis, Natalie Motise, 13, 14–15
Davis, Rebecca Miller, 4, 6–7
Debt peonage, 2
Decatur, Alabama, 11–12, 232, 261–86
Declaration of Independence, 186, 194–95
DeMint, Jim, 52
Democratic Party, 6–7, 8, 105; and civil rights, 6–9. *See also* Johnson, Lyndon; Kennedy, John F.; New Deal; Roosevelt, Franklin D.; Truman, Harry S.

Dent, Harry S., 8, 21; and Gerald Ford, 160–61; and Mississippi GOP, 152, 155
De Vries, Walter, 156–57, 173nn17,19
Dewey, Thomas E., 125, 128
Dies, Martin, 107. *See also* House Un-American Activities Committee (HUAC)
Disfranchisement, 2
Distinctiveness. *See* South: distinctiveness of
Dixiecrat Revolt, 7, 21, 42, 45, 115–16, 126–30; and local control, 47–48
Dixon, Rev. Thomas F., 5–6, 102, 106–7, 109, 196; and *The Flaming Sword*, 106–7, 118n9
Dobbins, W. O., 273–74
Doster, James, 235
Downs, Matthew L., 10, 11–12
Duffy, Joseph D., 187–89

Earle, Willie, lynching of, 40–41, 42, 61n46
Eastland, James O., 126, 134, 146n36, 150; and Mississippi GOP, 154
Economic development, 10–12
Economics. *See* Capitalism; Communism; Labor; Socialism
Edgar, Walter, 24
Edgerton, John, 104. *See also* Southern States Industrial Council
Edwards, James B., 47, 49
Egalitarianism, 308; attacked, 9, 181–82, 193–94, 198–99. *See also* Bradford, Melvin E.
Egerton, John, 304
"Eight-box system," 35
Eighth Amendment, 12, 297
Eisenhower, Dwight D., 45; and civil rights, 7, 33, 130–32; and relationship to South, 130–32. *See also* Little Rock
Elazar, Daniel, 14, 305–6, 319
Emerging Republican Majority, The, 7–8
Emmerich, J. Oliver, 128, 130, 135
Engerman, Stanley L., 192–93
Evers, Charles, 152, 153

Exceptionalism. *See* South: distinctiveness of

Fair Deal, 6
Fair Employment Practices Committee (FEPC), 110–11, 124, 126
Farmers: roads to market, 229–60
Fascism, 6
Faubus, Orval, 131; and prison reform, 293
Faulkner, William, 200n15
Federal Government, conflation of with "the North", 5
Federal investment in the South, 1–2, 3, 10, 11–12, 14, 325–41; roads and highways, 229–60
Federal judiciary: and penal reform, 287–300
Federal Road Aid Act of 1916, 11, 229–60
Federal Road Aid Act of 1921, 11, 229–60
Feldman, Glenn, 119n16
Finch, Cliff, 155–58, 162
Fleming, Thomas, 196–97
Florida, 120n29, 327–28; League of the South in, 211
Fogel, Robert W., 192–93
Football, college, 2; as a religion, 2
Ford, Gerald, 160–61
Fortas, Abe, 48
Fort Sumter, 31
Fourteenth Amendment, 291–92
Fowler, Don, 46
Fox-Genovese, Elizabeth, 202n36
Frank, Leo, lynching of, 5, 67–68, 71–78, 93; case of, 71–78; souvenirs from, 97n38
Franklin, John Hope, 206
Franklin, Webb, 168
Frederickson, Kari, 47–48
"Freedom of Choice," 48
"Freedom Riders," 136
"Freedom Summer," Mississippi, 1964, 7, 165
French Jacobins, 193
Gaughan, Anthony, 69–70
Gavagan, Joseph, 105–6

Gavagan-Wagner Anti-Lynching Bill, 105–6
Gender. *See* Frank, Leo; Masculine rhetoric; Women
Genovese, Eugene, 202n36; on capitalism and the Old South, 331
George, Walter, 105–6
Georgia, 5; and the 1964 election, 148n52; anti-capitalism in, 67–101; and resistance to military draft, 67–101. *See also* George, Walter; Russell, Richard; Talmadge, Eugene; Watson, Thomas E.
Georgia Farmers' Union, 69, 79–81, 98n50
Gerrymandering, 24, 167–71
Goldwater, Barry, 7, 150; and 1964 election, 46, 147n48, 148n52; appeal to white southerners on race, 7, 137–40; opposition to Civil Rights Act of 1964, 7, 137–39; opposition to NAACP, 7; opposition to U.S. Supreme Court, 7; support for stand at Ole Miss, 7; versus Lyndon Johnson, 137–39
Gore, Al, Sr., 44
Graham, Lindsey, 51–53
Grant, Ulysses S., 33
Graves, John Temple, 111
Great Depression, 11
Great Society, 117
"Great White Switch," 150, 171; second, 165–66
Gregory, Thomas W., 89
Guinier, Lani, 168

Hahn, Steven, 71, 95nn8,12
Hamer, Fannie Lou, 152
Hampton, Wade, 34–35, 58
Hardwick, Thomas W., 83–84
Harmon, Mose, Jr., 295, 298
Hart, Jeffrey, 189
Hayek, F. A., 113–14. *See also* Libertarianism
Hayes, Jack Irby, 39
Hayes, Rutherford B., 34
Haynesworth, Clement F., Jr.: Supreme Court nomination of, 48

Helms, Jesse, 187
Henderson, Charles, 242–43
Henley, J. Smith, 12–13, 287–300; judicial philosophy of, 296–97
Henry, Aaron, 157
Henry, Patrick, 1, 31
Hill, Lister, 279
Hill, Michael, 210–11, 218–24, 225n5
Hispanics. *See* Immigration; Latinos
Historical scholarship, 8–9. *See also* Nuance
Hollings, Fritz, 51–52
Home-schooling, 217
Hoover, Herbert, 105
House Un-American Activities Committee (HUAC), 107

Immigration, 9; as betrayal of true southerners, 9–10, 219–20
Indians. *See* Native Americans
Individualism, and self-reliance, 10, 14, 314, 322
Industrialism. *See* Capitalism; Southern States Industrial Council
Interposition, doctrine of, 4. *See also* Nullification Crisis

Jackson, Andrew, 1, 59n10, 148n56; Jacksonian ethos, 232; and "Nullification Crisis," 27–30
Jackson, Rev. Jesse, 167–69
Jaffa, Harry V., 183
Jansson, David R., 9–10
Jefferson, Thomas, 1, 194, 303, 318; and removal of slavery language from Declaration, 4, 20
Jews, 4, 5. *See also* Anti-Semitism
Jim Crow. *See* Segregation
Johnson, Andrew, 32–33
Johnson, Lyndon, 6–7, 148n56; and alienation of white Democrats, 46; and civil rights, 6–7, 44, 132–33, 137–40, 322; versus Goldwater, 137–39
Johnson, T. D., 278–79
Johnston, Olin, 39, 44, 53, 58; unseats "Cotton Ed" Smith, 40; use of *Smith v. Allwright*, 40
Johnston, Richard, 15n1; work reviewed, 15n1
Jones, Bob, 279

Kefauver, Estes, 44
Keith, Jeanette, 69–70
Kennedy, James Ronald, 211–12
Kennedy, John F., 45, 148n56; and civil rights, 7, 132–37; and JFK Profile in Courage Award, 50; and Ole Miss, 136–37, 147n44
Kennedy, Robert F., 136–37, 147n44
Kentucky, 1, 328; opposition to military draft in, 86
Kerry, John, 45
Kilby, Thomas E., 249
King, Martin Luther, Jr., 163; attacked, 195; holiday, 163
Kirby, John Henry, 102
Kirk, Russell, 184
Kitchen, Claude, 69–70, 82–83
Klein, Jo Ann, 164
Kluger, Richard, 43
Koch, Julianne, 330–31
Kosciuszko, Thaddeus, 56
Kristol, Irving, 188
Ku Klux Klan, 2, 77, 102; in Georgia, 77; praised, 197–98; in South Carolina, 20, 21, 33. *See also* Bradford, Melvin E.; Dixon, Rev. Thomas F.

Labor, 2, 107, 110–11, 150; and race purity, 104. *See* also Fair Employment Practices Committee (FEPC); Georgia Farmers' Union; New Deal
Lassiter, Matthew D., 15n1, 162; work reviewed, 15n1
Latinos, 9
League of the South, 9–10, 199, 207–26
Lee, "Light-horse" Harry, 56
Lee, Richard Henry, 1
Lee, Robert E., 31, 57
Leuchtenburg, William, 123, 126
Liberalism, 6, 7, 8, 48, 198–99; as

communism, 6; as fascism, 6; in Mississippi, 156–57; as totalitarianism, 6. *See also* Dixiecrat Revolt; Fair Deal; New Deal; Roosevelt, Franklin D.
Libertarianism, 2–3, 27. *See also* "Profitarianism"; Tea Party
Lilienthal, David, 11, 262, 267–69, 273, 278–81; dispute with Arthur Morgan, 263–65. *See also* Tennessee Valley Authority (TVA)
Lincoln, Abraham, 9, 32; attacked by Melvin E. Bradford, 9, 183, 185–86, 193–96. *See also* Bradford, Melvin E.
Little Rock, 130–32, 140
Locke, John, 289–90
Long, Huey, 37, 123
Lott, Trent, 124, 154, 161; and Reagan at Neshoba County, 165
Louisiana, 37, 120n29, 328; and the 1964 election, 148n52; and the Dixiecrat Revolt, 129, 144n23. *See also* Long, Huey
Lowndes, Joseph, 121n30
Lynching, 105–6. *See also* Earle, Willie; Frank, Leo

MacDonald, Forrest, 198
MacLean, Nancy, 96n28
Macon, Georgia. *See* National Grass Roots Convention
Madison, James, 1
Marion, Francis "Swamp Fox," 25
Marshall, John, 1
Marshall, Thurgood, 42, 43
Marx, Karl, 105
Masculine rhetoric, 115
Maybank, Burnet R., 39
McBride, Allen B., 13–14, 331
McBride, Eddie L., 154–55, 173n19
McCain, John: smeared by George W. Bush in South Carolina, 52
McWhiney, Grady, 198
Medicare, 14, 314, 337
Meredith, James, 136–37, 173n17
Mettler, Suzanne, 329–31, 334, 336
Militarism, 2, 3, 5; and anti-war sentiment in Georgia, 4–5, 67–101; resistance to draft, 90–92, 94nn5,7, 100n80; of Washington, 209–11
Mind of the South, The, 9
Mississippi, 22, 115, 120n29, 122–78, 327–28; and the Dixiecrat Revolt, 128, 129; opposition to military draft in, 86, 87, 100n80; Republicanization of, 6–9, 122–78. *See also* Barnett, Ross; Colmer, William; Lott, Trent; Neshoba County; Ole Miss; Sillers, Walter J.
Mississippi Freedom Democratic Party, 149–50, 152
Mobile, 232, 234
Monroe, James, 1, 27
Monsanto Chemicals, 277
Montgomery, Marion, 198
Morgan, Arthur: dispute with David Lilienthal, 263–65
Morgan, J. P., 79, 85, 98n54
Morse, Frank, 44
Mounger, William, 153, 154, 156–57, 161–63; and Ronald Reagan, 160, 165; and George Wallace, 163–64
Multiculturalism. *See* Immigration

Nashville Agrarians, 9, 182–85, 200n15, 218. *See also* Vanderbilt University
National Association for the Advancement of Colored People (NAACP), 7, 42, 102
National Endowment for the Humanities (NEH) 187–89
National Grass Roots Convention, 5–6, 102–4
Native Americans, 205
Nelson, Richard: on Tom Watson, 96n14
Neo-Confederacy, 9, 10, 181–204. *See also* Bradford, Melvin E.
Neoliberalism, 2–3, 113–14. *See also* Hayek, F. A.; Rand, Ayn
Neshoba County, Mississippi, 100n80, 164–65
New Deal, 5, 6, 39, 102–21; and communism, 5; as communistic, 5–6, 102–21; opposition to, 119n16; and race, 5–6,

102–21; and Reconstruction, 5; as slavery, 6; southern hostility toward, 5–6, 102–21. *See also* Fair Employment Practices Committee (FEPC); Tennessee Valley Authority (TVA); Works Progress Administration (WPA)
Nineteenth Amendment, 4
Ninety Six, South Carolina, 23–24, 53–58
Nixon, Richard, 8, 45, 139, 152; election of 1960, 133–37, 146n41, 148n56; reliance on Strom Thurmond, 46–47; and South Carolina, 48. *See also* "Southern Strategy"
Nofziger, Lyn, 156
North Carolina, 5; Hendersonville, 208; opposition to military draft in, 86. *See also* Dixon, Rev. Thomas F.; Helms, Jesse; Kitchen, Claude
Nuance, in historiography, 8–9
Nullification Crisis, 3, 4, 22, 27–30

Obama, Barack, 14, 139–40; referred to, 13, 140n1; and Tea Party, 13, 304, 309–14, 319
Obamacare. *See* Affordable Care Act
Occupy Movement, 303
Ogden, Florence Sillers, 138
Oklahoma, 188
Ole Miss, 7, 136–37, 147n44
Olliff, Martin T., 10–11

Parker, Frank R., 170
Patriotism, 2, 119n16
Patterson, John M., 229
Paul, Rand, 318
Paul, Ron, 318
Pelosi, Nancy, 316
People's Party. *See* Populism
Perdue, Sonny, 50
Perman, Michael, 130
Phagan, Mary, 72, 74–75
Phillips, Kevin P.: and the Republicanization of the South, 7–8
Phillips, Rubel, 148n55, 152, 154
Phillips, U. B., 230
Plain Whites. *See* Working-class whites
Polk, James K., 1

Poor Whites. *See* Working-class whites
Populism, 5, 13, 200n13; compared to Tea Party, 303–24
Populist Party, 95n12; antipathy to English capital, 98n44; in Georgia, 70–72
Prince, R. M., 114–15
Prisons: punishment and discipline, 293–95, 298–99; reform of, 12–13, 287–300
"Profitarianism," 2–3. *See also* Libertarianism; Neoliberalism
Progressive Movement, 38, 253

Race. *See* Bradford, Melvin E.; Capitalism: racialized versions of; Civil rights; Civil Rights Act of 1964; Convict lease; Disfranchisement; Dixiecrat Revolt; Dixon, Rev. Thomas F.; Ku Klux Klan; Lynching; New Deal: southern hostility toward; Republican Party: use of race; Rutledge, Archibald; Segregation; Slavery; "Southern Strategy"; Tea Party; Thurmond, J. Strom; Voting Rights Act of 1965; Wallace, George C.
Railroads, 10, 234–36
Ramsay, Claude, 150
Rand, Ayn, 5; recent popularity of, 5
Rand, Clayton, 113, 114, 120nn24,26
Randolph, A. Philip, 110. *See also* Fair Employment Practices Committee (FEPC)
Randolph, Edmund, 1
Randolph, John, 1
Reagan, Ronald, 9, 139–40, 140n1, 152, 178n72; and admiration for Melvin E. Bradford, 9, 201n20; and Mississippi, 160, 163–67, 178n72; and Neshoba County, 164–65; and USSR, 223; versus Carter, 48–49. *See also* Reynolds, William Bradford
Reconstruction, 185, 229, 318, 325; in South Carolina, 20, 32–36
Reconstruction Theology, 189–92
"Red Shirts," 20, 34–35, 58; black participation in, 34
Reed, Clarke, 8, 152–53, 156, 157, 160–61
Religion. *See* Arminianism; Calvinism;

Catholics; Comte, Auguste; Jews; Reconstruction Theology; Southern Baptists; South: religion and; Southern Methodists; Southern Presbyterians; Wesleyanism

Republican Party, 4, 9, 117, 292–93; and Confederate Battle Flag, 21; growing extremism of, 9; and Mississippi, 122–78; modern, 4; and the Republicanization of the South, 6–9, 122–78; use of race, 8. *See also* Atwater, H. Lee; Bradford, Melvin E.; Bush, George W.; Dent, Harry S.; Goldwater, Barry; Nixon, Richard; Reagan, Ronald; "Southern Strategy"; Tea Party; Thurmond, J. Strom

Reynolds, William Bradford: trip to Mississippi, 167–71, 178n72

Reynolds Metals Company, 267–68

Rhett, Robert Barnwell, 31

Richard, Gregory L., 10, 12–13

Roads and highways, 10–11, 229–60

Roe v. Wade, 316, 320

Rogers, S. Emory, 43

Romney, Mitt, 326–27

Roosevelt, Eleanor, 102, 114, 125

Roosevelt, Franklin D., 6, 39; and FEPC, 110–11; and "purge" elections, 39, 105–6; and race, 6, 7, 40, 123–26; south as "Nation's Number-One Economic Problem," 265–67; southern opposition to based on race, 102–21; and TVA, 263–65. *See also* New Deal

Roosevelt, Theodore, 71, 98n54

Rove, Karl, 21

Ruffin, Edmund, 31

Russell, Richard, 104–5

Rutledge, Archibald, 107–9

Santorum, Rick, 326

Saxton, Jim, 330–31

Schaller, Thomas F., 3–4

Schiff, Jacob, 79

Secession, 3, 4; and South Carolina, 22, 31

Segregation, 2

Sessions, Jeff, 326

Shafer, Byron, 15n1; work reviewed, 15n1

Shaw, Barton C., 77, 95n12

Shelton, Barrett, 11, 261–64, 270–72, 278–81

Sillers, Walter J., 111, 112

Simon, Bryant, 37

Sinha, Manisha, 29

Slaton, John M., 74–76, 77, 78

Slavery, 20, 30–31, 60n17; defended, 113, 192–93; and South Carolina, 22–23, 36, 59n2; and Virginia, 59n2. *See also* Bradford, Melvin E.; Civil War; Nullification Crisis

Smith, Ellison D. "Cotton Ed," 38; and "purge" election, 39, 105–6

Smith, Hazel Brannon. *See* Brannon, Hazel

Smith, Hoke, 72, 79, 83

Smith, John David, 118n9

Smith, Zachary C., 4, 5

Smith v. Allwright, 39, 124, 125

Socialism, 2, 116, 316; opposition to World War I, 82. *See also* New Deal

Social Security, 14, 314

Sons of Confederate Veterans, 199

South: contempt for Washington, 15, 325–41; culture and, 214–23, 304–8, 340; dependence on federal government, 15, 325–41; distinctiveness of, 1–2, 13–15, 223–24, 303; dual personality of, 15; as nation's "number-one economic problem," 105–6; psychology of, 15; relationship to federal government, 1–15, 205–26; religion and, 214–23, 331–32

South Carolina, 1, 3–4, 19–63, 115, 120n29; and the 1964 election, 148n52; and *Brown v. Board of Education*, 42–43; and Civil War, 30–32; and Dixiecrat Revolt, 42, 129; and Nullification Crisis, 3–4, 27–30; and Reconstruction, 32–33; and the "Red Shirts," 34–35; and relationship with federal government, 19–63; and slavery, 22–23, 59n2; and the "Southern Manifesto," 43–44. *See also* Atwater, H. Lee; Blease, Cole; Byrnes, James F.; Dent, Harry S.; Hampton, Wade; Johnston, Olin; Smith, Ellison D. "Cotton Ed";

Thurmond, J. Strom; Tillman, Benjamin "Pitchfork Ben"
South Carolina Exposition of Protest, 28–29
Southern Baptists, 14, 321
"Southern Manifesto," 43–44
Southern Methodists, 14
Southern National Congress, 10, 208–26
Southern Partisan, 196–98
Southern Presbyterians, 14. *See also* Reconstruction Theology
Southern States Industrial Council (SSIC): opposition to New Deal, 104
"Southern Strategy," of British, 25
"Southern Strategy," 8–9, 21, 117. *See also* Atwater, H. Lee; Dent, Harry S.; Nixon, Richard; Phillips, Kevin P.; Thurmond, J. Strom
Sparkman, John, 267, 279
Speer, Emory, 87–88, 89, 100n84
States' Rights, 2, 4, 27. *See also* Civil rights
Statute-Labor System, 10, 236–37
Stennis, John, 134, 146n36
Stephens, Dan, 293
Submerged State. *See* Mettler, Suzanne
"Suburban School," 15n1; discussed, 1–2, 165. *See also* Crespino, Joseph; Johnston, Richard; Lassiter, Matthew D.; Shafer, Byron
Suffrage, 4. *See also* Disfranchisement; Women
Sullens, Fred, 127–28, 128–29, 130–31, 132
Sumner, Charles, 20
Sumter, Thomas, 25
"Sun Belt" economy, 11–12, 261–86
"Sunbelt School," 11–12, 149. *See also* "Suburban School"

Talley, Winston, 295, 298
Talley v. Stephens, 292
Talmadge, Eugene, 5–6, 104–5, 123; criticism of the New Deal, 5–6, 102–4, 114
Tariffs. *See* Nullification Crisis
Taxes: and relation to Tea Party, 13–15; southern aversion toward, 3, 10–11, 13–15, 325–41. *See also* Tea Party

Tea Party, 13–15, 303–24, 325; and deservedness of aid recipients, 314, 317; and race, 13–14
Tennessee, 1, 44; Knoxville, 266; opposition to military draft in, 86
Tennessee Valley Authority (TVA), 11–12, 229, 261–86; in South Carolina, 39
Tenth Amendment, 26
Texas, 9, 115, 120n29, 188, 327–28; Austin, 86; opposition to military draft in, 86; San Antonio, 86. *See also* Bradford, Melvin E.; Dies, Martin; Johnson, Lyndon
Thernstrom, Abigail, 8
Thirteenth Amendment, 20
Thurmond, J. Strom, 8, 20, 34, 50–52, 53–56, 58; and 1960 election, 45; biographical sketch of, 41–42; conversion to GOP, 46, 62n64; and Dixiecrat Revolt, 21, 29, 41–42, 45, 128, 130, 144n23; length of career, 61n48; and the lynching of Willie Earle, 61n46; role in converting South to GOP, 45–48, 148n49; and "Southern Manifesto," 43–44; turns on New Deal, 116
Tilden, Samuel, 33–34
Tillman, Benjamin "Pitchfork Ben," 20, 34, 36, 39, 44, 58; honored in South Carolina, 53
Time on the Cross, 192–93
Tindall, George Brown, 79
Tories, colonial, 4, 20
Totalitarianism, 6, 103, 111
Truman, Harry S., 7; and civil rights, 7, 21, 40–41, 126–30; and Dixiecrat Revolt, 42, 126–30. *See also* Dixiecrat Revolt; Fair Deal
Tucker Prison Farm, 12, 291–300
Twenty-seventh Amendment, 59n8
Tyler, John, 1

United Daughters of the Confederacy, 57, 183
U.S. Constitution: and South Carolina, 25–26
U.S. Post Office: and road construction, 254
University of Mississippi. *See* Ole Miss

Van Buren, Martin, 27

Vanderbilt University, 9, 182, 184–85
Vardaman, James K., 123; opposition to World War I, 69–70, 83, 84, 87
Violence: resistance to draft in Georgia Upcountry, 90–92. *See also* Lynching
Virginia, 1, 120n29; and slavery, 59n2. *See also* Byrd, Harry F.; Henry, Patrick; Jefferson, Thomas; Lee, Richard Henry; Lee, Robert E.; Madison, James; Marshall, John; Monroe, James; Randolph, Edmund; Virginia Dynasty; Washington, George
Virginia Dynasty, 1
Voting rights, 35; abuses of, 59n7; enforcement of as a Machiavellian move, 7–8. *See also* Disfranchisement
Voting Rights Act of 1965, 7, 8, 322; importance of, 7; in Mississippi, 7, 149–51, 166–71; national consensus on, 170; and South Carolina, 22, 44–45. *See also* Johnson, Lyndon
Wagner, Robert, 105–6, 107
Walker, Prentiss, 7, 139, 150
Wallace, George C., 7, 9, 140n1, 147n48, 151, 166, 229, 320; admired by Melvin E. Bradford, 9; battle for white southern vote with Nixon, 46–47; as model for modern Republicans, 9; referred to, 8; and taxes, 325, 326. *See also* Bradford, Melvin E.
War. *See* Militarism
Ward, Jason Morgan, 4, 5–6
Warren, Earl, 43, 48, 61n52
Washington, George, 1
Watson, Robert W., 217–18
Watson, Thomas E., 4–5; anti-capitalism of, 67–101; and resistance to military draft, 67–101; suppression of newspaper, 89, 100n87. *See also* Capitalism; Frank, Leo; Militarism; Populist Party; Wilson, Woodrow
Weaver, Richard M., 189–90

Weinberger, Harry, 88–89
Wesleyanism, 14
White Citizens' Councils, 2, 133, 163
White Primary, 22. *See also* Smith v. Allwright
Williams, John Bell, 127, 152, 162
Wilson, Clyde, 196–97, 206, 207–8
Wilson, Woodrow, 5, 34, 98n54; attacked by Tom Watson, 68, 72, 78–79, 81, 85, 92–93; and federal road acts, 241, 243; and the League of Nations, 130
Winter, William, 162, 164
Wolters, Raymond, 178n72
Women, 20–21; and Leo Frank Case, 74–75, 96n28; in South Carolina, 21
Women's suffrage, 20–21, 38
Wood, Leonard, 98n54
Woodward, C. Vann, 4, 95n12, 98n50, 100n82, 229; criticized by Donald Davidson, 200n13; interpretation on Tom Watson disputed, 68–69; on Tom Watson, 4
Working-class whites, 35–37
Works Progress Administration (WPA), 104, 108, 113
World War I, 38; anti-capitalism during, 67–101; and resistance to military draft, 67–101
World War II, 6–7; and racial change, 111–15
Wormley House Bargain, 34
Wright, Fielding, 42, 128
Wright, Gavin, 230–31
Wyatt-Brown, Bertram, 96n28

Xenophobia, 92, 221

Yerger, Wirt, 150–54, 161

Zuczek, Richard, 32, 33

www.ingramcontent.com/pod-product-compliance
Lightning Source LLC
Chambersburg PA
CBHW021334230426
43666CB00006B/295